11

Research Methods
for Social Workers

An Introduction

Richard M. Grinnell, Jr.

Margaret Williams

Yvonne A. Unrau

Pair Bond Publications
652 Wynding Oaks
Kalamazoo, Michigan 49006
(269) 353-7100
www.PairBondPublications.com

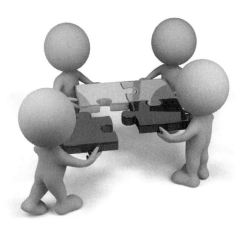

Preface

You don't have to burn books to destroy a culture.
Just get people to stop reading them.
~ Ray Bradbury

Time flies fast. The first edition of our book appeared nearly three decades ago. We've always intended for it to be used by beginning social work students as their first introduction to fundamental social work research methodology. As in the previous ten editions, our goal is to produce an inexpensive, "student-friendly" introduction to social work research methods couched within the positivistic and interpretive traditions—the two approaches most commonly used to generate relevant social work knowledge.

In sum, our book begins where every researcher begins: with finding a meaningful problem area to study and developing research questions and hypotheses. It then proceeds from measuring variables, selecting samples, and constructing research designs, to collecting and analyzing data, and report writing.

In a nutshell, our book is a primer, an introduction, a beginning. Our aim is to skim the surface of the research enterprise—to put a toe in the water, so to speak—and to give beginning social work students a taste of what it might be like to swim.

Book's Emphasis

As before, our emphasis continues to be on how the goal of evidence-based practice is furthered by the understanding of the two research approaches to knowledge development—positivistic (e.g., quantitative) and interpretive (e.g., qualitative). Thus, we firmly believe that students must thoroughly understand the nitty-gritty of these two research approaches in order for them to appreciate the concept of evidence-based practice. Thus, research in social work is presented as more than just a way to solve human problems, or to add to our knowledge base, or to guide evidence-based practice—although it is all of these.

Preparing Students for Advanced Research Courses

MOST, IF NOT ALL, entry-level research courses first cover basic research methodology as contained in this book. The students then go on and apply this content to more advanced research courses that specialize in single-system designs (case-level evaluation) or program evaluation (program-level evaluation). Thus, we have designed this book to provide students with the prerequisite foundational research knowledge they will need if they register for more advanced research/evaluation courses.

Highlights of Book

First and foremost, students will clearly understand our book; that is:

- Students will be able to easily follow what's being presented.

- Students will clearly appreciate how our book is organized.

- Students will be able to understand all the concepts.

- Students will appreciate the logic of the generic research process that we couch within the positivistic (quantitative) and interpretive (qualitative) traditions.

- Students will understand how the research enterprise will help them to become competent professionals.

- Students will appreciate that we use an abundant amount of social work examples throughout the entire book. Many of our examples center on women and minorities, in recognition of the need for social workers to be knowledgeable of their special needs and problems.

- Students will welcome our crisp writing style. In addition, our book is easy to teach *from* and *with.*

- Students will value our extensive student-oriented companion Web site that contains numerous student (and instructor) resources.

- Our book complies with the 2015 Council on Social Work Education's research requirements.

- Our book prepares students to become beginning critical consumers of the professional research literature. It also provides them with an opportunity to see how social work research studies are actually carried out.

- Abundant tables and figures provide visual representation of the concepts presented in our book.

- Numerous boxes are inserted throughout to complement and expand on the chapters; these boxes present interesting research examples, provide additional aids to student learning, and offer historical, social, and political contexts of social work research.

How did we accomplish the above? The answer is simple: This book contains only the *core* material that is realistically needed in order for beginning students to appreciate and understand the role of research in social work. Our guiding philosophy is to include only research-related content that students genuinely need to know to function as entry-level workers. Information overload is avoided at all costs. In short, we provide a straightforward view of the social work research enterprise while taking into account:

- The current pressures for accountability within the social services

- The current available research/evaluation technologies and approaches

- The present "research needs" of students as well as their needs in the first few years of their careers

◆ WHAT'S NEW?

Publishing an eleventh edition indicates that we may have attracted loyal followers over the years. Conversely, it also means that making major changes from one edition to the next can be hazardous to the book's long-standing appeal.

New content has been added to this edition in an effort to keep information current while retaining material that has stood the test of time. With the guidance of many social work research methods teachers and students alike, we have clarified material that needed further clarification, deleted material that needed deletion, and simplified material that needed simplification. All of this clarification, deletion, and simplification added an additional 112 pages to this edition.

Nevertheless, we continue to produce the least expensive research methods text on the market today, even with the additional pages. We feel that requiring students to purchase a higher-priced book is asking way too much of them, considering that their tuition and textbook costs have been increasing faster than their income levels.

As with all introductory social work research books, ours had to include *relevant* and *basic* research content. Our problem here was not so much what content to include as what to leave out. The research methodology and statistical content that we touch on in passing is treated in depth elsewhere. The following are a few of the additional modifications we have made from the last edition to this one:

◆ Study questions are included at the end of each chapter. The questions are in the order the content is covered in the chapter. This makes it easy for the students to answer the questions.

◆ A student self-efficacy quiz is included at the end of each chapter. Instructors can use each student's score as one of the measurements for a behavioral practice objective that can be reported to CSWE.

◆ Students are encouraged to take the chapter's self-efficacy quiz before reading the chapter and after they have read it. Taking the quiz before they read the chapter will prepare them for what to expect in the chapter, which in turn will enhance their learning experience—kind of like one of the threats to internal validly, *initial measurement effects.*

◆ We repeat important concepts throughout our book. Instructors who have taught research courses for several years are acutely aware of the need to keep reemphasizing basic concepts throughout the semester such as validity and reliability, constants and variables, randomization and random assignment, internal and external validly, conceptualization and operationalization, case-level evaluations and program-level evaluations, standardized and nonstandardized measuring instruments, confidentiality and anonymity, data sources and data collection methods, in addition to standards, ethics, and cultural considerations.

Thus, we have carefully tied together these major concepts not only within chapters but across chapters as well. There's deliberate repetition, as we strongly feel that the only way students can really understand fundamental research concepts is for them to come across the concepts throughout the entire semester—via the chapters contained in this book. Readers will, therefore, observe our propensity to explain research concepts in several different ways throughout the entire text.

ORGANIZATION

With the above in mind, our book is organized to follow the basic phases of the generic research process—from both the positivistic and interpretive perspectives (see Figures P.1 and P.2, respectively). Our book begins where every researcher begins—that is, with finding a meaningful problem area to study and developing research questions and hypotheses. It then proceeds from measuring variables to selecting samples, from constructing research designs and collecting and analyzing data to report writing.

LOGICAL AND FLEXIBLE TEACHING PLAN

THE BOOK IS ORGANIZED in a way that makes good sense when teaching fundamental research methods. Many other sequences that could be followed would make just as much sense, however. The chapters (and parts) in this book were planned to be independent of one another. They can be read out of the order in which they are presented, or they can be selectively omitted. However, they will probably make the most sense if read in the sequence presented because each chapter builds upon the knowledge presented in the preceding one.

The creative use of our book is highly encouraged. We only provide the minimal course content that we feel should be taught to beginning social work students. It is up to the instructor to add to our foundation through the use of the book's Web site and/or their own personal material, additional readings, videos, group assignments, guest lectures, and so forth.

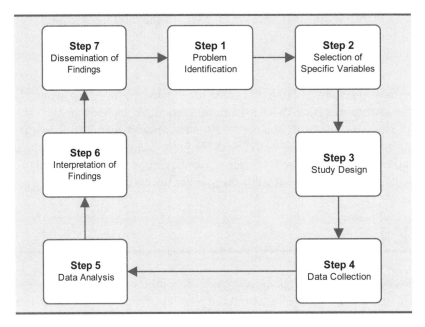

FIGURE P.1

Steps of the Positivistic (Quantitative) Research Approach

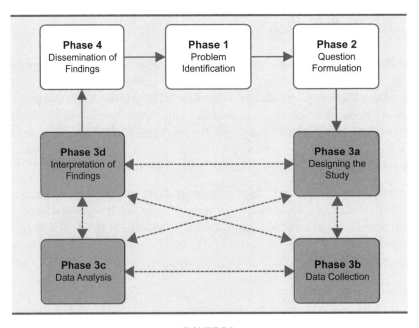

FIGURE P.2

Phases of the Interpretive (Qualitative) Research Approach

A FINAL WORD

We hope that the apparent levity with which we have treated the research process will be accepted in the same spirit as it was intended. Our goal was not to diminish research but to present the research process with warmth and humanness so that the students' first experience with it will be a positive one. After all, if wetting their big toes scares them, they will never learn to swim.

The field of research in our profession is continuing to grow and develop. We believe this edition will contribute to that growth. Another edition is anticipated, and suggestions for it are more than welcome. Please e-mail your comments directly to: rick.grinnell@wmich.edu.

If our book helps students to acquire basic research knowledge and skills and assists them in more advanced research/evaluation courses, our efforts will have been more than justified. If it also assists them to become effective social work practitioners our task will be fully rewarded.

Richard M. Grinnell, Jr.

Margaret Williams

Yvonne A. Unrau

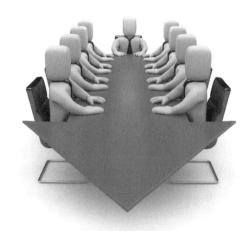

Contents in Brief

No man understands a deep book until he has seen
and lived at least part of its contents.
~ Ezra Pound

Contents in Detail

*No man understands a deep book until he has seen
and lived at least part of its contents.*
~ Ezra Pound

PART I
THE CONTEXTS OF SOCIAL WORK RESEARCH

Chapter 2: Formulating Research Questions   38

Chapter 3: Research Ethics 81

PART II
APPROACHES TO KNOWLEDGE DEVELOPMENT

Chapter 5: The Positivistic Research Approach   142

Chapter 6: The Interpretive Research Approach   177

PART III
MEASUREMENT

Chapter 7: Measuring Variables   202

PART IV
SAMPLING AND RESEARCH DESIGN

Chapter 9: Sampling   252

Chapter 10: Single-Subject Designs   272

Chapter 11: Group Designs   304

PART V
COLLECTING DATA

Chapter 13: Collecting Qualitative Data   372

Chapter 16: Analyzing Qualitative Data 438 Selfies

PART VII
RESEARCH PROPOSALS AND REPORTS

Chapter 17: Positivistic Proposals and Reports   464

PART I
The Contexts of Social Work Research

1

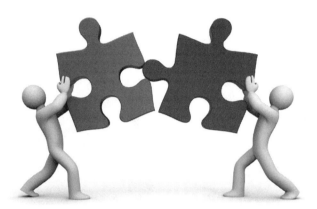

The Place of Research in Social Work

The whole of science is nothing more than
a refinement of everyday thinking.
~ Albert Einstein

Madame Cleo is a psychic consultant. She advertises widely on television, promising that her astounding insights into love, business, health, sex, and relationships will help her viewers achieve more fulfilling and gratifying lives. Ha! you think, I bet she can't do that for me! I bet she's just out for the money! But if she could, if she could only tell me . . . ! How do I know if she's for real or I'm just getting taken for a ride?

There's a parallel here with the clients who receive social services and you, the future social worker. Most of the people we help—in common with all those people who are never seen by social workers—would also like more fulfilling and rewarding lives. Like Madame Cleo's trusting clientele who get drawn into calling her on the phone, many of our clients also have personal issues, money issues, relationship issues, or health issues.

RESEARCH AND ACCOUNTABILITY

Unlike Madame Cleo, however, who has to be accountable only to her bank account, we as a profession are required to be accountable to society and must be able to provide answers to three basic accountability questions:

* How do our *clients* know that we can help them?

* How does our *profession* know that we have helped our clients?

* How do the *funding bodies* that fund our programs (which employ us) know how effectively their dollars are being spent?

What's the role that research plays in answering the three accountability questions? In one word: *significant!* That's the position of both the Council on Social Work Education (CSWE) and the National Association of Social Workers (NASW). These two prestigious national accountability organizations have a wide jurisdiction on what curriculum content is required to be taught in all accredited social work programs (CSWE) and how the students, after they graduate, practice their trade (NASW).

THE COUNCIL ON SOCIAL WORK EDUCATION

THE CSWE is the official *educational* organization that sets minimum curriculum standards for bachelor of social work (BSW) and master of social work (MSW) programs throughout the United States. Like your professors, this accreditation organization firmly believes that all social work students should know the basic principles of the scientific inquiry process.

For example, the latest version of the CSWE's *Baccalaureate and Master's Curriculum Policy Statements* (2015) contains the following competency statements related to research that all accredited social work programs must adhere to:

COMPETENCY 4

Engage in Practice-Informed Research and Research-Informed Practice
4A. use practice experience to inform scientific inquiry and research
4B. engage in critical analysis of quantitative and qualitative research methods and research findings

COMPETENCY 7

Assess Individuals, Families, Groups, Organizations, and Communities
7A. collect, organize, and critically analyze and interpret information from client systems
7D. select appropriate intervention strategies based on the assessment, research knowledge, and values and preferences of client systems

COMPETENCY 9

Evaluate Practice with Individuals, Families, Groups, Organizations, and Communities
9A. select and use appropriate methods for evaluation of outcomes
9B. critically analyze, monitor, and evaluate intervention processes and outcomes

With these six policy statements (i.e., 4a, 4b, 7a, 7d, 9a, 9b) in mind, you need to know research methodology so that you can be in compliance with the CSWE's requirements when it comes to their "research stuff." That is, no matter how you cut it, slice it, mince it, or dice it, it's extremely difficult for you to meet the CSWE's six policy statement goals without an elementary understanding of the scientific method—the contents of this book.

The research methods course you are currently taking should be complementary to the other courses in your social work program; that is, all of the courses in your program should help you achieve a beginning level of competency when it comes to the CSWE's research guidelines.

THE NATIONAL ASSOCIATION OF SOCIAL WORKERS

SIMILAR TO THE CSWE, THE NASW is a *practice* organization that works to enhance the professional growth and development of line-level social work practitioners. Like the CSWE for social work students, the NASW believes that practicing social workers should know the basics of research and evaluation principles as well. Do any of your other courses also address these principles? If so, which ones?

* Social workers should monitor and evaluate policies, the implementation of programs, and practice interventions.

* Social workers should promote and facilitate evaluation and research to contribute to the development of knowledge.

✴ Social workers should critically examine and keep current with emerging knowledge relevant to social work and fully use evaluation and research evidence in their professional practice.

✴ Social workers should report evaluation and research findings accurately. They should not fabricate or falsify results and should take steps to correct any errors later found in published data using standard publication methods.

✴ Social workers engaged in evaluation or research should be alert to and avoid conflicts of interest and dual relationships with participants, should inform participants when a real or potential conflict of interest arises, and should take steps to resolve the issue in a manner that makes participants' interests primary.

✴ Social workers should educate themselves, their students, and their colleagues about responsible research practices.

Unlike Madame Cleo, social work students and practitioners alike are expected to have a solid research knowledge base to guide and support their interventions. This course—along with all the other social work courses you are taking—will provide you with the content you will need to comply with the CSWE and NASW research standards. This knowledge base is generally derived from your social work education.

Of course, we as a profession tend to have more credibility than psychic consultants like Madame Cleo. We have graduated from accredited social work programs (CSWE) and have solid, recognized practice qualifications (NASW). In a nutshell, you're expected to have not only good intentions but also the skills and knowledge to convert your good intentions into desired practical results that will help your clients.

It all boils down to the fact that we have to be accountable to society, and to do so means that we need to acquire the knowledge and skills to help our clients in an effective and efficient manner.

How Do We Acquire a Knowledge Base?

The previous discussion focused on the need for our profession to become more accountable. As should be evident to you by now, one of the many ways to enhance our accountability is for you to become fully aware of how you actually go about obtaining the necessary knowledge base that you will use to help your various client systems (e.g., individual, family, group, community, or organization).

This should automatically lead to the question, "Where do I acquire the necessary knowledge to help my clients?" The answer is simple. You'll acquire the knowledge through the five highly interrelated sources listed here. The last one, the scientific method, is what this book is all about: all the chapters that follow are geared toward helping you to understand and appreciate this *one* way of generating knowledge for our profession:

— Authority

— Tradition

— Experience

— Beliefs and Intuition

— The Scientific Method (what this book is all about)

The most important thing to remember at this point is that all five of these "ways of knowing" highly overlap with each other. More importantly, you will use all five of the ways of knowing after you graduate.

AUTHORITY

THE FIRST WAY that you know something is someone in an authority position—like your research instructor—has told you so. That is, some things you "know" because someone in authority told you they were true. Had you lived in Galileo's time, for example, you would have "known" that there were seven heavenly bodies: the sun, the moon, and five planets. Because seven was a sacred number in the seventeenth century, the correctness of this belief was self-evident and was proclaimed by professors of philosophy.

When Galileo peeked through his telescope in 1610 and saw four satellites circling Jupiter, it was clear to those in authority that Galileo was wrong. Not only was he wrong, he had blasphemed against the accepted order. They denounced Galileo and his telescope, and they continued to comfortably believe in the sacredness of the number seven.

But the authorities could have looked through Galileo's telescope as well! They could have seen for themselves that the number of heavenly bodies had risen to eleven! In fact, they refused to look because it wasn't worth their while: they knew that they were right.

They had to be right because, in Galileo's time, the primary source of "how you knew something" was by authority—not by reason, and certainly not by observation. Today, this may seem a bit strange, and we may feel a trifle smug about the fact that in *our* time we rely on our own observations *in addition to* authority.

Questioning Authority Figures

All authority figures are not equal! Nevertheless, you have little choice but to rely on them in your quest for knowledge. You wouldn't progress very fast in your social work program if you felt it necessary to personally verify everything your professors said. Similarly, practicing social workers simply lack the time to evaluate the practice recommendations that are derived from research studies; they have no choice but to trust statements made by the researchers—the authority figures—who conducted the research studies and claimed their findings to be "true."

Experts can be wrong, however, and the consequences can sometimes be disastrous. A few decades ago, for example, authority figures in family therapy believed that children who had schizophrenia came from parents who had poor parenting skills. Researchers emphasized such causative factors as parental discord, excessive familial interdependency, and mothers with overprotective and domineering behaviors who did not allow their children to develop individual identities.

In accordance with these "research findings," many social workers assumed that all families who had a child with schizophrenia were dysfunctional, so many social workers focused their interventions on changing the family system. However, they often inadvertently instilled guilt into the parents and increased tensions rather than helping the parents to cope with their child's situation.

Recent research studies now show that schizophrenia is caused largely by genetic and other biological factors, not by bad parenting as once believed. According to these *current* findings, the most effective social work intervention is to support the family system by providing a nonstressful environment. This is what social workers *currently* do, again relying on *current* authority figures.

Most likely, the authorities are correct this time. However, they cannot be as exact *today* as they will be *tomorrow* when our knowledge of schizophrenia and good parenting has progressed even more. So what are we to do when we need to trust the experts but the experts may be wrong? Put simply, we need to evaluate the quality of their research studies. More specifically, we must be able to distinguish the good research studies from those that are bad and frankly awful. One of the main purposes of this book is to enable you, the future social worker, to adequately evaluate the quality of the research studies that produce "research findings."

You need to decide for yourself which good research findings you will clutch to your heart and use to help your clients, and which research findings you will disregard because they were generated from poorly designed studies. Remember, not every research study is a good one. Also remember that there are many good ones that generate relevant and quality knowledge that we can use with our clients. Simply put, good research studies have creditable evidence to substantiate their findings.

WHERE DOES CREDIBLE EVIDENCE (OR DATA) COME FROM? We always need to ask one very simple question: "Where did the evidence (or data) come from that was used to substantiate the study's findings?" The kind of evidence on which a practice statement is based, for example, must always be evaluated on the source of the data that was used to make the practice statement in the first place.

In addition, the media as a data source must always be questioned—especially Faux News. For example, we obtain knowledge by watching television shows and movies in addition to reading newspapers, journals, and magazine articles. These forms of communication provide rich information (right and wrong) about the social life of individuals and society in general.

Most people, for example, who have had absolutely no contact with criminals whatsoever, learn about crime from these forms of communication. As we know all too well, the media can easily perpetuate the myths of any given culture.

For example, the media show that most people who receive welfare are African American (most are actually not African American), that most people who are mentally ill are violent and dangerous (only a small percentage actually are), and that most elderly folks are senile and in nursing homes (a tiny minority are).

Television repeatedly shows low-income, inner-city African American youths using illegal drugs. Eventually, most people "know" that urban African Americans use illegal drugs at a much higher rate than other groups in the United States, even though this notion is false (Neuman, 2009).

TRADITION

THE SECOND WAY of adding to your social work knowledge base is simply through tradition. Obviously, authority and tradition are highly related to one another. For example, some things you "know" because your mother "knew" them and her mother before her, and they are a part of your cultural tradition. Your mother was also an authority figure who learned her bits and pieces through tradition and authority.

More often than not, people tend to accept cultural beliefs without much question. They may doubt some of them and test others for themselves, but for the most part they behave and believe as tradition dictates. To be sure, such conformity is useful, as our society could not function if each custom and belief was reexamined by each individual in every generation.

On the other hand, unquestioning acceptance of traditional dictates easily leads to stagnation and to the perpetuation of wrongs. It would be unfortunate, for example, if women were never allowed to vote because women had never traditionally voted, or if racial segregation and slavery were perpetuated because traditionally that's just the way it was. And don't forget that interracial marriages were illegal at one time. Some traditional beliefs are based on the dictates of authority carried on through time, such as opposition to same-sex marriages. The origins of other beliefs are lost in history.

Even in social service programs, whose history is relatively brief, things tend to be done in certain ways because they have always been done in those ways. When you first enter a social service program as a practicum student, for example, your colleagues will show you how the program runs.

You may be given a manual detailing your program's policies and procedures, which contains everything from staff holidays and locking up client files at night, to standard interviewing techniques with children who have been physically and emotionally abused. Informally, you will be told other things such as how much it costs to join the coffee club, whom to ask when you want a favor, whom to phone for certain kinds of information, and what form to complete to be put on the waiting list for a parking space.

In addition to this practical information, you may also receive advice about how to help your future clients. Your colleagues may offer you a few of their opinions about the most effective treatment intervention strategies that are used in your practicum setting.

If your practicum setting is a child sexual abuse treatment program, for example, it may be suggested to you that the nonoffending mother of a child who has been sexually abused does not need to address her own sexual abuse history in therapy in order to empathize with and protect her daughter. Such a view would support the belief that the best interventive approach is a learning one, perhaps helping the mother learn better communication skills in her relationship with her daughter.

Conversely, the suggestion may be that the mother's personal exploration into her psyche (whatever that is) is essential, so the intervention should be of a psychodynamic nature. Whatever the suggestion, it's likely that you, as a beginning social work student, will accept it, along with the information about the coffee club.

To be sure, you will want to fit in and become a valued member of the team. If the nonoffending mother is the first client you have really been responsible for, you may also be privately relieved that the intervention decision has been made for you. You may believe that your colleagues have more professional experience than you and surely should know best. In all likelihood, they probably do know best.

However, they also were once beginning social work students like yourself, and they probably formed their professional opinions in the same way you are presently forming yours. They too once trusted their supervisors' knowledge bases and their experiences (to be discussed shortly). In other words, much of what you will initially be told is based upon the way your practicum site has traditionally worked. This should not be a surprise to you.

This might be a good moment to use your newfound research skills to evaluate the literature on the best way to intervene with children who have been sexually abused. But if you do happen to find a different and more effective way to intervene, you may quickly discover that your colleagues are unreceptive or even hostile. They "know" what they do already works with their clients—they "know it works" because it has traditionally worked for years.

Thus, on the one hand, tradition is extremely useful. It simply allows you to learn from the achievements and mistakes of those who have done your job before you. You don't have to reinvent the wheel, as you've been given a head start. On the other hand, tradition can become way too comfortable. It can blind you to better ways of doing things.

EXPERIENCE

THE THIRD WAY of acquiring your knowledge base is through plain old-fashioned experience. You "know" that buttered bread falls when you drop it—buttered side down, of course. You "know" that knives cut and fire burns. You "know," as you gain experience in social work, that certain interventive approaches tend to work better than others with certain types of clients in certain types of situations. Such experience is of enormous benefit to your clients.

However, as with anything else, experience has its advantages and disadvantages. Experience in one area, for example, can blind you to the issues in another. Health planners from mental health backgrounds, for example, may see mental illness as the most compelling community health problem because of their experiences with the mentally ill.

Mental health issues may therefore command more dollars and attention than other public health issues that are equally deserving such as homelessness, poverty, and child abuse. Awareness of your own biases will allow you to make the most of your own experience while taking due account of the experiences of others.

BELIEFS AND INTUITION

AT THIS POINT, it's useful to differentiate among knowledge, beliefs, and intuition. Like everything else in life, they heavily interact with each other. *Knowledge* is an accepted body of facts or ideas mainly acquired through the use of the scientific method. We now have *knowledge* that the Earth is round, for example, because we have been into space and observed it from above.

A few centuries ago, we would have *known* that the Earth is flat because someone in authority said it is or because tradition had always held it to be flat—very flat indeed. Thus, knowledge is never final or certain. It's always changing as new facts come to our attention and new theories explaining the facts are developed, tested, and accepted or rejected.

Beliefs (or faith), on the other hand, are a body of facts or ideas that are acquired mainly through the reliance on tradition and/or authority. These are a way of thinking about something that has not been proven by the scientific method, and thus they are unscientific opinions at best.

Belief systems have remarkable staying power. Various beliefs about life after death, for example, have been held since the beginning of time by large numbers of people, and they will doubtless continue to be held, without much change, because there is nothing to change them.

More recently, the belief that one acquires worth through work has become strongly held in North American society. This belief holds that the harder you work, the more virtue you acquire by doing the work. At the same time, it's believed that people will avoid work if at all possible—presumably because they value ease over virtue—so many of the social service programs we have in place are designed to punish our clients' "idleness" and reward their "productivity."

Intuition is a natural ability or power that makes it possible to know something without any proof or evidence. It's a feeling that guides a person to act a certain way without fully understanding why. It can be described in a number of ways: revelation through insight, conviction without reason, or immediate apprehension without rational thought. In short, you "know" something without having a clue of how you know it. It has been suggested that intuition springs from a rational process at the subconscious level.

With the preceding discussion in mind, professional ethical concerns dictate that we should never rely *solely* on our beliefs and intuition when working with clients (Grinnell, 1985, 1995; Grinnell & Siegel, 1998). Take careful note of the word *solely*.

PROFESSIONAL ETHICAL CONCERNS

Let's use an example to illustrate a professional ethical concern. Suppose one day Jane goes to her family physician for a medical checkup because she has been feeling tired and depressed. After talking with her for a few minutes, the physician says, "My intuition tells me that you have high blood pressure," and then proceeds to give Jane hypertension medication. Following the physician's advice, Jane takes the medication for a few months and begins to feel better. Because she's now feeling better, Jane phones the physician and asks if it's all right to stop taking the medication. The physician says yes.

At no time did the physician take Jane's blood pressure, either to confirm the initial diagnostic intuitive hunch or to determine the effects of the medication later. Hence, it was entirely possible that Jane was taking a drug for which she had no need, or a drug that could actually harm her; alternatively, she may be stopping a medication that has been helping her. The point here is that the physician made crucial decisions about beginning and ending an intervention (treatment) without gathering all the necessary data.

Ethical social workers do not treat clients the way this physician did. Just as the wrong medication has the potential to harm, so does the wrong social work intervention. In the past, some studies have shown that the recipients of social work services have fared worse or no better than those who did not receive our services. Thus, we have a responsibility always to evaluate the effect of our interventions.

We must fully realize that we have no business intervening in other peoples' lives simply on the assumption that our good intentions lead to good client outcomes. Although we may mean well, our good intentions alone do not ensure that we really "help" our clients. We must integrate research and evaluation techniques in our practice so that we can measure the effects of our helping efforts.

We have a moral obligation to locate prior research studies and evaluate their results—even more so when the clients have not asked for our services. Truly professional social workers never rely *solely* on their good intentions, intuition, experiences, uninformed opinions, and subjective judgments. They also use the results of research findings that were derived from good research studies to guide their interventions, and they use the scientific method (to be discussed shortly) to assess their effectiveness.

THE SCIENTIFIC METHOD

AT LAST, you say: we have now come to the fifth and final way of knowing. This way of acquiring knowledge is through the use of the scientific method—the main focus of this book. It's sometimes called the *problem-solving process,* the *research method,* or the *research process.* When compared with the other four ways of knowing, the scientific method is the newest.

The scientific method is a way of knowing that is based on observable and/or measureable facts and objectivity. Simply put, it's a method of knowing that can be shared and objectively critiqued by others. It's the use of careful thought and the systematic use of sound data gathering and analytical procedures. This process makes a research study more easily verifiable and replicable by others compared with the other ways of knowing (Maschi & Youdin, 2012).

Aristotle, for example, was of the opinion that women had fewer teeth than men. The number of teeth possessed by women and men was a contentious issue in his day (believe it or not). Although he had been twice married, it never occurred to Aristotle to ask either of his two wives to open their mouths so he could observe and count the number of teeth each had.

Aristotle could have then simply compared the number of teeth each of his wives had with the number of teeth he had to determine whether woman had fewer teeth than men, but he didn't use the scientific method. By contrast, this type of solution would occur to anyone born in the twenty-first century because we are accustomed to evaluating our assumptions in light of our observations.

Presently, the social work profession is enamored with knowledge development through the use of the scientific method. Acquiring knowledge through the use of research findings that were derived from applying the scientific method is the most objective way of "knowing" something. Lawrence Neuman (2012) sums up what the scientific method is all about:

> The scientific method is not one single thing; it refers to the ideas, rules, techniques, and approaches that the scientific community uses. The method arises from a loose consensus within the community of scientists. It includes a way of looking at the world that places a high value on professionalism, craftsmanship, ethical integrity, creativity, rigorous standards, and diligence.

> It also includes strong professional norms such as honesty and uprightness in doing research studies, great candor and openness about how one has conducted a study, and a focus on the merits of the research study itself and not on any characteristics of the individuals who conducted the study.

THE SCIENTIFIC METHOD AND PROFESSIONAL JUDGMENTS

A professional judgment is a *conscious* process whereby facts, as far as they are known, are supplemented with the knowledge derived from all five ways of knowing to form the basis for rational decisions. In this eminently reasonable process, you know what facts you have and how reliable they are, you know what facts are missing, and you know what experiences you're using to fill in the gaps.

You are thus in a position to gauge whether your professional judgment is almost certainly right (you have all the facts), probably right (you have most of the facts), or possibly out to lunch (you know you are almost entirely guessing). A reasoned professional judgment on your part that utilizes all five ways of knowing, no matter how uncertain you may be, is far more beneficial to your client than only using one of the ways of knowing.

PHASES OF THE SCIENTIFIC METHOD

As we know by now, obtaining knowledge by the scientific method is one of the most objective approaches. The scientific method is a simple process that contains four phases, as illustrated in Figure 1.1.

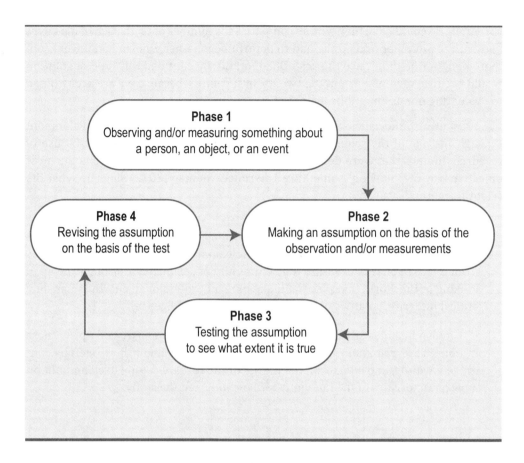

FIGURE 1.1
Phases of the Scientific Method

It begins with Phase 1: some kind of an observation and/or measurement. Suppose, for example, we find in the garage an unidentified bag of seeds, and we don't know what kind of seeds they are. We plant a random seed from the bag into the ground, and presto—it grows into a nice-looking petunia.

This might be a coincidence, but if we plant thirty-seven more seeds from the same bag, and all grow into petunias, we might assume that all the seeds in our bag are related to petunias. We have now reached Phase 2 in the scientific method: an assumption based on our observations.

In Phase 3, we test our assumption. This is done by planting yet another seed (the thirty-eighth) in the same way as before. If the thirty-eighth seed also becomes a petunia, we will be more certain that all the seeds in our bag will grow into petunias.

On the other hand, if the thirty-eighth seed grows into a cabbage, we will begin to se-riously question our original assumption—that the bag contains all petunia seeds—which is Phase 4 of the scientific method.

It's possible, of course, that we are quite mad and that we only imagined those petunias in the first place. We would be more certain of the real existence of those petunias if someone else had seen them as well. Thus, the more people who observe our results, the surer we become.

The scientific inquiry process holds that, in most cases, something exists if we can observe *and* measure it. To guard against objects that are "seen" without existing, such as cool pools of water observed by people dying of thirst in deserts, the scien-tific method has taken the premise one step farther: a thing exists if, and only if, we can measure it. A desert mirage's pool can be observed, for example, but it cannot be measured by a thermometer or a depth gauge.

Things that have always occurred in sequence, such as summer followed by fall, probably will continue to occur in sequence. In all likelihood, rivers will flow down-hill, water will freeze at zero degrees centigrade, and crops will grow if planted in the spring. Nothing is certain, however; nothing is absolute. It's a matter of slowly acquiring knowledge by making observations and taking measurements, deriving as-sumptions from those observations, and testing the assumptions with more observa-tions and measurements. Even the best-tested assumption is held to be true only until another observation comes along to disprove it.

Nothing is forever. It's all a matter of probabilities. Let's say you have lived your whole life all alone in a log cabin in the middle of a large forest. You have never ven-tured as far as a hundred yards from your cabin and have had no access to the outside world. You have observed for your entire life that all the ducks that flew over your land were white.

You have never seen a differently colored duck. Thus, you assume, and logically so, that all ducks are white. You would only have to see one nonwhite duck to dis-prove your white-duck assumption. Nothing is certain, no matter how long you "ob-jectively observed" it.

EXAMPLE OF THE SCIENTIFIC INQUIRY PROCESS

Suppose, for a moment, you're interested in determining whether the strength of a child's attachment to his or her mother affects the social skills of the child. In order to test your assumption (your hypothesis, if you will), you must now decide what you mean by "child" (say, under 6 years of age), and you need to find some young children and their respective mothers.

PHASE 1: OBSERVING AND/OR MEASURING. Next, you need to decide what you mean by "attachment," and you need to observe or measure how attached the children are to their mothers. Because you need to measure your observations, you will also need to come up with some system whereby certain observed behaviors mean "strong attachment," other behaviors mean "medium attachment," and still other behaviors mean "weak attachment." Then you need to decide what you mean by "social skills," and you now need to observe and measure the children's social skills. All of these definitions, observations, and measurements constitute Phase 1 of the research study (see Figure 1.1).

PHASE 2: ASSUMING. On the basis of your Phase 1 data, you might formulate an assumption, hunch, or hypothesis to the effect (for instance) that the stronger a child's attachment to his or her mother, the higher the child's social skills. Or to put it an-

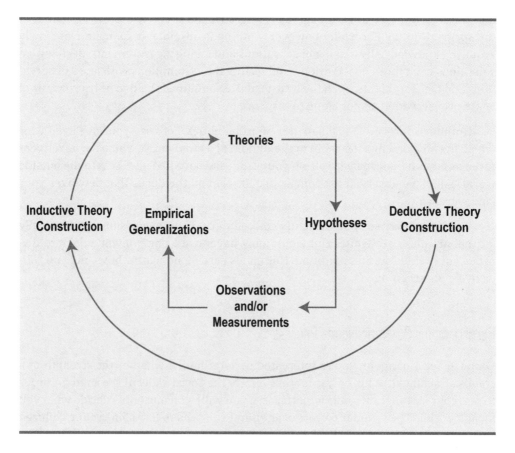

FIGURE 1.2
Inductive/Deductive Cycle of Theory Construction

other way, the children who have stronger attachments to their mothers will have more developed social skills than the children who have weaker attachments to their mothers.

This is Phase 2 of the scientific inquiry process, and it involves *inductive* logic. When using inductive logic, you simply begin with the detailed observations and/or measurements of the world obtained in Phase 1 and move toward more abstract generalizations and ideas (Figure 1.2).

If your assumption is correct, you can use it to predict that a particular child with a strong attachment to her mother will also demonstrate strong social skills. This is an example of *deductive* logic—you are deducing from the general to the particular.

PHASE 3: TESTING. In Phase 3, you set about testing your assumption, observing and measuring the attachment levels and social skills of as many other children as you can manage. Data from this phase may confirm or cast doubt upon your assumption. The data may also cause you to realize that "attachment" is not as simple a concept as you had imagined. It's not just a matter of the strength of the attachment; rather, the type of the attachment is also a factor (for instance, secure, insecure, or disorganized).

If you have tested enough children from diverse cultural backgrounds, you may also wonder whether your assumption holds up better in some cultures than it does in others. Is it more relevant, say, for children raised in nuclear families than for children raised in a more communal environment such as a First Nations reserve or an Israeli kibbutz?

PHASE 4: REVISING. The considerations in Phase 3 will lead you to Phase 4, where you revise your conjecture in light of your observations (inductive logic) and begin to test your revised hunch all over again (deductive logic). Hopefully, this will not be a lonely effort on your part.

Other researchers interested in attachment will also examine your assumption and the evidence you formulated it from, and they will conduct their own studies to see how right you really were. This combined work, conducted with honesty, skepticism, sharing, and freedom from entrenched beliefs, allows our knowledge base in the area of attachment to increase.

 # APPROACHES TO THE SCIENTIFIC METHOD

The scientific method contains two complementary research approaches—the positivistic approach (sometimes called the "quantitative approach") and the interpretive approach (sometimes called the "qualitative approach"). The two research approaches—positivistic and interpretive—generate their findings via the use of the scientific method. They just do it in very different ways, as outlined in Table 1.1. We will now turn our attention to the two approaches:

— Positivistic Research Approach to Knowledge Development

— Interpretive Research Approach to Knowledge Development

THE POSITIVISTIC APPROACH (CHAPTER 5)

THE POSITIVISTIC APPROACH is sometimes referred to as the *quantitative approach.* Positivistic research studies mostly rely on quantification in collecting and analyzing data and sometimes use statistics to test hypotheses established at the outset of the study. A garden-variety positivistic research study follows the general steps of the scientific method in a more or less straightforward manner, as outlined in Figure 5.1 in Chapter 5:

- First, a problem area is chosen, and a relevant researchable question (or specific hypothesis) is specified.

- Second, relevant variables within the research question (or hypothesis) are delineated.

- Third, a plan is developed for measuring the variables within the research question (or hypothesis).

- Fourth, relevant data are gathered for each variable and then analyzed to determine what they mean.

- Fifth, on the basis of the data generated, conclusions are drawn regarding the research question (or hypothesis).

- Finally, a report is written giving the study's findings, conclusions, and recommendations.

The study may then be evaluated by others and perhaps replicated (or repeated) to support or repudiate the application of the study's findings. In general, positivistic research studies are deductive in nature in that they attempt to draw large and representative samples of research participants so that their findings are "generalizable" to larger populations (Engel & Schutt, 2012).

TABLE 1.1

The Two Research Approaches in the Scientific Method

The Positivistic Research Approach (Chapter 5)	The Interpretive Research Approach (Chapter 6)
One objective reality	Many subjective realities
Seeks to be objective	Is admittedly subjective
Reality unchanged	Reality changed
Researcher put aside own values	Researcher recognizes own values
Social and physical sciences are a unity	Social and physical sciences are different
Passive roles for research subjects	Active roles for research participants
Many research subjects involved	Few research participants involved
Data obtained by observations and measurements	Data obtained by observations and asking questions
Data are quantitative in nature	Data are quantitative in nature
Deductive logic applied	Inductive logic applied
Casual information obtained	Descriptive information obtained
Tests hypotheses	Produces hypotheses
Seeks to explain or predict	Seeks to understand
Measuring instruments utilized	Researcher is the measuring instrument
High generalizability of findings	Limited generalizability of findings

THE INTERPRETIVE APPROACH (CHAPTER 6)

THE INTERPRETIVE APPROACH to knowledge development is sometimes referred to as the *qualitative approach.* Unlike positivistic studies, interpretive studies mostly rely on qualitative and descriptive methods of data collection and generate hypotheses and generalizations as a part of the research process. Meaningful problem areas also drive interpretive research studies. However, their direct relationship to the scientific method is somewhat different from the positivistic approach.

In a positivistic study, conceptual clarity about the research question (or hypothesis) usually precedes the collection and analysis of data. In contrast to positivistic studies, researchers doing interpretive studies do not use the data collection and analysis process simply to answer questions (or to test hypotheses).

Rather, the process is used first to discover what the most important questions are and then to refine and answer questions (or test hypotheses) that are increasingly more specific. The process is one of moving back and forth between facts and their interpretation, between answers to questions and the development of social work theory.

Using a holistic attitude, the interpretive research approach explores the richness, depth, and complexity of phenomena. Using an inductive process, interpretive methods generate narrative data from information-rich cases. They emphasize the deeper meanings of the research participants' experiences. Note that the positivistic research approach has steps (Figure 5.1) and the interpretive approach has phases (Figure 6.1).

See Figure 6.1 in Chapter 6 for how the interpretive research approach unfolds. Note how Phases 3a–d heavily interact with one another (see the arrows between the shaded phases). We will discuss in more detail of how to do an interpretive research study in Chapter 6.

 # CHARACTERISTICS OF RESEARCHERS

By now you should be familiar with how our profession can become more accountable by increasing your understanding of how you—as a future social worker—actually know something. And, more importantly, you should have an adequate appreciation of how the use of the scientific method generates more objective knowledge for our profession than the other four ways of knowing.

When researchers use the scientific method to generate knowledge via research findings, they must personally possess four important characteristics, which are embedded within the method itself. More specifically, social work researchers must:

— Be Aware of Their Own Values

— Be Skeptics

— Share Their Findings with Others

— Be Honest

Let's discuss each characteristic one at a time, even though they are all highly intertwined and comingled.

Value Awareness

LIKE A JUDGE—and not Judge Judy—you must be fully aware of and be able to set aside your values when you do a research study. You must be unbiased and impartial to the highest degree as possible. This means that you as a social work researcher should be able to put aside your personal values both when you are conducting research studies and when you are evaluating the research results obtained by other researchers.

If your personal values system dictates, for example, that health care should be publicly funded and equally available to everyone, you should still be able to use the scientific method to acquire knowledge about the advantages and disadvantages of a privatized system. If the evidence from your own or someone else's study shows that privatized health care is superior in some respects to the publicly funded system you support, you should be able to weigh this evidence objectively—even though it may conflict with your personal values system.

Skeptical Curiosity

NOW THAT YOU'RE A VALUELESS RESEARCHER, you must become an insatiably curious one as well. We now know that knowledge acquired using the scientific method is never certain. Scientific "truth" remains true only until new evidence comes along to show that it's not true or is only partly true.

Skeptical curiosity means that all findings derived from the scientific method should be—and, most importantly, *must* be—questioned. Wherever possible, new studies should be conducted by different researchers to see whether the same results are obtained again. In other words, research studies (whenever possible) should be replicated.

Replication of the same study with the same results by another researcher makes it less likely that the results of the first study were affected by bias, dishonesty, or just plain error. Thus, the findings are more likely to be "true" in the sense that they are more likely to reflect a reality external to the researchers.

We will come back to this business of external reality later on. For now, it's enough to say that the continual replication of research studies is a routine practice in the physical sciences, but it's far rarer in the social sciences, especially in the social work profession, for two main reasons:

- First, it's far more difficult to replicate a study of people than a study of physical objects.

- Second, researchers in the social sciences have a harder time finding money to do research studies than researchers in the physical sciences.

SHARING

AS YOUR MOTHER SAID, you must share your stuff with others. The results of a research study and the methods used to conduct it must be available to everyone so that the study's findings can be critiqued and the study replicated.

It's worth noting that sharing findings from a research study is a modern value. Remember that it wasn't that long ago that illiteracy among peasants and women was valued by those who were neither. Knowledge has always been a weapon as well as a tool. Those who know little may be less likely to question the wisdom and authority of those who are above them in the social hierarchy. Public education is thus an enormously powerful social force that allows people to access and question the evidence, or data, upon which their leaders make decisions on their behalf.

HONESTY

NOT ONLY MUST YOU BE A VALUELESS SKEPTICAL, have a curious nature, and share your research findings with others, you must also be honest in what you share. Honesty means, of course, that you're not supposed to fiddle with the results obtained from your study.

Honesty may sound fairly straightforward, but, in fact, the results of research studies are rarely as clear-cut as we would like them to be. Quite often, and in the most respectable research situations, theories are formulated on the basis of whether one wiggle on a graph is slightly longer than the corresponding woggle.

If "dishonesty" means a deliberate intention to deceive, then probably very few researchers are dishonest. If, however, it means that they have allowed their values systems and their preconceived ideas to influence their methods of data collection, analysis, and interpretation, then there are probably a few guilty ones among us.

In this sense, the term "honesty" includes an obligation on the part of researchers to be explicit about what their values and ideas are. They need to be sufficiently self-aware to both identify their values systems and perceive the effects of these upon their own work. Then they need to be sufficiently honest to make an explicit statement about where they stand so that others can evaluate the conclusions drawn from their research studies.

 # PURE AND APPLIED RESEARCH STUDIES

Research studies can also be classified into pure and applied (Grinnell, Rothery, & Thomlison, 1993). Sometimes a research study can be a pure one and an applied one at the same time.

PURE RESEARCH STUDIES

PURE RESEARCH STUDIES are motivated primarily by a researcher's curiosity. The questions they address are considered important because they can produce results that improve our ability to describe or explain phenomena. Successfully answering a pure research question advances theory.

Social workers with a sociological background may be interested, for example, in the organizational patterns that evolve in a social system, such as in the John Wilson Elementary School community when an intruder threatens children (see Box 1.1).

- What are the specific processes whereby the teachers formulate a coherent response to the threat?

- How are parents, often relatively marginal members of the school community, drawn into more central positions and made effective partners in the effort to maintain a defense?

- What differentiates this school, where the children reportedly cope with danger while maintaining good morale, from other schools where similar stresses would have more debilitating effects?

BOX 1.1
Another Kidnap Has Parents Nervous

INNISFAIL - Anxious parents are uniting to protect their kids after the fifth child abduction incident since June in this normally peaceful town.

And teachers are on red alert for strangers.

The drastic precautions have been forced on them by the latest kidnap bid—the attempted abduction last Friday of a seven-year-old girl inside the town's only elementary school.

As John Wilson Elementary School ended its day Tuesday, the parking lot was jammed with parents, big brothers, big sisters, friends, and neighbors.

"Now, everybody's coming to the school to pick up their kids—or other people's kids. Even parents that never used to come and get their kids are walking them to school every day now," said Jeanette Clark, waiting for her daughter.

"We have to make sure every child gets home safely now.

"This last abduction was really serious because the guy went right into the school," she said.

The culprit, described as a 50-year-old white male with brown hair and a moustache, walked into the school, grabbed the girl, who was just coming out of the bathroom, and demanded, "Come with me."

But the girl bit his arm and ran for help.

Laurie Moore, mother of a Grade 3 girl, said she and her friends with children are emphasizing "stay away from strangers" warnings.

"I tell my daughter not to talk to anyone, and if anyone comes near her she has to scream and run. It really is sad that we all have to ago through this," she said.

School Principal Bill Hoppins has created a volunteer program where parents can help each other by supervising kids on the playground during the morning.

Tim Belbin, whose daughter attends Grade 2, said he's willing to offer his time to watch his and other children.

"I find this all really disturbing . . . really scary."

The abduction attempt has also prompted teachers to supervise all the students in their classes as they leave the school grounds and make sure they can identify all adults in the area.

"If we don't know them, we have to go up and ask them, even if they don't like it," said Hoppins.

And Hoppins said that when students are absent without a parental notification, their homes are called immediately. "There have been a number of precautions taken here since the last abduction attempt. And we are working together with the parents.

Social workers with a psychological background also would be interested in responses to stress, but from a different perspective. If their focus is on the development of personality, they may attempt to identify traits that allow some children to cope more effectively with danger than others. If they focus on the perpetrators, they may try to learn what it is about such people that could explain why they behave in ways that are repellent to most other people.

All of these potential research questions are motivated by a desire to increase or improve the knowledge base of our profession. The questions have a theoretical relevance, and the purpose in seeking to answer them is to advance basic knowledge about how social systems organize themselves or how personality develops.

APPLIED RESEARCH STUDIES

THE ADVANTAGE OF APPLIED RESEARCH over pure research is highlighted in a defense of "useful" rather than "useless" facts presented by Sherlock Holmes to his companion, Dr. Watson, in Conan Doyle's story titled, *A Study in Scarlet:*

> "You see," he explained, "I consider that a man's brain originally is like a little empty attic, and you have to stock it with such furniture as you choose . . . It is a mistake to think that that little room has elastic walls and can distend to any extent . . . There comes a time when for every addition of knowledge you forget something that you knew before. It is of the highest importance, therefore, not to have useless facts elbowing out the useful ones."
>
> "But the Solar System!" I protested.
>
> "What the deuce is it to me?" he interrupted impatiently; "you say that we go round the sun. If we went round the moon it would not make a pennyworth of difference to me or to my work." (Doyle, 1901/1955, p. 11).

A social worker with professional responsibilities for knowing how to be helpful in circumstances like those at John Wilson Elementary School may have some sympathy for Holmes's position. Theory about the dynamics of social organizations or the development of personality is fine for those who have time to invest in such issues.

However, an applied researcher is more interested in the young girl who bit her assailant and ran for help. How did she know so clearly what to do that she could handle the attack against herself with such competence? Can anything be learned from her history that would help parents or teachers prepare other children to be equally effective should the need arise?

A researcher could also be interested in how the principal of the school handled the situation. Are there generalizable guidelines that can be extracted from the principal's approach to mobilizing teachers and parents? Should other professionals be informed about what the principal did to enable the children to keep their spirits up while at the same time alerting them to the danger?

Many practicing social workers would be interested in the long-term effects of this kind of experience on the children. Some children will certainly be more deeply affected than others, and it's important to know how they are affected and what kinds of attention to their emotional needs will help them cope adaptively with the experience and its aftermath. These questions are motivated in part by curiosity, as pure research questions are, but there is another need operating as well, and that is mastery.

In sum, the goal of *pure research studies* is to develop theory and expand our profession's knowledge base, and the goal of *applied research studies* is to develop solutions for problems and applications in practice. The distinction between theoretical results and practical results marks the principal difference between pure and applied research studies.

Now that we know that the sole purpose of social work research is to generate knowledge that is as value free and objective as possible via the scientific method, let's see how social work research can be defined.

 # DEFINITION OF SOCIAL WORK RESEARCH

So far, we have discussed the various ways of obtaining knowledge and briefly looked at the characteristics and phases of the scientific method. Armed with this knowledge, we now need a definition of *research,* which is composed of two syllables, *re* and *search*.

Dictionaries define the former syllable as a prefix meaning again, anew, or over again, and the latter as a verb meaning to examine closely and carefully, to test and try, or to probe (Duehn, 1985). Together, these syllables form a noun that describes a careful and systematic study in some field of knowledge, undertaken to establish facts or principles. Social work research therefore can be defined as follows:

> Social work research is a systematic and objective inquiry that uses the scientific method to solve human problems and creates new knowledge that is generally applicable to the social work profession.

We obtain much of our knowledge base from the findings derived from research studies that use the scientific method. However, all research studies have built-in biases and limitations that create errors and keep us from being absolutely certain about the studies' outcomes.

This book helps you to understand these limitations and to take them into account in the interpretation of research findings and helps you to avoid making errors or obtaining wrong answers. One of the principal products of a research study is obtaining "objective and systematic" data—via the scientific method—about reality as it is, "unbiased" and "error-free."

 # RESEARCH AND PRACTICE

Believe it or not, social work research and practice have much in common. They are both problem-solving processes. As can be seen in Figure 1.3 there are parallels between social work research and social work practice (Duehn, 1985).

All social work activities, both practice and research, are organized around one central assumption: there is a preferred order of thinking and action that, when rigorously followed, will increase the likelihood of achieving our objectives.

Social work practitioners and researchers base their conclusions on careful observation, systematic trial, and intelligent analysis. Both observe, reflect, conclude, try, monitor results, and continuously reapply the same problem-solving process until the problem (practice or research) is addressed satisfactorily.

 # RESEARCH ROLES

We have discussed the reasons why social workers need to use research findings that were derived by the scientific method. Because there are many different ways of actually engaging within the scientific method—and in the scientific community for that matter—it's useful to look at the three highly interrelated research roles that social workers might play:

— The Research Consumer

— The Creator and Disseminator of Knowledge

— The Contributing Partner

THE RESEARCH CONSUMER

YOUR FIRST SOCIAL WORK RESEARCH ROLE is that of the research consumer. If you go to your doctor to discuss your arthritis, for example, you expect the doctor to be aware of the most recent advances in the management and treatment of arthritis. All professionals, in all disciplines, are expected by their clients to keep up with the latest developments in their fields.

They do this by attending conferences, reading books and journals, and paying attention to the results derived from research studies. In other words, these professionals—which includes you as a social worker—are *research consumers*, and, as previously noted, they need to know enough about the scientific method to consume research studies wisely, separating the nutritious wheat from the junk food chaff.

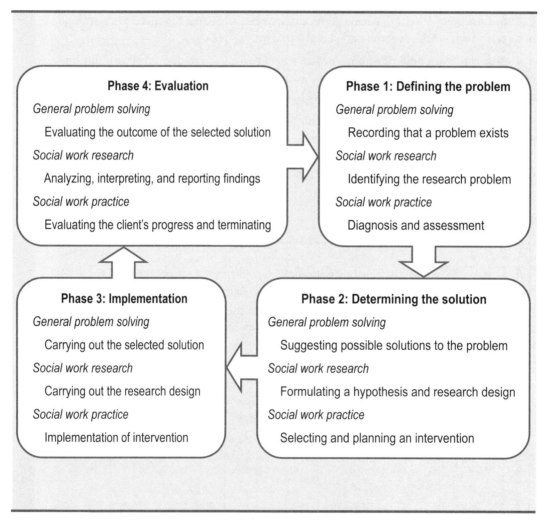

FIGURE 1.3

Parallels among General Problem Solving, Research, and Social Work Practice

THE CREATOR AND DISSEMINATOR OF KNOWLEDGE

YOU MAY BE QUITE DETERMINED that you will never yourself conduct a research study. "Never ever!" you say. But then you find that you are the only staff person in a small social service program that desperately requires a needs assessment if the program is to serve its clients and keep its funding base. You look up "needs assessment" in forgotten research texts, and you sweat and stumble through them because someone has to do the study and there is no one there but you.

This may seem like an unlikely scenario, but in fact many social service programs are very small and are run on a wing and a prayer by a few paid staff and a large volunteer contingent. They rise and flourish for a time and die, and death is often hastened along by their inability to demonstrate, in research terms, how much good they are doing on their clients' behalf, how little it's costing, and what the dreadful social consequences would be if they weren't there to do it.

You may escape being the sole social worker in a program that needs research know-how. But even if you are a mere cog in an immense machine of interlocking social workers, the time may come when you want to try something new. Most social workers do. Most of them, however, don't try that something in any structured way.

They don't write down exactly what the something is (perhaps a new intervention for raising Jody's self-esteem), they don't say why they need it (nothing else has been working), and they don't record how they tested it (they measured Jody's self-esteem before and after doing it) or how effective it was (Jody's self-esteem score rose triumphantly from X to Y, and was still at its higher level 3 months later).

Worse, they don't tell anyone else they did it, except for a few murmurs, rapidly forgotten, to a colleague over coffee. One consequence of this is that other Jody types, who might benefit from the same intervention, never have the opportunity to do so because their social workers don't know that it exists. Another consequence is that the social service program cannot use this newfound innovation as evidence of its effectiveness to place before its funders.

THE CONTRIBUTING PARTNER

IN REALITY, many social service programs conduct some kind of research studies from time to time, particularly evaluative studies. Many more agree to host studies conducted by researchers external to the program, such as university professors and their graduate students.

Unlike studies conducted by psychologists, social work research rarely takes place in a laboratory but instead is usually conducted in field settings. Data may be taken from the program's clients and/or their case files or may be collected in the program or in the clients' homes. Because social workers are usually employed by social service programs, they are often drawn into the program's research activities by default.

Such activities are normally conducted by a team, consisting of researchers and program staff members. Today, the solitary social work researcher, like the solitary mad scientist, is very much a thing of the past. Staff members who contribute to research inquiry may have specific skills to offer that they never imagined were research related.

One worker, for example, may be particularly astute and accurate when it comes to observing client behaviors. Another worker may perform well as a liaison between the clients and the researcher or between one program and another. Some social workers are cooperative in research endeavors, and others are less so, depending on their attitudes toward knowledge development through the use of the scientific method.

Those of us who know the most about scientific methods tend to be the most cooperative and also the most useful. Hence, the greater the number of social workers who understand research principles, the more likely it is that relevant studies will be successfully completed and that our knowledge base will be increased.

INTEGRATING THE THREE RESEARCH ROLES

JUST ABOUT EVERYTHING IN LIFE is interdependent on everything else. Chaos theory comes readily to mind concerning the idea of interdependence. The same holds true with the three research roles noted earlier—they are not independent of one another. They must be integrated if research is to accomplish its goals of increasing our profession's knowledge base and improving the effectiveness of our interventions with clients.

The issue is not whether we should consume research findings, produce and disseminate research results, or become contributing partners in research studies. Rather, it's whether we can engage the full spectrum of available knowledge and skills in the continual improvement of our practices. Social workers who adopt only one or two of the three research roles are shortchanging themselves and their clients (Reid & Smith, 1989):

> If research is to be used to full advantage to advance the goals of social work, the profession needs to develop a climate in which both doing and consuming research are normal professional activities. By this we do not mean that all social workers should necessarily do research or that all practice should be based on the results of research, but rather that an ability to carry out studies at some level and the facility in using scientifically based knowledge should be an integral part of the skills that social workers have and use.

Having a research base for our profession will not guarantee its public acceptance, but there is no doubt that the absence of such a base and the lack of vigorous research efforts to expand it will, in the long run, erode our credibility and be harmful to our clients.

MAKING A COMMITMENT TO LIFELONG LEARNING

Come on, go ahead and commit to lifelong learning. You can do it. It's easy. Don't become a slacker. You simply need to be a lifelong learner in order to become a professional social worker. Judy Krysik and Jerry Finn (2013) provide some fantastic tips on how to become lifelong learners:

> The expectations for producing and using research in professional social work practice are clear. The question that remains is: How? Entry-level social work jobs can be demanding, leaving little time for consultation, research, or even reflection. A social worker is more likely to use research if the employing agency or organization has a culture that supports it and if the worker is committed to making it happen. Will you commit yourself to a career of lifelong learning? If so, your very first step is to develop an action plan to make it happen. Here are a few tips that you might consider adopting.

- Join the National Association of Social Workers.

- Choose a conference that is relevant to your practice area and make a commitment to attend every year.

- Ask your manager or supervisor to subscribe to a professional journal(s).

- Join a Listserv dedicated to critiquing knowledge in your area of practice.

- Join your local library and spend at least one day a month in professional development reading about the latest research in your area.

- Initiate a brown-bag lunch session at your workplace at which you and your colleagues discuss research.

- Attend research-based training and workshops whenever possible.

- Continue your formal education by taking courses online or at a university or college.

- Make a presentation to share your research findings at a conference.

❄ Evaluate your day-to-day practices; that is, evaluate whether you are effective with your clients.

❄ Collaborate with others to evaluate the services provided by your agency or organization.

❄ Seek employment in agencies and organizations whose culture supports using research and evaluating practice.

 # SUMMARY

Knowledge is essential to human survival. Over the course of history, there have been many ways of knowing, from divine revelation, to tradition, to the authority of elders. By the beginning of the seventeenth century, people began to rely on a different way of knowing—the scientific method. Social workers obtain their knowledge from authority, tradition, professional experience, personal beliefs, and intuition as well as from findings derived from research studies that use the scientific method.

Expanding our research/practice base is also a way of enabling our profession to assert its place in the community of human service professionals. It's a way of carving out a niche of respectability, of challenging the insidious stereotype that social workers have their hearts in the right place but they are uninformed and ineffective.

Any profession (and especially ours) that bases its credibility on faith or ideology alone will have a hard time surviving. Although a research base for our profession will not guarantee us public acceptance, the absence of such a base and the lack of vigorous research efforts to expand it will—in the long run—undoubtedly erode our credibility.

Social workers engage in three main research roles. They can consume research by using the findings of others in their day-to-day practices, they can become contributing partners in the knowledge-generation enterprise, and they can produce and disseminate research results for others to use.

This chapter briefly explored the place of research in social work and advocated that our practices be based on quality research findings that are derived from the scientific method. The next chapter builds upon this one in that it discusses how researchers choose what problems to study in the first place.

Study Questions for Chapter 1

— First, answer each question only AFTER you have read the chapter.

— Second, indicate how comfortable you were in answering each question on a 5-point scale:

1	2	3	4	5
Very uncomfortable	Somewhat uncomfortable	Neutral	Somewhat comfortable	Very comfortable

If you rated any question between 1–3, please reread the section of the chapter where the information for the question can be found. If you're still uncomfortable answering the question, talk with your instructor and/or your classmates for more clarification.

Questions	Degree of comfort? (Circle one number)
1. Before you entered your social work program and before you read this chapter, how did you think our profession obtained its knowledge base? Provide as many examples as you can to justify your response.	1 2 3 4 5
2. In your own words, list the six CSWE research-related competencies that you are expected to master as a social work practitioner. Now discuss how you plan to integrate each competency into your daily social work activities when you graduate and become a professional social worker. You need to formulate a plan for how you are going to do this. Provide as many examples as you can to justify your position.	1 2 3 4 5
3. In your own words, list the six NASW research-related principles that you are expected to master as a social work practitioner. Now discuss how you plan to integrate each principle into your daily social work activities when you graduate and become a professional social worker. You need to formulate a plan for how you are going to do this. Provide as many examples as you can to justify your position.	1 2 3 4 5
4. List the five ways we obtain our knowledge base. Now discuss how you plan to use each one when you graduate and become a professional social worker. Provide an example for each one of the five ways of knowing.	1 2 3 4 5
5. What are the main differences among knowledge, tradition, beliefs, and intuition? Provide as many social work examples as you can to justify your response.	1 2 3 4 5

6.	What is professional judgment? Provide as many social work examples as you can to justify your response.	1 2 3 4 5
7.	Discuss why a professional judgment on your part, no matter how uncertain you may be, is far more beneficial to your client than just using your intuition.	1 2 3 4 5
8.	What is the "scientific method"? How is this method of knowing more "objective" than the other four ways of knowing? Provide as many social work examples as you can to justify your response.	1 2 3 4 5
9.	Take a look at Figure 1.1. Describe the phases of the scientific inquiry process in your own words using one common social work example throughout your discussion.	1 2 3 4 5
10.	What is inductive logic? What is deductive logic? Compare the two using one social work research example of your choice.	1 2 3 4 5
11.	List and discuss the four characteristics that social work researchers must possess. Identify any of the characteristics that surprised you. Identify one characteristic that you think you may have trouble with as a future social work practitioner and delineate the ways you could grow in this area.	1 2 3 4 5
12.	In reference to Question 11, do you feel that line-level social work practitioners should also possess these characteristics? If so, which ones?	1 2 3 4 5
13.	In reference to Question 11, what additional characteristics do you feel social work researchers should have?	1 2 3 4 5
14.	Look at Table 1.1. Compare and contrast the positivistic and interpretive research approaches to knowledge development in relation to each one of the 15 rows in the table. Provide social work examples throughout your discussion.	1 2 3 4 5
15.	What is the difference between pure and applied research studies? When would you use each of them? Provide as many examples as you can to justify your response.	1 2 3 4 5
16.	Provide your own definition of social work research. How does your definition differ from the one provided in the book?	1 2 3 4 5

17. Review our definition of social work research. Now, use Google to find a definition of social work research, and locate at least 5 other definitions of social work research. Compare and contrast the ones you found with ours. What are their commonalities? What are their differences?	1 2 3 4 5
18. Now the hard part: Revise your own definition of social work research by integrating our definition of social work research and the 5 definitions you found on the Internet. Don't be shy, go for it! Present your revised definition to the rest of the class. What were their comments? Did they help you refine your revised definition even further?	1 2 3 4 5
19. Look at Figure 1.3. In your own words describe how the social work research process is the same as the social work practice process. Use a social work example throughout your discussion.	1 2 3 4 5
20. List the three research roles you can take as a professional social work practitioner. Now discuss how you could be in each role as a social worker upon graduation. Use specific social work examples throughout your discussion.	1 2 3 4 5
21. What is lifelong learning? Provide an example.	1 2 3 4 5
22. Why is making a commitment to lifelong learning so important? Provide as many social work examples as you can to justify your response.	1 2 3 4 5
23. At this point in your course, how comfortable are you with discussing the place of research in social work with your field instructor (or your supervisor at work)? With your fellow classmates? Discuss in detail.	1 2 3 4 5

Assessing Your Self-Efficacy for Chapter 1

AFTER you have read the chapter AND have completed all the study questions, please indicate how knowledgeable you feel you are for each concept listed below.

1 Very uncomfortable	2 Somewhat uncomfortable	3 Neutral	4 Somewhat comfortable	5 Very comfortable

Major Concepts in Chapter	Knowledge Level? (Circle one number)
1. Accountability in the social work profession	1 2 3 4 5
2. How the research process enhances our accountability	1 2 3 4 5
3. The Council on Social Work Education	1 2 3 4 5
4. The National Association of Social Workers	1 2 3 4 5
5. How we obtain our knowledge base	1 2 3 4 5
6. The five ways of knowing what's "true"	1 2 3 4 5
7. The scientific method of knowledge generation	1 2 3 4 5
8. Phases of the scientific method	1 2 3 4 5
9. The benefits of the two research approaches to knowledge development	1 2 3 4 5
10. The positivistic research approach	1 2 3 4 5
11. The interpretive research approach	1 2 3 4 5
12. Characteristics of social work researchers	1 2 3 4 5
13. Pure and applied research studies	1 2 3 4 5
14. The definition of social work research	1 2 3 4 5
15. Commonalities between social work "research" and social work "practice"	1 2 3 4 5

16. The three social work research roles that social workers can take	1 2 3 4 5
17. The concept of lifelong learning as it pertains to professional social work practice	1 2 3 4 5

Add up your scores (Minimum = 17, Maximum = 85)	Total score =

A	76 — 85	= Social Work Manager in the making.
B	68 — 75	= Social Work Supervisor.
C	60 — 67	= Social Work Practitioner.
D	17 — 59	= Case Aide. Reread the chapter and redo the study questions.

2

Formulating Research Questions

The important thing is to never stop questioning.
~ Albert Einstein

I n the last chapter we discussed how we go about knowing something, and we placed a considerable emphasis on the fact that knowing something derived from the scientific method is more objective, if you will, than knowing that same thing through authority, tradition, experience, or beliefs and intuition.

In this chapter we discuss how to formulate research questions that can be answered through using the scientific method. Before you can even begin to start formulating a research question, however, you need to fully appreciate the direct and indirect factors that affect its construction.

Factors Affecting Research Questions

There are six highly overlapping factors that indirectly or directly affect the formulation of a social work research question (Grinnell & Williams, 1990; Williams, Grinnell, & Tutty, 1997). Obviously, these factors have a major impact on the way research questions are formulated. For the sake of clarity, these factors are presented separately, although in reality they always act in combination. The factors are:

— The Social Work Profession

— The Social Work Agency

— The Researcher

— The Social Work Practitioner

— Ethical and Cultural Considerations

— Political and Social Considerations

The Social Work Profession

THE FIRST FACTOR that affects how social work research questions are formulated is our very own profession. Doing a research study that answers a research question in a social work practice setting is enormously different from doing one in a scientific laboratory or in an artificial setting. Many social work research questions are geared toward our clients, who often participate in our research projects. They have special needs that we must take into consideration if we use them to collect data that will answer our research question. On a general level, our profession welcomes research studies that contain one or more of the following characteristics:

— Pure Questions That Increase Our Knowledge Base

— Applied Questions That Evaluate Our Social Work Interventions

— Social Problems Studied Must Be Changeable

PURE QUESTIONS THAT INCREASE OUR KNOWLEDGE BASE

We welcome *pure* research questions with open arms that are geared toward increasing our knowledge base. Identifying a body of social work knowledge, as distinct from sociological or psychological knowledge, is often a difficult task. Our profession has always been something of a poor relation among the social sciences, borrowing bits of information from psychology, anthropology, and sociology, pieces from political science and economics, and never finding much that can be classified as distinctly and uniquely social work.

However, we are hardly in a position to complain about this. The knowledge garnered from psychology is obtained largely from research questions that were answered from studies undertaken by psychologists. Similarly, the knowledge we borrow from anthropology, sociology, political science, and economics is gathered by people in these fields.

It seems only reasonable that the knowledge specific to our field should be obtained by social workers, who formulate their own research questions and conduct the subsequent research studies to answer them in their particular areas of expertise.

APPLIED QUESTIONS THAT EVALUATE OUR SOCIAL WORK INTERVENTIONS

Our profession is also likes *applied* research questions that evaluate our daily practices. As we established in the previous chapter, if we are to remain involved in the well-being of our clients, we must become more active in assessing the effectiveness and efficiency of our interventions. The social problem of domestic violence, for example, will not be solved by indiscriminate funding of emergency shelters for women who have been battered, by treatment for men who have been abusive toward their partners, by services for children who have been victimized, or by higher education for all and sundry. Good research questions are needed both to determine the most effective ways of helping people and to evaluate the usefulness of our social service programs currently being funded.

Evaluation of existing social service programs is no longer the rather lackadaisical affair that it once was. As recently as the 1970s, it would have been enough for a program's director to convince a funding body that the program it was funding was meeting its goal, keeping within its budget, and generally providing a useful service to the community, without having to produce detailed documentation to that effect.

Today, funders want "objective data" derived from research studies that determine whether the agency's goals are being met at the least possible cost. They want the results of evaluative studies, performed according to accepted research methods. They simply want proof. The demand for evaluation is so pervasive that if we do not evaluate our own programs, the evaluations will often be conducted for us by professional evaluators, hired by funding bodies. Until recently, all evaluations of social

BOX 2.1
Where Do Research Questions Come From?

So how do researchers come up with the idea for a research question? Probably one of the most common sources of research ideas is the experience of practical problems in our field. Many researchers are directly engaged in social, health, or human service program implementation, and they come up with their ideas based on what they see happening around them. Others aren't directly involved in service contexts, but they work with (or survey) people who are in order to learn what needs to be better understood.

Many of the ideas would strike the outsider as silly or worse. For instance, in health services areas, there is great interest in the problem of back injuries among nursing staff. It's not necessarily the thing that comes first to mind when we think about the health-care field. But if you reflect on it for a minute longer, it should be obvious that nurses and nursing staff do an awful lot of lifting in performing their jobs.

They lift and push heavy equipment, and they lift and push oftentimes heavy patients! If five or ten out of every hundred nursing staff were to strain their backs on average over the period of one year, the costs would be enormous—and that's pretty much what's happening. Even minor injuries can result in increased absenteeism. Major ones can result in lost jobs and expensive medical bills.

The nursing industry figures that this is a problem that costs tens of millions of dollars annually in increased health care. The health-care industry has developed a number of approaches, many of them educational, to try to reduce the scope and cost of the problem. So even though they might seem silly at first, practical problems that arise in practice can lead to extensive research efforts.

THE LITERATURE

Another source for research ideas is the literature (to be discussed shortly). Certainly, many researchers get ideas for research by reading the literature and thinking of ways to extend or refine previous research studies. Another type of literature that acts as a source of good research ideas is the Requests for Proposals (RFPs) that are published by government agencies. These RFPs describe some problem that the agency would like researchers to address—they are virtually handing the researcher an idea! Typically, the RFP describes the problem that needs addressing, the contexts in which it operates, the approach they would like to see taken to investigate and address the problem, and the amount they would be willing to pay for such a study. Clearly, there's nothing like potential research funding to get researchers to focus on a particular research topic.

And let's not forget the fact that many researchers simply think up their research topics on their own. Of course, no one lives in a vacuum, so we would expect that the ideas you come up with on your own are influenced by your background, culture, education, and experiences.

work programs were carried out by non–social workers who were skilled in such techniques as planning, programing, and budget systems (PPBS) but who knew very little about social work values and practices.

Few of our programs are cost efficient in the way that businesses must be in order to survive. The purpose of a business is to make a profit; the purpose of a social work program is to salvage human lives. Because of this distinction, social work administrators objected to the use of business cost-efficiency criteria to measure the worth of human services. They questioned the meaning of the word "efficient" in the human context: Did it mean efficient in terms of time, money, labor, suffering, human rights, or something else?

Eventually, we began to conduct evaluative studies and tried to reach a compromise between PPBS efficiency and client needs. The prestige of our profession has benefitted from the fact that we are now empowered to evaluate our own programs in light of our own value systems. Clients have also benefitted because now their needs are not sacrificed arbitrarily to costs. These gains are lost, however, if the agency's staff ignores evaluations until they are imposed upon them from outside the agency.

In sum, it benefits both social workers and their clients if we take more responsibility for formulating research questions and conducting the subsequent research studies that answer them on our own programs. This provides us with the authority to advocate for our clients, to be heard by other professionals with regard to clients, to maintain control over the programs serving clients, and to bring about needed change.

In this present age of accountability, there is no doubt that a profession that strives for status must be accountable. To some degree it's a question of "the more accountability, the more status," because accountability *is* status. It symbolizes power. It's apparent, therefore, that if our profession wishes to crawl up the status ladder, its driving force must be accountability. The way to achieve accountability is by answering well-formulated, well-thought-out research questions.

However, we must never forget that accountability is not all a facade. As we know from the previous chapter, the scientific method—as one of the five ways of knowing—is not just a path to authority and status. It also allows us to determine how best to serve our clients, how to determine the effectiveness of our services, and how to improve the services we offer.

SOCIAL PROBLEMS MUST BE CHANGEABLE

We strongly invite research questions that will help solve social problems. However, the problems must be changeable—and have a solution. In the last chapter, we talked about what motivates social workers to do research studies. Your supervisor may want you to do one, or you might have to for the sake of your clients, or you could be just interested in a particular topic or area. Sometimes the research question is mostly already there, and it only remains for you to word it more precisely so that it can become researchable.

Perhaps, for example, your social service program provides substance abuse treatment to First Nations adolescents, and it wants to know whether the spirituality component it has recently introduced makes the treatment more effective. At other times, you begin more generally with a broad topic area—poverty, for example—and then you will need to decide what particular aspects of your general topic area you want to address before you can formulate a sound research question.

Simply put, social work research topics—and the research questions they generate—deal with social problems. A social problem is something we wish we didn't have. We do not define a social problem in the first place unless we believe that change both ought to and probably can occur.

This may not sound particularly profound, but consider for a moment what it is that causes some social circumstances and not others to be defined as "problems." In our day, poverty is seen as a social problem. In earlier times, poverty certainly existed, but it was not considered a problem in the sense that we felt we ought to do something about it. The attitude was very much that the poor are always with us—they always have been, they probably always will be, and that is just the way life is.

Knowing that our profession is the first factor that affects research questions, we now turn our attention to the second, the social work agency where the practitioners work.

The Social Work Agency

THE SECOND FACTOR affecting research questions is the social work agency—the place where we work. This factor heavily overlaps with the previous one—the social work profession itself. Most of us are employed by a social work program housed within an agency. A child protection agency, for example, may run an investigation program whose sole purpose is to investigate alleged cases of child abuse and neglect.

The same agency may provide in-home support services to families who have abused or neglected their children—a second program. The agency may run a survivor-witness program for children and nonoffending parents who have to appear in court—a third program.

Research studies that answer research questions are usually conducted within the confines of a program. The word "confines" is used advisedly because no study can be undertaken without the support, or at least the toleration, of the program's director. Some program directors are supportive of research studies while others shiver at the merest mention, but there are some things that all of them have in common. The first of these is that they all worry about money.

Program directors of social work agencies have very little money. They worry that in the coming year they may have even less money—that their funding will be cut or even terminated, their clients will suffer, and their staff will be unemployed. They worry that all these disasters will follow in the wake of an evaluative research study. People doing research studies often have access to client files and to clients.

BOX 2.2
Show Ignores Native Stereotypes

GIBSONS, B.C. (CP)—Native actress Marianne Jones had to fight to keep from laughing when a script once called for her to utter the line: "Him shot six times."

"It was really a difficult thing to say," recalls Jones, who now plays Laurel on CBC's Beachcombers.

That, she says, is typical of the way natives are portrayed on TV and films.

And that, she says, is what's different about Beachcombers.

"It's one of the only shows that portrays native people on a day-to-day basis," says Jones.

"No other series has that sort of exposure. When you think of how many native people there are in the country, it's amazing that there isn't more."

Television's portrayal of natives touches a nerve in Jones.

The striking actress with shoulder-length raven hair cherishes her Haida heritage. She identifies her birthplace as "Haida Gwaii—that's the Queen Charlotte Islands, the real name."

The four natives in Beachcombers are depicted as people rather than stereotypes.

"I've done a lot of other shows and they sort of want to put you in a slot: You're a noble savage, you know, the Hollywood stereotypes that have been perpetuated forever."

She admits that natives are struggling with their identity these days; wrestling with tradition and the attractions of the 20th century.

"We're all weighing the traditional life, the spirituality, against being human . . . . We're living today."

"Everybody has a fridge, so to speak," she adds with a raspy laugh.

Jones is doing her part by venturing into video production, starting with a documentary on a Haida artist.

"For a long time, native people have not been allowed or able to define their own images."

"We need to take control to get rid of those Hollywood stereotypes, and to change native people on television to real people."

We sometimes talk to staff and examine agency procedures. We are in an excellent position to embarrass everyone by breaching client confidentiality, making inappropriate statements at the wrong times to the wrong people, and writing reports that comment on the program's weaknesses but disregard its strengths. All programs, like all people, have flaws. Few are efficient in the business sense, and most are open to doubt concerning their effectiveness. Program directors know this. They work to improve programs, serving their clients as best they can with limited resources and knowledge that is patchy at best—because the knowledge has not been gained and the research studies necessary to gain it have not been undertaken.

It's not surprising, then, that program directors find themselves torn with regard to the place of the research enterprise in our profession. They understand that increased knowledge, via answering research questions, is necessary in order to serve clients better, but sometimes they wish that the knowledge could be gathered somewhere else: not through their programs, not with their client files, not using their scarce resources, and not taking up the time of their staff. They correctly argue that resources given to research studies are resources taken away from client services.

They may think, privately, that research reports are useful only to those engaged in the studies in the first place. There is an upside to all of this gloom, however. It's possible that the research report might reflect the program in a good light, delighting its funders and improving its standing in the public eye. In addition, the study might reveal a genuinely practical way in which the program could improve its services to its clients or do what it does more efficiently.

Many program directors will therefore give permission for research studies to be conducted, provided that the person(s) doing the study is of good standing in the social work community, the proposed study meets the staff's approval, and agreements are entered into concerning confidentiality and the use of staff and financial resources. Larger agencies often have special committees to evaluate research requests (to be discussed in the following chapter). Few, if any, of our programs are designed with the notion that someday the program will be engaged in the research process.

In some programs, client files have become more ordered with the advent of the computer, but frequently data are difficult both to find and to interpret. The entries in client files may be made by different workers at different times, in writing ranging from copperplate to scrawl, with different viewpoints on the people and events involved, and sometimes with vital data missing.

Policies and procedures manuals, long outdated, may bear little relationship to the policies presently in place and the procedures actually undertaken. When this occurs, we must often become dependent upon the goodwill of staff to provide guidance and explanations, even when the original plan was just a quiet session with client files. A researcher's positive relationships with program staff cannot be overemphasized. If you don't possess sound social skills, you'll never be given permission to do a research study within a social work agency.

THE RESEARCHER

THE THIRD FACTOR affecting the formulation of research questions is the person actually doing the study—the researcher. To illustrate how social work researchers are motivated to come up with specific research questions, two articles from Canadian newspapers will be used as examples (Grinnell, Rothery, & Thomlison, 1993).

What motivates social workers to pose research questions? One way to answer this question is by examining possible reactions to the articles reproduced in Boxes 1.1 and 2.2. As you know, the article reproduced in Box 1.1 in the previous chapter concerned the attempted abduction of a child in an elementary school at Innisfail, Alberta, and the article in Box 2.2 in this chapter remarks on the unusual lack of stereotyping of Native Indians in a Canadian television program. The two articles can easily be applied to the problems of child abuse and racism throughout the world.

Readers will have different reactions to the story about the kidnapped child. Parents of young children, for example, may feel fear and anxiety about the safety of their children because they may be reminded that in their communities there are those who could harm them. They and others may experience anger toward those who victimize children and a desire to see them caught, restrained, or punished. They may feel concern for the abducted seven-year-old, mixed with feelings of relief that she was returned to her family.

An adult who was victimized as a child, for example, may be likely to have more complex and strong emotional reactions than a person who was not victimized as a child. Teachers, social workers, and police officers whose jobs entail responsibility for such situations may experience professional curiosity.

With the second article (Box 2.2), a reader may react with admiration for Marianne Jones, who has overcome the barriers imposed by racism to establish herself in a difficult career. Those of you who are members of a minority group may well applaud more enthusiastically than those of you who are not; you may even share her success in some way. An administrator in a school system that serves minority students may sense an opportunity—a chance to answer a meaningful research question into what images of minorities are perpetuated through the educational system and what impact this has on the students.

Some readers may have little or no reaction, however; if nothing in their past history or current involvements is linked to the issues of child abuse (Box 1.1) or racism (Box 2.2), they may merely glance at the articles and pass them over quickly. A great variety of responses to these two news items is possible, each shaped by the reader's history and circumstances.

It is in reactions such as these that research questions are born. We may be drawn into projects simply because they are there—the support is available to conduct a particular study, or our careers will benefit from seizing the opportunities.

Nevertheless, a research question would not be formulated without someone, somewhere, sometime, confronting a situation or event and finding it relevant. Potential researchers begin with the sense (often vaguely formulated) that there is more to be known about a problem area; a question exists that is important enough to justify investing time and other resources in the search for an answer.

The most important thing to know before doing any research study is what implications the study's findings might produce that will advance the knowledge base of social work practice, education, and policy.

Value Systems of the Researchers

At every stage in the research process, there are decisions to be made based on the knowledge and value systems of the person formulating the research question and conducting the research study. If we are investigating poverty, for example, and believe that poverty results from character flaws in the poor, we might study treatment interventions designed to overcome those flaws.

On the other hand, if we believe that ghettos are a factor, we might prefer to focus on environmental causes. In short, the research questions we finally select are determined by our own value systems as well as by the social and political realities of the hour.

Another factor in our study of poverty is how we define "poor." What annual income should a person earn in order to be categorized as poor? We may decide that "poor," in the context of our study, means an annual income of less than $10,000, and that we do not need to talk to anyone who earns more than that. If we decide that the upper limit should be $20,000, we are automatically including many more people as potential participants for our study. Thus, the data collected about "the poor" will depend largely on whom is defined as poor.

Our final report will probably include recommendations for change based on our study's findings—based off of our research question, of course. These recommendations, too, will depend on our personal value systems, modified by social, political, and economic realities.

It may be our private opinion that welfare recipients should be given only the absolute minimum of resources necessary to sustain life in order to motivate them to find work. On the other hand, we may believe that a decent standard of living is every human being's birthright. Whatever our opinion, it's likely that we will clothe it in suitable phraseology and incorporate it somehow into our recommendations.

Personal value systems are particularly evident in program evaluations. Our programs are often labeled as ineffective not as a result of poor goal achievement, but because there is disagreement about the goal itself. Is a drug prevention program "successful" if it reduces drug use among its clients, or must clients abstain altogether before success can be claimed?

Then there is the question of how much success constitutes "success." Is a job placement program worth funding if it finds jobs for *only* 50 percent of its clients? Should an in-home support program be continued if the child is removed from the home in 30 percent of the cases?

Next, there is the matter of what types of clients are the most deserving. Should limited resources be used to counsel people dying of cancer, or would the money be better spent on those who are newly diagnosed? Is it worthwhile to provide long-term treatment for one family whose potential for change is small, while other families with more potential linger on the waiting list? These types of value-based questions are endless.

THE SOCIAL WORK PRACTITIONER

SOCIAL WORKERS' BELIEFS AND ATTITUDES also affect how research questions are formulated that will be answered in agency settings. Some social workers, for example, refuse to have an observer present at an interview with a client on the grounds that the client will be unable to speak freely and the social worker–client relationship will be disrupted.

This difficulty can be resolved in facilities with one-way mirrors; but if no such mirror exists, a person wishing to answer a research question that determines the effectiveness and efficiency of a treatment intervention, for example, may not be able to watch the intervention in a practical, clinical setting.

An alternative to the physical presence of the person doing the study is a video recorder. A few social workers—whose belief in disruption leads them to be disrupted—also object to video recorders; indeed, some social workers seem to believe that there is a sort of an aura surrounding practice relationships that is shattered by such devices, even though experience has shown that most clients ignore video recorders after the first few curious glances.

To a degree, it's true that the act of measuring alters what it measures, but often the change is neither great nor long-lasting. When video recorders, paper-and-pencil questionnaires, and computer question-and-answer programs are shunned out of hand, the effectiveness of the intervention can never be objectively established.

The opinions and attitudes of social workers in regard to research practices thus play a vital part in the formulation of research questions. It's not just our attitude that makes a difference—it's the attitudes of everyone involved in the study.

ETHICAL AND CULTURAL CONSIDERATIONS

THE FIFTH IMPORTANT FACTOR affecting the formulation of social work research questions is ethical and cultural considerations. Physical scientists are by no means exempt from ethical considerations. Consider Robert Oppenheimer and other atomic scientists, who learned too late that their scientific findings about splitting the atom were used to create an atomic bomb—a purpose the scientists themselves opposed.

A physical scientist who wishes to run tests on water samples, for example, does not have to consider the feelings of the water samples or worry about harming them. No large dilemma is presented if one of the water samples must be sacrificed to the cause of knowledge building.

For people engaged in social work research studies, however, the ethical issues are far more pervasive and complex. It's a fundamental principle of formulating a social work research question: increasing our knowledge base is much to be desired, but it must never be obtained at the expense of human beings. Because many of our research questions revolve directly around human beings, safeguards must be put in place to ensure that our research participants are never harmed, either physically or psychologically.

Clients participating in studies trust the individual practitioners who involve them in the studies. It's therefore incumbent upon all of us to be familiar with ethical principles so that our client's trust will never be betrayed.

Essentially, there are three precautionary ethical measures that must be taken before beginning any research study that will answer any research question. These are (1) obtaining the participant's informed consent, (2) designing the study in an ethical manner, and (3) ensuring that others will be properly told about the study's findings. All of these concerns are discussed in detail in the following chapter on research ethics.

POLITICAL AND SOCIAL CONSIDERATIONS

THE LAST FACTOR that affects social work research questions is political and social considerations. Ethics and politics are interrelated, but a useful distinction exists in that ethics has to do with the methods employed in answering the research question, whereas politics is concerned with the practical costs and uses of the study's findings.

Consider, for example, the area of race relations. Most social researchers in the 1960s supported the cause of African American equality in America. In 1969, Arthur Jensen, a Harvard psychologist, examined data on racial differences in IQ test results and concluded that genetic differences between African Americans and Caucasians accounted for the lower IQ scores of African Americans. Jensen was labeled a racist, and such was the furor surrounding his study that other people were reluctant to pursue any line of inquiry involving comparisons between Caucasians and African Americans.

Consequently, a needed investigation into the higher rate of mortality seen in African American women with breast cancer as compared with similarly afflicted Caucasian women was not conducted. The study may have revealed racial differences in genetic predispositions to breast tumors, and the National Cancer Institute, at that time, was understandably reluctant to use the word "genetic" in connection with African Americans. It's not infrequently the case that sensitivity about vulnerable populations leads to avoidance of research studies that might benefit those groups.

Politics plays an important role not only in what research studies are funded or conducted but in what findings are published. Contrary opinions or unpopular opinions are no longer punished, as they were in Galileo's day, by the Inquisitional Tribunal or the rack, but they are still punished.

Punishment may be delivered in the form of articles and books that are never published, invitations to present research papers that are never offered, academic appointments that are never given—and research proposals that are never funded.

The answer to a research question can be an extremely expensive endeavor. If a funding body cannot be found to support the research proposal, the study may never be conducted. Funding bodies tend either to be governments or to be influenced by government policies; and a person doing a research study is as interested as anyone else in money, recognition, and professional advancement. It's therefore often the case that funded studies follow directions consistent with the prevailing political climate.

Studies under one government may inquire into ways of improving social services and better designs for public housing. Under another government, attention may shift to the efficiency of existing programs, as measured through program evaluations.

It's important to remember, though, that not all research studies are expensive and many can be conducted without the aid of government money. No large amounts of extra funding are needed to integrate evaluation into the normal routine of clinical practice. Program evaluations do not cost large amounts of money when conducted by program staff themselves.

In sum, social work research questions are affected not only by the personal biases of the person conducting the study to answer the questions, but also by prevailing beliefs on such sensitive issues as race, gender, poverty, disability, sexual orientation, violence, and so forth. Government positions both shape and are shaped by these beliefs, leading to support of some research questions but not of others.

Legitimate inquiry is sometimes restricted by fear that data uncovered on one of these sensitive issues will be misinterpreted or misused, thereby bringing harm to vulnerable client groups.

THE KNOWLEDGE-LEVEL CONTINUUM

Once your research question is formulated it then must be answered. We will now turn our attention to how the positivistic and interpretive research approaches answer various types of research questions. All research studies fall anywhere along the knowledge-level continuum depending on how much is already known about the research question under investigation (Figure 2.1).

How much is known about the research question determines the purpose of the study. If you didn't know anything, for example, you will merely want to explore the research area, gathering basic data. Studies like this, conducted for the purpose of exploration, are known, logically enough, as exploratory studies and fall at the bottom of the knowledge-level continuum as can be seen in Figure 2.1. Exploratory research questions usually adopt an interpretive research approach. However, they can adopt a positivistic approach as well.

When you have gained some knowledge of the research topic area through exploratory studies, the next task is to describe a specific aspect of the topic area in greater detail, using words (interpretive) and/or numbers (positivistic). These studies, whose purpose is description, are known as descriptive studies and fall in the middle of the knowledge-level continuum as presented in Figure 2.1.

They can adopt a positivistic and/or interpretive research approach. After descriptive studies have provided a substantial knowledge base in the research topic area, you will be in a position to ask very specific and more complex research questions—causality questions. These kinds of studies are known as explanatory studies.

The division of the knowledge continuum into three parts—exploratory, descriptive, and explanatory—is a useful way of categorizing research studies in terms of their purpose, the kinds of questions they can answer, and the research approach(s) they can take in answering the questions.

However, as in all categorization systems, the three divisions are totally arbitrary, and some social work research studies defy categorization, falling nastily somewhere between exploratory and descriptive, or between descriptive and explanatory. This defiance is only to be expected because the knowledge-level continuum is essentially that—a continuum, not a neat collection of categories. The continuum contains three types of research studies:

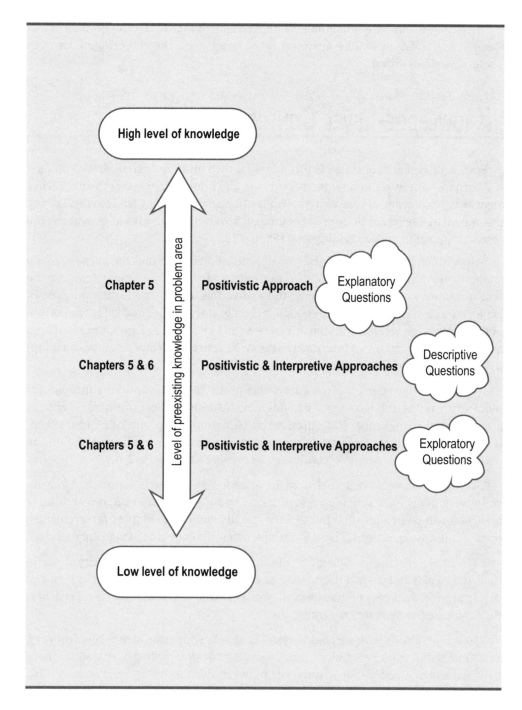

FIGURE 2.1
The Knowledge-Level Continuum, Approaches to
the Scientific Method, and Types of Questions Answered

— Exploratory Research Studies

— Descriptive Research Studies

— Explanatory Research Studies

EXPLORATORY RESEARCH STUDIES

EXPLORATORY STUDIES are most useful when the research topic area is relatively new. In the United States during the 1970s, for example, the development of new drugs to control the symptoms of mental illness, together with new federal funding for small, community-based mental health centers, resulted in a massive discharge of people from large state-based mental health institutions.

Some folks applauded this move as restoring the civil liberties of the mentally ill. Others were concerned that current community facilities would prove inadequate to meet the needs of the people being discharged and their families. Social workers active in the 1970s were anxious to explore the situation, both with an eye on influencing social policy and in order to develop programs to meet the perceived needs of this group of people.

The topic area here is very broad. What are the consequences of a massive discharge of people who are psychiatrically challenged and were recently institutionalized? Many different questions pertaining to the topic can be asked.

Where are these people living now? Alone? In halfway houses? With their families? On the street? Are they receiving proper medication and nutrition? What income do they have? How do they spend their time? What stresses do they suffer? What impact have they had on their family members and the communities in which they now reside? What services are available to them? How do they feel about being discharged?

No single study can answer all these questions. It's a matter of devising a sieve-like procedure where the first sieve with the biggest holes identifies general themes. Each general theme is then put through successively finer sieves until more specific research questions can be asked.

Let's take a closer look at Figure 2.2. You might begin to explore the consequences of the massive discharge by gathering together a group of these discharged people and asking them a basic exploratory question: What have been your experiences since you were discharged? (What are the components that make up the discharge experience?) The question will be answered using qualitative data. Individual answers via words—not numbers—will generate common themes.

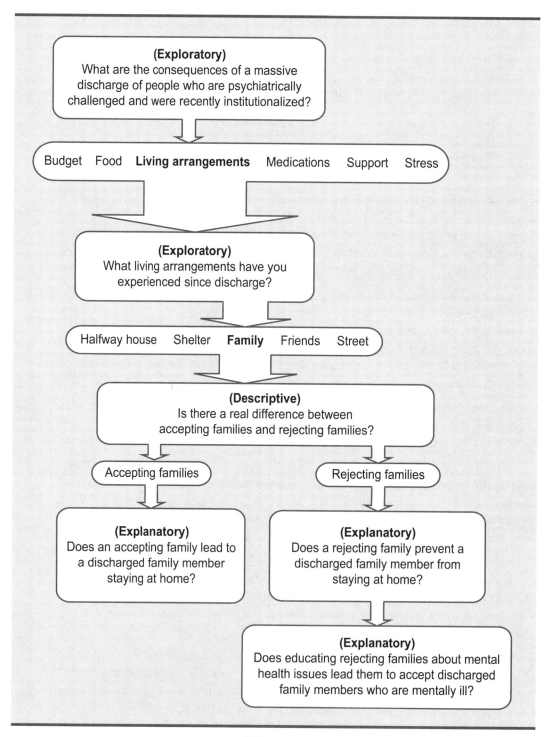

FIGURE 2.2

Example of a Sieving Procedure

At this point, you might feel a need for numbers. How many of them are living where? How many times have they moved on average? What percentage of those who moved in with their families stayed there? These are descriptive questions, aimed at describing, or providing an accurate profile, of this group of people.

You are now moving up the knowledge continuum in Figure 2.1 from the exploratory to the descriptive category, but, before we go there, let's summarize the general goals of exploratory research studies (Neuman, 2009):

- ❈ Become familiar with the basic facts, people, and concerns involved.

- ❈ Develop a well-grounded mental picture of what is occurring.

- ❈ Generate many ideas and develop tentative theories and conjectures.

- ❈ Determine the feasibility of doing additional research.

- ❈ Formulate questions and refine issues for more systematic inquiry.

- ❈ Develop techniques and a sense of direction for future research.

DESCRIPTIVE RESEARCH STUDIES

AT THE DESCRIPTIVE LEVEL, suppose you have decided to focus your research questions on those people who moved in with their families. You have an idea, based on your previous exploratory study, that there might be a relationship between the length of time spent in the institution and whether this group of people moved in with their families after discharge.

You would like to confirm or refute this relationship by using a much larger group of respondents than you used in your exploratory study (Figure 2.2). Another important tentative relationship that emerged at the exploratory level was the relationship between staying in the family home and the level of acceptance shown by the family.

You would like to know whether this relationship holds with a larger group. You would also like to know whether there is a real difference between accepting and rejecting families: is group A different from group B? And what factors contribute to acceptance or rejection of the discharged family member?

Eventually, you would like to know whether there is anything social workers can do to facilitate acceptance, but you don't have enough data yet to be able to usefully ask that question. In general, the goals of descriptive research studies are as follows (Neuman, 2009):

✳ Provide an accurate profile of a group.

✳ Describe a process, mechanism, or relationship.

✳ Give a verbal or numerical picture (e.g., percentages).

✳ Find information to stimulate new explanations.

✳ Create a set of categories or classify types.

✳ Clarify a sequence, set of stages, or steps.

✳ Document information that confirms or contradicts prior beliefs about a subject.

EXPLANATORY RESEARCH STUDIES

SUPPOSE YOU HAVE LEARNED from your descriptive studies that there are real differences between accepting and rejecting families and that these differences seem to have a major impact on whether the discharged person stays at home. Now you would like to ask two related explanatory, or causality, questions:

EXPLANATORY RESEARCH QUESTIONS (FIGURE 2.2)

1. Does an accepting family lead to a discharged family member staying at home?

2. Does a rejecting family prevent a discharged family member from staying at home?

In both cases, the answers will probably be yes, to some extent. Perhaps 30% of staying at home is explained by an accepting family, and the other 70% remains to be explained by other factors: the severity of the discharged person's symptoms, for example, or the degree of acceptance shown by community members outside the family.

Now, you might want to know whether acceptance on the part of the family carries more weight in the staying-at-home decision than acceptance on the part of the community. The answer to this question will provide a direction for possible intervention strategies. You will know whether to focus your attention on individual families or on entire communities.

Suppose that you decide, on the basis of your own and other explanatory studies, to focus on the families, and that the intervention that you choose for increasing their acceptance is education about mental illness. To evaluate the effectiveness of your intervention, you will eventually need to ask another explanatory question:

EXPLANATORY RESEARCH QUESTION (FIGURE 2.2)

Does educating rejecting families about mental health issues lead them to accept discharged family members who are mentally ill?

With the answer to this question, you have concluded your sieving procedures, as outlined in Figure 2.2. You have moved from a broad exploratory question about discharge experiences to a tested intervention designed to serve the discharged people and their families. In general, these are the goals of explanatory research studies (Neuman, 2009):

- Determine the accuracy of a principle or theory.

- Find out which competing explanation is better.

- Link different issues or topics under a common general statement.

- Build and elaborate a theory so that it becomes more complete.

- Extend a theory or principle into new areas or issues.

- Provide evidence to support or refute an explanation.

CLASSIFICATION OF RESEARCH QUESTIONS

Figures 2.2 and 2.3 show how research questions can be placed on a continuum from simple (exploratory studies) to complex (explanatory studies). Not surprisingly, we need to ask simple questions first. When we have the answers to these simple questions, we then proceed to ask more complex ones. We are thus moving from "little knowledge about our research question" to "more knowledge about our research question."

Figure 2.3 presents the knowledge continuum (from high to low—middle arrow), seven general classifications that research questions can take (left side), and the research approach (right side) that is most appropriate to answer each question classification. On a general level, there are seven types of questions that research studies can answer:

- Existence

- Composition

— Relationship

— Descriptive-Comparative

— Causality

— Causality-Comparative

— Causality-Comparative Interaction

EXISTENCE QUESTIONS

SUPPOSE FOR A MOMENT you have an assumption that there is an association between low self-esteem in women and spousal abuse. You are going to study this topic—over a number of studies—starting at the beginning. The beginning, at the bottom of the knowledge continuum, is an existence question. In fact, there are two existence questions because your assumption involves two concepts: (1) self-esteem and (2) spousal abuse.

First, knowing nothing whatsoever about either self-esteem or spouse abuse, let alone whether there is an association between them, you want to know if self-esteem and spousal abuse actually exist in the first place. Self-esteem and spouse abuse are concepts—they are nothing more than ideas, human inventions, if you like—that have become very familiar to social workers, and it's tempting just to say, "Of course they exist. I know they exist."

But there must have been a time when self-esteem was no more than a vague idea, held among students of human nature, that some people seem to feel better about themselves than other people do. It would then have been just a matter of contacting Ms. Smith—and Ms. Jones, and Ms. Tasmania—and asking them, "Do you feel good about yourself?"

This interpretive study, more commonly referred to as qualitative—and many others like it, conducted by different researchers over time—would have provided an indication that yes indeed, some people do feel better about themselves than other people do. Self-esteem, if that is what you want to call (or label) the feeling, does in fact exist. The same process can be done to determine whether spouse abuse exists. However, spouse abuse can be more easily observed and measured.

COMPOSITION QUESTIONS

THE SECOND QUESTION, "what is it that makes you feel good about yourself?" is an attempt to find out what particular personal attributes contribute to self-esteem. That is, it answers the composition question next on the knowledge continuum. Interpretive studies exploring this dimension may have discovered that people who feel good about themselves in general also specifically feel that they are liked by others, that they are competent, intelligent, caring, physically attractive, and have a host of other attributes that together make up the concept "self-esteem."

Thus, interpretive studies provide descriptive, or qualitative data, indicating that self-esteem exists and what it is. Similarly, they indicate that women are in fact sometimes abused by their partners and what particular forms such abuse can take.

RELATIONSHIP QUESTIONS

GOING UP ONE MORE NOTCH on the list, you next come to *relationship questions.* What, if any, is the relationship between women's self-esteem and spousal abuse? Here, you might begin with another interpretive study, trying to determine, on an individual basis, whether there seems to be any connection between having low self-esteem and being abused.

If there does seem to be enough evidence to theorize that such a relationship may exist, you might then use the positivistic research approach to see if the relationship holds for a larger number of women rather than just the small number you interviewed in your interpretive study.

DESCRIPTIVE-COMPARATIVE QUESTIONS

NEXT ON THE CONTINUUM you come to *descriptive-comparative questions:* Is Group A different from Group B? Here, you might go in a number of directions. You might wonder, for example, whether there is any difference in self-esteem levels between women in heterosexual relationships and women in lesbian relationships.

Does self-esteem differ between First Nations women and non-First Nations women? Do women with different sexual orientations or from different cultural groups also differ in how often they are abused, or how severely, or in what particular way?

Because you are asking about differences between social groups, which involve large numbers of people, you will need positivistic methods to address these questions. These will be discussed in Chapter 5.

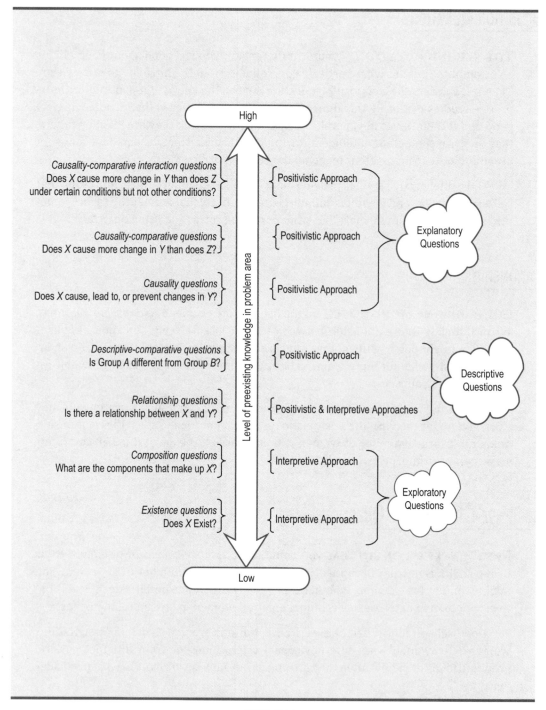

FIGURE 2.3

**Types of Research Questions, the Knowledge-Level Continuum,
and Approaches to the Scientific Method**

Similarly, it's unlikely that having low self-esteem leads inevitably to being abused. Positivistic studies here, with their use of impressive statistics, can tell us what percentage of the abuse can be explained by low self-esteem and what percentage remains to be explained by other factors.

CAUSALITY QUESTIONS

THIRD FROM THE TOP of the continuum are the *causality* questions. Does low self-esteem actually cause women to be abused? Or, for that matter, does being abused cause low self-esteem? Most complex behaviors don't have single causes. Being abused might certainly contribute to having low self-esteem, but it's highly unlikely to be the sole cause.

Similarly, it's unlikely that having low self-esteem leads inevitably to being abused. Positivistic studies here, with their use of impressive statistics, can tell us what percentage of the abuse can be explained by low self-esteem and what percentage remains to be explained by other factors.

CAUSALITY-COMPARATIVE QUESTIONS

IF THERE ARE FACTORS other than low self-esteem that cause abuse, it would be nice to know what they are and how much weight they have. Perhaps heavy drinking on the part of the abuser is a factor. Perhaps poverty is, or the battering suffered by the abuser as a child. Once these possible factors have been explored, using the same process you used in your exploration of self-esteem and spousal abuse, positivistic methods can again tell us what percentage of abuse is explained by each factor.

If low self-esteem accounts for only 2 percent, say, and heavy drinking accounts for 8 percent, you will have answered the *causality-comparative question*. You will know, on the average, that heavy drinking on the abuser's part has more effect on spousal abuse than does the woman's self-esteem level.

CAUSALITY-COMPARATIVE INTERACTION QUESTIONS

AT THE TIP-TOP OF THE CONTINUUM are the *causality-comparative interaction questions*. They ask whether your research findings only hold up under certain conditions. For example, if it's true that heavy drinking contributes more to spousal abuse than does the woman's level of self-esteem, perhaps that is only true for couples who are living in poverty. Or it's only true for couples with children. Or it's only true if the abuser was himself abused.

This final type of question, again answered through positivistic methods, reflects the highest aim of social work research: explanation. If we are to give our clients the best possible service, we need to know about causes and effects. What action or attribute on the part of whom causes how much of what effect, and under what conditions? What type of treatment will cause most change in a particular type of client in a particular situation?

CRITERIA FOR GOOD RESEARCH QUESTIONS

From the preceding discussion you now know how a research question springs to life and how such questions can be classified. Your research question now needs to be evaluated. Every research question must be:

— Relevant

— Researchable

— Feasible

— Ethical and Culturally Sensitive

If it doesn't pass muster on all four criteria, it's worthless and must be discarded like an old pair of sneakers.

RELEVANCE

RELEVANCE IS ONE OF THOSE THINGS, like efficiency, that is never absolute. The same research question may be less or more relevant depending on who is defining what is meant by "relevant" in what particular context. A research question about Chinese pottery, for example, might be relevant to researchers who are interested in Chinese potters or to archeologists, but it will be less relevant to social workers.

To social workers, a relevant research question is one whose answers will have an impact on policies, theories, or practices related to the social work profession. Within this framework, the degree of relevance of any particular study is usually decided by the organization who funds it, the program who houses it, and the research team who undertakes it.

RESEARCHABILITY

SOME VERY INTERESTING QUESTIONS cannot be answered through the research process, either because of the nature of the question or because of the difficulties inherent in collecting the necessary data. For example, a research study cannot answer the question "Does God exist?" Neither can it answer the question, "Is abortion wrong?" With respect to the latter, we may be able to collect evidence related to the effects of experiencing or being denied an abortion, but we cannot answer the underlying moral question.

In general, questions concerning faith or moral decisions are outside the province of research. Then there is the matter of technical difficulties inherent in the research question itself. For example, Aristotle believed that children would be healthier if conceived when the wind was from the north.

We are as interested in the health of children as Aristotle was, but, even supposing that we accepted the direction of the wind at conception as a possible contributing factor to healthier children, the question would not be researchable because of the practical difficulties associated with determining the direction of the wind at conception in a large enough number of cases. Thus, researchability has to do with whether the research question is appropriate for scientific enquiry and whether it's possible to collect the valid, reliable data that would be needed to answer the question.

FEASIBILITY

FEASIBILITY CARRIES the "collection of the necessary data" issue one step farther. Perhaps it's possible to collect data about the direction of the wind at conception (wind socks attached to every home combined with careful record keeping), but it's not possible for you to do it, given your limited resources, your inability to influence homebuilding, and the current protection of privacy standards. The question about the relationship between the wind and the health of children might therefore be researchable, but it's not feasible as far as you are concerned.

Your available resources have a profound effect on the scope of the research study you are able to mount and thus on the questions you are able to answer. In other words, given all these things, could you practically do what you have planned?

ETHICAL AND CULTURALLY SENSITIVITY

THERE IS A POTENTIAL FOR HARM not just in the way the study is conducted but in the way the research question is phrased as well. Researchers are in a wonderful position to offend just about everyone if they fail to pay attention to the cultural, gender, and sexual orientation aspects of their research questions. Not only might they offend people, but they might cause harm not just to research participants but to entire groups of people.

We will discuss ethics in depth in the next chapter (Chapter 3), and in Chapter 4 we will address the cultural considerations that must be taken into account when doing research studies. For now, just remember that your research question must be ethical and culturally sensitive in addition to being relevant, researchable, and feasible.

Now that you know how to formulate a general social work research question, you need to have an understanding of how to use the existing literature to help you to answer your research question and develop your research study—the topic of the following section.

 # Reviewing the Literature

All social work research studies must draw upon the literature. Yours is no exception. A literature review is an essential early step in refining your research question or writing a research proposal. Our discussion of how to review the literature has been written by Vivienne Bozalek and Nelleke Bak.

This section of this chapter demystifies the literature review process by focusing on what it is, how it's perceived by social work students, why you are required to undertake a literature review when doing a research study (or writing a research proposal), how to go about doing a literature review, and finally what the characteristics of a good literature review may look like.

Doing a research study can be seen as an entry into an academic conversation that has been going on in professional social work journals and books. Just as you would do when joining any other conversation, you'll first listen to what the conversation is about, figure out what the main issues of debate are, and determine who is responding to whom—and in what way.

The literature review section of your research study or proposal is a way of reporting to your reader on the academic conversation in which you are planning to participate. In the simplest of forms, a literature review generally involves the search for and documentation of primary (original) sources of scholarship, rather than secondary sources, which are reports of other people's work. Cooper and Hedges (1994) describe the literature review as:

> A literature review reports on primary or original scholarship. The primary reports used in a literature review may be verbal, but in the vast majority of cases

they are written documents. The types of scholarship may be empirical, theoretical, critical/analytical, or methodological in nature. Second, a literature review seeks to describe, summarize, evaluate, clarify, and/or integrate the content of primary reports.

This should give you some idea of what a literature review may involve. Reviewing the literature is a continuous process. It begins before a specific research question has been finalized, and it continues until the final report is finished. To summarize:

- The literature review draws mainly on primary sources.

- It can have a variety of purposes:

  - to help you identify a suitable topic for study

  - to help you identify relevant literature for your study

  - to help you get an idea of what the main debates are on your topic area

  - to help you understand the issues involved

  - to help inform your own ideas about your research problem area

  - to gain familiarity with the accepted research approaches and methods in our profession

  - to become a critical co-conversant in the "academic conversation"

- It's a continuous process, which begins before a research question is finalized and continues to the end.

- It's a well-written, coherent product, appropriate to the purpose for which you need it.

Now that you have some idea of what a literature review is, the question that must be looked at more closely concerns the reasons for engaging in a literature review: Why is it regarded as an essential part of your research study?

THE PURPOSE OF LITERATURE REVIEWS

A LITERATURE REVIEW is based upon the assumption that doing a research study is not something that happens in isolation. It's something that is done and developed by a community of academic researchers. (Think of the academic conversation analogy: you can't have a conversation all on your own!) This means that knowledge development is seen to be a cumulative activity, and you can learn from what other researchers and writers have done before you.

What you are researching in the present must be built upon the knowledge of what has been researched in the past. Researchers read previous studies to compare, replicate, or criticize the findings of other writers. When you are participating in the academic conversation—by doing a research study or writing a research proposal—you are responding to issues raised, drawing links between what various authors have said, showing where there might be some contradictions, or raising some considerations that haven't been addressed before.

But you can do this only if you know what the conversation has been and is about. So you must know what the past and current debates are in the literature. Ranjit Kumar (1994) has put together a useful list of seven potential uses of literature reviews:

— Helping to Bring Clarity and Focus to the Research Question

— Helping to Identify Gaps

— Preventing Duplication of Knowledge

— Helping to Broaden the Knowledge Base

— Helping to Contextualize the Research Project

— Helping to Improve a Study's Methodology

— Assisting in Identifying Opposing Views

Helping to Bring Clarity and Focus to the Research Question

You cannot undertake a literature review unless you know what you want to find out. On the other hand, a literature review is also necessary in helping you to shape and narrow your research question. This is because reviewing the literature helps you to better understand your subject area, and thus helps you to conceptualize your research question much more clearly and precisely.

A literature review helps you to understand the relationship between your research question and the body of existing knowledge in that area. In other words, the literature contributes to your understanding of why your research question is a problem. When you do a literature review, you can identify more information and ideas that might be directly relevant to your study.

BOX 2.3
Literature Review Tips

One of the most important early steps in a research project is conducting the literature review. This is also one of the most humbling experiences you're likely to have. Why? Because you're likely to find out that just about any worthwhile idea you will have has been thought of before, at least to some degree. Every time I teach a research methods course, I have at least one student come to me complaining that they couldn't find anything in the literature that was related to their topic. And nearly every time they have said that, I was able to show them that was only true because they had looked for articles that were exactly the same as their research topic.

A literature review is designed to identify related research, to set the current research project within a conceptual and theoretical context. When looked at that way, there is almost no topic that is so new or unique that we can't locate relevant and informative related research. Below are two tips for conducting the literature review.

Tip 1: Concentrate your efforts on the scientific literature. Try to determine what the most credible research journals are in your topic area and start with those. Put the greatest emphasis on research journals that use a blind review system. In a blind review, authors submit potential articles to a journal editor, who in turn asks several reviewers to provide a critical review of the paper. The paper is sent to these reviewers with no identification of the author so that there will be no personal bias (either for or against the author). Based on the reviewers' recommendations, the editor can accept the article for publication, reject it, or recommend that the author revise and resubmit it. Articles in journals with blind review processes can be expected to have a fairly high level of credibility.

Tip 2: Do your review early in the research process. You are likely to learn a lot during the literature review that will help you in making the trade-offs you'll need to face. After all, previous researchers also had to face trade-off decisions.

WHAT SHOULD YOU LOOK FOR IN A LITERATURE REVIEW?

1. You might be able to find a study that is quite similar to the one you are thinking of doing. Because all credible research studies have to review the literature themselves, you can check their literature review to get a quick-start on your own.

2. Prior research will help ensure that you have included all the major relevant constructs in your study. You may find that other, similar studies have routinely looked at an outcome that you might not have included. If you did your study without that construct, it would not be judged credible because it ignored a major construct.

3. The literature review will help you to find and select appropriate measuring instruments. You will readily see what measurement instruments researchers have been using in contexts similar to yours.

4. The review will help you to anticipate common problems in your research context. You can use the prior experiences of others to avoid common pitfalls.

HELPING TO IDENTIFY GAPS

To identify the obvious gaps in your general problem area, you have to know the literature. In doing a literature review, you become aware of what has already been done and what remains to be done in your study's area. Be careful of claiming that there are gaps in the knowledge when you have not done a thorough review of the literature.

PREVENTING DUPLICATION OF KNOWLEDGE

You may feel excited about a particular idea—your research question that was derived from a general problem area—and believe that you are the only person to have had this idea. More often than not, after you read the existing literature, you will quickly discover that your research question has indeed been thought of before.

A good literature review helps you to avoid reinventing the wheel. In other words, it can keep you from merely answering research questions that were previously answered by other researchers before you. Of course, planning to replicate studies (a legitimate form of research) or aiming to study an issue for which there is no definitive answer (e.g., the link between mind and brain) is not merely duplicating research studies. You are contributing to the body of knowledge by either validating previous studies or contributing some new insights on a longstanding issue. Very few research studies produce a definitive answer to a research question.

Thus, don't think because your research question has been previously written about that the final answer also has been discovered. A literature review is also useful to get to know what has worked—and what has not—in terms of scientific methodology so that you can avoid making the same mistakes as others may have made.

HELPING TO BROADEN THE KNOWLEDGE BASE

You should read widely in the subject area in which you intend to conduct your research study. It's important that you know what other researchers have found, who the authors considered to be movers and shakers are, what the seminal works are in your research study's problem area, what the key issues and crucial questions are, and what theories have been put forward in the relevant body of knowledge.

You will also be able to see how others have defined concepts that you will be using, and what the widely accepted definitions (or interpretations) are. You will be in a better position to work out interpretations of your key concepts that suit your study's purposes from this existing knowledge base.

Our profession has, over the years, developed basic research practices and conventions. Consult the literature to familiarize yourself with the acceptable research conventions and approaches adopted in the research literature. When you undertake a degree in social work, you are supposed to be an expert in your concentration area, or at least an apprentice who demonstrates mastery in your area of study. The more you know, the better the position you are in to study your topic.

Helping to Contextualize the Research Project

You must provide a signpost to let your readers know where your research question (and the methodological research approach that will answer the question) are coming from. This signposting allows readers to see which theories and principles have been influential in shaping your approach to your research study or research proposal. As has already been indicated, the literature review enables you to build a platform based on existing knowledge from which you can carry on and explain what your contribution will be to the field when your research study is finished.

The literature review can put your study into historical and other perspectives, and can provide an intellectual context for your work. This enables you to position your study in relation to what others have written. Context reviews help you to (1) place your project in the larger picture, (2) establish links between your topic and the existing body of knowledge, (3) establish the relevance and significance of your research question, and (4) establish the possible implications of your position.

Helping to Improve a Study's Methodology

Going through the existing literature helps you to acquaint yourself with the various scientific methodologies that others have used to answer research questions similar to those you are investigating. You can see what has worked and what has not worked for others who were using similar procedures and methods, and what problems they faced.

In learning about the scientific methodologies that others have used, you will be more able to select a methodology that is capable of giving you reliable and valid answers to your research question and that is appropriate for the problem area in which you are studying (Kumar, 1994).

Assisting in Identifying Opposing Views

A literature review helps identify differences between your study and previous studies. The idea that your research study builds on earlier work does not necessarily imply that it extends, flows, or approves of earlier work found in the literature. Your work might be highly critical of earlier work and even seek to discredit it.

However, even if you are critical of a particular theory or methods of conducting a research study, you will still need to review the literature to argue the weaknesses of the previous studies and the benefits of the alternative approach that you have chosen. In a nutshell, you cannot justifiably reject or criticize something if you don't clearly understand (and demonstrate to your readers that you clearly understand) what it is you are rejecting or criticizing.

WHERE AND HOW TO SEARCH FOR INFORMATION

YOU NEED TO KNOW how to use the computers in your university or college library and how to use indexes and abstracts. You can organize searches based on subjects, themes, or keywords. Find out who your subject librarians are and make friends with them. Interlibrary loans are extremely useful and provide an efficient service.

When searching electronic databases and the shelves of the library, it's important to establish the credibility of the source you find. Is it an academically acknowledged database? Are the entries still relevant? The date of the publication is important. For empirical studies, you should concentrate on the latest publications and work backward from these as they become outdated.

Remember, researchers build on the work of those who have gone before them (just as you need to do in your own study.) With theoretical articles, it's not as important to have the most current articles as you might be drawing on classic texts that are more dated. The quickest way of getting an overview of the trends in the debates is to look at the professional journals in your problem area.

You will eventually get an idea of what will make a successful study in your study's problem area. You can compare the studies you find and any publications that come from them with what you intend to do in your study. More important authors tend to be quoted more frequently, and you will be able to tell who the highly regarded authors are in your study's problem area simply by perusing the literature.

INTERNET SEARCHES

The Internet is a terrific tool for obtaining information. However, you need to know your way around it if you want to avoid drawing on inappropriate sites. Most professional journals are now available in electronic form online, and you should check which of these are available at your university or college. Although some journals are available in this form, it should not be seen as an alternative to searching the print versions of journals and books in your university or college library. This is because some of the literature is still only available in printed form.

The Internet is also useful for "gray material," which is information such as government policy documents, speeches, press releases, and so forth. The advantage of the Internet is its immediacy of access, and the information is often very recent. But you must be careful of what you find on the Internet because anyone can write anything there—so unless you know that a site is an academically acknowledged one, you can't be sure of the credibility of information you find there.

STORING AND MANAGING INFORMATION

IN SEARCHING THE LITERATURE, it's very important to develop some sort of filing system—either as hardcopy or on a computer. Remember to store all details so that you don't have to go back to the original sources. This can be a very annoying task, but outstanding or incomplete references must be tracked down when you write your final research report or develop your research proposal. Details on the following should be kept and arranged alphabetically:

- Author(s) (surname and initial)

- Title of the book (if a chapter in an edited collection is used, note the chapter title as well)

- Journal title (and title of article)

- Relevant pages

- Journal volume

- Month of publication

- Year of publication

- Publisher

- Library where information is found

- How the item relates to your research project

It's important to keep these sources accurate and consistent. You can either write the details of each reference separately on a blank index card (on sale in any stationery store), which you will file alphabetically, or you can use one of the many inexpensive software programs such as EndNote (www.endnote.com) to enter your references. We suggest using software programs.

READING FOR A LITERATURE REVIEW

THERE IS NO SHORTCUT to doing a good research study. You must read—period, full stop. There is simply no way around it. But there are different ways of reading. The process of reading has three different aspects:

— *Preview,* in which you do a broad and superficial sweep of the literature

— *Overview,* in which you slightly engage with the material

— *Inview,* in which you read very carefully for understanding of the material

PREVIEW

Plenty of books, journals, and Internet information are available to you as a university or college student. It's possible to waste hundreds of hours reading irrelevant information and, in this way, procrastinate about getting down to writing. You need to become skilled at selecting the right sources for your purposes.

To do so, you need to be able to preview books and journal articles quickly by looking at the title, date of publication, author, organization responsible for publication, and the contents pages. You do this while keeping in mind your purposes for reading:

* *The title.* From the title, you can predict whether some of the information for your research question may be covered.

* *Table of contents/subheadings.* Will some of the necessary information for your research question be covered? Will it be directly relevant to your topic, or will it just give you a broad overview? Which chapter(s) or sections of a book look relevant to your research study?

* *Date and place of publication.* Is the book or journal article fairly current and up to date?

* *The author(s)/organization/publisher.* Are they reputable? Have you heard of them before? Is there any information on them? Are they attached to a credible institution?

In the preview stage, to locate literature it helps if you jot down your research question, what you know about it, what you would like to know about it, any questions you have about it, and the value it may have for your literature review.

OVERVIEW

Once you have selected a book or journal article you want to read, the best way to begin to understand it is to get a sense of how the whole book or journal article (or sections of it) is structured. You can do this by overviewing the work. This will give you a sense of its whole framework (or structure) so that when you read it in detail you will be able to fit what you read into the whole context of the work.

Not only will the overview help you to find information quickly, it will assist your understanding as you read. In doing a survey or overview, you should concentrate on headings, subheadings, introductions, conclusions, the opening and closing sentences of sections, graphs, tables, and any summaries that the piece provides.

INVIEW

The inview involves a detailed and careful reading of the subject matter—ensuring that you understand the concepts and follow the argument. Take clear and detailed notes of everything you read. Keep your research question in mind, and don't record pages of information that aren't directly and meaningfully relevant to your study's research question.

You could keep summaries of your readings in a particular file or in a software program. Don't forget, at the same time, to record all the necessary details of the reference. In your summaries, you might include what the main issues and arguments are, a critical comment, and how the content relates to your proposed research study.

You should read broadly and deeply in your field of study before beginning to write a literature review. This helps you to locate your study in a wider theoretical landscape. Then read deeply in the narrower field of your research question so that you have a detailed account of existing literature as it relates to your study's problem area.

After reading in an intensive way, you need to make notes of your own, draw a mind-map, and respond—you begin to prepare an argument for your literature review. Select a suitable structure for organizing the literature, and use subheadings— lots of subheadings.

You could begin your inview of the literature by finding an introductory book or key articles that introduce the main concepts and theoretical language in the problem area that you are going to study. Try to identify the concepts that you don't understand, and discuss these with your fellow students and instructor.

You should develop a conceptual map and try to fit new readings into this map. Pull together themes and issues that belong together. Once you have developed a map, a rough structure of your draft framework, keep slotting in information under the headings and subheadings that you develop. Kumar (1994) suggests the following:

- Note the theories put forward, the criticisms of these and their basis, and the methodologies adopted (e.g., study design, sample size and its characteristics, measurement procedures) and the criticisms of them.

- Examine to what extent the findings can be generalized to other situations.

- Notice where significant differences of opinion exist among researchers, and give your view about the validity of these differences.

- Ascertain the areas in which little or nothing is known—the gaps that exist in the body of knowledge.

Developing a Theoretical Framework

STUDENTS STRUGGLE with developing theoretical frameworks. A possible reason for this is that there is not a "correct" and clear-cut theoretical framework that exists. The question about which framework is the most appropriate one in and of itself is a question of debate within the literature.

Nevertheless, the theoretical framework is where you highlight the main thrust of the academic conversation you are entering. Note the similarities and differences between themes and theories, agreements and disagreements among authors, and the bearing that these have on your research topic. Use these as a basis for developing the theoretical framework that is best suited to the purpose of your study.

A theoretical framework sets up key concepts, interpretations, approaches, claims, foundations, principles, and other items that will influence the design of your structure, and how you will sort the information and analyze the findings of your study. Unless you review the literature in relation to this framework, you won't be able to develop a focus in your literature search. In other words, the theoretical framework provides you with a guide as you read (Kumar, 1994).

You must first go through the literature to develop this framework, and then have the framework in hand while you go through the literature. A good idea is to go through some of the literature to develop this framework, then use this skeleton framework to guide your readings further. As you read more, you may change the framework, but if you don't have some structure, you will be bogged down in a lot of unnecessary readings and note taking that aren't directly relevant to your study.

The theoretical framework is the basis of your research problem. Of course, competing theoretical frameworks are put forward to explain the issue you will be researching, so you will need to discuss—based on the arguments put forward by other authors—why this particular framework is appropriate for your purposes.

Writing and Organizing a Literature Review

Your writing should be signposted at every point; that is, you should say what you are going to do, then do it, then say what you have done. You will need to do and redo things—the process of research and writing is messy and doubles back on itself. Only in the end does it appear as seamless and linear.

Even the best authors have reworked their text many, many times before it was finally printed. Coherence only emerges over time. Unfortunately, there are no shortcuts. In the literature review, you should present an exposition (a clear and coherent summary with a particular purpose) of the issue you are studying, which you then use as the base for an argument. Rather than just stating facts, use an argument to persuade the reader to a particular interpretation.

You can use the findings of other authors to support your claims. You should have a central argument (the main point you want to put forward), then use each paragraph to develop a part of the main argument. You must state the argument early on and sum it up in the conclusion. All your points should link to your main argument. You can organize your literature review:

* *By date of study.* Here, you would start with older studies and work toward the latest. This is the least ordered of the literature reviews.

* *By school of thought/theory.* This is a review of the theoretical positions of scholars, which forms the theoretical framework. You could organize it from oldest to most recent, or you could start with the approaches or definitions that you feel to be inappropriate, or that have been discredited by recent scholarship. You would then follow this with a discussion of those points that would form the frame of reference for your study.

* *By themes that have emerged from the literature.* The headings and subheadings should be based on the literature and should be precise, be descriptive of contents, and follow a logical progression. Substantiations and contradictions should be clearly referenced. Your arguments should be conceptually clear, highlighting the reasons for and against, and referring to the main findings, gaps, and issues.

�֍ *By method.* You can, for example, compare past positivistic (Chapter 5) and interpretive studies (Chapter 6) in your study's area and show how these two different methodologies produced different sets of results, if any.

Try to answer the following questions:

✖ What do you consider to be the most important theories and perspectives to arise from the literature? How have these affected your understanding of your topic?

✖ How does your research question link with the state of knowledge as reflected in the literature?

✖ What questions are raised by the literature that your research study addresses?

✖ Has anyone ever done this before? What partial answers to your research question have been found before? How did previous researchers go about asking such questions? What methodological issues are raised by the literature in question?

✖ In what way is your topic valid, important, and doable? How will your research study add to the literature?

If you're still undecided on how to construct your literature review, here is a suggestion on how to get started. Go back to your research proposal and the ten keywords (or phrases) you have noted as capturing the main concepts of your study. Jot them down in a column. Then, for each concept jotted down, ask yourself, "What does the literature say about this?"

Next to each one, identify three or four readings that address this concept. Make clear and honest summaries of each reading. Then critically engage with your summaries, noting the trends, similarities, differences, gaps, and implications.

Rewrite this draft into flowing text. Do this for each listed concept (the concept can be a subheading), and you'll have the first draft of your literature review. You should keep a log or a journal of information that you gathered during your whole writing process. You need to ignore references that aren't relevant any more and pare the references down if needed.

CRITERIA OF A GOOD LITERATURE REVIEW

YOUR LITERATURE REVIEW must cover the main aspects of your study and be fair in its treatment of authors. The literature review should do justice to an author's arguments before critiquing them. (You can't agree or disagree with something if you don't have a clear idea of what it is you're agreeing or disagreeing with!) It should be topical.

The review shouldn't be confined to Internet sources. It should be well organized around your research questions and key concepts, rather than being summaries of what you have read. Take note of the authority of authors and the reliability and validity of the research methods they used to answer their research questions.

There's a delicate balance between discussing what others have said and found, and developing your own voice. You are neither just listing what others have said, nor are you merely "telling your own story." You need to demonstrate that you have an informed voice. So don't quote too many studies or begin with "Smith (2012) found that . . ." as it shifts the focus of your own argument onto that of others.

It's better to develop a theme and then cite the work of relevant authors to reinforce your argument. Don't be tempted to report everything you know—be selective about what you report. Every reference you use must build on the evidence you are presenting to support your case. Using your own words to describe difficult concepts will help convince yourself and others that you really understand the material.

SUMMARY

This chapter started out discussing the factors that affect formulating social work research questions. We then went on to present the three main forms that research studies can take: exploratory, descriptive, and explanatory. Next, we talked about how research studies can be classified via the research questions they address. We then went on to discuss the various considerations that all research questions must contain: relevance, researchability, feasibility, ethical acceptability, and cultural sensitivity.

Finally, we presented a very brief discussion on how the professional literature can be used to formulate research questions. Your literature review should be specific, current, of historical interest, coherent, interesting, and well organized around your research question and key concepts, rather than being a mere summary of what you have read. It should be a critical discussion of relevant information from different sources.

Do you remember that your research question must be ethical? Well, the next chapter describes how ethics plays a significant role not only in formulating research questions but also during the entire research process itself.

Study Questions for Chapter 2

— First, answer each question only AFTER you have read the chapter.

— Second, indicate how comfortable you were in answering each question on a 5-point scale:

1	2	3	4	5
Very uncomfortable	Somewhat uncomfortable	Neutral	Somewhat comfortable	Very comfortable

If you rated any question between 1–3, please reread the section of the chapter where the information for the question can be found. If you're still uncomfortable answering the question, talk with your instructor and/or your classmates for more clarification.

Questions	Degree of comfort? (Circle one number)
1. Before you entered your social work program and before you read this chapter, how did you think our profession formulated research questions? Provide as many examples as you can to justify your response.	1 2 3 4 5
2. List each one of the factors that affect social work research studies. Discuss how they are highly related to one another using one common social work example throughout your discussion.	1 2 3 4 5
3. What social work research question would you like answered? Why? Discuss how it was influenced by each one of the factors presented in the book.	1 2 3 4 5
4. Discuss what the knowledge-level continuum is all about. Provide specific social work examples for each of the three levels.	1 2 3 4 5
5. What is the sieving procedure all about, as illustrated in Figure 2.2?	1 2 3 4 5
6. Write a social work research question for each of the seven classifications that research studies can fall under (Figure 2.3). Use one common social work example throughout your discussion.	1 2 3 4 5
7. For each question you formulated for Question 6, evaluate it with the four criteria found in the book. Discuss in detail.	1 2 3 4 5

8. In your own words, describe the purpose of a literature review using the points that are outlined in the chapter. Use social work examples to illustrate your points.	1 2 3 4 5
9. Discuss how you read for a literature review as outlined in this chapter. Discuss the concepts of preview, overview, and inview. Provide examples to aid in your discussion.	1 2 3 4 5
10. Discuss the four options that you can select from when writing a literature review. Provide an example of each one.	1 2 3 4 5
11. What are five major questions you need to ask and answer when writing and organizing your literature review?	1 2 3 4 5
12. At this point in your course, how comfortable are you with discussing the process of constructing social work research questions with your field instructor (or your supervisor at work)? With your fellow classmates? Discuss in detail.	1 2 3 4 5
13. At this point in your course, how comfortable are you with describing the literature review the process with your field instructor (or your supervisor at work)? With your fellow classmates? Discuss in detail.	1 2 3 4 5
14. At this point in your course, how comfortable are you with describing the knowledge-level continuum with your field instructor (or your supervisor at work)? With your fellow classmates? Discuss in detail.	1 2 3 4 5
15. At this point in your course, how comfortable are you with describing the classification of research questions with your field instructor (or your supervisor at work)? With your fellow classmates? Discuss in detail	1 2 3 4 5
16. At this point in your course, how comfortable are you with describing the criteria that are utilized for evaluating research questions with your field instructor (or your supervisor at work)? With your fellow classmates? Discuss in detail.	1 2 3 4 5

Assessing Your Self-Efficacy for Chapter 2

AFTER you have read the chapter AND have completed all the study questions, please indicate how knowledgeable you feel you are for each concept listed below.

1	2	3	4	5
Very uncomfortable	Somewhat uncomfortable	Neutral	Somewhat comfortable	Very comfortable

Major Concepts in Chapter	Knowledge Level? (Circle one number)
1. Factors that affect social work research studies	1 2 3 4 5
2. The knowledge-level continuum	1 2 3 4 5
3. Exploratory research studies	1 2 3 4 5
4. Descriptive research studies	1 2 3 4 5
5. Explanatory research studies	1 2 3 4 5
6. Classification of social work research questions	1 2 3 4 5
7. Exploratory research questions	1 2 3 4 5
8. Descriptive research questions	1 2 3 4 5
9. Explanatory research questions	1 2 3 4 5
10. Criteria for good research questions	1 2 3 4 5
11. Literature reviews	1 2 3 4 5

Add up your scores (Minimum = 11, Maximum = 55)	Total score =

A   50 — 55 = Social Work Manager in the making.
B   44 — 49 = Social Work Supervisor.
C   38 — 43 = Social Work Practitioner.
D   11 — 37 = Case Aide. Reread the chapter and redo the study questions.

3

Research Ethics

*Ethics is knowing the difference between what
you have a right to do and what is right to do.*
~ Potter Stewart

The first chapter of this book discussed the five ways of acquiring knowledge and stressed how you should obtain your knowledge from findings that were derived from the scientific method whenever possible. We also indicated that you should never ignore the other four ways of knowing. Remember, professional judgments are always based on utilizing all five ways of knowing.

The last chapter presented how to formulate social work research questions that can be answered by using the scientific method. As you know, we presented four criteria that you must apply when evaluating any question you want to research—and one of the five criteria was ethics, the purpose of this chapter.

USING CLIENTS AS RESEARCH PARTICIPANTS

Many social work research studies use clients as research participants, sometimes inappropriately called *subjects*. When using clients within our research studies, we need to be extremely careful not to violate any of their ethical rights. Sounds simple, you say. Well, read on.

Consider Aristotle, for example. He believed that horses would become severely ill if they were bitten by pregnant shrewmice. He never tested his belief via the scientific method. If he wanted to he could have done a simple research study that arranged for a group of horses to be bitten by pregnant shrewmice (experimental group) and a group of horses that would not be bitten (control group). He then could have compared the illness rate of the horses in the experimental group to the illness rate of the horses in the control group.

If he did this simple study, however, he would have had to solve the resulting ethical dilemma. Was he justified in subjecting a few horses to the discomfort of being bitten by pregnant shrew mice just to gain enough knowledge to help all horses in the future?

Now suppose the horses were people. To social workers, the answer is apparent: No, we are not justified! Increasing the sum of knowledge is a worthy aim, but the client, or research participant, must not be harmed in the process. We are not in the business of committing lesser evils for the sake of greater goods.

Not harming our clients, by commission or omission, is a cardinal rule of the research process and imposes a major limitation. There are a number of bodies devoted to ensuring that harm does not occur. All universities, for example, have ethics committees, or institutional review boards (IRBs), and many large social service programs do as well.

There are also various professional associations and lay groups that focus on protecting research participants. However, it's likely that the participants in your research study will never have heard of any of these bodies. They will do what you ask them to do either because they trust you or because they think they have no other choice but to participate.

The responsibility of not hurting any of your research participants is squarely on your shoulders. We will now turn our attention of obtaining their informed consent to participate in your research study, with an eye to doing no harm to them whatsoever. You must always remember that their safety comes first and your research project second.

OBTAINING INFORMED CONSENT

Before you involve any human being in a research study, you must obtain the person's informed consent. The key word here is *informed*. The word "informed" means that all of your potential research participants must fully understand what is going to happen in the course of your study, why it's going to happen, and what its effect will be on them.

If the person is psychiatrically challenged, mentally delayed, or in any other way incapable of full understanding, your study must be fully and adequately explained to someone else—perhaps a parent, guardian, social worker, spouse, or someone to whom the participant's welfare is important.

All written communications must be couched in simple language that all potential participants will understand. Some researchers, particularly academics, have a tendency to confuse obscurity with profundity. They use technical terms so firmly embedded in convoluted sentence structures that the meaning falters and disappears altogether at the second comma.

It's clear that no research participant may be bribed, threatened, deceived, or in any way coerced into participating in your study. Questions must be encouraged, both initially and throughout the course of the study. People who believe they understand may have misinterpreted your explanation or understood it only in part.

They may say they understand when they do not, in an effort to avoid appearing foolish. They may even sign documents they do not understand to confirm their supposed understanding, and it's your responsibility to ensure that their understanding is real and complete.

It's extremely important for potential participants to know that they are not signing away their rights when they sign a consent form. They may decide at any time to withdraw from the study *without penalty*, without so much as a reproachful glance. When completed, the study's results must also be made available to them.

BRIBERY, DECEPTION, AND OTHER FORMS OF COERCION

IT GOES WITHOUT SAYING that consent must never be obtained through bribery, threats, deception, or any form of coercion. You may feel insulted that such a possibility would even be mentioned in a text addressed to social workers, but consider what constitutes bribery. For example, if you offer $100 to the chief executive officer of an agency to persuade her to take part in your study, this is bribery.

If you want to know how your research participants *really* behave when no one else is looking, you will have to deceive them into believing that they are *not* being watched. You might think you can do this using an interview room with a one-way mirror, or you might pretend to be an ordinary member of a group when you are, in fact, a glint-eyed observer. Neither of these behaviors is ethically acceptable.

The only conditions under which deception might be countenanced—and it's a very large *might*—are when the data to be obtained are vitally important and there is no other way to get them. If you can persuade the various ethics committees that review your research proposal that both these conditions exist, you *might* be given permission to carry out the study.

Even then, you would have to be sure that the deception was thoroughly explained to all the participants when the study was over and that arrangements had been made—free counseling, for example—to counter any harm they might have suffered.

Last, but not least, there are threats. No researcher would ever persuade potential participants to cooperate by threatening that, if they do not, worse things will befall them. But a *perceived* threat, even if not intended, can have the same effect. For example, a woman awaiting an abortion may agree to provide private information about herself and her partner because she believes that, if she does not, she will be denied the abortion. It's of no use to tell her that this is not true; she may simply feel she is not in a position to take any chances.

There are captive populations in prisons, schools, and institutions who may agree out of sheer boredom to take part in a research study. Or they may participate in return for certain privileges or because they fear some reprisal. There may be people who agree because family members pressure them into it, or they want to please their social workers, or they need some service or payment that they believe depends on their cooperation. Often, situations like these cannot be changed, but at least you can be aware of them and do your best to deal with them in an ethical and straightforward manner.

INGREDIENTS OF AN INFORMED CONSENT FORM

A **WRITTEN CONSENT** form should be only part of the process of informing research participants of their roles in the study and their rights as volunteers. As we have said before, it must give potential participants a basic description of the purpose of the study, the study's procedures, and their rights as voluntary participants. A consent form must provide in plain and simple language:

* that participants are being asked to participate in a research study

* that their participation is voluntary, and that they may discontinue participation at any time without penalty or loss of benefits to which they are otherwise entitled (e.g., in their standing as a patient, student, or employee)

* the names of the investigators and their affiliations

* the purposes of the research study, simply explained

* what the study's procedures will be

* the expected duration of their participation

* any reasonably foreseeable risks or discomforts

* any safeguards to minimize the risks

* any benefits to the participants or to others that may reasonably be expected from the research study. (In most cases, the study is not being performed for the benefit of the participants but for the potential benefit of others. This broader social benefit to the public should be made explicit.)

* in cases where an incentive is offered, a description of the incentive and of how and under what conditions it is to be obtained

* appropriate alternative procedures or courses of treatment, if applicable

* the extent, if any, to which confidentiality of records identifying the participants will be maintained (not an issue unless participants can be identified)

* any restrictions on confidentiality. (For example, if any of the information gained during the study might have to be disclosed as required by law, as in instances of child abuse, absolute confidentiality cannot be ensured.)

* what monetary compensation or medical or psychological treatment will be provided for any research-related injury (if more than minimal risk)

* contact information for questions about the study (name, office address, and phone contacts for the researcher, faculty advisor, and IRB staff). Do not include home phone numbers.

* that the researcher will keep one copy of the signed consent form and give another signed copy to the participants

Using the preceding points, Box 3.1 provides an example of an actual consent letter written to the social workers who were the legal guardians of foster care adolescents in a residential treatment facility. The letter was written to "persuade" the social workers to have their clients (foster care adolescents) participate in a research study.

In this study, the adolescents' biological parents were not involved because the adolescents were wards of the state. If a social worker agreed to have his adolescents participate in the study, then the adolescents would be given assent forms to sign (Box 3.2).

BOX 3.1
Example of a Consent Form

NOTE: This consent form was given to social workers who were the legal guardians of the foster youth (clients) whom we wanted to participate in our workshop. We asked the workers whether they would agree to have their clients participate in our workshop BEFORE we could ask the youth whether they wanted to participate.

If a worker agreed via this consent form that we could contact his clients, we then asked the youths via an assent form (Box 3.2) whether they wanted to participate. If a worker did not agree to have her clients participate in our workshop, we did not ask those youths to participate.

(Letterhead)

You are invited to have your clients participate in Chatham-Kent Children's Services (CKCS) Help-Seeking Project for Adolescents in Out-of-Home Placement. The project is funded by the Provincial Centre of Excellence for Child and Youth Mental Health. The primary person in charge of the project is Mike Stephens, Chief Executive Officer of CKCS.

This handout describes our project and will help you decide if you want to have your clients participate. You are 100% free to choose whether or not you will have your clients take part in the study. Before you decide, however, you need to know what will be expected of them if you agree to have them participate and the risks and benefits of their participation. Please take time to read this handout.

There are no negative consequences for either you or your clients in reference to your decision as to their potential participation. Your clients can drop out of the study at any time. The services they receive from CKCS will not be affected by your decision to have them participate in this project.

If you agree to have your clients take part in the project they will be asked to sign a separate assent form. The assent form is a shorter version of this consent form and contains important information about the project. When they sign the assent form, they give their "consent," which means that they agree to participate in the project.

WHAT'S THE PROJECT ABOUT ANYWAY?

The main purpose of our project is to find out whether a workshop on help-seeking for youth living in out-of-home placement at CKCS will help them become more skilled at asking for help when personal or emotional problems arise. We don't yet know whether our help-seeking workshop works. So we have designed a project that will involve about 120 youth, ages 12 years and older, who are living at CKCS.

Half of the youth who participate in the project will attend a special workshop, and the other half will not. The workshop will give them information and ideas about how to seek help when personal or emotional problems arise. We will then compare the help-seeking skills of those youth who attended the workshop with those who did not in order to learn whether the workshop was helpful.

As you can see below, they will be assigned, by chance, to a group who attend the workshop, or to a group who do not attend. That is, they may or may not attend the workshop even though they agree to participate in the project (via an assent form). If we learn that the workshop is helpful in the way we expect, then all youth that did not get to attend the workshop will be offered a chance to attend it at a later date, as long as they are still living at CKCS.

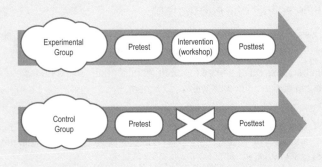

In total, about 120 youth will participate in the project. Everyone will be asked to complete a set of questionnaires at four different times: this week, 5 weeks from now, 10 weeks from now, and 5 months from now. Step by step, this is what will happen if you agree to have your clients participate in the project AND they have also agreed.

1. They will be contacted twice by telephone. Sometime this week, and then again 5 months from now, a CKCS staff member will call them by telephone and ask them questions. The phone interview takes about 30 minutes and includes questions about common emotional and behavioral problems experienced by teenagers. They do not have to answer any questions they don't want to.

2. They will be asked to come to CKCS four times over the next 5 months and to complete four other surveys. These surveys are completed at the CKCS computer lab using a special computer program. Sitting at their own computers and wearing headphones, they will see each question appear on the computer screen and hear the question being read through the headphones.

3. They will answer the questions by clicking the computer mouse. The computer surveys should take about 30 to 40 minutes to complete each time. As we said above, they do not have to answer any questions that they don't want to. They will be paid for their participation. They will receive $10 the first time they answer the survey questions, $15 the second time, $20 the third time, and $30 the fourth time.

4. Snacks also will be provided at each meeting, and bus fare to CKCS will be available if they need it. In addition to the above surveys, a project staff member will review their CKCS case files for information such as their placements, services they have received, and family contacts.

5. By chance, half of the youth participating in the project will invited to attend a 2- to 3-hour workshop that will include six youths at a time. The workshop will take place at CKCS and be run by a CKCS staff member. The purpose of the workshop is to give them additional information about how they can best get help for their personal or emotional problems while living in a CKCS placement.

6. If they leave CKCS within 5 weeks of the start of the project, their participation in the project will automatically end.

HOW WILL THEIR PRIVACY BE PROTECTED?

Confidentiality describes what we do to keep information gathered about your clients completely private. In order to protect their privacy in this project:

1. We use numbers instead of names (or other identifiers) on all the data we obtain so that no one can connect the data with you or them.

2. The data collected for this project will be sent to researchers at Western Michigan University. Once again, the data will not include anything that would individually identify you or them. The researchers and their staff have been trained in protecting everyone's confidentiality.

3. No CKCS staff member will have access to the data that your clients provide as part of this project. None of the data collected from your clients will be shared with you (their Children's Service Worker and legal guardian), their foster parents or caregivers, or any other workers at CKCS. The data collected will only be used for this project.

4. All data will be stored in a safe, locked area. The computers for this project are protected by a firewall system.

5. All the adolescents' answers will be kept absolutely private unless a staff member thinks they might be in danger of hurting themselves. For example, if an adolescent tells us that he or she is using illegal drugs, or is thinking of harming him or herself or someone else, project staff are obligated to inform you because you are his or her legal guardian and CKCS Children's Service Worker.

6. The information from the project will be used to write papers, make presentations, and work with other education or research centers to improve out-of-home services for youth. Please remember that their names, or any information that could identify them, will never be used. We will evaluate the survey answers "as a group" and not for any one individual. They will not be identified (for example, by name or social security number) in any reports or publications of this project.

WILL THEIR INFORMATION BE SHARED WITH OTHERS?

Yes. As we have said before, if we know or think we know that one of your clients is being abused, under law we must take action to protect that person. We also must report if we hear that an individual intends to harm himself or herself or someone else. We will inform you immediately if this is the case.

WHAT ARE THEIR RIGHTS AS A PARTICIPANT IN OUR PROJECT?

As participants in our project, your clients have certain rights that protect them from potential harm. After you, as their legal guardian, have provided your consent to have them participate in the project (via signing this form), their specific rights are as follows:

1. It is up to them to decide if they want to be in our project. That means their participation is completely voluntary.

2. They have the right to change their mind at any time about being in the project. If they decide to leave the project, there will be no penalty of any kind.

3. They have the right to refuse to answer any question(s). Some questions might be personal or sensitive to them. These questions are important to our project, and we would like them to answer the questions honestly. However, if there are questions they do not want to answer, they may skip them and move on to other questions.

4. They will be given copies of this project description (your consent form). If they want to participate in our project, they will also sign an assent form.

5. Their assent forms will also be explained verbally to them. If they have any difficulty in reading these forms, a staff person will read them to your client.

6. At any time they can ask any staff member questions about our project. They may also call collect Mike Stephens (x-xxx-xxx-xxxx, extension xxx).

7. If they would like to contact someone outside the project staff with questions or concerns, they can call Yvonne Unrau at xxx-xxx-xxxx or Rick Grinnell at xxx-xxx-xxxx, who are the two Western Michigan University researchers involved with the project. They may also contact the Chair of the Human Subjects Institutional Review Board (xxx-xxx-xxxx) or the Vice President for Research (xxx-xxx-xxxx) at Western Michigan University if questions or problems arise during the course of the study. They may call collect.

RISKS ASSOCIATED WITH PARTICIPATING IN THIS PROJECT

There are very few risks in this project. The adolescents may, however, feel a little embarrassed or uncomfortable because of the personal nature of some questions on the surveys or due to certain project activities such as role-plays in the workshop.

Remember, they do not have to answer any questions or take part in any activities at any time.

WHAT ARE THE BENEFITS TO THEM?

Many people find it helpful to think and talk about personal information about themselves and their families. Being in the project gives them a chance to do this. The project may improve our knowledge about how youth in care can better seek help when they need it. The information gained may help us understand more about how parents, foster parents, and CKCS can work together to help teenagers who are placed in foster or group care.

This information might be used to prevent problems for teenagers in the future and to help those that are having trouble. As a participant, they will be part of a valuable project that might help other people in the future. Please sign below to show that you have reviewed this project description, that you consent to have your clients participate, and that you have had all your questions answered.

_____

Social worker's signature (as legal guardian) and date

BOX 3.2

Example of an Assent Form

NOTE: *This assent form was given to the foster youth after their respective social workers had provided us with permission to contact them via a consent from (Box 3.1).*

(Letterhead)

I have been invited to be part of a study entitled "Chatham-Kent Children's Services (CKCS) Help-Seeking Project for Adolescents in Out-of-Home Placement."

The main purpose of the study is to see whether a workshop and additional support given to youth living at CKCS will make them more skilled at asking for help with personal or emotional problems. In this study:

1. I will be phoned by a CKCS staff member twice over 20 weeks and be asked to answer questions on the phone. This will take about 15 minutes each time.

2. I will be invited to come to CKCS four times over the next 20 weeks to answer questions from four other survey questionnaires about my help-seeking behaviors using a special computer program at CKCS.

3. After the first testing, CKCS will pay me $10 (or equivalent).

4. After the second testing point, CKCS will pay me $15 (or equivalent).

5. After the third testing point, CKCS will pay me $20 (or equivalent).

6. After the fourth (and final) time, CKCS will pay me $30 (or equivalent).

7. CKCS will provide food snacks at each testing time.

8. A project staff member will look at my case file to obtain basic information about me such as my age, sex, time in care, etc.

9. My name will not be recorded; instead of recording my name, a number code will be used.

10. I also may be invited to participate in a 2- to 3-hour workshop with a small group of about five other youth in care. The workshop will take place at CKCS and will be run by a CKCS mental health worker and possibly someone who formerly lived in an out-of-home placement.

11. At the workshop, I will get information and ideas about asking for help related to personal or emotional problems that are common with teenagers.

12. If I don't want to participate at this time, the service I receive from CKCS will not be affected.

13. Even if I agree today to participate by signing this form, I can change my mind at any time and withdraw from the study, and there will be no effect on the service I receive from CKCS.

14. If I choose to complete any or all of the questionnaires for the study, then my scores will be sent to researchers at Western Michigan University in Kalamazoo, Michigan.

15. As mentioned previously, my name will not be on any of the surveys that are sent to Michigan. The researchers will use a code number instead of my name. The researchers will keep a list of names and code numbers that will be destroyed once the researchers have looked at all the questionnaires.

16. All my answers will be kept private, which means even my Children's Service Worker or caregivers won't know what I say unless project staff members think I might be in danger of hurting myself or others. Then project staff will need to tell my Children's Service Worker.

17. My signature below indicates that I have agreed to be interviewed by phone and take the surveys on the computer.

YOUR SIGNATURE ALSO INDICATES THAT YOU AGREE:

1. to have your case file at CKCS reviewed for information it contains.

2. to be assigned to participate in a special help-seeking workshop for this project, if selected.

3. to allow CKCS to give the researchers your survey results and case file information (your name will not be sent to the researchers).

4. that you have had a chance to ask any questions you may have.

_____

Print your name on above line.

_____ (Date: _____)

Sign your name on the above line and put in today's date

Assent obtained by: _____

In a nutshell, consent forms need to be signed by adults, and assent forms must be signed by non-adults—children and adolescents. If your study is going to use children and/or adolescents as research participants, you will have to obtain the consent of at least one of their parents or legal guardians (via consent forms) in addition to your research participants' consent (via assent forms).

In this case you will have to write two forms, one for the adolescents' legal guardians (consent form) and one for the adolescents (assent form). Writing consent and assent forms takes an astronomical amount of time—never underestimate how much time it will take.

ANONYMITY VERSUS CONFIDENTIALITY

A promise of particular concern to many research participants is that of anonymity. A current illegal drug user may be afraid of being identified. Folks receiving social services may be concerned whether anyone else might learn that they are receiving them. Also, there is often some confusion between the terms "anonymity" and "confidentiality."

Some research studies are designed so that no one, not even the person doing the study, knows which research participant gave what response. An example is a mailed survey form bearing no identifying marks whatsoever and asking the respondent not to provide a name. In a study like this, the respondent is *anonymous.*

It's more often the case, however, that we do in fact know how a particular participant responded and have agreed not to divulge the information to anyone else. In such cases, the information is considered *confidential.* Part of our explanation to a potential research participant must include a clear statement of what information will be shared and with whom it will be shared (e.g., Boxes 3.1 and 3.2).

ENSURING CONFIDENTIALITY

THE FIRST STEP in the process for ensuring confidentiality is often to assign a code number to each participant. The researcher and her assistants alone know that Ms. Smith, for example, is number 132. All data concerning Ms. Smith are then combined with data from all the other participants to produce summary aggregated results that do not identify Ms. Smith in any way. No one reading the final research report or any publication stemming from it will know that Ms. Smith took part in the study at all.

Sometimes, however, complete confidentiality cannot be guaranteed. In a study undertaken in a small community, for example, direct quotes from an interview with "a" social worker may narrow the field to three because there are only three social workers there. Then the flavor of the quote may narrow it again to Mr. Jones, who said the same thing in church last Sunday. If there is any risk that Mr. Jones might be recognized as the source of the quote, this possibility must be clearly acknowledged in the letter of consent that Mr. Jones is asked to sign.

Although the ideal is to obtain written consent from the potential participant before the study begins, it's not always possible to obtain the consent in writing. In a telephone interview, for example, the information that would have been contained in a letter of consent is usually read to the participant, and oral consent is obtained.

If a number of participants are to be interviewed by telephone, the same information, set out in exactly the same way, must be read to them all. A mailed questionnaire is sent out with an accompanying introductory letter. This letter contains a statement that filling out the questionnaire and sending it back constitutes consent.

 # DESIGNING THE STUDY IN AN ETHICAL MANNER

Once you have obtained informed consent from your research participants, you then need to actually carry out your research study in an ethical manner. During every step in any proposed social work research study, you will be called upon to make numerous ethical decisions. Andre Ivanoff and Betty Blythe have authored this section of this chapter. There are eight overlapping steps that we need to take when conducting any research study.

This section covers each of the steps and discusses the ethical issues we need to address for each one. Each step overlaps with the other steps. Thus, it's impractical to discuss ethical issues that need to be addressed within each step in a complete vacuum, isolated from the other steps: all steps are influenced by the ethical decisions made in the others, as depicted in Figure 5.1 for positivistic studies and Figure 6.1 for interpretive ones.

— Step 1: Develop the Research Question

— Step 2: Select a Research Approach

— Step 3: Specify How Variables Are Measured

— Step 4: Select a Sample

— Step 5: Select a Research Design

— Step 6: Select a Data Collection Method

— Step 7: Analyze the Data

— Step 8: Write and Disseminate the Research Report

STEP 1: DEVELOP THE RESEARCH QUESTION

AS WE KNOW FROM CHAPTER 2, we must address a simple question: What is the purpose of our research study in the first place? Will it increase our understanding of the problem we are investigating? Is it likely to benefit individuals (or groups) in need?

Sometimes a research study can *directly benefit* those who participate in it—that is, the research participants themselves. In addition, it may *indirectly benefit* others who share the same or a similar condition or problem but are not actually participating in the study; that is, they are not directly involved in the study as research participants.

If the study does not directly or indirectly benefit its participants, then it must contribute to our professional social work knowledge base. If the research question posed already has been answered, however, what's the argument for answering it again?

The researcher may believe it's important to replicate clinical findings and/or generalize the study's findings to other populations, or to simply replicate the study using a more rigorous and creditable research design, which in turn would produce more trustworthy findings.

Research training is another acceptable reason for conducting a research study that may not directly benefit its participants. In many universities and research institutions alike, providing opportunities for students to learn how to conduct research studies is an important function.

The National Association of Social Worker's *Code of Ethics* (1999) also contains an ethical standard that requires students to be educated in research methodology. In cases where there may be little direct or indirect benefit to the research participants, the level of risk posed by their participation in research studies should be minimal; that is, there should be little to no chance that their participation in the research studies could harm them in any way.

REFINE THE RESEARCH QUESTION THROUGH THE LITERATURE

After identifying a research question, the next goal is to refine it further by surveying the relevant literature, as discussed in the previous chapter. This involves a thorough review of the theory and other research studies related to the research question. It's important to base any research inquiry on a solid understanding of what came before: "What do we already know about the potential research question under investigation?" Critical to refining the initial research question *is asking an answerable question.* For example,

What social work intervention(s) will decrease gang-related "tagging" (graffiti) on public school grounds?

As we know from Chapter 2, once we have a question that can be answered, such as this one, we can then refine it a bit more. This part of the research process is roughly analogous to the assessment phase in clinical social work practice. Once the client's presenting problem (the research question) is posed, we then proceed to identify the parameters of the problem and explore its impact on the client's functioning.

As newer and more specific client information is drawn out during the assessment phase of social work practice, we then refine and increase the clarity and precision of the original problem statement. This process in clinical assessment is called *targeting*. Basing our choice of intervention on conclusions drawn quickly and imprecisely about the target problem compromises ethical practice.

EVALUATE THE LITERATURE

What is *acceptable* knowledge? Is all information found on Google "good"? Is one search engine or bibliographic resource superior to another in the value of the information it generates? And what impact do the answers to these questions have on the services we provide to our clients? Even many elementary schools now inform their students that Wikipedia is *not* an acceptable reference source to be used in an academic paper.

Using search engines to find treatments for depression, for example, yields numerous links to psychotropic medication before psychosocial treatments are even cited. Indeed, information on how to commit suicide exists side by side with scholarly papers on factors related to preventing suicide!

Evaluating sources of knowledge was much easier (however inefficient) before the advent of the World Wide Web. Professional journals and books, along with professional consensus, were considered the building blocks of our profession's knowledge base. These were available by subscription and in bookstores; most of us had to go to libraries or buy books to access this information. The Internet has broadened and extended our information sources beyond expectation and, at the same time, has made it much more difficult to critically assess the information found there.

Today, credible sources of practice information are available on the Internet, such as the Cochrane Collaboration (www.cochrane.org) and the Campbell Collaboration (www.campbellcollaboration.org). These organizations' Web sites include both systematic reviews and meta-analyses covering the assessment and treatment of health, mental health, and social welfare problems.

Evidence-based practice guidelines represent the best of scholarly consensus and are available for mental health, substance abuse, and other areas of social work practice. What's the best kind of evidence to inform our day-to-day practice? An evidence credibility hierarchy continuum exists that stretches from lowest to highest.

It starts with anecdotal case reports (lowest) and moves up to randomized clinical trials (highest). This hierarchy is helpful in guiding our choice of what intervention to use in solving a client's problem. The most robust type of evidence to support a particular intervention for a particular client problem is the most ethical one to use.

STEP 2: SELECT A RESEARCH APPROACH (CHAPTERS 5 AND 6)

AS WE REFINE OUR RESEARCH QUESTION in Step 1, the research approach finally used will become much clearer. Figure 2.2 provides a diagram of how research questions are refined. Certain questions can be better answered by a positivistic approach, such as those described in Chapter 5. Others may require an interpretive approach, such as those contained in Chapter 6.

Our literature review, discussed in Chapter 2, will probably suggest what approach may be the most appropriate for our particular topic area and the intended population (research participants) we wish to explore. Sometimes our own biases about research approaches or the biases of the larger research community influence us as we select a research approach.

For example, some researchers do not have a high regard for interpretive approaches, whereas others have a strong preference for them. As we know from the preceding chapters, a research approach should not be dictated by this kind of sophomoric thinking. As we noted at the outset of this section, our selected research approach—and the ethical issues contained within it—should strive to reduce, not introduce, bias.

All too often, a randomized clinical trial is held up as the gold standard of scientific inquiry. In certain fields of inquiry, a rich history of research and development exists, and a social work intervention might be ready for a randomized experimental study like those discussed in Chapter 11.

But what about an intervention that has not yet been described as a detailed proceduralized or manualized treatment? In this case, it's unethical to choose a randomized control research design because the intervention is clearly not ready to be tested. We have a responsibility to our research participants—as well as to the larger professional community—to select a research approach that will produce useful, reliable, and valid findings.

STEP 3: SPECIFY HOW VARIABLES ARE MEASURED (CHAPTERS 7 AND 8)

MANY OF THE GUIDELINES for specifying the measurement of variables (covered in Chapters 7 and 8) are helpful in avoiding the potential ethical pitfalls in Step 3. For example, we need to avoid measurement methods and instruments with obvious biases, such as the biases related to gender, age, sexual orientation, and culture. If we are studying the sexual habits of men and women, for example, the language of the questions we formulate should not assume that all the research participants are heterosexual.

In fact, our *Code of Ethics* stresses the need for us to understand and respect the full extent of social diversity found within our client systems. This understanding and respect for individual differences must be reflected in the selection and measurement of the variables we wish to study.

In selecting the variables to study, we also need to base our selection on the literature and not conduct a fishing expedition in which every variable imaginable is included in the study in an effort to search for something of significance. Having specific research questions and hypotheses guiding each phase of the study is not just good research practice, it's also good ethical practice. In a nutshell, research participants should not be asked to provide a wealth of information that may or may not address the central question(s) of the research study.

BE AWARE OF CULTURAL ISSUES (CHAPTER 4)

As we will see in the next chapter, a study that fails to take into account cultural issues is unlikely to produce valid and reliable findings. Cultural issues must be considered at every step of the research process, from developing the research question to disseminating the study's findings. As we know from our social work practice classes, perceptions and definitions of child sexual abuse are socially constructed and are shaped by specific cultural, social, and historical perspectives.

Thus, we must take into account how our potential study's participants perceive and understand child sexual abuse, in addition to the cultural customs about discussing such a sensitive topic. These cultural contexts influence how the research questions are asked, how study participants are recruited, and how data are collected and finally analyzed.

We may find that little or no information is available on the social problem being addressed in the culture of the population in which we are interested. In this case, we need to consult representatives from the group we are studying for advice and guidance. *Focus groups* with these individuals will help to clarify many potential issues.

Pilot testing the measuring procedures using people from the group of interest is absolutely essential in an effort to avoid any misunderstandings, the possibility of offending our study's participants, and, ultimately, the production of data that are not reliable and valid.

EXAMPLES OF CULTURAL ISSUE AWARENESS. A proposed research study of the experiences of political refugees to the United States from former Soviet Bloc countries may be a relatively novel area of inquiry, with limited advice available in the professional literature. Thus, in designing a research questionnaire, we would likely find that talking to the immigrants and the social service staff who works with refugees will be the most helpful in understanding the challenges faced by this particular population.

Another example of an extremely important topic under the general area of cultural issues is that of language. If the data collection method(s), such as those discussed in Chapters 12 to 14, involve gathering data directly from our research participants, then we need to be sensitive to issues related to language.

Even when collecting data from participants who speak the same language as the social worker, we must be sensitive to regional dialects, the age of the respondents, and the like. When doing research studies with adolescents or "Millennials," for example, you have to consider the trade-off between using Standard English, slang, Web speak, or other types of communication they commonly use.

As we know from earlier in this chapter, when obtaining informed consent from potential research participants, we must strive to explain our study's procedures in terms that can be easily understood by prospective participants. Our *Code of Ethics* and the next chapter clearly address the importance of considering cultural issues when designing a research study. We are reminded to respect the cultural and ethnic backgrounds of the people with whom we work.

This includes recognizing the strengths that exist in all cultures—which is critical when designing research questions and hypotheses, selecting variables to be studied, and conducting all other steps of the research process itself. Thus, the above-mentioned study of political refugees needs to consider their strengths as well as their challenges and difficulties.

STEP 4: SELECT A SAMPLE (CHAPTER 9)

HOW WE SELECT RESEARCH PARTICIPANTS for potential participation in our research studies is a very important ingredient of the research process. Although sampling methods are primarily driven by the study's purpose, sampling decisions also are influenced by our own personal values and sometimes by convenience. Ethical concerns include whether the potential research participants are representative of the target population we really want to study.

In other words, is this the group most affected by the problem we are trying to answer via the research study? As we will see in Chapter 9 on sampling, it's important to ask whether the group is diverse enough to represent those who are affected by the problem.

Research studies with samples lacking in cultural diversity may limit generalization to the broader population under study, and they also compromise social work ethical tenets that address social justice and increased inclusion. Intentionally or inadvertently excluding certain individuals or groups from participating in a research study can markedly affect the data gathered and the conclusions drawn about the phenomena under study.

For instance, a research study of immigrants that excludes non–English-speaking individuals, nonreaders, and agency clients who come in before or after regular hours for the convenience of the researchers introduces several types of sampling biases that will directly affect the generalizability of study's results. This example also ignores the mandate that all social workers must engage in culturally competent practice and research that respects client diversity.

Recruitment

How potential research participants are recruited also requires an ethical lens. Assessing all possible ways that a potential research participant might feel undue influence to participate—such as a personal appeal, a financial incentive, the status of being part of a special group, other tangible or intangible benefits, or just plain-old fear of repercussions—can be a daunting task, to say the least.

Who is actually recruiting the participants? Does the gatekeeper—or the process of the recruitment effort itself—exert pressure, subtle or direct, to participate or not to participate? Social workers hold an ethical obligation to examine the fairness or *equity* of recruitment strategies within target populations and the representativeness (or diversity) of the sample finally selected to be included in the study.

As we know from earlier portions of this chapter, our *Code of Ethics* includes standards that mandate that we obtain potential research participants without threatening to penalize anyone who refuses to participate—and without offering inappropriate rewards for their participation. Just as clients have the right to self-determination in social work practice, so too do participants who volunteer for research projects.

Take a look at Boxes 3.1 and 3.2, which provide examples of consent (Box 3.1) and assent (Box 3.2) forms. Do you see any possibility that the foster youth were unduly influenced to participate and/or would not receive services if they did not participate? Why or why not? And speaking of ethical recruitment, take a look at Box 3.3.

STEP 5: SELECT A RESEARCH DESIGN (CHAPTERS 10 AND 11)

THE RESEARCH DESIGN that is finally chosen also warrants examination from an ethical perspective. In intervention or evaluation research, in which participants are randomized to either an intervention group or a control group, concerns often arise about withholding treatment or providing a less potent intervention for control group members.

The ability to randomly assign research participants to groups significantly strengthens arguments about whether a particular intervention is responsible for the change (if any) that has occurred for the individuals in the intervention group.

This decision, however, must be weighed against the reality of the participant's life or problem situation. Clients can be randomly assigned to two groups: one group receives the intervention (experimental group), and the other group does not receive it (control group). If the experimental group does better than the control group after the study is completed, the control group would then receive the same intervention that the experimental group received earlier.

Because the control group receives the intervention at a later date, there are no ethical violations present in this particular research design when implemented correctly. However, a delay must always be weighed against the benefit, as some delays may be detrimental or even fatal.

The following diagram illustrates the kind of study that was used with the foster care adolescents described in Boxes 3.1 and 3.2. The experimental group received the social work intervention or workshop (top arrow), and the control group did not (bottom arrow).

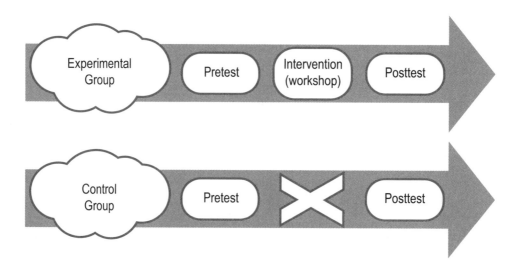

One important fact that we may lose sight of is that a new, untested intervention may not necessarily be better than no treatment at all. It is, as they say, an "empirical question" and deserves testing. What is clear is that individuals applying for social work services have the right to receive the best known evidence-based interventions at that time.

In other words, it's unethical to withhold an intervention that has already been demonstrated to be effective. Protecting clients from deprivation of services and ensuring that they have access to the best interventions is also a mandate of our *Code of Ethics.*

Individuals applying for experimental or innovative services of any type have the right to know the availability of alternative forms of interventions and the risks and benefits of each intervention. Exploring the use of different kinds of control conditions and determining which is best, both for the clients and for answering the research question, is an important ethical task.

BOX 3.3
Heart's in the Right Place but Head Isn't

Let's begin our venture into recruiting research participants from an ethical perspective with a short vignette that illustrates how a beginning graduate-level social work student, Margaret, wanted to recruit clients (research participants) for a research study.

In her field practicum, Margaret is helping her professor recruit families for a research study that is aimed at providing an intervention to improve the parenting skills of pregnant and parenting teenagers. She recruits potential research participants at the local public social services office (her practicum setting), where the pregnant teenagers meet weekly with their child protection workers.

According to the research study's recruitment protocol, recruitment takes place via colorful flyers handed out to clients by the receptionist as they enter the agency. The clients are asked by the receptionist to talk with Margaret to get further information on an "important" study in which they may wish to participate.

One day, Margaret notices a young pregnant teenager crying in the waiting room and asks her if she can do anything to help. Listening to her story, Margaret unwittingly finds herself strongly encouraging the teenager to participate in the research project (a new intervention, yet to be tested) by telling her how much the intervention would improve her parenting skills.

She also suggests that her participation in the research study would reflect favorably on the child protection worker's evaluation of the teen. At this point, do you see anything wrong with Margaret's behaviors?

Margaret responded to the client's sad story with encouragement that she believed to be in the client's best interests—participating in the research study. Margaret increases the client's motivation to participate by telling her it will improve her parenting skills.

In addition, Margaret asserts that the client's participation would favorably impact the child protection worker's assessment of the teen. Although Margaret's intentions may be understandable to the novice, she has in fact violated the ethical principles of both practice and research in one brief three-minute conversation. More specifically, and in no particular order, Margaret:

1. assumed she understood the client's problem without conducting an adequate assessment.

2. did not fully disclose the purpose of the research study.

3. exerted coercive influence over the client to participate by telling her the intervention will work for her without actually knowing if it would.

4. suggested that the client's participation in the study would favorably affect the agency's perception of her.

5. did not realize that the young woman may have felt that she had to participate in the research study to receive the services she was asking for by coming into the agency in the first place.

6. did not tell the client that she may be randomly assigned to a control group (those who do not receive the treatment) and, thus, may receive no intervention whatsoever (at this time, that is).

7. did not obtain the consent of the teen's parents or legal guardian.

Oh, by the way, this incident actually happened!

BENEFICENCE

Central to the consideration of the ethical issues in experimental designs is the question of *beneficence*. Researchers and the IRBs that guide them must consider how to maximize the benefit and minimize harm to participants when considering how best to test the effectiveness of a social work intervention. The possibility of other viable treatment methods must be considered as well, as opposed to offering no treatment. Again, our *Code of Ethics* mandates that we must protect both clients and research participants from deprivation of access to evidence-based services.

EQUIPOISE, OR THE UNCERTAINTY PRINCIPLE

Highly related to providing the most effective services as possible is the concept of *equipoise*, also called the *uncertainty principle*. This principle maintains that research studies that randomize their research participants to different treatment groups should be conducted only if there is a true uncertainty about which of the treatment alternatives is most likely to benefit them. Some questions are easy to answer, but some pose serious dilemmas to the researcher.

For instance, if an intervention being tested is known to be superior to an alternative inferior intervention, it's unethical to assign individuals to the inferior intervention. Similarly, an experimental research study that contains two interventions is unethical if a third intervention exists that is known to be more effective, unless the researchers have questions about the efficacy of the effective intervention for a particular subgroup of clients.

All too often, however, a consideration of beneficence and equipoise raises challenging questions for social work researchers, especially those working in fields where there are relatively few data to support the effectiveness of alternative interventions. Moreover, if the usual intervention has little or no evidence to support its effectiveness, can it be considered an appropriate comparison treatment?

DECEPTION

Deception is another aspect of a study's research design that requires ethical forethought. Let's consider an example to illustrate this point. José wanted to study racial/ethnic bias in employment practices in family service agencies in Chicago. He mailed numerous fake application letters to all family service agencies in Chicago that had current openings for full-time clinicians. Each letter contained the exact same qualifications, but he would change his name to reflect four different groups of people: African American, Latino, Asian, or Irish heritage.

In short, everything was the same except his name. José planned to simply count the number of interview requests he received, broken down by each group. Sounds harmless, you say? Read on.

In no way in his cover letter for employment did José indicate he was conducting a research study. To José's surprise, all of Chicago's executive directors of family service agencies met at a local conference and started talking about good job candidates they were going to follow up on. José's name came up several times in the conversation.

The executive directors soon became angry when they found out they had been duped by José. Several of them had not interviewed other qualified individuals because they were holding slots open to interview José when time permitted.

José, his school, his dean, and the federal government all became involved in addressing the consequences of his unethical use of deception. José's actions ignored a key concept of our *Code of Ethics*: Whether acting as a practitioner or a researcher, social workers are mandated to act with integrity and in a trustworthy manner.

Generally, it's good practice to avoid deception whenever possible. Although it sounds reasonable to say that good social work researchers should *never* lie to their potential research participants or provide them with less than a full disclosure about the methods of their studies, in reality this is not always desirable. As an example, a social worker assessing bias toward developmentally delayed clients by staff employed at correctional institutions understandably initially might not want to disclose the entire purpose of the study because it might affect how the custodial staff responds.

We need to ask the ethical question: Is deception absolutely necessary to carry out the study? In other words, is deception necessary to prevent participants from trying to respond in a contrived and/or socially desirable manner?

Next, we need to ask whether there is a possibility that the deception will harm our research participants, in either the short or long term. If the deception causes or encourages participants to react in ways they might not otherwise, or allows them to make choices at odds with their personal views of themselves (e.g., a decision-making study that allows a participant to lie, cheat, or steal), learning later about their behavior might be psychologically distressing.

Our *Code of Ethics* mandates not only that we protect our research participants from mental distress but also that we protect our clients from all harm to the fullest extent possible. The majority of deception that is approved in research studies is of minimal risk to research participants and is far less dramatic than José's study of racial/ethnic bias in hiring practices.

For example, Jennifer would have been wiser if she had used *more* deception in her study that monitored children's seat belt use on school buses. Climbing onto a school bus after the young children had boarded, she announced, "I am doing a research study for your principal, and I'm counting the number of safe and smart children on this bus who buckle up!"

In this one simple very honest sentence she immediately gave away the purpose of her study, which resulted in an immediate flurry of seat belt buckling—thus defeating her ability to get an accurate and realistic count of those children who would not have buckled up if it weren't for her disclosure of the study. On another topic: Do you think Jennifer needed permission from the children's parents to do her simple head count? Why or why not? After all, the children were minors.

DEBRIEFING. One of the ways in which we can appropriately counteract the use of deception is by using debriefing procedures after the study is over. Debriefing involves explaining the true purpose of the research study to the participants after the study is completed, along with *why* the deception was necessary in the first place. If there is a concern about psychological distress as a result of having been deceived by the study, for example, then participants must be offered adequate means of addressing this distress.

In some cases of minimal-risk research involving deception, debriefing participants about the true nature of the study and their responses may cause greater distress than not fully understanding their actions in the study.

Also, experienced mental health professionals and IRBs might disagree on whether distressing self-knowledge can be mitigated effectively and how this should best be done, or even whether a study should be conducted in view of the psychological risks to potential participants. One possible way that our *Code of Ethics* offers to mitigate the situation is to offer participants "appropriate supportive services" after the study.

STEP 6: SELECT A DATA COLLECTION METHOD (CHAPTERS 12–14)

STEP 6 OF THE RESEARCH PROCESS, data collection, contains the ethical issues that surround it:

— How Data Are Collected

— Who Will Collect the Data

— The Frequency and Timing of Data Collection

HOW DATA ARE COLLECTED

As we will see in Chapter 14, a researcher's choice of how to collect the data that best answer the research question can introduce unintended bias, coercing some and potentially excluding other desired participants. Awareness is the key to understanding the ethical implications of data collection.

EXAMPLE 1. Aiesha wants to do a follow-up study with juveniles released from custody in her state's detention facilities. She conducts a phone survey during the hours she's at work (standard business hours) and calls the youths' "home" phone numbers. Aiesha is unaware that she is missing the youths who (1) do not have phones, (2) have phones but simply do not answer them, (3) do not hang out at home during the day, (4) operate primarily from cell phones, and (5) she is possibly inadvertently informing housemates who answer that the person being called was formerly detained.

EXAMPLE 2. One of Aiesha's colleagues, Barbara, is using an "anonymous" Internet-based survey to examine the educational aspirations of young adults. As part of her study, she asks participants about their recreational drug use and about any knowledge they might have about their parents' recreational use of illegal substances.

Although she does not ask for names or other identifying information, it's possible to trace respondents by their computers' Internet protocol (IP) addresses. Barbara forgot that all researchers must protect their participants' identities, just as practitioners must protect clients' privacy, according to our *Code of Ethics.*

Further, although the youths have consented to participate via completion of the Internet survey itself, Barbara also was gathering data about the youths' parents. The parents have not consented to have their children give Barbara data about them.

Collecting data about parental substance abuse via their children without the parents' consent is not a good idea to say the least. A situation similar to this one resulted in the temporary shutdown of all federal research at one eastern university after a very irate parent contacted the U.S. Department of Health and Human Services' Office for Human Research Protection.

WHO WILL COLLECT THE DATA

Who is actually going to collect the data that will answer the research question constitutes yet another ethical decision to be made. Anyone in a position of power or authority over the participant, such as teachers, social workers, health-care officials, administrators—anyone who can either supply or deny the resources that research participants need—introduces the potential for undue influence.

Coercion can easily result in less-than-willing participation. It also may influence the quality of the data collected because the participants may respond differently than they normally would if they believe that individuals who have authority over them may see their responses.

Paper and pencil surveys about anger and urges to act impulsively that are completed by clients arrested for interpersonal violence are an example. Our *Code of Ethics* also asserts that the presence of coercion violates the tenets of voluntary participation in both practice and research activities.

FREQUENCY AND TIMING OF DATA COLLECTION

Finally, the choice we make about the frequency and timing of data collection activities also may raise privacy issues. Some research designs call for collecting data at additional intervals after the main part of the study has been completed with all research participants. In situations such as these, the consent and/or assent letter(s) (e.g., Boxes 3.1 and 3.2) must inform potential research participants that they will be contacted in the future.

Step 7: Analyze the Data (Chapters 15 and 16)

DATA ANALYSIS and, indeed, even drawing conclusions about data results is, unfortunately, one step in the research process that many social workers most often wish to outsource or turn over to others. Those of us who are not research oriented are often unfamiliar with data analysis beyond basic statistics and may avoid reading the results section of journal articles, skipping ahead to the discussion section and assuming that the author will review what is most important.

We rely heavily on the peer review process in professional publications for assurance that appropriate methods of data analysis are used. However, does this excuse us from not knowing statistics? Some have suggested that ethical data analysis begins with our moral responsibility to *understand* the analyses that data undergo before we make use of the research results.

Ethical problems in data analysis are rooted, broadly speaking, in the research environment. Don't be more invested in supporting your theories than in testing them! The researcher's personal attachment to specific theories, followed by the importance of obtaining statistical significance so that the research results can be published or receive other indicators of peer approval, are real parts of the research environment.

Our common understanding of research "success" is based on the outcomes of the study—that is, whether the study's findings support the researcher's hypotheses. Hearing a researcher say the project did not "turn out" generally means that the results did not support the researcher's theories.

The following are a few guidelines related to data analysis:

* Research findings and results should be presented openly and honestly. This includes avoiding leaving out or omitting contradictory findings.

* Untrue or deceptive statements should be avoided in reports.

* The limits and boundaries of inference used should be delineated clearly. This may include considerations of the subjects sampled for participation or the levels of experimental variables.

* Complete and clear documentation should be provided, including how the data were edited, the statistical procedures used, and the assumptions made about the data.

* The role of data analyst ideally is neutral so that statistical procedures may be applied without concern for a favorable outcome.

Social workers wishing to employ ethical analysis strategies should incorporate these five principles into their own work. Much more will be said about analyzing quantitative data in Chapter 15 and qualitative data in Chapter 16.

STEP 8: WRITE AND DISSEMINATE THE RESEARCH REPORT

THE FINAL STEP, writing and disseminating the research report, is fraught with potential ethical dilemmas. To begin, all too often we neglect to write a report and disseminate the findings of our research studies. Somehow we get caught up in our busy schedules and the need to move on to the next project, and we fail to attend to this crucial last step. Not reporting findings is a disservice to everyone who participated in and funded the study.

Moreover, our *Code of Ethics* calls for us to facilitate informed participation in the general community for shaping public social policy and human service institutions, as well as to engage in social and political action ourselves. Depending on the nature of the research study, the findings might be important in advocating for social justice for our constituents, such as providing equal access to benefits and resources that will meet their basic needs and allow them to realize their full potential.

In addition to reporting to the community at large, we have a responsibility to report our findings to our research participants and our community, who are supposed to benefit from our study's findings. In particular, if our recruitment process involved promising to make a report available to potential study participants, it's critical that we share our findings with them in clear, understandable language.

There are a host of methods for disseminating research findings, including research summaries, journal articles, books, press releases, flyers, posters, brochures, letters of thanks to study participants, study newsletters, local conferences, and seminars. Social workers need to consider the goal of the reporting and the needs of the target audience in selecting a distribution method.

For a broader audience, we need to find ways to make the content comprehensible and interesting. We need to be good storytellers when communicating research findings while taking care not to distort them. As we will see in the following chapter, we must also find culturally sensitive ways to report our study's findings to both our research participants and communities, when appropriate.

Our *Code of Ethics* also provides a thorough discussion of the importance of protecting clients' right to privacy. Providing feedback to our participants, while still maintaining their confidentiality, can be challenging in certain situations. To illustrate, our research participants may have been in domestic violence shelters, mental health institutions, or juvenile justice placements, and then were returned home or released to more open settings. Simply obtaining a current address is often difficult, but even when the address is obtained, involuntary clients often do not want others to know that they have received social services.

Hence, participants may not wish to receive a research report, which in some way labels them as affiliated with a particular agency or service. A cover letter thanking a woman for her involvement in an interpersonal violence study can "out" her and may even create a dangerous situation. Incarcerated youth, who were once eager to see the results of a study they participated in, may feel awkward and embarrassed 18 months later when the report arrives mailed to their homes.

Another ethical dilemma that we sometimes face arises when there's a conflict between the participants' agency, policy makers, advocacy groups, and/or the group that funded the study and the researcher. If stakeholders are displeased with certain findings, or with the way in which the researcher has interpreted them, this can seriously complicate the dissemination of the findings. Our *Code of Ethics* highlights our responsibility to report accurately our evaluation and research findings—and, it should go without saying, not to fabricate the results.

To the extent possible, we should come to some general agreement in the early stages of planning our research study about how these issues will be resolved. In fact, our *Code of Ethics* cautions us to identify potential conflicts of interest, inform the participants when a real or potential conflict of interest develops, and place primary importance on the participants' interests in resolving any conflicts of interest.

Often, the sharing of findings will be a delicate matter. Agency staff may be reluctant to hear, for example, that their program may be less effective than they had thought. If they were not engaged in the research process in the first place and they know little about the research methods, they may be tempted to dismiss the findings and block any attempt on the part of the researcher to discuss recommendations for improvement. Thus, findings must be presented carefully, to the right people, in the right order, and at the right time.

Practitioners wrestle every day with a similar problem. Mr. Yen might not want to be told that his daughter is still threatening to run away despite all those parenting classes and family therapy sessions he attended. His daughter might not want him to know. His wife might not want him to know either, in case this bit of data spurs him to inappropriate disciplinary steps. The social worker must decide whom to tell, as well as how, when, and how much. The same holds true when doing research studies.

 # ETHICS AND OUR SOCIAL SERVICE PROGRAMS

We noted in Chapter 1 that one thing all agency administrators have in common is worry. They worry about how effectively they are serving their clients and how they can demonstrate their effectiveness to funders. They worry about offending people. They worry about whether they will be seen to be doing the right thing, with the right people, in the right place, at the right time. All these worries have ethical and political overtones.

Take effective service to clients, for example. There is nothing absolute about effectiveness. The same service may be deemed to be effective or ineffective depending on how effectiveness is defined and who does the defining. For instance, the aim of a drug rehabilitation program might be to ensure that every client who comes through its doors will absolutely and positively abstain 100% from using any type of drug forevermore.

This aim, though worthy, is probably impossible to achieve. The program's actual achievement—in terms of the percentage of clients who completely abstained, partially abstained, or did not abstain from using a particular drug over a particular period—will be seen as successful or not depending on the political climate.

If marijuana is currently viewed as a gateway to hell, for example, the program's lack of success in curtailing its use will be judged more harshly than in a more tolerant climate. If a more immediate concern is gas sniffing among First Nations children, the program is likely to be judged on how well it's dealing with solvent abuse. Effectiveness thus tends to be defined and evaluated with respect to the external political and social issues of the hour.

There are also the internal politics of the program to be considered. Staff members will each have their individual views about which of the many issues facing the program should be given priority, how scarce resources should be used, which treatment modality is best, what the reporting structure ought to be, and, in general, who ought to do what, where, how, and when. These inevitable tensions affect the research climate within the program.

Most social service programs will be less or more receptive to research endeavors at different times, depending on their internal political situations and their current level of staff morale. When staff are feeling overworked, underpaid, and unappreciated, they will be less inclined to cooperate with research efforts, but, at the same time, this is the moment when they might benefit most from an evaluative study designed to improve client service delivery or to optimize the organizational structure.

Conversely, when morale is low due to conflicts with administrators, an evaluative study might just serve to exacerbate the conflicts. Researchers, like all social workers, have the potential to help or to harm. If they are to help, they must be sensitive to internal and external political considerations so that they can conduct a useful study in the right way, in the right place, at the right time.

MISUSES OF RESEARCH RESULTS

It might be worthwhile here to consider the misuses of research results. A study that sets out to be useful can turn out to be harmful if the results are used in an unethical way. There are four primary ways in which research results may be misused within social service programs:

— To Justify Decisions Already Made

— To Safeguard Public Relations

— To Appraise the Performance of Staff

— To Fulfill Funding Requirements

Justifying Decisions Already Made

We said earlier that a common aim among agency administrators is to avoid offending people. In our opinion, there is no one on earth who is more politically correct than an agency's executive director. Indeed, in the present political climate where services to clients are increasingly community based, programs make it a priority to establish and maintain good relationships with community stakeholders. There are usually a large number of stakeholder groups, each with its own agenda, so maintaining good relationships with all of them requires a great deal of tact.

For example, mindful of the needs of its client group, the agency might propose to build a hospice for AIDS patients in a nearby residential area. The homeowners in the area object. In company with other public-spirited citizens, they approve of hospices for AIDS patients—and rehabilitation programs for young offenders, and homes for pregnant adolescents—but they don't want them in their own backyards. Sound familiar?

The agency, trapped between its duty to its clients and its duty to its neighbors, will go through the normal processes of convening meetings, establishing committees, collecting comments, and issuing reports. It's also quite likely that a research study will be commissioned into the advisability of building the hospice as proposed.

Again, the researchers need to be sensitive to the political currents both within and outside the agency setting. Probably some stakeholders have already decided that they want the hospice built and are looking to the research report to confirm this opinion.

Other stakeholders will not want the hospice built in their neighborhood and also expect that the research report will support their position. Trapped, like the agency, between a rock and a hard place, the researchers will need to consider very carefully the uses that are likely to be made of their research results.

If the results will be used solely to justify a decision that has already been made on other grounds, then it's unethical to undertake the study. On the other hand, if it's possible that an objective, bias-free appraisal of the advantages and disadvantages of building the hospice will actually sway the decision, then the study should be done. The researchers must decide whether to undertake the study based on their judgment of the ethical and political factors involved.

Safeguarding Public Relations

Another of the worries shared by agency administrators is negative publicity. Perhaps a worker in a group home has been indicted for the sexual abuse of residents, or a foster parent has abused a child. These kinds of incidents inevitably attract intense media scrutiny, and it's tempting for administrators to immediately commission an evaluative study to investigate the problem, declining to comment until the research results become available.

Now, there's nothing wrong with an evaluative study. It may, indeed, be the best way to determine why the problem occurred and what can be done to prevent it from occurring again in the future. But if the sole purpose of the study is to delay comment until the furor has died down, then it's simply not ethical for a researcher to undertake the study. Neither is it ethical if there is an unspoken expectation that the researcher will discover only what the foster care program wants.

If parts of the report are taken out of context in order to show the program in a good light, or if the results are distorted to avoid public embarrassment, then the integrity of the study will obviously be compromised. In such a situation, the researcher will be at fault as well.

It used to be the case that researchers were not held responsible for the uses made of their study results and recommendations. Their jobs were merely to produce them. Now, however, it's considered essential for researchers to do the best they can to ensure that results are used in an ethical way.

Appraising Staff Performance

The third possible misuse of research results is for performance appraisals. Again, there is nothing wrong with a performance appraisal. Most workers are required to undergo an annual evaluation of how well they performed during the previous year. However, a performance appraisal and a research study are two separate things.

For example, consider a research study designed to document overall client progress within a program by aggregating (or adding up) the progress made by the clients of each individual social worker. Before they are aggregated, the study results have the potential to demonstrate that the clients of one social worker made more progress overall than the clients of another. And this, in turn, may be taken to indicate that one social worker is more competent than the other.

In a study of this kind, it's not ethical for researchers to release results before they have been aggregated—that is, before they are in a form that will protect the confidentiality of the social workers who participated in the study. In the event that they are prematurely released, it's certainly not ethical for administrators to use the information to appraise a particular social worker. Nevertheless, there have been instances when research results have been used for political purposes, to promote or undermine a specific worker or program, so researchers need to be wary of this.

FULFILLING FUNDING REQUIREMENTS

Most evaluation studies are used, at least in part, to demonstrate accountability to funders. Indeed, almost all social service programs, particularly new or pilot projects, are funded with the stipulation that they should be evaluated. It's not unethical, therefore, to use evaluation research to fulfill funding requirements. But it is unethical to use evaluation research solely to fulfill funding requirements without any real intention of using the information gathered to improve the program.

 SUMMARY

This chapter briefly looked at a few of the ethical factors that affect the social work research enterprise. You now know how research is used in social work (Chapter 1), how to formulate research questions through the literature (Chapter 2), and how to behave in an ethical manner when doing a research study (this chapter). You're now an ethical researcher who can formulate good social work research questions, but you need to be a culturally sensitive one as well—the topic of the next chapter.

Study Questions for Chapter 3

— First, answer each question only AFTER you have read the chapter.

— Second, indicate how comfortable you were in answering each question on a 5-point scale:

1	2	3	4	5
Very uncomfortable	Somewhat uncomfortable	Neutral	Somewhat comfortable	Very comfortable

If you rated any question between 1–3, please reread the section of the chapter where the information for the question can be found. If you're still uncomfortable answering the question, talk with your instructor and/or your classmates for more clarification.

Questions	Degree of comfort? (Circle one number)
1. List and discuss in detail the ethical issues that are involved in the early stages of doing a research or evaluation study. Provide one common social work example throughout your entire discussion.	1 2 3 4 5
2. What is informed consent? Discuss why this is important in a research study. Provide examples.	1 2 3 4 5
3. What are consent forms? Why are they necessary when conducting a research study? What are their ingredients? Provide as many examples as you can to justify your response. Are there any other topics that you think should be included in a consent form? If so, what are they?	1 2 3 4 5
4. What are assent forms? Why are they necessary when conducting a research study? What are their ingredients? Provide as many examples as you can to justify your response. Are there any other topics that you think should be included in an assent form? If so, what are they?	1 2 3 4 5
5. What are the differences between a consent form and an assent form? Discuss in detail.	1 2 3 4 5
6. What are bribery and deception? When can you ethically bribe or deceive a research participant? Provide examples to illustrate your points.	1 2 3 4 5
7. What is the difference between anonymity and confidentiality? Provide as many examples as you can to justify your response.	1 2 3 4 5

8.	Discuss the ethical issues that may arise in Step 1 of the research process. Discuss them in detail and apply a social work example throughout.	1 2 3 4 5
9.	Discuss the ethical issues that may arise in Step 2 of the research process. Discuss them in detail and apply a social work example throughout.	1 2 3 4 5
10.	Discuss the ethical issues that may arise in Step 3 of the research process. Discuss them in detail and apply a social work example throughout.	1 2 3 4 5
11.	Discuss the ethical issues that may arise in Step 4 of the research process. Discuss them in detail and apply a social work example throughout.	1 2 3 4 5
12.	Discuss the ethical issues that may arise in Step 5 of the research process. Discuss them in detail and apply a social work example throughout.	1 2 3 4 5
13.	Discuss the ethical issues that may arise in Step 6 of the research process. Discuss them in detail and apply a social work example throughout.	1 2 3 4 5
14.	Discuss the ethical issues that may arise in Step 7 of the research process. Discuss them in detail and apply a social work example throughout.	1 2 3 4 5
15.	Discuss the ethical issues that may arise in Step 8 of the research process. Discuss them in detail and apply a social work example throughout.	1 2 3 4 5
16.	Discuss the ethical issues that surround the misuse of research results in relation to justifying decisions already made. Provide a social work example throughout your discussion.	1 2 3 4 5
17.	Discuss the ethical issues that surround the misuse of research results in relation to public relations. Provide a social work example throughout your discussion.	1 2 3 4 5
18.	Discuss the ethical issues that surround the misuse of research results in relation to performance appraisals. Provide a social work example throughout your discussion.	1 2 3 4 5

19. Discuss the ethical issues that surround the misuse of research results in relation to fulfilling funding requirements. Provide a social work example throughout your discussion.	1 2 3 4 5
20. In groups of four, create a hypothetical research study that would require the participation of social work clients. Decide on the study's purpose and the research methodology. Discuss how you would protect the participants from harm, ensure confidentiality, provide adequate information about the study, and encourage voluntary participation. Draft an informed consent statement that addresses your ethical concerns. Read the statement to the class. (Use information from the entire chapter.)	1 2 3 4 5
21. At this point in your course, how comfortable are you with discussing the various ethical issues that you need to be aware of when doing a social work research study with your field instructor (or your supervisor at work)? With your fellow classmates? Discuss in detail.	1 2 3 4 5
22. At this point in your course, how comfortable are you with describing consent and assent forms with your field instructor (or your supervisor at work)? With your fellow classmates? Discuss in detail.	1 2 3 4 5

Assessing Your Self-Efficacy for Chapter 3

AFTER you have read the chapter AND have completed all the study questions, please indicate how knowledgeable you feel you are for each concept listed below.

1	2	3	4	5
Very uncomfortable	Somewhat uncomfortable	Neutral	Somewhat comfortable	Very comfortable

Major Concepts in Chapter	Knowledge Level? (Circle one number)
1. Using clients as research participants	1 2 3 4 5
2. Obtaining informed consent	1 2 3 4 5
3. Obtaining informed assent	1 2 3 4 5
4. Bribery, deception, and other forms of coercion	1 2 3 4 5
5. Ingredients of consent forms	1 2 3 4 5
6. Ingredients of assent forms	1 2 3 4 5
7. Anonymity	1 2 3 4 5
8. Confidentially	1 2 3 4 5
9. Ethical considerations in each of the eight steps of the research process	1 2 3 4 5
10. The four major misuses of research results	1 2 3 4 5
Add up your scores (Minimum = 10, Maximum = 50)	Total score =

A   45 — 50 = Social Work Manager in the making.
B   40 — 44 = Social Work Supervisor.
C   35 — 39 = Social Work Practitioner.
D   10 — 34 = Case Aide. Reread the chapter and redo the study questions.

4

Culturally Competent Research

A nation's culture resides in the hearts and in the soul of its people.
~ Mahatma Gandhi

You now know how the research process is used in our profession (Chapter 1), how to formulate research problems through the literature (Chapter 2), and how to abide by ethical principles when doing research studies (Chapter 3). Using the three previous chapters as background, this chapter explores basic culture issues that also need to be taken into account when doing a social work research study. As you know from reading the previous chapter on ethics, many cultural and ethical issues are highly intertwined.

This chapter is a logical extension of the previous one in that we provide a brief overview of culture and cultural competence, followed by a discussion of key issues in culturally competent research practices. As the issues are discussed, we make use of examples of worldview perceptions, communications, and behaviors that may be characteristic of particular cultures. These are intended only as examples of cultural patterns and not to suggest that any characteristics describe all members of the group.

We fully recognize that cultures are not monolithic and that a variety of cultural patterns may exist within broadly defined cultural groups. The descriptions provided within this chapter are for illustrative purposes only and are not meant to be stereotypical of the members of any culture.

We also know that each individual is unique, and we recognize that within any culture a wide range of individual perceptions, communications, and behaviors may exist. In social work research, as in any other human interactive process, there is no substitute for meeting each person with openness and acceptance, regardless of cultural background.

OUR VILLAGE

Our village has grown to encompass the world. Faster means of transportation (e.g., air travel) and communication (e.g., Internet, social media), the expansion of trade, and the human desire to seek a better life have created societies that no longer find their roots in one cultural tradition or their voice in one common language. Rather, migration trends and globalization activities have laid the foundations for complex, culturally diverse societies with representation from several racial, ethnic, and cultural groups.

Diversity is reflected throughout our society: in schools, in the workplace, and within all types of formal and informal organizations. Social service organizations are no exception; there is increasing diversity both among staff and also among service recipients. Of course, diversity also has an impact on social work research; the challenge for researchers is to work effectively in culturally diverse settings.

WORKING WITH STAKEHOLDERS OR RESEARCH TEAMS

AS IS MADE CLEAR throughout this book, doing a research study is more than the technical practice of formulating research questions, organizing and implementing data collection activities, analyzing data, and reporting findings. Although these are important research activities, researchers also need to work effectively with a variety of stakeholders or research teams in a wide range of organizations. The tasks include working with research teams to clarify expectations, identify interests, reconcile differences, and win cooperation.

You must therefore be adept at establishing interpersonal and working relationships in addition to bringing technical expertise to the research process. When working with different cultural groups or in different cultural settings, you must be culturally competent and also have the ability to adapt the technical aspects of the research procedures so that they are appropriate for your specific research setting and research participants alike. To achieve community involvement with a lens toward culturally sensitivity, the following questions should be considered when forming a research team that will guide you through your study:

- What history (e.g., prior practice and research, knowledge of group and/ or community) does the research team have with the racial/ethnic group members included in your study?

- What efforts have been made to ensure the inclusion of the perspective of racial/ethnic group members in the design, conduct, and analysis of the study?

- What is the race/ethnicity of the research team, including the principal investigator, consultants, data collectors, and coders?

- Have potential biases of research team members been recognized?

- What efforts have been made to counter potential biases of the research team in working with racial/ethnic minority groups?

It's not necessary for the researcher to be a member of the racial/ethnic group being studied, but achieving culturally competent research knowledge of the community is crucial. Cross-cultural research is strengthened when researchers study the beliefs, values, and social structures that form the context of the participants' worldview and when they incorporate that knowledge into the design and conduct of their studies.

 # THE IMPACT OF CULTURE

Culture is many things: a set of customs, traditions, and beliefs, and a worldview. It's socially defined and passed on from generation to generation (Porter & Samovar, 2006; Thomas & Inkson, 2009). Culture is manifested in the perceptions through which we view our surroundings and the patterns of language and behavior through which we interact with others. Culture exists at two levels:

- *Micro-level.* Micro-level culture is found with individuals and is reflected in their personal values, beliefs, communication styles, and behaviors.

- *Macro-level.* Macro-level culture exists within organizations, institutions, and communities; it's manifested in mandates, policies, and practices.

Fundamentally, culture acts as a filter through which people view, perceive, and evaluate the world around them. At the same time, it also provides a framework within which people process information, think, communicate, and behave. Because different cultures establish different frameworks for perceiving and judging as well as for thinking and acting, misperceptions, miscommunications, and conflicts are not only possible but also likely. Where people are unaware of how culture filters thinking, actions, perceptions, and judgments, the likelihood for misunderstanding is even greater.

The Japanese, for example, have traditionally used bowing as a form of greeting, but in North America handshakes are prevalent; in certain European countries, hugging and kissing are customary. It's easy to see that what is meant as a friendly gesture in one culture may be viewed as an intrusion in another. In a meeting, for example, a statement that is meant as a hypothetical example in one culture may be viewed as a firm commitment in another.

Unless you sit at the table and know the rules the group operates by, you could develop a research study that misses the point. You need to start off with a model that is culturally informed in order to come up with data and meaningful recommendations that will be helpful and relevant to the community you are working in.

In North America, for example, there is considerable emphasis on the "bottom line," which may translate to outcomes in a positivistic research study. Thus, social work evaluations are often concerned with assessing the outcomes of a social service program. In some cultures, however, the fact that a program has been created and now operates and provides employment for community members may be viewed as at least as important as the actual results of the social services it delivers.

BRIDGING THE CULTURE GAP

Under the principle "respect for people," as set out by the American Evaluation Association, researchers are expected to be aware of—and respect differences among—people and to be mindful of the implications of cultural differences on the research or evaluation processes. Social work researchers thus need:

* A clear understanding of the impact of culture on human and social processes generally and on evaluation processes specifically

* Skills in cross-cultural communication to ensure that they can effectively interact with people from diverse backgrounds

Cultural Awareness

As the previous discussion makes clear, culture provides a powerful organizing framework that filters perceptions and communications and also shapes behaviors and interactions. To practice effectively in different cultural settings, researchers need a general awareness of the role that culture plays in shaping our perceptions, ideas, and behaviors.

Further, we need fundamental attitudes of respect for difference, a willingness to learn about other cultures, and a genuine belief that cultural differences are a source of strength and enrichment rather than an obstacle to be overcome. In particular, social work researchers need cultural awareness: they need to be on guard that their perceptions, communications, and actions are not unduly influenced by ethnocentrism, enculturation, and stereotyping—processes that act as barriers to effective communication and relationships.

Ethnocentrism

Because our own history is inevitably based in our own culture, and because we generally continue to be immersed in that culture, a natural human tendency is to judge others and other cultures by the standards of our own beliefs and values. This is known as *ethnocentrism,* and it leads to defining the world in our own terms. Thus, we might tend to view as normal that which is typical in our own culture; the different practices, structures, or patterns that may be typical in other cultures are likely then to be viewed as "abnormal" or even problematic (Neuliep, 2000).

Among some social groups, for example, child rearing is viewed as a community responsibility, with extended family and other community members taking an active role when necessary. This is seldom typical in urban North American culture, where high mobility often places families in communities without extended family or other support networks.

Thus, in a large urban setting, an appropriate outcome for family support programs may be that the family remains intact, but in communities located in rural or remote areas or on Native American reservations, a more appropriate outcome might be that suitable caregiving arrangements are identified within the family's kinship or community network. An ethnocentric researcher might unwittingly apply mainstream North American values to a Native American family support program, which would clearly result in a distortion in the evaluation process.

ENCULTURATION

Enculturation is a close cousin to ethnocentrism. It's a related process, which refers to the fact that, as children, we learn to behave in ways that are appropriate to our culture. We also come to adopt a variety of core beliefs about human nature, human experience, and human behavior.

This process teaches us how to behave, interact, and even think. Of course, other cultural groups will have different ways of thinking, behaving, and interacting. In some Asian cultures, for example, people value discussion, negotiation, and relationship, whereas in North America, people tend to be more direct and task-oriented (Hall, 1983). Similarly, some cultures such as the Swiss and Germans emphasize promptness, whereas in some Southern U.S. cultures, a meeting is seldom expected to start at the appointed time, but only after everyone has arrived (Lewis, 1997).

The differences in behavior patterns and interactions are real; however, it's important for researchers to recognize that others' patterns are as legitimate and appropriate as their own. When we are unable to do this, stereotyping may occur, resulting in misunderstanding and misjudgment.

For example, a social work researcher may become frustrated because it's difficult to start meetings on time in a community or because it's not possible to keep to a tight schedule, and she may begin to stereotype the group she is working with as uninterested, uncooperative, and disorganized. Obviously, such stereotypes will have the effect of creating additional barriers to communications and interactions and will hinder the research process.

INTERCULTURAL COMMUNICATION

AWARENESS OF THE IMPACT of culture is important, but effective relationships depend on the actual communications. Because social work research is as much a relationship process as a technical matter, effective communication is always important, particularly so in communication across cultures.

There are many models of intercultural communication. One of the more useful ones is offered by Porter and Samovar (2006). In this model, perceptions are regarded as the gateway to communication; they are the means by which people select, evaluate, and organize information about the world around them.

Perceptions, of course, depend in large part upon an individual's worldview, which is, in part, formed as a result of his or her cultural experiences. Perceptions help us select, organize, and interpret a variety of external stimuli, including the communications that others direct toward us.

After we process the communications that are directed toward us, we usually respond. Different cultures support different communication patterns and styles, and thus our response is also shaped and formed, at least in part, by our cultural background. Communications, then, are inextricably bound with culture. The opportunity for misunderstanding, ever present in any communication, is even greater when individuals from different cultural backgrounds interact.

Intercultural communication takes place at both the nonverbal and verbal levels. Anyone who interacts with members of another culture needs an understanding of both nonverbal and verbal communication patterns typical in that culture. We will briefly look at communication at each of these levels.

NONVERBAL COMMUNICATION

An important part of human communication takes place nonverbally. Facial expressions, time, use of space, and gestures convey much information and are deeply based in culture. Without an understanding of the meaning of nonverbal communication symbols used by a culture, it's all too easy to misinterpret signs.

A hand gesture that has virtually no meaning in one culture can easily be a vulgar symbol in another culture. For example, the OK sign, widely used in North America, is a circle formed by the thumb and the first finger; this sign is considered to be offensive and unacceptable in Brazil, and to mean money in Japan (Morrison, Conway, & Borden, 1994).

One's physical position in relation to another person may result in an inadvertent message of disinterest or aggression. North Americans usually feel comfortable standing at a distance of about two and a half to four feet from others. However, members of some cultures, among them Arabic societies, prefer to stand much closer when engaged in conversations (Hall, 1983). Researchers who position themselves at a North American distance may be perceived as cold, aloof, and uninterested by members of such cultures.

Similarly, the use of eye contact carries culturally specific meaning. In European-based cultures, eye contact is used extensively to demonstrate interest and to confirm that one is listening. Many other cultures, however, do not use eye contact extensively and may perceive it as disrespectful and even threatening. For example, prolonged eye contact in Japanese is considered to be rude (Samovar, Porter, & Stefani, 1998).

VERBAL COMMUNICATION

On the verbal level, words also derive much of their meaning through culture. As language is the primary means through which a culture communicates its values and beliefs, the same words may have different meanings within different cultures.

For example, the Japanese use the word *hai,* meaning "yes," to indicate that they have heard what was said and are thinking about a response. Because, in many circumstances, it's considered impolite to openly express disagreement, *hai* is used even when the listener actually disagrees with what is being said (Koyama, 1992). Thus, the meaning assigned to "yes" is quite different than that commonly understood by North Americans, who consider "yes" to mean that the listener is in agreement.

The social work research process uses an extensive transmission of information through communications. Thus, it's vital that verbal communications be accurate and effective. Without an understanding of intercultural communication generally and an ability to understand the specific patterns used by the group with whom the researcher is dealing, communication problems may arise and derail the research process.

CULTURAL FRAMEWORKS

As we have seen, culture often defines a group's values and beliefs, and creates its communication patterns. In addition, culture also provides frameworks for other complex structures and processes. Different cultural groups, for example, have different methods of gathering data and of making decisions.

An understanding of these patterns is essential to ensure that data collection and analytical processes are appropriate and final research reports are practical and relevant. This section briefly looks at cultural frameworks regarding:

— Orientation to Data

— Decision Making

— Individualism

— Tradition

— Pace of Life (and Concepts of Time)

ORIENTATION TO DATA

SOME CULTURES THRIVE on "hard data" and greatly value processes, such as research studies, that produce data that can then be considered and acted upon (Lewis, 1997; Thomas & Inkson, 2009). These cultures, which include the North American mainstream culture, are considered data oriented.

On the other hand, some cultures such as Middle Eastern and Latin American cultures are viewed as "dialogue oriented," in that they pay more attention to relationships and process than to data (Lewis, 1997). These groups tend to view statistics and data with some suspicion and regard them as only part of a picture. Such cultures consider relationships and context to be more important than numbers.

Decision Making

In many Western cultures, logic and rationality are highly valued and used extensively in making decisions about important matters (Hoefstede, 1997; Lewis, 1997). The positivistic research approach (Chapter 5) is an example of this style of "scientific" thinking. However, some cultures are less impressed by "hard science" and prefer a softer, more personal approach to knowledge development, often called the interpretive research approach (Chapter 6).

When researchers prepare a report for people whose culture supports a scientific orientation to thinking, quantitative data with statistical analyses are quite appropriate; however, if the users are people who come from a culture that prefers more subjective and intuitive approaches to decision making, a report organized around the presentation of strictly quantitative results can easily become useless and/or incomprehensible.

Individualism

Although most cultures support both individualistic and collectivistic tendencies, there is in every culture a bias toward one or the other (Hoefstede, 1997). In individualistic cultures, such as the mainstream North American culture, people work toward individual goals, and initiative, competition, and achievement are highly valued.

In collectivistic cultures, people are group oriented; loyalty, relationships, and overall community development are valued while individual goals are downplayed. In such cultures, the family, organizations with which people are affiliated (including the workplace), and the community are particularly important.

Keeping in perspective an organization's cultural view on individualism versus collectivism is important in understanding the behaviors, interactions, work processes, and structures that may be found in the course of a research or evaluation study. What may appear from an individualistic perspective to be an unwieldy work processes involving too many people may, in fact, be explained by a culture-based desire not to leave anyone out and to create as wide a network of involvement as possible.

TRADITION

SOME CULTURES are more traditional and value the status quo and conformity while others encourage innovation and view change as necessary if progress is to be made (Dodd, 1998). Change-oriented cultures such as mainstream North American society encourage experimentation, risk taking, and innovation. They consider change to be an opportunity to improve.

In other cultures, such as some traditional Asian cultures, values are centered on tradition and continuity. The young are expected to give way to the wishes of the older generation, and new ideas are not encouraged because they might disrupt the structure of society.

You should readily recognize that the research process, as a change- and improvement-oriented activity, is grounded in Western cultural values. As such, the concept of "research" itself may seem alien to those steeped in more traditional cultures. After all, research and evaluations are concerned with identifying areas for improvement, which therefore implies change, but traditional cultures value stability and continuity.

Inevitably, social work researchers will sometimes work with organizations that are based in a tradition-oriented culture. In such circumstances, we need to be sensitive to the fact that there may not exist a common understanding even about the basic premises of the research processes.

PACE OF LIFE

IN NORTH AMERICA, especially in larger cities, we live our lives at an accelerated pace. Our schedules are jammed with many activities; agendas are overloaded, and there is an expectation that everything is a priority and must be done immediately. Time is viewed as linear and rigid; we live with the sense that if we miss an event it's forever gone. In such cultures, which are called monochronic, people tend to organize their lives by the clock (Hall, 1983).

Clearly, in such cultures it's important to be on time for meetings, to meet deadlines, and to stay on schedule (Cooper, Calloway-Thomas, & Simonds, 2007; Samovar, Porter, & Stefani, 1998). In a sense, time is so central that members of the culture are hardly aware of its importance, but all things, including personal relationships, take second place to successful time management.

On the other hand, in polychronic cultures life is lived at a slower pace; activities grind to a halt on weekends, during rest times, and during festivals and important celebrations. Slower-paced cultures—for example, those in Latin America, the Middle East, and Indonesia—tend to be less aware of time and hold less of a concept of it as a commodity that must be managed.

Time may be seen as circular and flexible; the Indonesians even refer to it as "rubber time" (Harris & Moran, 1996). In polychronic cultures, time is not nearly as important an organizing force in people's lives as it is in monochronic cultures; if the scheduled start time passes without the event taking place, people are not unduly disturbed as another appropriate start time can be set. "Time is money" could not have arisen as a central idea in these cultures, which focus on relationships and interactions. Time management and business come second in such cultures (Hall, 1983); rather, it's vital to establish a personal relationship before conducting business.

Obviously, researchers need to have a good understanding of the concept of time that is held within the setting where they conduct their work. Tight schedules that provide few opportunities for cementing working relationships and that disregard widely observed rest periods, holidays, and celebrations are obviously unrealistic and will be unsuitable in polychronic cultures. Attempting to impose such a schedule will be regarded as thoughtless and will impede rather than facilitate the research process.

Further, in assessing the achievement of milestones and other accomplishments, we need to take into account the concept of time and the pace of life prevalent in the particular culture. In setting up a new social service program, for example, planning, procedure, policy development, initial staffing, and other preparatory activities may be accomplished in a much briefer period of time in one setting than in another. Both the concepts of time and the pace of life might be, in fact, equally appropriate when the cultural orientation toward time is taken into account.

CULTURALLY COMPETENT RESEARCHERS

Although some researchers come from minority backgrounds, many do bring a mainstream North American cultural orientation to their work. This orientation will result in part from their own cultural background and in part from their formation and education as researchers. The methods of social work research are, to a large degree, based in a Western or North American cultural tradition. Inevitably, researchers will bring their own culturally based beliefs, values, and perspectives as well as their culturally based toolkit to their work.

More and more research studies are conducted in settings that are culturally different from mainstream North American culture. Research studies are conducted on reservations, at women's shelters, in organizations serving immigrants, and at agencies that grew from the needs and aspirations of minority communities and reflect the cultures of those communities.

Those of us who undertake a research study in a culturally different setting, or among people from different cultural backgrounds, require the skills to effectively conduct the work and to make the research process more meaningful within those settings. The essential competencies for a researcher to be culturally sensitive are:

— Cultural Awareness

— Intercultural Communication Skills

— Specific Knowledge about the Culture in Which We Hope to Work

— An Ability to Appropriately Adapt Evaluation Methods and Processes

Cultural Awareness

TO BE EFFECTIVE in intercultural work, social work researchers need a degree of cultural awareness that provides them with an understanding of the impact of culture on all human values, attitudes, and behaviors as well as interactions and processes. They need to understand how culture filters communications and how the research process itself is a culture-based activity. Further, we should have an understanding of concepts such as ethnocentrism, enculturation, and stereotyping—all of which may subtly, or not so subtly, raise barriers to effective communication and relationships.

In addition, we need to bring attitudes of openness and acceptance to our work as well as a genuine belief that cultural differences need not pose barriers but rather can strengthen and enrich the research process. Researchers who wish to practice in diverse settings also need a high degree of self-awareness as well as an understanding of their own cultural values and experiences, and the impact of these values and experiences on their communication patterns, relationships, and professional work.

Cultural awareness increases through contact with other cultures and through experiencing differences. Traveling, working in culturally different settings, and living in diverse communities are ways that you can develop your awareness and attitudes.

Intercultural Communication Skills

THE ABILITY to approach others with openness and acceptance is foundational to effective communication, regardless of setting; in intercultural communication, it's particularly important. However, effective intercultural communication also requires specific knowledge of the other culture and its communication symbols.

As we now know, the meaning of nonverbal or verbal symbols is culturally defined. It's therefore important to know the meaning of common nonverbal and verbal communication symbols to ensure accuracy in both the transmission and the reception of messages.

Social work researchers can prepare for their work by reading novels set in the culture, watching high-quality movies, and perusing books and guides that describe prevailing communication patterns. The use of cultural guides, discussed in the following section, is also helpful in learning to understand the meaning of common communication symbols.

SPECIFIC KNOWLEDGE ABOUT THE CULTURE

IN THE PREVIOUS SECTION, the importance of developing specific understandings about prevailing communication patterns in a specific culture was discussed. However, a researcher who wishes to be effective in a culturally different setting must understand more than communication patterns. Specific knowledge about various details of the culture is important to ensure that effective relationships can be established, that the work is planned in a realistic manner, and that the resulting products will have utility.

Among other things, it's important to have some sense of the history of the group who comprise the culture in which the research study will be conducted. On Native American reservations, for example, the history of oppression and dislocation is vitally important and has framed their values, attitudes, and beliefs. Among certain immigrant groups, escape from oppression is a dominant theme, and an emphasis on newly found freedoms and opportunities frames these individualistic and achievement-oriented cultures.

Beyond history, the specific values, beliefs, and perspectives that shape individuals' and groups' perceptions and communications are vital to understand, as are the cultural structures, processes, and frameworks that are characteristic of the group. For example, in working with Native American groups on reservations, it's customary to include elders on advisory committees and to listen with respect to the ideas and opinions that they express.

Concepts of time have been discussed previously; it's sufficient to say that the scheduled starting time for meetings may or may not be firmly fixed, depending on the setting. Meetings on reservations may begin with a prayer to the Creator rather than a review of the agenda as is the case in most Western-oriented institutions.

There are myriad other details about culture, some of which may be important to understand to work successfully in the setting. For example, one of the authors of this book conducted an evaluation on a reservation and had the opportunity to observe restorative justice circles in action. The program had been conceived carefully with extensive use of traditional symbols. One of these symbols was the circle itself, which symbolized a teepee; a convention had developed over time that participants entered and left the circle in one particular place, which symbolized the entry to the teepee.

Entering or leaving the circle in any other place was regarded as the equivalent of walking through the walls of the teepee. Of course, a social work researcher coming from the outside would not have been aware of this and would inevitably have committed a cultural faux pas. Happily, the researcher's team included a member from the community itself, who served as a cultural guide and briefed the researcher on the meaning of the cultural symbols involved as well as the appropriate behaviors.

In general, specific cultural knowledge can be obtained through the same methods as suggested for understanding the specifics of communication patterns: travel, reading guidebooks and histories by writers from the culture, and watching movies. Engaging collaborators from within the cultural group, even if not from within the organization itself, is perhaps the most effective way of learning about values, beliefs, traditions, behavior patterns, and the detailed texture of another culture.

APPROPRIATELY ADAPTING RESEARCH STUDIES

DEVELOPING CULTURAL AWARENESS, intercultural communication skills, and specific knowledge of the culture of the group with which researchers are involved is foundational to conducting effective research studies. The final set of skills involves adapting the research process so that it will be appropriate and meaningful within the culture of the organization where the study is being conducted. Adapting research studies involves:

— Working with Stakeholders

— Ensuring That the Work Processes Are Appropriate

— Ensuring That the Products Are Meaningful

WORKING WITH STAKEHOLDERS

As discussed throughout this book, a variety of groups—including funders, staff members, program participants, and community members—may have an interest in how a social work research study is done and, consequently, in the final results. Different groups of stakeholders are likely to have different interests, and this will particularly be true in the case of conducting evaluations in settings with culturally different stakeholders.

Generally, funders represent powerful institutions such as governments and foundations within mainstream society. They will therefore articulate their interests from a North American or Western cultural perspective. For example, funders for a social service program will likely be interested in data that shed light on the extent to which the program is delivering the services that had been contracted and with what effect. Further, they will prefer to have the data packaged as a formal report, replete with quantitative data and statistics as well as specific recommendations for improvement.

On the other hand, if the setting is based in a different culture, staff members, service recipients, and community members may be more interested in understanding the role that the program is playing within the community. If they come from a dialogue-oriented culture, they may be interested in descriptions of the service process and the service recipients' stories about their experiences with the service and its impact on their families. They will be looking not so much to receive data for the purpose of making changes but rather to develop a broader and deeper understanding of the program and its place in the community.

Researchers need to work at understanding each stakeholder group's perspectives, expectations, and interests and to realize that these may be fundamentally different from one another. A culturally competent researcher must be committed to accommodating the different perspectives and interests of the diverse stakeholders within the research process.

ADAPTING PROCESSES

A program evaluation, for example, always involves obtaining the cooperation of staff members and other stakeholder groups in carrying out the required research procedures—particularly for the data collection system. The effectiveness of such a system depends on staff members carrying out their assigned roles in the research process in a knowledgeable and consistent manner. It's therefore very important that the work processes be designed so that they are congruent with the culture within the organization.

For example, we need to take into account the cultural meaning of time in the organization. If the organization is polychronic and operates at a relatively relaxed pace, the scheduling of research activities such as data collection must take this into account. A schedule that is appropriate in an organization that operates from a monochronic cultural perspective may be totally unfeasible within a polychronic culture. Attempting to impose such a schedule will likely create tensions and stresses: at best, it may result in an inconsistent implementation of the research activities; at worst, the entire research study may be discredited and collapse.

It's thus important that we design work processes in a manner that is congruent with the cultural meaning of time. Scheduling should take into account the concept of time and orientation to time so as not to impose a burden that would be regarded by the culture as unduly stressful or inappropriate. The process should ensure that holidays, community celebrations, and festivals are taken into account when setting schedules.

Similarly, data collection activities need to take into account both the cultural orientation of the staff members who are likely to collect the data and the research recipients who are likely to provide the data. In dialogue-oriented cultures, the collection of highly quantitative data involving the use of standardized measures, rating scales, and structured surveys may be inappropriate and result in inconsistent data collection at best.

At worst, research participants and staff members will go through the motions of providing and collecting data without really understanding why the data are needed or how they are to be used. The reliability and validity of such data, of course, are likely to be low, compromising the entire research effort.

Data collection protocols and procedures need to take into account whether research participants are oriented to "data" or "dialogue" and should be designed to be as meaningful and culturally appropriate as possible. In dialogue-oriented cultures, it may not be entirely possible or advisable to avoid the collection of quantitative data, but such data collection methods should be used sparingly. Ample explanations and support should also be provided to research participants so that they can find meaning in these tasks and carry them out effectively.

PROVIDING MEANINGFUL PRODUCTS

Ultimately, research studies are undertaken to generate information products that stakeholders will find useful. It's particularly important that the final products be appropriate to the culture of stakeholders. As discussed earlier, funders are likely to find reports useful when they address the extent to which the social service program meets its contractual obligations for providing services and describe the outcomes of those services. Further, funders will look for quantitative data and statistical analyses that support the findings of the report. Managers who regularly deal with funders may also favor reports of this type.

However, other stakeholder groups may not find such products useful or understandable. This will be especially the case if stakeholders come from cultural backgrounds that are dialogue oriented. Reports with descriptions, stories, illustrations, and even pictures are likely to prove more meaningful to such stakeholders.

Culturally competent researchers should accommodate all stakeholder groups who have a legitimate interest in the results derived from a research study. Tailoring final reports to funders' needs alone is a poor practice and is unlikely to result in meaningful program change. Program development necessarily comes from the inside and is based primarily on the initiative of the managers and staff.

The final products from a research study should support the efforts of managers and staff to develop the program by providing data that are meaningful, practical, and useful. It's usually the case that positivistic (Chapter 5) and interpretive (Chapter 6) approaches can be combined within a single study. Although matters that interest funders are likely to be more suited to quantitative data collection and analyses, increased understanding can result from including descriptively oriented material that focuses on contextual matters.

Statistics describing the demographic makeup of clients, for example, can be supplemented by providing more detailed descriptions of a few selected clients. Often this can be accomplished by providing people with the opportunity to tell their stories in their words.

To sum up the research process with a culturally based lens, Kiki Sayre provides the following guidelines (2002):

- *Develop specific cultural knowledge.* Know the relationship between variables and behaviors in the group being evaluated. Only when the norms and values are clearly delineated can they be given proper consideration.

- *Explicitly examine the theoretical framework that is the foundation of your research study.* Communicate clearly your own values, beliefs, approach, and worldview as the researcher. Acknowledge and address how these may differ from the perspectives of the group to be studied. Whenever possible, have someone on the research team who has knowledge and understanding of the group being studied.

- *Define and measure ethnicity in a meaningful manner.* To the degree possible, also define and measure key constructs, such as socioeconomic status, that are known to covary with ethnicity.

- *Choose measures that are appropriate for all the ethnic groups in your study and/or check those measures you use for their equivalence across groups.* Make sure the measuring instruments you are using have cross-cultural equivalence.

- *Make sure your analyses reflect your study's research questions and that you have sufficient data to get accurate answers.* The goal is to accurately interpret the experiences of particular groups of people in order to minimize errors throughout the study. For this reason, the research team needs to be involved from the beginning of the study.

- *Interpret results to reflect the lives of the people studied.* Have someone with knowledge of the particular group analyze the data alongside the researchers in order to point out variables that should be considered.

- *Define the population precisely*. Understand a group's country of origin, immigration history, sociopolitical status, level of education, and rules and norms. Without a clear understanding of the group's background, it's best to develop a research team group that has this background.

- *Develop collaborations with the people you are studying.* Community members need to be involved in the planning and implementation of the research study. Define the pertinent research questions at the outset of the study.

- *Encourage buy-in.* Know the community well and understand the pressures and external constraints operating among the population. State the goals of the research team, and determine the goals of the people being studied. Describe how the data will be used. Conduct interviews in a location that is comfortable to the group and without bias.

- *Provide timely feedback and results in clear, useful formats conveyed through culturally appropriate methods.* Ask those involved how best to disseminate the study's results. For example, you could share the results of your research study with a Native American population in New Mexico in a "give-back" ceremony that uses storytelling and visuals, with no written material.

- *Consider acculturation and biculturalism in interpretation and utilization of data.* Acculturation measures are often linear and one-dimensional. Bicultural adaptation—or the adoption of some majority culture attitudes and practices coupled with the retention of ethnic group cultural practices and identity—is now considered a more useful measurement. Cultural identity can be bicultural or even tricultural. People generally do not lose one culture to gain another.

- *Know when to aggregate the within-group data from a heterogeneous sample and still maximize external validity.* Conduct within-group analyses that consider groups independently of each other to ensure that important data are not overlooked. Only aggregate the data when convincing similarities can be found.

- *Avoid deficit model interpretations.* Abandon stereotypes and models that measure diverse groups against a monocultural standard.

SUMMARY

Armed with all the ethics knowledge you gained from the last chapter and combined with this one, you should now have a sound grasp of how to do ethical and culturally competent research studies. Conducting an ethical and culturally sensitive social work research study is an extremely complex endeavor, and undertaking research that involves stakeholders from different cultural backgrounds adds considerable complexity.

Study Questions for Chapter 4

— First, answer each question only AFTER you have read the chapter.

— Second, indicate how comfortable you were in answering each question on a 5-point scale:

1	2	3	4	5
Very uncomfortable	Somewhat uncomfortable	Neutral	Somewhat comfortable	Very comfortable

If you rated any question between 1–3, please reread the section of the chapter where the information for the question can be found. If you're still uncomfortable answering the question, talk with your instructor and/or your classmates for more clarification.

Questions	Degree of comfort? (Circle one number)
1. Discuss in detail why it's important to know the cultural makeup of the stakeholders who are on your research team. How does this affect the research process? Provide as many examples as you can to justify your response.	1 2 3 4 5
2. List and discuss the specific "social work" skills you think you will need when working with your stakeholders or research group. Provide examples to illustrate your points.	1 2 3 4 5
3. Discuss how social work research can be affected by culture at both the micro level (e.g., research participants, researchers) and at the macro level (e.g., your organization, institutions, the greater community). What cultural type of barriers exist at these levels, and how would you work through them? Provide as many examples as you can to justify your response.	1 2 3 4 5
4. Discuss how your biases as a social work researcher can affect the research process in relation to ethnocentrism. Provide as many examples as you can to justify your response.	1 2 3 4 5
5. Discuss how your biases as a social work researcher can affect the research process in relation to enculturation. Provide as many examples as you can to justify your response.	1 2 3 4 5

6. List and discuss in detail the issues you will need to consider to actually become a culturally competent social work researcher. In your own words, define a culturally competent researcher. Use a common social work example throughout your discussion.	1 2 3 4 5
7. When doing a social work research study, discuss the practical strategies we can use to produce an accurate portrayal and understanding of minorities and disadvantaged groups. Use a common social work example throughout your discussion.	1 2 3 4 5
8. Discuss in detail how you will become a competent social work researcher in relation to "intercultural communication skills." Use a common social work example throughout your discussion.	1 2 3 4 5
9. Discuss in detail how you will become a competent social work researcher in relation to "specific knowledge about the culture in which you hope to study." Use a common social work example throughout your discussion.	1 2 3 4 5
10. Discuss in detail how you will become a competent social work researcher in relation to your "ability to appropriately adapt evaluation methods and processes." Use a common social work example throughout your discussion.	1 2 3 4 5
11. Discuss how you will go about developing specific cultural knowledge about your research participants. Provide as many examples as you can to illustrate your points.	1 2 3 4 5
12. Discuss how you will go about explicitly examining with a cultural lens the theoretical framework that is the foundation of your research study. Provide as many examples as you can to illustrate your points.	1 2 3 4 5
13. Discuss how you will go about defining and measuring "ethnicity" in a meaningful manner. Why is this important? Provide as many examples as you can to illustrate your points.	1 2 3 4 5
14. Discuss how you will go about choosing measuring instruments that are appropriate for all the ethnic groups in your study. Why is this important? Provide as many examples as you can to illustrate your points.	1 2 3 4 5
15. Discuss how you will go about making sure that you will interpret your study's results to accurately reflect the lives of your research participants. Why is this important? Provide as many examples as you can to illustrate your points.	1 2 3 4 5

16.	Discuss how you will precisely define the population of your research participants. Why is this important? Provide as many examples as you can to illustrate your points.	1 2 3 4 5
17.	Discuss how you will go about developing meaningful collaborations with your research participants. Why is this important? Provide as many examples as you can to illustrate your points.	1 2 3 4 5
18.	Discuss how you will go about encouraging buy-in with all of your stakeholders. Why is this important? Provide as many examples as you can to illustrate your points.	1 2 3 4 5
19.	Discuss how you will go about providing timely feedback of your study's results in a clear and useful format conveyed through culturally appropriate methods. Why is this important? Provide as many examples as you can to illustrate your points.	1 2 3 4 5
20.	Discuss how you will avoid deficit model interpretations. Why is this important? Provide as many examples as you can to illustrate your points.	1 2 3 4 5
21.	At this point in your course, how comfortable are you with discussing how to do culturally competent social work research with your field instructor (or your supervisor at work)? With your fellow classmates? Discuss in detail.	1 2 3 4 5

Assessing Your Self-Efficacy for Chapter 4

AFTER you have read the chapter AND have completed all the study questions, please indicate how knowledgeable you feel you are for each concept listed below.

1	2	3	4	5
Very uncomfortable	Somewhat uncomfortable	Neutral	Somewhat comfortable	Very comfortable

Major Concepts in Chapter	Knowledge Level? (Circle one number)
1. Working with stakeholders or research groups	1 2 3 4 5
2. Micro- and macro-level cultures	1 2 3 4 5
3. The impact of culture	1 2 3 4 5
4. Cultural awareness	1 2 3 4 5
5. Ethnocentrism	1 2 3 4 5
6. Enculturation	1 2 3 4 5
7. Intercultural communication	1 2 3 4 5
8. Verbal and nonverbal communication patterns	1 2 3 4 5
9. Criteria to become a culturally competent researcher	1 2 3 4 5
Add up your scores (Minimum = 9, Maximum = 45)	Total score =

A 40 — 45 = Social Work Manager in the making.
B 36 — 39 = Social Work Supervisor.
C 31 — 35 = Social Work Practitioner.
D   9 — 30 = Case Aide. Reread the chapter and redo the study questions.

PART II
Approaches to Knowledge Development

5

The Positivistic Research Approach

*You can use all the quantitative data you can get, but you still have to
distrust it and use your own intelligence and judgment.*
~ Alvin Toffler

As we know from the previous chapters in this book, social work knowledge is best
generated through the use of the scientific method. This method contains two
complimentary approaches: the positivistic approach, sometimes called the *quantitative approach*, which is the topic of this chapter, and the interpretive approach, sometimes called the *qualitative approach*, which is the topic of the next chapter.

No matter which approach we use to obtain our professional knowledge base,
knowledge gained from employing either approach is much more objective than
knowledge derived from the other four ways of "knowing" (i.e., authority, tradition,
experience, or beliefs and intuition). Before we discuss the positivistic approach to
knowledge development, however, you need to thoroughly understand and appreciate how this approach is embedded within the positivist way of thinking.

WHAT IS THE POSITIVIST WAY OF THINKING?

Our discussion on how positivists think has been adapted and modified from Grinnell and Williams (1990), Krysik and Grinnell (1997), Williams, Tutty, and Grinnell (1995), Williams, Unrau, and Grinnell (1998), and Unrau, Grinnell, and Williams (2008). In a nutshell, the positivist way of thinking strives toward:

— Measurability

— Objectivity

— Reducing Uncertainty

— Duplication

— The Use of Standardized Procedures

STRIVING TOWARD MEASURABILITY

THE POSITIVIST WAY of thinking tries to study only those things that can be objectively measured. That is, knowledge gained through this belief is based on *objective measurements* of the real world, not on someone's opinions, beliefs, hunches, intuitions, or past experiences. Conversely, and as you know from Chapter 1, knowledge gained through tradition or authority depends on people's opinions and beliefs and not on "objective" measurements of some kind.

Entities that cannot be measured or even seen—such as the id, ego, or superego—are not amenable to a positivistic-orientated research study but rather rely on tradition and authority. In short, a positivistic principle would be that the things you believe to exist must be able to be measured. However, at this point in our discussion, it's useful to remember that researchers doing studies within a positivistic framework believe that practically everything in life is measurable. In fact, some say that a thing—or a variable, if you will—doesn't exist unless it can be measured.

STRIVING TOWARD OBJECTIVITY

THE SECOND IDEAL of the positivistic belief is that research studies must be as objective as possible. The variables that are being observed and/or measured must not be affected in any way by the person doing the observing or measuring. Physical scientists have observed inanimate matter for centuries, confident in the belief that objects do not change as a result of being observed.

In the subworld of the atom, however, physicists are beginning to learn what social workers have always known: things do change when they are observed. People think, feel, and behave very differently as a result of being observed. Not only do they change, they change in different ways depending on who is doing the observing and/ or measuring.

There is yet another problem. Some observed behaviors, for example, are open to interpretation by the folks doing the observing. To illustrate this point, let's take a simple example: a client you are seeing, named Ron, is severely withdrawn. He may behave in one way in your office during individual treatment sessions but in quite another way when his mother joins the interviews.

You may think that Ron is unduly silent, while his mother remarks on how much he is talking. If his mother wants him to talk, perhaps as a sign that he is emerging from his withdrawal, she may perceive him to be talking more than he really is.

All folks doing research studies with the positivistic framework go to great lengths to ensure that their own hopes, fears, beliefs, and biases do not affect their research results, and that the biases of others do not affect them either. Nevertheless, as discussed in later chapters, complete objectivity is rarely possible in social work research despite the many strategies that have been developed over the years to achieve it.

Suppose, for example, that a social worker is trying to help a mother interact more positively with her child. The worker, together with a colleague, may first observe the child and mother in a playroom setting, recording how many times the mother makes eye contact with the child, hugs the child, criticizes the child, makes encouraging comments, and so forth on a 3-point scale: discouraging, neutral, or encouraging. The social worker may perceive a remark that the mother has made to the child as "neutral," while the colleague thinks it was "encouraging."

As you will see throughout this book, in such a situation it's impossible to resolve the disagreement. If there were six objective observers, for example, five opting for neutral and only one for encouraging, the sole "encouraging observer" was more likely to be wrong than the other five, so it's very likely that the mother's remark was neutral. As you know from Chapter 1, as more people agree on what they have observed, the less likely it becomes that the observation was distorted by bias, and the more likely it is that the agreement reached is "objectively true."

As should be obvious by now, objectivity is largely a matter of agreement. There are some things, usually physical phenomena, about which most people agree. Most people agree, for example, that objects fall when dropped, water turns to steam at a certain temperature, and sea water contains salt.

However, there are other things—mostly to do with values, attitudes, and feelings—about which agreement is far rarer. An argument about whether Beethoven is a better composer than Willie Nelson, for example, cannot be objectively resolved.

Neither can a dispute about the rightness of capital punishment, euthanasia, same-sex marriage, or abortion. It's not surprising, therefore, that physical researchers who work with physical phenomena are able to be more objective than social work researchers, who work with human beings.

STRIVING TOWARD REDUCING UNCERTAINTY

POSITIVISTIC-ORIENTATED RESEARCH STUDIES try to totally rule out uncertainty. Because all observations and/or measurements in the social sciences are made by human beings, personal bias cannot be entirely eliminated. There is always the possibility that an observation and/or measurement is in error, no matter how many people agree about what they saw or measured.

There is also the possibility that the conclusions drawn from even an accurate observation or measurement will be wrong. A huge number of people may agree, for example, that an object in the sky is a UFO when in fact it's a meteor. Even if they agree that it's a meteor, they may come to the conclusion—probably erroneously— that the meteor is a warning from angry extraterrestrials.

In the twentieth century, most people do not believe that natural phenomena have anything to do with extraterrestrial beings. They prefer the explanations that modern researchers have proposed. Nevertheless, no researcher would say—or at least be quoted as saying—that meteors and extraterrestrial beings are not related for certain.

When we are using the scientific method of knowledge development, nothing is certain. Even the best-tested theory is only tentative and accepted as true until newly discovered evidence shows it to be untrue or only partly true. All knowledge gained through the scientific method is thus provisional. Everything presently accepted as true is true only with varying degrees of probability.

STRIVING TOWARD DUPLICATION

POSITIVISTIC RESEARCHERS try to do research studies in such a way that their studies can be duplicated by other researchers. Suppose, for a moment, you are running a twelve-week intervention program to help fathers who have abused their children to manage their anger without resorting to physical violence. You have put a great deal of effort into designing your program, and believe that your intervention (the program) is more effective than other interventions that are geared toward anger-management.

You develop a method of measuring the degree to which the fathers in your group have learned to dissipate their anger in nondamaging ways, and you find that, indeed, the group of fathers shows marked improvement. Improvement shown by one group of fathers, however, is not convincing evidence for the effectiveness of your intervention.

Perhaps your measurements were in error, and the improvement was not as great as you hoped for. Perhaps the improvement was a coincidence, and the fathers' behaviors changed because they had joined health clubs and each had vented his fury on a punching bag. To be more certain, you duplicate your intervention and measuring procedures with a second group of fathers. In other words, you replicate your study.

After you have used the same procedures with a number of groups and obtained similar results each time, you might expect that other social workers will eagerly adopt your anger-management intervention. However, as presented in the previous chapters, tradition dies hard. Other social workers have a vested interest in their own interventions, and they may suggest that you found the results you did only because you wanted to find them.

To counter any suggestion of bias, you ask another, independent social worker to use your same anger-management intervention and measuring methods with other groups of fathers. If the results are the same as before, your colleagues in the field of anger management may choose to adopt your intervention method (the program).

Whatever your colleagues decide, you are excited about your newfound intervention. You wonder whether your methods would work as well with women as they do with men, with adolescents as well as with adults, with Native Americans, Asians, or African Americans as well as with Caucasians, with mixed groups, larger groups, or groups in different settings. In fact, you have identified a lifetime project because you will have to apply your intervention and measuring procedures repeatedly to all these different groups of people.

Striving Toward the Use of Standardized Procedures

FINALLY, a true-to-the-bone positivistic researcher tries to use well-accepted, "research-type" standardized procedures. For a positivistic-oriented research study to be creditable and before others can accept its results, they must be satisfied that your study was conducted according to accepted scientific standardized procedures. The allegation that your work lacks objectivity is only one of the criticisms they might bring.

In addition, they might suggest that the group of fathers you worked with was not typical of abusive fathers in general, and thus your results are not applicable to other groups of abusive fathers. It might be alleged that you did not make proper measurements, or that you measured the wrong variables, or that you did not take enough measurements, or that you did not analyze your data correctly, and so on.

To negate these kinds of criticisms, over the years social work researchers have agreed on a set of standard procedures and techniques that are thought most likely to produce "true and unbiased" knowledge—which is what this book is all about. Certain steps must be performed in a certain order. Foreseeable errors must be guarded against.

Ethical behavior with research participants and colleagues must be maintained, as outlined in Chapter 3. These procedures must be followed if your study is both to generate usable results and to be accepted as useful by other social workers.

 # STEPS OF THE POSITIVISTIC RESEARCH APPROACH

The preceding discussion is only the philosophy behind the positivistic research approach to knowledge building, as was clearly explained on the left side of Table 1.1. With this philosophy in mind, we now turn our attention to the seven general sequential steps (in a more or less straightforward manner) that all positivistic researchers follow, as outlined in Figure 5.1.

The most important thing to remember at this point is that all the steps in Figure 5.1 are highly intertwined to various degrees and that it's difficult, if not impossible, to describe a single step in isolation from the remaining six steps. However, for the sake of simplicity, we'll describe each step in a sequential manner:

— Step 1: Identifying the Problem

— Step 2: Selecting Variables

— Step 3: Designing the Study

— Step 4: Collecting Data

— Step 5: Analyzing Data

— Step 6: Interpreting Findings

— Step 7: Disseminating Findings

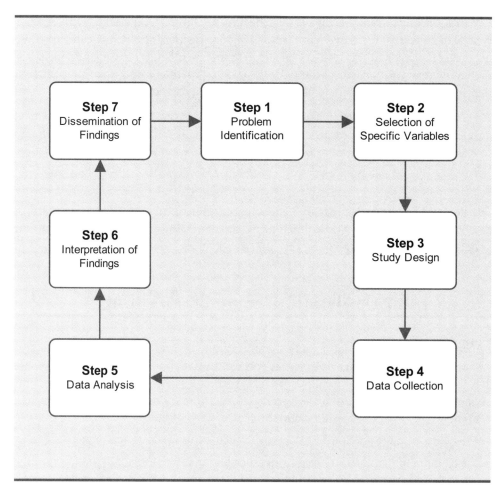

FIGURE 5.1

Steps of the Positivistic (Quantitative) Research Approach

These steps yield a very useful format for obtaining knowledge in our profession. The positivistic research approach is a tried and tested method of scientific inquiry. In a nutshell, most of the critical decisions to be made in a positivistic research study occur *before* the study is ever started. This means that the researcher is well aware (or should be aware!) of all the study's limitations before the study actually begins.

It is possible, therefore, for a researcher to decide that a positivistic study has simply too many limitations and to come to the eventual conclusion that it should not be performed. Regardless of whether a proposed study is ever carried out, the process always begins with choosing a research topic and focusing the research question (the topic of Chapter 2).

Step 1: Identifying the Problem (Chapter 2)

As can be seen in Figure 5.1, the first step of the positivistic approach to knowledge development is to identify a general problem area to study and then to refine this general area into a research question that can be answered or a hypothesis that can be tested.

Positivistic-type of studies are usually deductive processes; that is, they usually begin with a broad and general query about a general social problem then pare it down to a specific research question or hypothesis. For instance, your general research problem may have started out with curiosity about racial discrimination within public social service agencies. Your general problem area could be written simply as:

General Problem Area

Racial discrimination within public social service agencies

Step 2: Selecting Specific Variables (Chapter 2)

You may have noticed through your professional practice as a medical social worker in a local hospital, for example, that many of the patients in your hospital are from ethnic minority backgrounds who have the following variables:

- High unemployment rates

- A large proportion of their members living under the poverty level

- Low levels of educational attainment

You believe that these three conditions alone should increase the likelihood of them utilizing the hospital's social service department where you work. Conversely, and at the same time, you have also observed that there are more ethnic majorities than minorities who are seen in your hospital's social service department.

Where the research study actually takes place is called the *research setting*. So your research setting for this study is the hospital where you're employed.

Your personal observations may then lead you to asking whether discrimination against ethnic minorities exists when it comes to them having access to your hospital's social service department. You can easily test the possibility of such a relationship by using the positivistic research approach.

As should be evident by now, Steps 1 and 2 are highly intertwined and comingled, and they usually take place at the same time. Step 2 within the positivistic research process has eight sub-steps:

— Step 2a: Determining What Others Have Found

— Step 2b: Refining the General Problem Area

— Step 2c: Developing Concepts

— Step 2d: Identifying Variables within Concepts

— Step 2e: Defining Attributes of Variables

— Step 2f: Defining Independent and Dependent Variables

— Step 2g: Constructing a Hypothesis

— Step 2h: Evaluating the Hypothesis

STEP 2A: DETERMINING WHAT OTHERS HAVE FOUND

The next phase in focusing your research question is visiting the library and using the Internet to review the literature related to your two concepts:

CONCEPTS
1. Racial discrimination within social services (concept 1)
2. Access to social services (concept 2)

You will want to read the literature related to your two main concepts within the general research question: racial discrimination within social service agencies and access to them. You will want to learn about how various theories explain both of your main concepts in order to arrive at a meaningful research question. It may be, for example, that many ethnic minority cultures are unlikely to ask strangers for help with life's personal difficulties.

STEP 2B: REFINING THE GENERAL PROBLEM AREA

Furthermore, you may learn that most social service programs are organized using bureaucratic structures, which require new potential clients to talk to several strangers (e.g., telephone receptionist, waiting-room clerk, intake worker) before they are able to access social services.

Given that you know, via the literature, that ethnic minorities do not like talking with strangers about their personal problems, and that social services are set up for people to deal with a series of strangers, you could develop a very simple positivistic research question:

POSITIVISTIC RESEARCH QUESTION

Do patients who come from ethnic minority backgrounds have difficulty accessing my hospital's social service department?

STEP 2C: DEVELOPING CONCEPTS

The very broad general problem area of racial discrimination has become much more specific via the construction of a more specific research question. In short, you have narrowed down your first global concept, racial discrimination, to a somewhat much more specific concept, a person's ethnicity. At this point, you have yet to refine your second concept in your research question, access to your hospital's social services. This will be done later on. For now, let's review the concept of *concepts.*

CONCEPTS. What are concepts anyway? They are nothing more than ideas. When you speak of a client's ethnic background, for example, you have in mind the concept of *ethnicity*. When you use the word *ethnicity*, you are referring to the underlying idea that certain groups of people can be differentiated from other groups in terms of physical characteristics, customs, beliefs, language, and so on.

A female patient in your hospital, for example, has just been referred to your social service department. She is a *patient* in the hospital, she is a *woman,* and she is now also your *client.* If she's married, she is a *wife.* If she has children, she is a *mother.* She may be a *home owner,* a *committee member,* an *Asian,* and a *Catholic.* She may even be *hostile, demanding,* or *compassionate.*

All of her characteristics are concepts. They are simply ideas that all members of a society share—to a greater or lesser degree, of course. Some concepts are perceived the same way by all of us. On the other hand, some concepts give rise to huge disagreements. The concept of being a mother, for example, involves the concept of children and, specifically, the concept of having given birth to a child. Today, most people would agree that giving birth to a child is only *one* way of defining a mother.

The idea of motherhood in Western society involves more than simply giving birth. Also involved in motherhood are the concepts of loving, of caring for the child's physical needs, of offering the child emotional support, of advocating for the child with others, of accepting legal and financial responsibility for the child, and of being there for the child in all circumstances and at all times.

Some of us could easily argue that a woman who does all of these things is a mother, whether she has given birth or not. Others would say that the biological mother is the *only* real mother, even if she abandoned her child at birth.

Like many other qualities of interest to social workers, ethnicity is a highly complex concept with many possible dimensions. Intelligence is another such concept, as are alienation, morale, conformity, and a host of others.

Step 2d: Identifying Variables within Concepts

You can now break down your global concept—ethnicity of patients who seek out your hospital's social service department—into a variable by breaking down ethnicity into different ethnic groups. Some patients will belong to one ethnic group, some to another, some to a third, and so on. In other words, these people *vary* with respect to which ethnic group they belong to. Any concept that can vary, logically enough, is called a *variable*. So your variable name is *ethnic group*.

Step 2e: Defining Attributes of Variables

You now have gone from your general concept of ethnicity to a variable, ethnic group. Finally, you need to think about which particular ethnic groups will be useful for your study. Perhaps you know that Asians are patients within your hospital, as are Caucasians, Latinos, African Americans, and Native Americans. This gives you five attributes, for your ethnic group variable:

ATTRIBUTES FOR ETHNIC GROUP VARIABLE
1. Asian
2. Caucasian
3. Latino
4. African American
5. Native American

During your positivistic study—or more accurately, during the quantitative portion of your study—you will ask all the hospital's patients which one of the five ethnic groups they belong to; or perhaps these data will be recorded on the hospital's intake forms, and you will not need to ask the patients at all.

In any case, the resulting data will be in the form of numbers or percentages for each attribute. You will have succeeded in measuring the variable *ethnic group* by describing it in terms of five attributes. You will note that these five categories only provide one possible description. You could also have included Pacific Islanders, for example, if there were any receiving medical treatment in your hospital, and then you would have had six attributes of your ethnic group variable instead of only five:

ATTRIBUTES FOR ETHNIC GROUP VARIABLE

1. Asian
2. Caucasian
3. Latino
4. African American
5. Native American
6. Pacific Islanders

If you were afraid that not all clients receiving medical treatment would fit into one of your six categories, then you could include a seventh miscellaneous category, *other,* to be sure you had accounted for everyone:

ATTRIBUTES FOR ETHNIC GROUP VARIABLE

1. Asian
2. Caucasian
3. Latino
4. African American
5. Native American
6. Pacific Islanders
7. Other

By reviewing the literature and your knowledge of your social service unit, you have more or less devised a direction for your study in relation to your ethnicity concept. From the general problem area of racial discrimination, you have come up with a concept, a variable, and six attributes for your variable:

General Problem Area: Racial Discrimination

Concept: Ethnicity

Variable: Ethnic group

Attributes:

1. Asian
2. Caucasian
3. Latino
4. African American
5. Native American
6. Pacific Islanders

As you know, ethnicity is not the only concept of interest in your study. There is also *access to social work services,* which is the idea that some people, or groups of people, are able to access social work services more readily than other people or groups.

You might think of access simply in terms of how many of the patients receiving medical treatment within your hospital actually saw a social worker. Clients will *vary* with respect to whether they saw a social worker, so you have the variable—*saw social worker*—and two attributes of that variable:

Yes, the patient saw a social worker
No, the patient did not see a social worker

You could, for example, ask each patient upon leaving the hospital a very simple question:

Did you see a social worker while you were in the hospital?
1. Yes
2. No

If you wish to explore access in more depth, you might be interested in the factors affecting access. For example, perhaps your review of the literature has led you to believe that some ethnic groups tend to receive fewer referrals to social work services than other groups. If this is the case in your hospital, clients will vary with respect to whether they received a referral, and you immediately have a second variable—*referral*—and two attributes of that variable:

Yes, the patient was referred
No, the patient was not referred

Once again, this variable can take the form of a very simple question:

When you were a patient within the hospital, were you at any time referred to the hospital's social service department?
1. Yes
2. No

However, there is more to accessing hospital social work services than just being referred. Perhaps, according to the literature, certain ethnic groups are more likely to follow up on a referral than other groups because of cultural beliefs around the appropriateness of asking non-family members for help. In that case, you have a third variable, *follow-up of referral,* with two attributes of its own:

Yes, the client followed up

No, the client did not follow up

This also can be put into a question form:

If you were referred to social work services while you were a patient in the hospital, did you follow up on the referral and actually see a social worker?
1. Yes
2. No

In addition, those who do try to follow up on referrals may meet circumstances within the referral process that are more intimidating for some than for others. Perhaps they are obliged to fill out a large number of forms or tell their stories to many unfamiliar people before they actually succeed in achieving an appointment with a social worker.

If this is the case, they *vary* with respect to how intimidating they find the process, which gives you a fourth variable: *feelings of intimidation around the referral process.* The attributes here are not so immediately apparent, but you might decide on just three:

Not at all intimidated
Somewhat intimidated
Very intimidated

This also can be put into the form of a simple question that you would ask all patients who were referred to social services:

How intimidated were you when you were referred to the social services department?
1. Not at all intimidated
2. Somewhat intimidated
3. Very intimidated

By reviewing the literature and your knowledge of your hospital's social service department, you have more or less devised a direction for your study in relation to your access concept. You have come up with a concept, four variables, and attributes for each one of the four variables:

Concept: Access to social work services

> *First Variable:* Saw social worker?
> > *Attributes:* 1. Yes
> > 2. No

> *Second Variable:* Referral?
> > *Attributes:* 1. Yes
> > 2. No

> *Third Variable:* Follow-up of referral?
> > *Attributes:* 1. Yes
> > 2. No

> *Fourth Variable:* Feelings of intimidation
> > *Attributes:* 1. Not at all intimidated
> > 2. Somewhat intimidated
> > 3. Very intimidated

STEP 2F: DEFINING INDEPENDENT AND DEPENDENT VARIABLES

A simple positivistic research study may choose to focus on the relationship between only two variables, called a *bivariate relationship.* The study tries to answer, in general terms, Does variable X affect variable Y? Or how does variable X affect variable Y? This would be a great time for you to review Figure 2.3 in Chapter 2.

If one variable affects the other, the variable that does the affecting is called an *independent variable*, symbolized by X. The variable that is affected is called the *dependent variable*, symbolized by Y. If enough is known about the topic, and you have a good idea of what the effect will be, the question may be phrased, If X occurs, will Y result? If variable X affects variable Y, whatever happens to Y will depend on X.

NO INDEPENDENT OR DEPENDENT VARIABLES. Some positivistic research studies are not concerned with the effect that one variable might have on another. Perhaps it's not yet known whether two variables are even associated, and it's far too soon to postulate what the relationship between them might be. For example, your study might try to ascertain the answer to a simple question:

SIMPLE RESEARCH QUESTION

How intimidated do ethnic minority patients feel when they are referred to my hospital's social service department?

In this simple question, there is no independent variable; neither is there a dependent variable. There is only one variable: degree of intimidation felt by one group of people, the ethnic minorities. You could even include ethnic majorities as well and ask this question:

SIMPLE RESEARCH QUESTION

How intimidated do *all* patients feel when they are referred to my hospital's social service department?

STEP 2G: CONSTRUCTING A HYPOTHESIS

There are many types of hypotheses, but we will only briefly discuss two:

— Nondirectional

— Directional

NONDIRECTIONAL HYPOTHESES. A nondirectional hypothesis (also called a two-tailed hypothesis) is simply a statement that says you expect to find a relationship between two or more variables. You're not willing, however, to stick your neck out as to the specific relationship between them. A nondirectional hypothesis for each one of your access variables could be, for example:

Nondirectional Research Hypothesis 1: Saw a Social Worker
Ethnic minorities and ethnic majorities see hospital social workers differentially.

Nondirectional Research Hypothesis 2: Referral
Ethnic minorities and ethnic majorities are referred to the hospital's social service department differentially.

Nondirectional Research Hypothesis 3: Follow-up
Ethnic minorities and ethnic majorities vary to the degree they follow up on referrals.

Nondirectional Research Hypothesis 4: Intimidation
Ethnic minorities and ethnic majorities feel differently on how intimidated they were about the referral process.

DIRECTIONAL HYPOTHESES. Unlike a nondirectional hypothesis, a directional hypothesis (also called a one-tailed hypothesis) specifically indicates the predicted direction of the relationship between two variables. The direction stated is based on an existing body of knowledge related to the research question.

You may have found out through the literature (in addition to your own observations), for example, that you have enough evidence to suggest the following directional research hypotheses:

- Directional Research Hypothesis 1: Saw a Social Worker
  Ethnic majorities see hospital social workers more than ethnic minorities.

- Directional Research Hypothesis 2: Referral
  Ethnic majorities are referred to the hospital's social service department more than ethnic minorities.

- Directional Research Hypothesis 3: Follow-up
  Ethnic majorities follow up with social service referrals more than ethnic minorities.

- Directional Research Hypothesis 4: Intimidation
  Ethnic minorities are more intimidated with the referral process than ethnic majorities.

As you shall see in this book, many research questions have at least one independent variable and one dependent variable. You could easily design your positivistic study to have one independent variable, ethnicity (i.e., ethnic minority or ethnic majority), and one dependent variable, difficulty in accessing social services (i.e., yes or no). You could easily organize your variables in this way because you are expecting that a person's ethnicity is somehow related to his/her difficulty in accessing social services.

It would be absurd to say the opposite—that the degree of difficulty that people have in accessing social services influences their ethnicity. You could write your directional hypothesis as follows:

DIRECTIONAL HYPOTHESIS

Ethnic minorities have more difficulty than ethnic majorities in accessing my hospital's social service department.

Having set out your hypothesis in this way, you can plainly see that your research design will compare two groups of folks (ethnic minorities and ethnic majorities) in terms of whether or not (yes or no) each group had difficulty accessing your hospital's social service department. Your research design is the blueprint for the study. It's a basic guide to deciding how, where, and when data will be collected.

STEP 2H: EVALUATING THE HYPOTHESIS

You must now evaluate your hypothesis. Our discussion on how to evaluate hypotheses has been adapted and modified from Grinnell and Williams (1990), Williams, Tutty, and Grinnell (1995), and Williams, Unrau, and Grinnell (1998). Hypotheses have to be:

— Relevant

— Complete

— Specific

— Testable

— Ethically and Culturally Sensitive

RELEVANCE. It's hardly necessary to stress that a useful hypothesis is one that contributes to the profession's knowledge base. Nevertheless, some social work problem areas are so enormously complex that it's not uncommon for people to get so sidetracked in reading the professional literature that they develop very interesting hypotheses totally unrelated to the original problem area they had wanted to investigate. They needlessly run down a bunch of rabbit holes. The relevancy criterion is a reminder that the hypothesis must be directly related to the research question, which in turn must be directly related to the study's general problem area.

COMPLETENESS. A hypothesis should be a complete statement that expresses your intended meaning in its entirety. The reader should not be left with the impression that some word or phrase is missing, such as:

AN INCOMPLETE HYPOTHESIS
Moral values are declining.

Other examples would include a whole range of comparative statements without a reference point. The statement "Males are more aggressive," for example, may be assumed to mean "Men are more aggressive than women," but someone investigating the social life of animals may have meant "Male humans are more aggressive than male gorillas."

SPECIFICITY. A hypothesis must be unambiguous. The reader should be able to understand what each variable contained in the hypothesis means and what relationship, if any, is hypothesized to exist between them. Consider, for example, this hypothesis:

A BADLY WORDED HYPOTHESIS

Badly timed family therapy affects success.

Badly timed family therapy may refer to therapy offered too soon or too late for the family to benefit; or to the social worker or family being late for therapy sessions; or to sessions that are too long or too short to be effective. Similarly, "success" may mean resolution of the family's problems as determined by objective measurement, or it may mean the family's—or the social worker's—degree of satisfaction with the therapy, or any combination of these.

With regard to the relationship between the two variables, the reader may assume that you are hypothesizing a negative correlation; that is, the more badly timed the therapy, the less success will be achieved. On the other hand, perhaps you are only hypothesizing an association. Bad timing will invariably coexist with lack of success. Be that as it may, the reader should not be left to guess at what you mean by a hypothesis. If you are trying to be both complete and specific, you may hypothesize, for example:

A PROPERLY WORDED HYPOTHESIS

Family therapy that is undertaken *after* the male perpetrator has accepted responsibility for the sexual abuse of his child is more likely to succeed in reuniting the family than family therapy undertaken *before* the male perpetrator has accepted responsibility for the sexual abuse.

This hypothesis is complete and specific. It leaves the reader in no doubt as to what you mean, but it's also somewhat wordy and clumsy. One of the difficulties in writing a good hypothesis is that specific statements need more words than unspecific or ambiguous statements.

POTENTIAL FOR TESTING. The fourth criterion for judging whether a hypothesis is good and useful is the ease with which the truth of the hypothesis can be verified. Some statements cannot be verified at all with presently available measurement techniques. "Telepathic communication exists between identical twins" is one such statement.

A hypothesis of sufficient importance will often generate new data-gathering techniques, which will enable it to be eventually tested. Nevertheless, as a general rule it's best to limit hypotheses to statements that can be tested immediately by current and available measurement methods.

ETHICALLY AND CULTURALLY SENSITIVE. Well, if we have to explain this criterion you don't belong in social work. Read Chapter 3 on ethics and Chapter 4 on cultural competence to review all the ethical and cultural issues that must be dealt with in a research study—especially when it comes to formulating research questions and hypotheses.

STEP 3: DESIGNING THE STUDY

AFTER ALL OF THE NECESSARY WORK has been done in relation to formulating your research question and/or hypothesis, you need to actually state how your study is going to unfold; that is, you now need to describe how you are going to measure your variables and select your research sample. Like Step 2 discussed previously, Step 3 also has sub-steps:

— Step 3a: Measuring Variables

— Step 3b: Deciding on a Sample

— Step 3c: Addressing Ethical and Cultural Issues

STEP 3A: MEASURING VARIABLES (CHAPTERS 7 AND 8)

All your variables must be able to be objectively measured. This means that you must precisely record the variable's frequency, and/or its duration, and/or its magnitude (intensity). Think about your ethnic minority variable for a minute. As noted earlier, you could simply operationalize this variable into two categories: ethnic minority and ethnic majorities:

Are you an ethnic minority?
1. Yes
2. No

Here you are simply measuring the presence (ethnic minority) or absence (ethnic majority) of a trait for each research participant within your study. You also needed to measure the difficulty in accessing the hospital's social service department variable. Once again, you could have measured this variable in a number of ways. You chose, however to measure it where each person could produce a response to a simple question:

> Did you have difficulty in accessing our hospital's social service department?
> 1. Yes
> 2. No

Step 3b: Deciding on a Sample (Chapter 9)

Sampling is nothing more than selecting units (e.g., people, organizations) from a specific population of interest so that by studying the sample you can generalize your results back to the population from which the sample was drawn.

Step 3c: Addressing Ethical and Cultural Issues (Chapters 3 and 4)

It goes without saying that you must review all the ethical and cultural issues in every step of your proposed research study before you collect one speck of data. So the main two questions you need to ask yourself at this point are:

- Is my proposed research study ethical (Chapter 3)?
- Is my proposed research study culturally sensitive (Chapter 4)?

Step 4: Collecting the Data (Chapters 12–14)

Only after you decide that your study is ethical and culturally sensitive can you start to collect your data. Data collection is where the rubber hits the road. The data you collect must reflect a condition in the *real* world and should not be biased in any way by the person collecting the data.

In your positivistic study, the research participants produce the data—not you, the researcher. That is, you only record the data that each participant individually provides (probably through a questionnaire of some type) for both of your variables:

- "Ethnic Minority" or "Ethnic Majority" for the ethnicity variable
- "Yes" or "No" for the access to social service variable

Your data collection procedures must be able to be duplicated by others. In other words, they must be sufficiently clear and straightforward that other researchers could use them in their research studies.

Data collection is a critical step in the research process because it's the link between theory and practice. Your research study always begins with an idea that is molded by a conceptual framework, which uses preexisting knowledge about your study's problem area.

Once your research question has been refined to a researchable level, data are sought from a selected source(s) and gathered using a data collection method. The data collected are then used to support or supplant your original study's conceptions about your research problem under investigation.

STEP 5: ANALYZING THE DATA (CHAPTER 15)

ONCE YOU HAVE COLLECTED your data via the previous step, you need to analyze them. You asked your research participants to fill out a simple two-question questionnaire that only asked two questions:

Question 1: Are you an ethnic minority?
1. Yes
2. No

Question 2: Did you have difficulty in accessing our hospital's social service department?
1. Yes
2. No

There are two major types of quantitative data analyses:

— Descriptive statistics

— Inferential statistics

DESCRIPTIVE STATISTICS

As presented in Chapter 15, descriptive statistics describe your study's sample or population. Consider your ethnicity variable for a moment. You can easily describe your research participants in relation to their ethnicity by stating how many of them fell into each attribute of the variable. Suppose, for example, that 40 percent of your sample is in the ethnic minority category and the remaining 60 percent are in the ethnic majority category as shown:

ATTRIBUTES

Ethnic Minority..............40%
Ethnic Majority.............60%

These two percentages will give you a picture of what your sample looks like in relation to their ethnicity. A different picture could be produced where 10 percent of your sample are ethnic minorities and 90 percent are not:

ATTRIBUTES

Ethnic Minority..............10%
Ethnic Majority.............90%

This describes only one variable—ethnicity. A more detailed picture is given when data for two variables are displayed at the same time (Table 5.1). Suppose, for example, that 70 percent of your research participants who are ethnic minorities reported that they had difficulty in accessing your hospital's social services, compared with 20 percent of those who are the ethnic majority.

Other descriptive information about your research participants could include variables such as average age, percentages of males and females, average income, and so on. Much more will be said about descriptive statistics in Chapter 15 when we discuss how to analyze quantitative data—data that are in the form of numbers.

INFERENTIAL STATISTICS

Inferential statistics determine the probability that a relationship between the two variables within your sample also exists within the population from which it was drawn. Suppose that in your positivistic study you find a statistically significant relationship between the ethnicity of your research participants (your sample) and whether they successfully accessed social services within your hospital setting.

The use of inferential statistics will permit you to say whether the relationship detected in your study's sample exists in the larger population from which it was drawn. Much more will also be said about inferential statistics in Chapter 15.

STEP 6: INTERPRETING THE FINDINGS

ONCE YOUR DATA have been analyzed and put into a visual display, they need to be interpreted; that is, what do they mean—in words? You could come up with the following simple interpretation:

TABLE 5.1
Difficulty in Accessing Social Services

Ethnicity	Having Difficulty?	
	Yes	No
Ethnic Minority	70%	30%
Ethnic Majority	20%	80%

As can be seen in Table 5.1, ethnic minorities had more difficulty in accessing social services than ethnic majorities.

STEP 6A: COMPARING RESULTS WITH FINDINGS FROM PREVIOUS STUDIES

Your findings now need to be compared with what other studies have found. This is the time to review the literature once again, as discussed in Chapter 2. At this point, you need to state how your study's findings are either consistent or inconsistent with the findings from similar studies.

STEP 6B: SPECIFYING THE STUDY'S LIMITATIONS

At this point, you need to state the limitations of your study. You will need to state how well your study addressed all the threats to internal and external validities, as discussed in Chapter 11.

STEP 7: DISSEMINATING THE STUDY'S FINDINGS

QUANTITATIVE FINDINGS are easily summarized in tables, figures, and graphs. When data are disseminated to lay people, we usually rely on straightforward graphs and charts to illustrate our findings. As discussed in Chapter 17, presentation of statistical findings is typically reserved for professional journals. Much more will be said on writing and disseminating positivistic study results in Chapter 17.

An Extended Example

Let's set aside racial discrimination and access to social services within your hospital for a moment and focus on an example involving poverty, domestic violence, substance abuse, and homelessness.

What's the Problem?

LET'S PRETEND for a moment that you're a social worker in a large social service agency. The past three years of agency intake data reveal that many of the clients you serve experience similar social issues. More specifically, most clients seeking services from your agency regularly present with one or more of the following problems:

- Poverty
- Domestic Violence
- Substance Abuse
- Homelessness

Your agency's Executive Director establishes a "Practice Informed by Research" Committee that is charged with the following mandate:

MANDATE

To design a research study involving agency clientele so that workers at the agency will be better informed about the complex relationship between the issues of poverty, domestic violence, substance abuse, and homelessness

You are asked to chair the Practice Informed by Research Committee. Gladly, you accept and begin leading your committee through the remaining steps of the research process, as outlined in Figure 5.1.

Formulating Initial Impressions

AS CHAIR of the Practice Informed by Research Committee, your first step is to invite open discussion with your committee members about what they "know" about each of the four presenting problems, or issues, and the relationship between them.

Drawing upon your task-group facilitation skills learned in one of your social work practice classes, you help your committee members tease out the source(s) of their collective wisdom (or knowledge) as a group.

Questions about possible relationships among the presenting problems are discussed, and efforts are made to determine whether the committee's answers are based on authority, tradition, experience, intuition, or the scientific method. During this process of discussion, the committee learns some very important things, such as how much of their present knowledge set is based on empirical knowledge versus other ways of knowing; what biases, values, or beliefs are active among committee members; and how the scientific method can be used to advance the current knowledge base among workers at the agency. Some possible questions you could formulate are as follows:

- Is poverty related to domestic violence?

- Is poverty related to substance abuse?

- Is poverty related to homelessness?

- Is domestic violence related to substance abuse?

- Is domestic violence related to homelessness?

- Is substance abuse related to homelessness?

DETERMINING WHAT OTHERS HAVE FOUND

GIVEN YOUR SUPERB SKILLS as a group facilitator, you have energized your committee members and stimulated their curiosity such that they are eager to read the latest research about poverty, domestic violence, substance abuse, and homelessness. Each committee member accepts a task to search the literature for articles and information that report on the relationship between one or more of the four presenting problems of interest.

Committee members search a variety of sources of information such as professional journals, credible Web sites, and books (see Chapter 2). Using quality criteria to evaluate the evidence of information gathered, the committee synthesizes the knowledge gathered from empirical sources. If so desired, the committee might endeavor to systematically assess the literature gathered through meta-analyses. Below are two general questions that you need to address in relation to your problem area:

Research Questions

1. What does the available literature have to say about poverty, domestic violence, substance abuse, and homelessness?

2. Has it been established that any two or more of these variables are, in fact, related? And if so, what is the relationship between or among them?

With a synthesis of the literature gathered, the Practice Informed by Research Committee is in an excellent position to make an informed statement about up-to-date knowledge on the relationship between poverty, domestic violence, substance abuse, and homelessness.

Refining the General Problem Area

By this point, the excitement of your committee members has waned somewhat. As it turned out, the task of reviewing the literature was more onerous than anticipated. Indeed, the number of research studies investigating poverty, domestic violence, substance abuse, and homelessness was overwhelming. Committee members had to agree on the parameters of their search.

For example, a search for research on the topic of domestic violence required committee members to define "partner" in domestic violence and decide whether the research studies to be reviewed would include gay and lesbian partnerships as well as heterosexual partners. Moreover, applying criteria to evaluate individual studies was not as straightforward as initially thought.

Nevertheless, your committee trudged through and indeed was successful at finding relevant empirical articles. To recharge the committee and keep the momentum of the research process going, you work with committee members to set priorities for the remainder of your work together. In short, you decide what research question(s)—exploratory, descriptive, or explanatory—will be the focus of your investigation.

In turn, you decide what research design is best suited to investigating the proposed research question. As the above suggests, the committee decides to focus on the descriptive relationship between only two presenting problem areas—domestic violence and substance abuse. One of the many oversimplified examples from the preceding four highly interrelated variables (i.e., poverty, domestic violence, substance abuse, and homelessness) might be:

Descriptive Relationship between Two Variables

Clients with substance abuse problems will also have domestic violence issues.

Measuring the Variables

You now need to review with your committee members the work already accomplished in the previous steps and note that planning thus far has largely been a conceptual exercise. When you start to define and decide on how to measure your variables, you soon realize that the tasks for the committee become much more specific in nature, particularly as related to the research process. With respect to measurement, committee members must develop a way to measure the two presenting problems, or variables (i.e., substance abuse and domestic violence), that will be studied and find measuring instruments for each variable.

It must be pointed out that you really need to know how other studies measured their variables. If you feel that the previous studies measured their variables properly, then you can use the method they used to measure your variables, too. There is no need to reinvent the wheel if the previous measurements are valid and reliable. Your committee believes that the previous studies measured the two variables well, so you decide also to use them in your study.

As you can see, the end result of this step is the selection of the Domestic Violence Inventory (DVI) to measure domestic violence and the Substance Abuse Questionnaire (SAQ) to measure substance abuse. You have decided, through the literature and your past experiences, that your two variables will be measured as follows:

Measurement of Variables

1. Substance abuse: *Substance Abuse Questionnaire* (SAQ)
2. Domestic violence: *Domestic Violence Inventory* (DVI)

Selecting a Sample

With a clear research hypothesis, a solid understanding of other research studies, and the selection of measuring instruments for key variables, the next step for the committee is to decide on the sampling procedures that will be used in the study. At this point, research and practice knowledge come together to decide which parameters for the sample will be most meaningful.

For example, it turns out that intake data show that most (but not all) clients presenting with either substance abuse or domestic violence problems at intake report that they have been living together for more than one year. The intake data show that only a handful of coupled clients are in new relationships of less than one year. Consequently, this characteristic of clients at the agency becomes a criterion to define the population, and consequently the sample, to be studied.

Once all of the sampling criteria are established, the committee must decide the particular sampling method to use. The aim is to select a sample that is representative (e.g., similar in age, race, marital status, and service history) of *all* clients that fit the eligibility criteria.

After reviewing the literature and evaluating all the logistics in relation to administering the measuring instruments, you have decided to administer them as follows:

PROTOCOL FOR ADMINISTERING THE MEASURING INSTRUMENTS TO A SAMPLE

The SAQ and DVI will be administered to all partners living together for more than one year who are receiving social services from XYZ agency from July 1, 2016, to June 30, 2017. Both measuring instruments will be administered by the intake worker during the client's second visit to the agency.

ADDRESSING ETHICAL AND CULTURAL ISSUES

AS AN ETHICAL SOCIAL WORK PRACTITIONER who adheres to the NASW *Code of Ethics*, you are aware that not one speck of data for the study will be collected until proper procedures have developed and independently reviewed. After reading Chapters 3 and 4 of this text and Section 5 of the NASW *Code of Ethics*, the committee gets to work on developing proper consent forms and research protocols as well as on obtaining all necessary ethics approvals. Remember that you must:

- Write the research participant consent form and/or assent form.

- Obtain written permission from XYZ agency.

- Obtain official written approvals from appropriate institutional review boards.

COLLECTING THE DATA

AT THIS POINT in the positivistic research process, your study should be ethically and culturally sound. As discussed in Chapter 3, you can only collect data after you have obtained written consent and/or assent from your research participants. Data collection is a step that indicates the study is under way. There are many different methods of data collection available, and each has particular advantages and disadvantages, as discussed in Chapter 14. Continuing with our simple example, data collection involves administering the SAQ and DVI instruments to sampled partners who have been living together for more than one year.

Once the study is under way, the protocols established for data collection should be carried out precisely so as to avoid errors. Moreover, data collection procedures should not be changed. If changes are necessary, then they must be approved by the ethical oversight bodies involved *before* those changes are implemented.

Your committee's focus at this point is only to monitor that the study is being carried out as planned and to use research principles to troubleshoot any problems that arise. Chapter 12 presents the various data collection methods that could be used to collect quantitative data.

ANALYZING THE DATA

GATHERING AND ANALYZING your data is an exciting process because this is when you and your committee get the answer to your stated hypothesis: Clients who have substance abuse issues will also have domestic violence issues (and vice versa). It will reveal two key facts or results from your study that indeed support this hypothesis.

Before it was possible to produce these results, your committee was hard at work ensuring that data were properly entered into an appropriate computer program and analyzed. Chapters 15 and 16 discuss data analysis in detail: Chapter 15 on quantitative analyses and Chapter 16 on qualitative analyses. Your quantitative data analysis could be as simple as the following:

DATA ANALYSIS

1. There were a total of 200 couples in the study; 150 had domestic violence issues, and 50 did not have any domestic violence issues.

2. Of the 150 couples who had domestic violence issues, 85% of them had at least one partner also experiencing substance abuse issues.

INTERPRETING THE DATA

GETTING AN ANSWER to your research question and deciding on the usefulness of the answer are two separate steps. The committee will go beyond the reported "facts," as stated previously, and make a conclusive statement such as:

CONCLUSION FROM DATA ANALYSIS

Substance abuse and domestic violence are co-occurring problems for most clients served by the agency. Thus, social work practitioners must be skilled in treating both presenting problems.

COMPARING RESULTS WITH FINDINGS FROM PREVIOUS STUDIES

AS CHAIR of the Practice Informed by Research Committee, you are aware that every research study is only a single piece in the puzzle of knowledge development. Consequently, you ask that the committee to consider the findings of your study in the context of the other research studies that were reviewed as well as any new studies published while your study was under way.

By contrasting your findings with what others have found, your committee builds on the existing knowledge base. Simply put, your findings need to be compared with what others have found. For example,

COMPARING YOUR STUDY'S FINDINGS WITH FINDINGS FROM OTHER STUDIES

1. The findings from this study are consistent with the findings from other studies; that is, domestic violence and substance abuse issues are highly related to one another.

2. This study adds new knowledge by finding this relationship for couples who have been living together for more than one year.

SPECIFYING THE STUDY'S LIMITATIONS

YOU ALSO REALIZE that no study is perfect, and that includes yours. Many study limitations are predetermined by the particular research design that was used. For example, threats to internal and external validity are limitations commonly discussed in research reports and journal articles (Chapter 11).

Acknowledging your study's limitations can be a humbling experience. Although you may be better informed at the conclusion of your study, you will not have found the magic cure to alleviate your clients' struggles and suffering by means of only one research study. The limitation section of your research report could read something like this:

LIMITATIONS OF YOUR STUDY

1. The limitations of this descriptive research design do not permit any inference of causation. We will never know whether substance abuse causes domestic violence, or whether domestic violence causes substance abuse.

2. Also we will never know how poverty and homelessness play a role in domestic violence and substance abuse because these two variables were never included in the study.

WRITING AND DISSEMINATING THE STUDY'S RESULTS

A FINAL, IMPORTANT STEP in the research process is sharing the new knowledge learned in your study. In the academic world, dissemination most often refers to publication of the study in a peer-reviewed journal. Although some practitioners also publish in peer-reviewed journals, dissemination in the practice world more commonly refers to sharing findings at conferences or local meetings.

The idea of dissemination is to make your study's results available to others who are working in the same area—whether as practitioners, researchers, policy makers, or educators. As chair of the Practice Informed by Research Committee, you will want to share your study's results with others in your agency.

The knowledge gained might be used to develop new procedures in the agency (e.g., intake, training, or referrals). Whatever the route of dissemination, the aim is to have completed your research study at the highest level of integrity so that the dissemination of your results will be most useful to others.

Even with all the limitations of your study's research design, some data are better than none; that is, no matter how many threats to internal and external validity (Chapter 11), as long as the study's procedures and limitations are clearly spelled out in the final report, the study's findings will be useful to others.

 # SUMMARY

As we know from the left-hand side of Figure 2.3, social work research questions can be placed on a continuum depending on how much knowledge is already known about the subject. The right-hand side indicates the research approach(es) that can be utilized to answer these questions.

As can be easily seen, there are seven main types of questions that positivistic research approaches can answer: existence questions, composition questions, relationship questions, descriptive-comparative questions, causality questions, causality-comparative questions, and causality-comparative interaction questions. However, as you know via reading this chapter qualitative data can easily be gathered within positivistic studies as well.

This chapter briefly discussed the positivistic research approach to knowledge building. The next chapter is a logical extension of this one in that it presents how the interpretive research approach can be used to build upon our knowledge base.

Study Questions for Chapter 5

— First, answer each question only AFTER you have read the chapter.

— Second, indicate how comfortable you were in answering each question on a 5-point scale:

1	2	3	4	5
Very uncomfortable	Somewhat uncomfortable	Neutral	Somewhat comfortable	Very comfortable

If you rated any question between 1–3, please reread the section of the chapter where the information for the question can be found. If you're still uncomfortable answering the question, talk with your instructor and/or your classmates for more clarification.

Questions	Degree of comfort? (Circle one number)
1. Discuss why the positivistic research approach is useful to knowledge generation.	1 2 3 4 5
2. In your own words, define the positivistic research approach. Provide a social work example to illustrate your points.	1 2 3 4 5
3. Discuss why the positivistic research approach to knowledge generation places such a heavy emphasis on the measurability of variables within research studies. Discuss in detail using a social work example to illustrate your points.	1 2 3 4 5
4. Discuss why the positivistic research approach to knowledge generation places such a heavy emphasis on objectivity within research studies. Discuss in detail using a social work example to illustrate your points.	1 2 3 4 5
5. Discuss why the positivistic research approach to knowledge generation places such a heavy emphasis on trying to reduce uncertainty within research studies. Discuss in detail using a social work example to illustrate your points.	1 2 3 4 5
6. Discuss why the positivistic research approach to knowledge generation places such a heavy emphasis on the duplication of research studies. Discuss in detail using a social work example to illustrate your points.	1 2 3 4 5
7. In your own words, describe the positivistic research process (Figure 5.1) by using one social work example throughout your discussion.	1 2 3 4 5

8. What are concepts? Provide a few social work examples of them.	1 2 3 4 5
9. What are variables? Provide a few social work examples of them.	1 2 3 4 5
10. What is the main difference between concepts and variables?	1 2 3 4 5
11. What are attributes of variables? Provide social work examples to illustrate your points.	1 2 3 4 5
12. What are independent variables? What are dependent variables? What is the main differences between them? Provide social work examples to illustrate your points.	1 2 3 4 5
13. What are nondirectional hypotheses? Provide a few social work examples of them.	1 2 3 4 5
14. What are directional hypotheses? Provide a few social work examples of them.	1 2 3 4 5
15. List and discuss the five criteria that you will use to evaluate all social work hypotheses. Provide a social work example for each criterion.	1 2 3 4 5
16. At this point in your course, how comfortable are you with discussing the positivistic research approach to knowledge generation with your field instructor (or your supervisor at work)? With your fellow classmates? Discuss in detail.	1 2 3 4 5

Assessing Your Self-Efficacy for Chapter 5

AFTER you have read the chapter AND have completed all the study questions, please indicate how knowledgeable you feel you are for each concept listed below.

1	2	3	4	5
Very uncomfortable	Somewhat uncomfortable	Neutral	Somewhat comfortable	Very comfortable

Major Concepts in Chapter	Knowledge Level? (Circle one number)
1. The positivistic way of thinking	1 2 3 4 5
2. Steps within the positivistic research approach to knowledge generation	1 2 3 4 5

3.	Reviewing the literature	1 2 3 4 5
4.	Selecting variables to study	1 2 3 4 5
5.	Concepts and variables	1 2 3 4 5
6.	Attributes of variables	1 2 3 4 5
7.	Independent and dependent variables	1 2 3 4 5
8.	Nondirectional hypotheses	1 2 3 4 5
9.	Directional hypotheses	1 2 3 4 5
10.	Measuring variables	1 2 3 4 5
11.	Selecting a sample or research participants	1 2 3 4 5
12.	Collecting data from research participants	1 2 3 4 5
13.	Analyzing data	1 2 3 4 5
14.	Interpreting data	1 2 3 4 5
15.	Comparing a study's results with the results from other studies	1 2 3 4 5
16.	Specifying a study's limitations	1 2 3 4 5
17.	Presenting and disseminating a study's findings	1 2 3 4 5

Add up your scores (Minimum = 17, Maximum = 85)	Total score =

A   76 — 85 = Social Work Manager in the making.
B   68 — 75 = Social Work Supervisor.
C   60 — 67 = Social Work Practitioner.
D   17 — 59 = Case Aide. Reread the chapter and redo the study questions.

6

The Interpretive Research Approach

*You may have heard the world is made up of atoms and molecules, but it's
really made up of stories. When you sit with an individual that's been here,
you can give quantitative data a qualitative overlay.*
~ William Turner

The previous chapter presented a brief discussion of how the generation of social
work knowledge is acquired via the positivistic research approach. As you know,
this approach uses quantitative data—that is, data that contain numbers. This chapter is a logical extension of the last one in that we now focus our attention on the
interpretive research approach that uses qualitative data—that is, data that contain
words, diagrams, illustrations, pictures, and stories.

As we know from the previous chapter, the positivistic approach to knowledge development is embedded within the positivistic way of thinking or viewing
the world. In direct contrast to the positivistic approach, the interpretive approach
to knowledge development is embedded within the interpretive way of thinking or
viewing the world. We will now turn our attention to the interpretive way of thinking.

What Is the Interpretive Way of Thinking?

The interpretive approach to knowledge development is the second approach to obtaining knowledge in our profession (see right side of Figure 2.1). It basically discards the positivistic notion that there is only one external reality waiting to be discovered. Instead, the interpretive research approach is based on the interpretive perspective that states that reality is defined by the research participants' interpretations of their own realities.

In sum, it's the subjective reality that is studied via the interpretive research approach rather than the objective one studied by the positivistic approach. Empiricism—the belief that science must be founded on observations and measurements, another tenet of positivism—is thus discarded.

As you will see in Chapters 12 to 14, the differences between the philosophies of the positivistic approach and the interpretive approach to knowledge development naturally lead to different data collection methods. Subjective reality, for example, cannot be easily explored through the data collection methods of mailed surveys, structured observations, and analyzing existing statistics (Chapter 12). However, there are a few good data collection methods we can use to determine the subjective reality of participants: interviewing, participant observations, secondary text data, and historical data (Chapter 13).

Numbers versus Words

THE INTERPRETIVE APPROACH says that the only real way to find out about the subjective reality of our research participants is to ask them, and the answer will come back in words, not in numbers. In a nutshell, interpretive research approaches produce qualitative data in the form of text. Positivistic research methods produce quantitative data in the form of numbers. As Creswell (2010) points out:

> *Positivistic research* is a means for testing objective theories by examining the relationship among variables. These variables, in turn, can be measured, typically on measuring instruments, so that numbered data can be analyzed using statistical procedures. The final written report has a set structure consisting of introduction, literature and theory, methods, results, and discussion. Those who engage in this form of inquiry have assumptions about testing theories deductively, building in protections against bias, controlling for alternative explanations, and being able to generalize and replicate the findings.

> *Interpretive research* is a means for exploring and understanding the meaning individuals or groups ascribe to a social or human problem. The process of

research involves emerging questions and procedures, data typically collected in the participant's setting, data analysis inductively building from particulars to general themes, and the researcher making interpretations of the meaning of the data. The final written report has a flexible structure. Those who engage in this form of inquiry support a way of looking at research that honors an inductive style, a focus on individual meaning, and the importance of rendering the complexity of a situation.

Data ≠ Information

Here, it's worth pausing for a moment to discuss what is meant by data. Data are plural; the singular is datum from the Latin dare, to give. A datum is thus something that is given, either from a quantitative observation and/or measurement or from a qualitative discussion with Ms. Smith about her experiences in giving birth at her home.

A number of observations and/or measurements with the positivistic approach, or a number of discussions with the interpretive approach constitute data. The most important thing to remember at this point is that both approaches to the research method produce data. They simply produce different kinds of data. Data are not the same thing as information, although the two words are often used interchangeably.

Information is something you hope to get from the data once you have analyzed them—whether they are numbers or words. You might, for example, collect data about the home-birthing experiences of a number of women, and your analysis might reveal commonalties between them: perhaps all the women felt that their partners had played a more meaningful role in the birthing process at home than would have been possible in a hospital setting.

The enhanced role of the partner is information that you, as the researcher, have derived from the interview data. In other words, data are pieces of evidence, in the form of words (qualitative data) or numbers (quantitative data), that you put together to give you information—which is what the research method is all about.

So, in a nutshell, information is how you interpret the facts. For example, if it's 86 degrees Fahrenheit outside, this is a fact measured by a thermometer. Someone who lives in Phoenix may interpret this fact by saying it's "mild," while someone in Fargo may say it's "very hot." The interpretation of facts depends on one's individual reality. Information is nothing more than the subjective interpretation of objective facts.

One Reality versus Many

AS YOU KNOW about the positivistic standpoint as presented in the last chapter, if you do not accept the idea of a single reality—which is not changed by being observed and/or measured, and from which you, the researcher, are "detached" from the study—then you are not a "real researcher" doing a "real research study." Thus, as a nonresearcher doing a nonresearch study, your findings are not considered to be of much use.

Many of the supposed "nonresearchers" whose views were not thought to be valid were women and/or came from diverse minority groups. Feminists, for example, have argued that there is not only one reality—there are many realities. They contend that men and women experience the world differently and so they both exist in different realities, constructed by them from their own perceptions.

Changing Realities

As we know from Chapter 4, people from various cultural groups view "their worlds" from their individual perspectives, beliefs, and traditions, which means they will experience their own realities. As for the idea that reality is not changed by being observed and/or measured, feminists have argued that a relationship of some kind is always formed between the researcher and the research participant (subject), resulting in yet another mutual reality constructed between the two of them. In any study involving human research participants, there will thus be at least three realities:

- The researcher's reality

- The research participant's reality

- The mutual reality they (researcher and research participant) both create and share

Moreover, all three realities are constantly changing as the study proceeds and as further interactions occur. The positivistic notion of a single unchanged and unchanging reality, some feminists have argued, was typically a male idea, probably due to the fact that men view human relationships as being less important than do women.

This is a low blow that will quite properly be resented by the many men who do in fact ascribe importance to relationships. But, that aside, perhaps the problem lies less with phenomenalism (a single unchanged reality as opposed to multiple changing realities) than it does with scientism (the idea that the physical and social sciences can be approached in the same way).

Subjects versus Research Participants

HAVING DEALT with what data are (don't ever write "data is"), let's go back to the implications of collecting data about people's subjective realities. Because it's the research participant's reality you want to explore, the research participant is a very important data source.

The positivistic approach may seem like it tends to relegate the research participant to the status of an object or subject. In a study of caesarian births at a hospital during a certain period, for example, Ms. Smith will not be viewed as an individual within the positivistic approach to knowledge development, but only as the seventeenth woman who experienced such a birth during that period. Details of her medical history may be gathered without any reference to Ms. Smith as a separate person with her own hopes and fears, failings, and strengths.

Conversely, an interpretive approach to caesarian births will focus on Ms. Smith's individual experiences. What was her experience? What did it mean to her? How did she interpret it in the context of her own reality?

Compared with the positivistic approach to knowledge building where research participants (subjects) are more passive than active, the interpretive approach actively engages the research participants to vigorously engage and guide the studies as they go along. So, at the risk of sounding simplistic, think of it this way: the positivistic approach gathers numbers from passive subjects whereas the interpretive approach gathers words from active research participants.

RESEARCHERS' VALUES

IN ORDER TO DISCOVER the truth of Ms. Smith's reality, however, you must be clear about the nature of your own reality. We discussed in Chapter 1 about value awareness as one of the characteristics that distinguish the research method from the other four ways of knowledge development. As you know, value awareness is the ability for you to put aside your own values when you are conducting research studies or when you are evaluating the results obtained by other researchers. This is sometimes called disinterestedness.

Researchers who are disinterested are ones who are able to accept evidence, or data, that run against their own values. From a hardline positivistic perspective, this putting aside of values seems more akin to sweeping them under the carpet and pretending they don't exist.

Researchers engaged in positivistic studies will deny that their own values are important. They claim their values have nothing to do with the study. In a nutshell, their values cease to exist. In contrast, interpretive researchers take a very different view. Their values are not only a part of their own realities but also a part of the mutual reality that is constructed through their interactions with their research participants.

An interpretive researcher's values thus must be acknowledged and thoroughly explored so that the mutual shaping of realities resulting from the interaction with their research participants may be more completely and honestly understood.

The term value awareness, while important to both research approaches, is thus understood in different ways. To positivistic researchers, it means putting values aside so they don't affect the study. To interpretive researchers, it means an immersion in values so that their inevitable effect is understood and their research participants' realities emerge more clearly.

COMMONALITIES OF ALL INTERPRETIVE RESEARCH STUDIES

LESLIE TUTTY, MIKE ROTHERY, AND RICK GRINNELL (1996) present a few characteristics that most interpretive research studies have in common:

* Research studies that are conducted primarily in the natural settings where the research participants carry out their daily business in a "non-research" atmosphere.

* Research studies where variables cannot be controlled and experimentally manipulated (though changes in variables and their effect on other variables can certainly be observed).

* Research studies in which the questions to be asked are not always completely conceptualized at the outset (though they can be).

* Research studies in which the data collected are heavily influenced by the experiences and priorities of the research participants, rather than being collected by predetermined and/or highly structured and/or standardized measurement instruments.

* Research studies in which meanings are drawn from the data (and presented to others) using processes that are more natural and familiar than those used in the positivistic method. The data need not be reduced to numbers and statistically analyzed (though counting and statistics can be employed if they are thought useful).

PHASES OF THE INTERPRETIVE APPROACH

Like positivistic researchers, interpretive researchers make a major commitment in terms of time, money, and resources when they undertake research studies. As can be seen in Figure 5.1, a positivistic study has basic sequential steps that must be followed to produce useful quantitative data. As can be seen in Figure 6.1, an interpretive study does not have these specific steps—the activities are more phases than

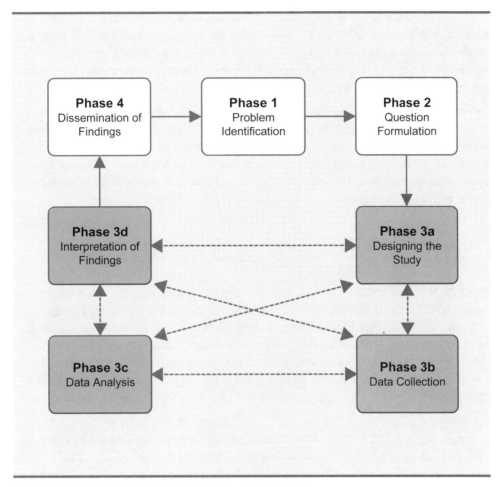

FIGURE 6.1
Phases of the Interpretive (Qualitative) Research Approach

steps, as many of the phases highly interact with one another as the study progresses from one phase to the next. Take a look at how Phases 3a through 3d interact between and among one another. In short, they all are done at the same time. See the dashed arrows between the shaded phases that show how Phases 3a through 3d highly interact with one another.

One of the major differences between the two research approaches is how they utilize the literature. In a positivistic study, for example, the literature is utilized mostly within the first three steps of the research method. In an interpretive study, the literature is heavily utilized in all of the phases. The interpretive research approach is akin to exploring a social problem maze that has multiple entry points and paths.

You have no way of knowing whether the maze will lead you to a place of importance or not, but you enter into it out of your own curiosity and perhaps even conviction. You enter the maze without a map or a guide; you have only yourself to rely on and your notebook to record important events, observations, conversations, and impressions along the way.

You will begin your journey of an interpretive inquiry by stepping into one entrance and forging ahead. You move cautiously forward, using all of your senses in an effort to pinpoint your location and what surrounds you at any one time. You may enter into dead-end rooms within the maze and have to backtrack. You may also encounter paths that you did not think possible. In some cases, you may even find a secret passageway that links you to a completely different maze.

PHASES 1 AND 2: PROBLEM IDENTIFICATION AND QUESTION FORMULATION

INTERPRETIVE STUDIES are generally inductive and require you to reason in such a way that you move from a part to a whole or from a particular instance to a general conclusion (see Figure 6.1). Let's return to the research problem introduced in the last chapter—racial discrimination within the social services. You begin the interpretive research process, once again, from your observations and/or hunches—ethnic minorities are among the highest groups for unemployment, poverty, and low education; however, Caucasians outnumber ethnic minorities when seeking assistance from social services.

You can focus your interpretive research question by identifying the key concepts in your question. These key concepts set the parameters of your research study—they are the outside boundaries of your maze. As in the positivistic research approach, you would want to visit the library and review the literature related to your key concepts. Your literature review, however, takes on a very different purpose. Rather than pinpointing exact variables to study, you review the literature to see how your key concepts are generally described and defined by previous researchers.

Going with the maze example for the moment, you might learn whether your maze will have rounded or perpendicular corners, or whether it will have multiple levels. The knowledge you glean from the literature assists you with ways of thinking that you hope will help you move through the maze in a way that you will arrive at a meaningful understanding of the problem it represents.

Because you may never have been in the maze before, you must also be prepared to abandon what you think you know and accept new experiences as you go. Let's revisit your research question:

RESEARCH QUESTION

Do ethnic minorities have difficulty in accessing social services?

In your literature review, you would want to focus on definitions and theories related to discrimination within the social services. In the positivistic research approach, you reviewed the literature to search for meaningful variables that could be measured. You do not want, however, to rely on the literature to define key variables in your interpretive study. Rather, you will rely upon the interpretive research process itself to identify key variables and how they relate to one another. Remember, the identification and refinement of these variables will be coming from your research participants.

In rare occasions, hypotheses can be used in an interpretive research study. They can focus your research question even further. A hypothesis in an interpretive study is less likely to be outright accepted or rejected, as is the case in a positivistic study. Rather, it's a working hypothesis and is refined over time as new data are collected. Box 6.1 describes how to formulate interpretive research questions.

Your hypothesis is changed throughout the interpretive research process based on the reasoning of the researcher, not on any statistical test. So all of this leads us to ask the question, "What do interpretive researchers actually do when they carry out a research study?" Neuman (2012) has outlined several activities that interpretive researchers engage in when carrying out their studies:

- Observes ordinary events and activities as they happen in natural settings, in addition to any unusual occurrences.

- Is directly involved with the people being studied and personally experiences the process of daily social life in the field.

- Acquires an insider's point of view while maintaining the analytic perspective or distance of an outsider.

- Uses a variety of techniques and social skills in a flexible manner as the situation demands.

- Produces data in the form of extensive written notes, as well as diagrams, maps, or pictures to provide detailed descriptions.

- Sees events holistically (e.g., as a whole unit, not in pieces) and individually in their social context.

- Understands and develops empathy for members in a field setting, and does not just record "cold" objective facts.

- Notices both explicit and tacit aspects of culture.

✱ Observes ongoing social processes without upsetting, disrupting, or imposing an outside point of view.

✱ Is capable of coping with high levels of personal stress, uncertainty, ethical dilemmas, and ambiguity.

PHASE 3A: DESIGNING THE RESEARCH STUDY

YOU CAN ENTER into an interpretive research study with general research questions or working hypotheses. However, you are far less concerned about homing in on specific variables. Because interpretive research studies are inductive processes, you do not want to constrain yourself with preconceived ideas about how your concepts or variables will relate to one another.

Thus, while you will have a list of key concepts, and perhaps loosely defined variables, you want to remain open to the possibilities of how they are defined by your research participants and any relationships that your research participants may draw. In short, your research participants will refine the variables as your study progresses.

An interpretive study is aimed at an in-depth understanding of a few cases, rather than a general understanding of many cases or people. Thus, more often than not, the number of research participants in an interpretive study is much smaller than in a positivistic one. As discussed in Chapter 9, you will probably want to use a purposeful sampling strategy to select your research participants: a process that selects the "best-fitting" people to provide data for your study.

The interpretive research approach is about studying a social phenomenon within its natural context. As such, the case study is a major interpretive research design. A case can be a person, a group, a community, an organization, or an event. You can study many different types of social phenomena within any one of these cases. Any case study design can be guided by different interpretive research methods.

SELECTING AN INTERPRETIVE RESEARCH APPROACH

Punch (2009) suggests you ask yourself a series of questions before finally selecting an interpretive research approach to answer your research question:

1. What exactly am I trying to find out? Different questions require different methods to answer them.

2. What kind of focus on my topic do I want to achieve? Do I want to study this phenomenon or situation in detail? Or am I mainly interested in making standardized and systematic comparisons and in accounting for variance?

3. How have other researchers dealt with this topic? To what extent do I wish to align my project with this literature?

4. What practical considerations should sway my choice? For instance, how long might my study take, and do I have the resources to study it this way? Can I get access to the single case I want to study in depth? Are quantitative samples and data readily available?

5. Will I learn more about this topic using positivistic or interpretive methods? What will be the knowledge payoff of each method?

6. What seems to work best for me? Am I committed to a particular research model, which implies a particular methodology? Do I have a gut feeling about what a good piece of interpretive research looks like?

BOX 6.1

Formulating Interpretive Research Questions

Interpretive analyses seek to capture the richness of people's experiences in their own terms. Understanding and meaning emerge from in-depth analysis of detailed descriptions and verbatim quotations. The following example, one nurse's responses to a closed- and open-ended question on a survey, illustrates what is meant by depth, detail, and meaning. The first question was from a closed-ended question on a survey questionnaire:

Quantitative Question:

Accountability, as practiced in our primary health-care system, creates an undesirable atmosphere of anxiety among nurses.

___1. Strongly agree

___2. Agree

___3. Disagree

___4. Strongly disagree

One nurse marked "strongly agree" to the above question. Now compare this response (1) to her response to the following open-ended question:

Qualitative Question:

Please add any personal comments you'd like to make in your own words about any part of the primary health-care system's accountability approach.

> **Her Response:**
>
> "Fear" is the word for "accountability" as applied in our system. Accountability is a political ploy to maintain power and control us. The disappointment in our system is incredible. You wouldn't believe the new layers of administration that have been created just to keep this system going. Come down and visit us in hell sometime.
>
> These two responses illustrate one kind of difference that can exist between qualitative data derived from responses to open-ended questions and quantitative measurement. Quantitative measures are succinct and easily aggregated for analysis; they are systematic, standardized, and easily presented in a short space.
>
> By contrast, qualitative responses are longer and more detailed; analysis is difficult because responses are neither systematic nor standardized. The open-ended response permits one to understand the world as seen by the respondent.
>
> Direct quotations are a basic source of raw data in interpretive studies. They reveal the respondent's level of emotion, and his/her thoughts, experiences, and basic perceptions.
>
> It's important to keep in mind that the purposes and functions of qualitative and quantitative data on questionnaires are different, yet complementary. The statistics from standardized items make summaries, comparisons, and generalizations quite easy and precise. The narrative comments from open-ended questions are typically meant to provide a forum for explanations, meanings, and new ideas.

Answering the six questions shows that an interpretive research approach is not always appropriate to every research problem. For example, following Item 2, if you are mainly interested in making systematic comparisons in order to account for the variance in some phenomenon (e.g., crime or suicide rates), then a positivistic research study is indicated.

Equally, and as a general rule, if it turns out that published research on your topic is largely positivistic (Item 5), does it pay to swim against the tide? It makes a lot of sense if you can align your work with a previous classic study. The last thing you want to do is to try to reinvent the wheel!

PHASE 3B: COLLECTING THE DATA

INTERPRETIVE RESEARCHERS are the principal instruments of data collection. This means that the data collected are somehow "processed" through the person collecting them. Interviewing, for example, is a common data collection method that produces text data. Data collection in the interview is interactive, where you can check out your understanding and interpretation of your participants' responses as you go along. To collect meaningful text data, you want to be immersed into the context or setting of the study.

You want to have some understanding, for example, of what it's like to be a client of social services before you launch into a dialogue with clients about their experiences of discrimination, if any, within the social services. If you do not have a grasp of the setting in which you are about to participate, then you run the risk of misinterpreting what is told to you.

Given that your general research question evolves in an interpretive study, the data collection process is particularly vulnerable to biases of the data collector. There are three principles to guide you in your data collection efforts:

- *First,* you want to make every effort to be aware of your own biases. In fact, your own notes on reactions and biases to what you are studying are used as sources of data later on, when you interpret the data (Chapter 16).

- *Second,* data collection is a two-way street. The research participants tell you their stories, and, in turn, you tell them your understanding or interpretation of their stories. It's a process of checks and balances.

- *Third,* interpretive data collection typically involves multiple data sources and multiple data collection methods. In your study, you may see clients, line-level social workers, and supervisors as potential data sources. You may collect data from each of these groups using interviews, observation, and existing documentation (data collection methods).

PHASES 3C AND 3D: ANALYZING AND INTERPRETING THE DATA

COLLECTING, ANALYZING, AND INTERPRETING qualitative data are highly intermingled. Let's say that, in your first round of data collection, you interview a number of ethnic minority clients about their perceptions of racial discrimination in the social services. Suppose they consistently tell you that to be a client of social services they must give up many of their cultural values. You could then develop more specific research questions for a second round of interviews in an effort to gain more of an in-depth understanding of the relationship between cultural values and being a social service client.

Overall, the process of analyzing qualitative data is an iterative one. This means that you must read and reread the volumes of data that you collected. You simply look for patterns and themes that help to capture how your research participants are experiencing the problem you are studying.

The ultimate goal is to interpret data in such a way that the true expressions of your research participants are revealed. You want to explain meaning according to the beliefs and experiences of those who provided the data. The aim is for you to walk the walk and talk the talk of your research participants and not to impose outside meaning on the data they have provided. Much more will be said about analyzing and interpreting qualitative data in Chapter 16.

PHASE 4: DISSEMINATION OF FINDINGS

INTERPRETIVE RESEARCH REPORTS are lengthier than positivistic ones. This is because it's not possible to strip the context of an interpretive study and present only its findings. The knowledge gained from an interpretive endeavor is nested within the context from which it was derived. Furthermore, text data are more awkward and clumsy to summarize than numerical data.

Unlike positivistic studies, you cannot rely on a simple figure or table to indicate a finding. Instead, you display text usually in the form of quotes or summary notes to support your conclusions. Much more will be said about the presentation and dissemination of interpretive research studies in Chapter 18.

COMPARING APPROACHES

Both research approaches can be compared on their philosophical differences. By comparing the philosophical underpinnings of positivistic and interpretive research approaches, you can more fully appreciate their important differences. Each approach offers you a unique method of studying a social work–related problem, and the same research problem can be studied using either approach.

Suppose for a moment that you are interested in a broad social problem such as racial discrimination. In particular, let's say you are interested in studying the social problem of racial discrimination within public social service programs. Let's now look at the major differences between the two approaches and see how your research problem, racial discrimination, could be studied under both approaches when taking the following four concepts into account:

— Perceptions of Reality

— Ways of Knowing

— Value Bases

— Applications

PERCEPTIONS OF REALITY

✻ *Positivistic.* Ethnic minorities share similar experiences within the public social service system. These experiences can be described objectively; that is, a single reality exists outside any one person.

✻ *Interpretive.* Individual and ethnic group experiences within the public social service system are unique. Their experiences can only be described subjectively; that is, a single and unique reality exists within each person.

WAYS OF KNOWING

✻ *Positivistic.* The experience of ethnic minorities within public social services is made known by closely examining specific parts of their experiences. Scientific principles, rules, and tests of sound reasoning are used to guide the research process.

✻ *Interpretive.* The experience of ethnic minorities within public social services is made known by capturing the whole experiences of a few cases. Parts of their experiences are considered only in relation to the whole of them. Sources of knowledge are illustrated through stories, diagrams, and pictures that are shared by the people with their unique life experiences.

VALUE BASES

✻ *Positivistic.* The researchers suspend all their values related to ethnic minorities and social services from the steps taken within the research study. The research participant "deposits" data, which are screened, organized, and analyzed by the researchers who do not attribute any personal meaning to the research participants or to the data they provide.

✻ *Interpretive.* The researcher is the research process, and any personal values, beliefs, and experiences of the researcher will influence the research process. The researcher learns from the research participants, and their interaction is mutual.

APPLICATIONS

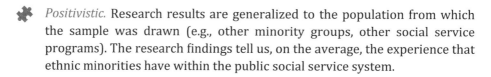

Positivistic. Research results are generalized to the population from which the sample was drawn (e.g., other minority groups, other social service programs). The research findings tell us, on the average, the experience that ethnic minorities have within the public social service system.

Interpretive. Research results tell a story of a few individuals' or one group's experience within the public social service system. The research findings provide an in-depth understanding of a few people. The life context of each research participant is key to understanding the stories he or she tells.

SIMILAR FEATURES

SO FAR we have been focusing on the differences between the two research approaches. They also have many similarities. First, they both use careful and diligent research processes in an effort to discover and interpret knowledge. They both are guided by systematic procedures and orderly plans.

Second, both approaches can be used to study any particular social problem. The positivistic approach is more effective than the interpretive approach in reaching a specific and precise understanding of one aspect (or part) of an already well-defined social problem. The positivistic approach seeks to answer research questions that ask about quantity, such as:

Are women more depressed than men?

Does low income predict one's level of self-concept?

Do child sexual abuse investigation teams reduce the number of times an alleged victim is questioned by professionals?

Is degree of aggression related to severity of crimes committed among inmates?

An interpretive research approach, on the other hand, aims to answer research questions that provide you with a more comprehensive understanding of a social problem from an intensive study of a few people. This approach is usually conducted within the context of the research participants' natural environments (Rubin & Babbie, 2010). Research questions that would be relevant to the interpretive research approach might include:

❋ How do women experience depression as compared with men?

❋ How do individuals with low income define their self-concept?

❋ How do professionals on child sexual abuse investigation teams work together to make decisions?

❋ How do federal inmates describe their own aggression in relation to the crimes they have committed?

As you will see throughout this book, not only can both approaches be used to study the same social problem, they both can be used to study the same research question. Whichever approach is used clearly has an impact on the type of findings produced to answer a research question (or to test a hypothesis).

USING BOTH APPROACHES IN A SINGLE STUDY

Given the seemingly contradictory philosophical beliefs associated with the two research approaches, it's difficult to imagine how they could exist together in a single research study. As it stands, most research studies incorporate only one approach. The reason may, in part, relate to philosophy, but practical considerations of cost, time, and resources are also factors.

It's not unusual, however, to see quantitative data used within an interpretive study or qualitative data in a positivistic one. Just think that, if you were to use a positivistic approach, there is no reason why you could not ask research participants a few open-ended questions to more fully explain their experiences. In this instance, your positivistic research report would contain some pieces of qualitative data to help bring meaning to the study's quantitative findings.

Let's say you want to proceed with an interpretive research study to examine your research question about discrimination within the public social service system. Surely you would want to identify how many research participants were included, as well as important defining characteristics such as their average age, the number who had difficulty accessing social services, or the number who were satisfied with the services they received.

Although it's possible to incorporate interpretive research activity into a positivistic study (and positivistic research activity into an interpretive study), the approach you finally select must be guided by your purpose for conducting the study in the first place. Ultimately, all research studies are about the pursuit of knowledge. Just what kind of knowledge you are after is up to you.

WHAT DO YOU REALLY WANT TO KNOW?

AS MENTIONED PREVIOUSLY, both research approaches have their advantages and disadvantages, and both shine in different phases within the research method. Which approach you select for a particular study depends not on whether you are a positivist or an interpretivist but on what particular research question your study is trying to answer. Are you looking for descriptions or explanations? If the former, an interpretive study will be spot on; if the latter, a positivistic one will do the trick.

Human nature being what it is, we are always looking, in the end, for explanation. We want to know not only what reality is like but also what its interconnections are and what we can do to change it to make our lives more comfortable and safer. However, first things first: description comes before explanation. Before you can know whether poverty is related to child abuse, for example, you must be able to describe both poverty and child abuse as fully as possible. Similarly, if you want to know whether low self-esteem in women contributes to spousal abuse, you must know what self-esteem is and what constitutes abuse.

By now, because you are a social worker interested in people and not numbers, you may be ready to throw the whole positivistic research approach out the window. But let's be sure that you don't throw out the baby with the bath water. Social work values dictate that you make room for different approaches to knowledge development, different opinions, and differing views on what reality really is. Believe us, the two different approaches each have value in their own way, depending on what kind of data (quantitative and/or qualitative) you hope to gain from a particular research study.

EXAMPLE OF USING BOTH APPROACHES IN A SINGLE STUDY

SUPPOSE, FOR EXAMPLE, you have an assumption that caesarian operations are being conducted too often and unnecessarily for the convenience of obstetricians rather than for the benefit of mothers and their babies. To confirm or refute this hunch (it has yet to be proven), you would need data on the number of caesarian births in a particular time frame, and on how many of them were justified on the basis of medical need. Numbers would be required—quantitative data.

The questions about how many and how often could not be answered solely by descriptions of Ms. Smith's individual experiences. On the other hand, Ms. Smith's experiences would certainly lend richness to the part of your study that asked how far the hospital's services took the well-being of mothers into account.

Many of the best research studies use positivistic and interpretive methods within the same study. It's important to remember that the former provides the necessary numerical data while the latter provides the human depth that allows for a richer understanding of the numbers in their particular context.

Sometimes, therefore, depending on the research question (assumption) to be answered, Ms. Smith will be seen as no more than a number. At other times, her individuality will be of paramount importance. If she is seen as a number, for example, her role will be passive. She will be one of a large number of persons.

On the other hand, if she is seen as an individual, her part in the research study will be far more active. It's her reality that you are now exploring. She will be front and center in a research study that is driven by her and not the researcher. Even the language will change. She is no longer a subject—or possibly an object—but a full and equal participant, along with the researcher.

Advantages and Disadvantages

According to Colorado State University's Writing Center (2011), interpretive research has several advantages and disadvantages.

ADVANTAGES

- Accounts for the complexity of group behaviors

- Reveals interrelationships among multifaceted dimensions of group interactions

- Provides context for behaviors

- Reveals qualities of group experience in a way that other forms of research cannot

- Helps determine questions and types of follow-up research

- Reveals descriptions of behaviors in context by stepping outside the group

- Allows interpretive researchers to identify recurring patterns of behavior that participants may be unable to recognize

Interpretive research expands the range of knowledge and understanding of the world beyond the researchers themselves. It often helps us see why something is the way it is, rather than just presenting a phenomenon. For instance, a positivistic study may find that students who are taught composition using a process method receive higher grades on papers than students taught using a product method. However, an interpretive study of composition instructors could reveal why many of them still use the product method even though they are aware of the benefits of the process method.

DISADVANTAGES

* Researcher bias can bias the design of a study.

* Researcher bias can enter into data collection.

* Sources or participants may not all be equally credible.

* Some participants may have been previously influenced and may affect the outcome of the study.

* Background information may be missing.

* Study group may not be representative of the larger population.

* Analysis of observations can be biased.

* Any group that is studied is altered to some degree by the very presence of the researcher, which somewhat skews any data collected.

* Building trust with participants to facilitate full and honest self-representation takes time. Short-term observational studies are at a particular disadvantage where trust building is concerned.

* The quality of the data alone can be problematic. Ethnographic research is time consuming, potentially expensive, and requires a well-trained researcher.

* Too few data can lead to false assumptions about behavior patterns. Conversely, a large quantity of data may not be effectively processed.

* The data collector's first impressions can bias data collection.

* Narrative inquiries do not lend themselves well to replicability and are not generalizable.

* Narrative inquiries are considered unreliable by experimentalists. However, ethnographies can be assessed and compared for certain variables to yield testable explanations, which is as close as ethnographic research gets to being empirical in nature.

Interpretive research is neither prescriptive nor definite. Such research provides significant data about groups or cultures and prompts new research questions, but narrative studies do not attempt to answer questions, nor are they predictive of future behaviors.

SUMMARY

As we know from the left side of Figure 2.3, social work research questions can be placed on a continuum depending on how much knowledge is already known about the subject. The right side indicates the research approach(es) that can be used to answer these questions.

As can be easily seen, there are three main types of questions that interpretive research approaches can answer: existence questions, composition questions, and relationship questions. However, as you know from reading this chapter, qualitative data can easily be gathered within positivistic studies as well.

This chapter briefly discussed the interpretive research approach to knowledge building and also highlighted a few differences and similarities between the positivistic and interpretive research approaches. These two complementary and respected research approaches are divergent in terms of their philosophical principles. Yet they both generate useful knowledge for our profession. They simply complement each other by providing different kinds of data (quantitative via positivistic studies, and qualitative via interpretive studies).

The most important thing to remember is that the research question finally proposed determines which research approach(es) is(are) utilized to answer the question; that is, the question always guides the research approach—the research approach should never guide the question.

This is the last chapter in Part II of our book, which is devoted to the generation of knowledge via briefly describing two research approaches. In a nutshell, both research approaches measure variables (in their own way, of course), and these variables need to be measured to produce data—the focus of Part III.

Study Questions for Chapter 6

— First, answer each question only AFTER you have read the chapter.

— Second, indicate how comfortable you were in answering each question on a 5-point scale:

1	2	3	4	5
Very uncomfortable	Somewhat uncomfortable	Neutral	Somewhat comfortable	Very comfortable

If you rated any question between 1–3, please reread the section of the chapter where the information for the question can be found. If you're still uncomfortable answering the question, talk with your instructor and/or your classmates for more clarification.

Questions	Degree of comfort? (Circle one number)
1. Discuss the interpretive way of thinking. Now discuss the positivistic way of thinking. Compare and contrast the two ways of thinking using one common social work example throughout your discussion.	1 2 3 4 5
2. What kind of data do positivistic research studies produce? What kind of data do interpretive research studies produce? Provide social work examples for each research approach.	1 2 3 4 5
3. How many realities do positivistic researchers believe to exist? How many for interpretive researchers? Compare and contrast their differential perceptions of realities. Use as many social work examples that you can think of to illustrate your points.	1 2 3 4 5
4. Discuss the differential roles that research participants play within positivistic and interpretive research studies. Provide examples to illustrate your points.	1 2 3 4 5
5. Discuss the differences between data and information. Use a social work example throughout your discussion.	1 2 3 4 5
6. Discuss the term "value awareness" in reference to positivistic and interpretive studies. Provide social work examples to illustrate your points.	1 2 3 4 5
7. List, discuss, and provide social work examples of the commonalities in all interpretive research studies.	1 2 3 4 5

8.	List, discuss, and provide specific social work examples of all the phases within the interpretive research approach.	1 2 3 4 5
9.	Provide one common social work example when comparing both research approaches in reference to their philosophical differences.	1 2 3 4 5
10.	Provide one common social work example when comparing both research approaches in reference to their differential perceptions of reality.	1 2 3 4 5
11.	List, discuss, and provide specific social work examples of the two research approaches in reference to their similarities.	1 2 3 4 5
12.	Discuss in detail how you would go about combining both research approaches in a single social work study.	1 2 3 4 5
13.	At this point in your course, how comfortable are you with discussing the interpretive research approach to knowledge generation with your field instructor (or your supervisor at work)? With your fellow classmates? Discuss in detail.	1 2 3 4 5
14.	List and discuss the five criteria that you will use to evaluate all social work hypotheses. Provide a social work example for each criterion.	1 2 3 4 5
15.	At this point in your course, how comfortable are you with discussing the positivistic research approach to knowledge generation with your field instructor (or your supervisor at work)? With your fellow classmates? Discuss in detail.	1 2 3 4 5

Assessing Your Self-Efficacy for Chapter 6

AFTER you have read the chapter AND have completed all the study questions, please indicate how knowledgeable you feel you are for each concept listed below.

1	2	3	4	5
Very uncomfortable	Somewhat uncomfortable	Neutral	Somewhat comfortable	Very comfortable

Major Concepts in Chapter	Knowledge Level? (Circle one number)
1. The interpretive way of thinking	1 2 3 4 5
2. Data verses information	1 2 3 4 5
3. Realities	1 2 3 4 5
4. Commonalities of all interpretive research studies	1 2 3 4 5
5. Phases of the interpretive research approach	1 2 3 4 5
6. Criteria for selecting an interpretive research approach to knowledge generation	1 2 3 4 5
7. Philosophical differences between the positivistic and interpretive research approaches	1 2 3 4 5
8. Using both a positivistic and an interpretive research approach within the same study	1 2 3 4 5
9. Advantages of the interpretive research approach to knowledge generation	1 2 3 4 5
10. Disadvantages of using the interpretive research approach to knowledge generation	1 2 3 4 5
Add up your scores (Minimum = 10, Maximum = 50)	Total score =

A   45 — 50 = Social Work Manager in the making.
B   40 — 44 = Social Work Supervisor.
C   35 — 39 = Social Work Practitioner.
D   10 — 34 = Case Aide. Reread the chapter and redo the study questions.

PART III
Measuring Variables

7

Measurement

The ultimate measure of a man is not where he stands in moments of comfort and convenience, but where he stands at times of challenge and controversy.
~ Potter Stewart

The measurement of variables is the cornerstone of all social work positivistic research studies. Shining and formidable measuring instruments may come to mind, measuring things to several decimal places. The less scientifically inclined might merely picture rulers, but, in any case, measurement for most of us means reducing something to numbers. As we know, these "somethings" are called variables, and all variables can take on different measurement levels.

 ## LEVELS OF MEASUREMENT

Our discussion of measurement levels has been adapted and modified from Williams, Tutty, and Grinnell (1995). As we know from Chapter 5, the characteristics that describe a variable are known as its *attributes*. The variable *gender*, for example, has only two attributes—*male* and *female*—because gender in humans is limited to male and female, and there are no other categories or ways of describing gender.

The variable *ethnicity* has a number of possible attributes: *African American, Native American, Asian, Latino American,* and *Caucasian* are just five examples of the many attributes of the variable ethnicity. A point to note here is that the attributes of gender differ in kind from one another—male is different from female—and, in the same way, the attributes of ethnicity are also different from one another.

Now consider the variable *income*. Income can only be described in terms of amounts of money: $15,000 per year, $288.46 per week, and so forth. In whatever terms a person's income is actually described, it still comes down to a number. Because every number has its own category, as we mentioned before, the variable income can generate as many categories as there are numbers, up to the number covering the research participant who earns the most.

These numbers are all attributes of income, and they are all different, but they are not different in *kind*, as male and female are, or Native American and Latino; they are only different in *quantity*. In other words, the attributes of income differ in that they represent more or less of the same thing whereas the attributes of gender differ in that they represent different kinds of things.

Income will, therefore, be measured in a different way from gender. When we want to measure income, for example, we will be looking for categories (attributes) that are *lower* or *higher* than each other; on the other hand, when we measure gender, we will be looking for categories (attributes) that *are different in kind* from each other.

Mathematically, there is not much we can do with categories that are different in kind. We cannot subtract Latinos from Caucasians, for example, whereas we can quite easily subtract one person's annual income from another and come up with a meaningful difference. As far as mathematical computations are concerned, we are obliged to work at a lower level of complexity when we measure variables like ethnicity than when we measure variables like income. Depending on the nature of their attributes, all variables can be measured at one (or more) of four measurement levels:

— Nominal

— Ordinal

— Interval

— Ratio

NOMINAL MEASUREMENT

NOMINAL MEASUREMENT is the lowest level of measurement and is used to measure variables whose attributes are different in kind. As we have seen, gender is one variable measured at a nominal level, and ethnicity is another. *Place of birth* is a third, because "born in California," for example, is different from "born in Chicago," and we cannot add "born in California" to "born in Chicago," or subtract them or divide them, or do anything statistically interesting with them at all.

ORDINAL MEASUREMENT

ORDINAL MEASUREMENT is a higher level of measurement than nominal and is used to measure those variables whose attributes can be rank ordered: for example, socioeconomic status, sexism, racism, client satisfaction, and the like. If we intend to measure *client satisfaction*, we must first develop a list of all the possible attributes of client satisfaction: that is, we must think of all the possible categories into which answers about client satisfaction might be placed.

Some clients will be *very satisfied*—one category, at the high end of the satisfaction continuum; some will be *not at all satisfied*—a separate category, at the low end of the continuum; and others will be *generally satisfied*, *moderately satisfied*, or *somewhat satisfied*—three more categories, at differing points on the continuum, as illustrated:

1. Not at all satisfied

2. Somewhat satisfied

3. Moderately satisfied

4. Generally satisfied

5. Very satisfied

The preceding is a 5-point scale with a brief description of the degree of satisfaction represented by the point (i.e., 1, 2, 3, 4, 5). Of course, we may choose to express the anchors in different words, substituting *extremely satisfied* for *very satisfied*, or *fairly satisfied* for *generally satisfied*. We may select a 3-point scale instead, limiting the choices to *very satisfied*, *moderately satisfied,* and *not at all satisfied*; or we may even use a 10-point scale if we believe that our respondents will be able to rate their satisfaction with that degree of accuracy.

Whichever particular method is selected, some sort of scale is the only measurement option available because there is no other way to categorize client satisfaction except in terms of more satisfaction or less satisfaction. As we did with nominal measurement, we might assign numbers to each of the points on the scale. If we used the 5-point scale as illustrated above, we might assign:

- ✳ 5 to *very satisfied*

- ✳ 4 to *generally satisfied*

- ✳ 3 to *moderately satisfied*

- ✳ 2 to *somewhat satisfied*

- ✳ 1 to *not at all satisfied*

Here, the numbers do have some mathematical meaning. Five (*very satisfied*) is in fact better than 4 (*generally satisfied*), 4 is better than 3, 3 is better than 2, and 2 is better than 1. The numbers, however, say nothing about *how much better* any category is than any other. We cannot assume that the difference in satisfaction between *very* and *generally* is the same as the difference between *generally* and *moderately*.

In short, we cannot assume that the intervals between the anchored points on the scale are all the same length. Most definitely, we cannot assume that a client who rates a service at 4 (*generally satisfied*) is twice as satisfied as a client who rates the service at 2 (*somewhat satisfied*).

In fact, we cannot attempt any mathematical manipulation at all. We cannot add the numbers 1, 2, 3, 4, and 5, nor can we subtract, multiply, or divide them. As its name might suggest, all we can know from ordinal measurement is the order of the categories.

INTERVAL MEASUREMENT

SOME VARIABLES, such as client satisfaction, have attributes that can be rank-ordered—from *very satisfied* to *not at all satisfied*, as we have just discussed. As we saw, however, these attributes cannot be assumed to be the same distance apart if they are placed on a scale; and, in any case, the distance they are apart has no real meaning. No one can measure the distance between *very satisfied* and *moderately satisfied*; we only know that the one is better than the other.

Conversely, for some variables, the distance, or interval, separating their attributes *does* have meaning, and these variables can be measured at the interval level. An example in physical science would is the Fahrenheit or Celsius temperature scales. The difference between 80 degrees and 90 degrees is the same as the difference between 40 and 50 degrees. Eighty degrees is not twice as hot as 40 degrees; nor does zero degrees mean no heat at all.

In social work, interval measures are most commonly used in connection with standardized measuring instruments, as presented in Chapter 8. When we look at a standardized intelligence test, for example, we can say that the difference between IQ scores of 100 and 110 is the same as the difference between IQ scores of 95 and 105, based on the scores obtained by the many thousands of people who have taken the test over the years. As with the temperature scales, a person with an IQ score of 120 is not twice as intelligent as a person with a score of 60, nor does a score of 0 mean no intelligence at all.

RATIO MEASUREMENT

THE HIGHEST LEVEL of measurement, ratio measurement, is used to measure variables whose attributes are based on a true zero point. It may not be possible to have zero intelligence, but it's certainly possible to have zero children or zero money. Whenever a question about a particular variable might elicit the answer "none" or "never," that variable can be measured at the ratio level.

The question "How many times have you seen your social worker?" might be answered "Never." Other variables commonly measured at the ratio level include length of residence in a given place, age, number of times married, number of organizations belonged to, number of antisocial behaviors, number of case reviews, number of training sessions, number of supervisory meetings, and so forth. With a ratio level of measurement, we can meaningfully interpret the comparison between two scores.

A person who is 40 years of age, for example, is twice as old as a person who is 20 and half as old as a person who is 80. Children aged 2 and 5, respectively, are the same distance apart as children aged 6 and 9. Data resulting from ratio measurement can be added, subtracted, multiplied, and divided. Averages can be calculated, and other statistical analyses can be performed.

It's useful to note that although some variables *can* be measured at a higher level, they may not need to be. The variable *income*, for example, can be measured at a ratio level because it's possible to have a zero income, but, for the purposes of a particular study, we may not need to know the actual incomes of our research participants, only the range within which their incomes fall.

A person who is asked how much he or she earns may be reluctant to give a figure ("mind your own business" is a perfectly legitimate response) but may not object to checking one of a number of income categories, choosing, for example, between:

1. less than $5,000 per year

2. $5,001 to $15,000 per year

3. $15,001 to $25,000 per year

4. $25,001 to $35,000 per year

5. more than $35,000 per year

Categorizing income in this way reduces the measurement from the ratio level to the ordinal level. It will now be possible to know only that a person checking Category 1 earns less than a person checking Category 2, and so on. We will not know *how much* less or more one person earns than another and we will not be able to perform statistical tasks such as calculating average incomes, but we will be able to say, for example, that 50 percent of our sample falls into Category 1, 30 percent into Category 2, 15 percent into Category 3, and 5 percent into Category 4. If we are conducting a study to see how many people fall in each income range, this may be all we need to know.

In the same way, we might not want to know the actual ages of our sample, only the range in which they fall. For some studies, it might be enough to measure age at a nominal level—to inquire, for example, whether people were born during the Depression, or whether they were born before or after 1990. When studying variables that can be measured at any level, the measurement level chosen depends on what kind of data are needed, and this in turn is determined by why the data are needed, which in turn is determined by our research question.

DESCRIBING VARIABLES BY MEASURING THEM

The purpose of measuring a variable is to describe it as completely and accurately as possible. Often, the most complete and accurate possible description of a variable involves not only numbers but also words—numbers through the positivist approach and words through the interpretive approach.

When doing any research study—positivistic or interpretive—we need to describe the variables we are studying as accurately and completely as possible for four reasons:

— Correspondence

— Standardization

— Quantification

— Duplication

CORRESPONDENCE

CORRESPONDENCE MEANS making a link between what we measure and/or observe and the theories we have developed to explain what we have measured and/or observed. For example, the concept of attachment theory can easily explain the different behaviors (variables) of small children when they are separated from—or reunited with—their mothers.

Measuring and recording children's behaviors in this context provide a link between the abstract and the concrete—between attachment (an unspecific and nonmeasurable concept) and its indicators, or variables, such as a child's behaviors (a more specific and more measurable variable).

STANDARDIZATION

VARIABLES CAN BE COMPLEX, and the more complex they are the more likely it is that people will interpret the exact same variable in different ways. Like concepts, a single variable can at times mean different things to different people, even when using the same words.

"Self-esteem," for example, can mean different things to different people. However, the perceptions linked to self-esteem (that is, the empirical indicators of self-esteem) may be drawn together in the form of a measuring instrument, as they are in Hudson's *Index of Self-Esteem* (Figure 7.1).

You may or may not agree that all of the 25 items, or questions, contained in Hudson's *Index of Self-Esteem* together reflect what you mean by self-esteem—but at least you know what Hudson meant, and so does everyone else who is using his measuring instrument. By constructing this instrument, Hudson has *standardized* a complex variable so that everyone using his instrument will mean the same thing by the variable and measure it in the same way.

Moreover, if two or more different researchers use his instrument with the same research participants, they ought to get approximately the same results. The use of the word "approximately" here means that we must allow for a bit of error—something discussed at the end of this chapter.

QUANTIFICATION

QUANTIFICATION MEANS nothing more than defining the level of a variable in terms of a single number, or score. The use of Hudson's *Index of Self-Esteem*, for example, results in a single number, or score, obtained by following the scoring instructions. Reducing a complex variable such as self-esteem to a single number has disad-

Name:_____   Today's Date:_____

This questionnaire is designed to measure how you see yourself. It is not a test, so there are no right or wrong answers. Please answer each item as carefully and as accurately as you can by placing a number beside each one as follows:

> 1 = None of the time
> 2 = Very rarely
> 3 = A little of the time
> 4 = Some of the time
> 5 = A good part of the time
> 6 = Most of the time
> 7 = All of the time

1. ____ I feel that people would not like me if they really knew me well.
2. ____ I feel that others get along much better than I do.
3. ____ I feel that I am a beautiful person.
4. ____ When I am with others I feel they are glad I am with them.
5. ____ I feel that people really like to talk with me.
6. ____ I feel that I am a very competent person.
7. ____ I think I make a good impression on others.
8. ____ I feel that I need more self-confidence.
9. ____ When I am with strangers I am very nervous.
10. ____ I think that I am a dull person.
11. ____ I feel ugly.
12. ____ I feel that others have more fun than I do.
13. ____ I feel that I bore people.
14. ____ I think my friends find me interesting.
15. ____ I think I have a good sense of humor.
16. ____ I feel very self-conscious when I am with strangers.
17. ____ I feel that if I could be more like other people I would have it made.
18. ____ I feel that people have a good time when they are with me.
19. ____ I feel like a wallflower when I go out.
20. ____ I feel I get pushed around more than others.
21. ____ I think I am a rather nice person.
22. ____ I feel that people really like me very much.
23. ____ I feel that I am a likeable person.
24. ____ I am afraid I will appear foolish to others.
25. ____ My friends think very highly of me.

_____

Copyright © 1993, Walter W. Hudson Illegal to Photocopy or Otherwise Reproduce
3, 4, 5, 6, 7, 14, 15, 18, 21, 22, 23, 25

FIGURE 7.1

Hudson's *Index of Self-Esteem*

AUTHOR: Walter W. Hudson

PURPOSE: To measure problems with self-esteem.

DESCRIPTION: The ISE is a 25-item scale designed to measure the degree, severity, or magnitude of a problem the client has with self-esteem. Self-esteem is considered as the evaluative component of self-concept. The ISE is written in very simple language, is easily administered, and is easily scored. Because problems with self-esteem are often central to social and psychological difficulties, this instrument has a wide range of utility for a number of clinical problems.

The ISE has a cutting score of 30 (+ or −5), with scores above 30 indicating the respondent has a clinically significant problem and scores below 30 indicating the individual has no such problem. Another advantage of the ISE is that it is one of nine scales of the *Clinical Measurement Package* (Hudson, 1982), all of which are administered and scored the same way.

NORMS: This scale was derived from tests of 1,745 respondents, including single and married individuals, clinical and nonclinical populations, college students and nonstudents. Respondents included Caucasians, Japanese, and Chinese Americans, and a smaller number of members of other ethnic groups. Not recommended for use with children under the age of 12.

SCORING: For a detailed description on how to score the ISE, see: Bloom, Fischer, and Orme (2009) or go to: www.walmyr.com.

RELIABILITY: The ISE has a mean alpha of .93, indicating excellent internal consistency, and an excellent (low) S.E.M. of 3.70. The ISE also has excellent stability with a two-hour test-retest correlation of .92.

VALIDITY: The ISE has good know-groups validity, significantly distinguishing between clients judged by clinicians to have problems in the area of self-esteem and those known not to. Further, the ISE has very good construct validity, correlating well with a range of other measures with which it should correlate highly, e.g., depression, happiness, sense of identity, and scores on the *Generalized Contentment Scale* (depression).

PRIMARY REFERENCE: Hudson, W.W. (1982). *The clinical measurement package: A field manual.* Chicago: Dorsey.

FIGURE 7.1A

Basic Information about the *Index of Self-Esteem*

vantages in that the richness of the variable can never be completely captured in this way.

However, it also has advantages in that numbers can be used in statistics to search for meaningful relationships between one variable and another. For example, you might hypothesize that there is a relationship between two variables: self-esteem and marital satisfaction.

Hudson has *quantified* self-esteem, allowing the self-esteem of any research participant to be represented by a single number. He has also done this for the variable of marital satisfaction. Because both variables have been broken-down to two numbers, you can use statistical methods (discussed in Chapter 15) to see whether the relationship you hypothesized actually does exist.

DUPLICATION

IN THE PHYSICAL SCIENCES, experiments are routinely replicated. For example, if you put a test-tube containing 25 ounces of a solution into an oven to see what is left when the liquid evaporates, you may use five test-tubes containing 25 ounces each, not just one. Then, you will have five identical samples of solution evaporated at the same time under the same conditions, and you will be much more certain of your results than if you had just evaporated one sample. The word *replication* means doing the same thing more than once at the same time.

In our profession, we can rarely replicate research studies, but we can *duplicate* them. That is, a second researcher can attempt to confirm a first researcher's results by doing the same thing again later on, as much as is practically possible under the same conditions. Duplication increases certainty, and it's only possible if the variables being studied have been *standardized* and *quantified*.

For example, you could duplicate another researcher's work on attachment only if you measured attachment in the same way. If you used different child behaviors to indicate attachment and you assigned different values to mean, say, weak attachment or strong attachment, you may have done a useful study, but it would not be a duplicate of the first.

CRITERIA FOR SELECTING AN INSTRUMENT

NOW THAT YOU KNOW why you need to measure variables, let us go on to look at *how* you measure them in the first place. To measure a variable, you need a measuring instrument to measure it with—much more about this topic in the following chapter. Most of the measuring instruments used in social work are paper and pencil instruments like Figure 7.1.

Many other people besides Hudson have come up with ways of measuring self-esteem, and if you want to measure self-esteem in your study, you will have to choose between the various measuring instruments that are available. The same embarrassment of riches applies to most of the other variables you might want to measure. Remember that a variable is something that varies between research participants. Participants will vary, for example, with respect to their levels of self-esteem. What you need are some criteria to help you decide which instrument is best for measuring a particular variable in any given particular situation. There are five criteria that will help you to do this:

— Utility

— Sensitivity to Small Changes

— Nonreactivity

— Reliability

— Validity

UTILITY

IN ORDER TO COMPLETE Hudson's *Index of Self-Esteem* (Figure 7.1), for example, a research participant must preferably be able to read. Even if you, as the researcher, read the items to the participants, they must be able to relate a number between 1 and 7 (where 1 = none of the time, and 7 = all of the time) to each of the 25 items, or questions.

Further, they must know what a "wallflower" is before they can answer Item 19. If the research participants in your study cannot do this for a variety of reasons, then no matter how wonderful Hudson's *Index of Self-Esteem* might be in other respects, it's not useful to you in your particular study.

Hudson's *Index of Self-Esteem* may take only a few minutes to complete, but other instruments can take far longer. The Minnesota Multiphase Personality Inventory (the MMPI), for example, can take three hours or more to complete, and some people may not have the attention span or the motivation to complete the task. In sum, a measuring instrument is not useful if your research participants are unable or unwilling to complete it for whatever reasons. If they do complete it, however, you then have to score it.

The simple measuring instrument contained in Figure 7.1 is relatively quick and simple to score, but other instruments are far more complex and time consuming.

Usually, the simple instruments—quick to complete and easy to score—are less accurate than the more demanding instruments, and you will have to decide how far you are prepared to sacrifice accuracy for utility.

The main consideration here is what you are going to do with the measurements once you have obtained them. If you are doing an assessment that might affect a client's life in terms of treatment intervention, referral, placement, and so on, accuracy is paramount, and you will need the most accurate instrument (probably the longest and most complex) that the client can tolerate.

On the other hand, if you are doing an exploratory research study where the result will be a tentative suggestion that some variable may be related to another, a little inaccuracy in measurement is not the end of the world, and utility might be more important.

Sensitivity to Small Changes

SUPPOSE THAT one of your practice objectives with your 8-year-old client Johnny is to help him stop wetting his bed during the night. One obvious indicator of the variable—bedwetting—is a wet bed. Thus, you hastily decide that you will measure Johnny's bedwetting behavior by having his mother tell you when Johnny has—or has not—wet his bed during the week. That is, Did he or did he not wet his bed at least once during the week?

However, if Johnny has reduced the number of his bed-wetting incidents from five per week to only once per week, you will not know whether your intervention was working well because just the one bedwetting incident per week was enough to officially count as "wetting the bed." In other words, the way you chose to measure Johnny's bedwetting behavior was sensitive to the large difference between wetting and not wetting in a given week, but insensitive to the smaller difference between wetting once and wetting more than once in a given week.

In order to be able to congratulate Johnny on small improvements, and of course to track his progress over time, you will have to devise a more sensitive measuring instrument, such as one that measures the number of times Johnny wets his bed per week. Often, an instrument that is more sensitive will also be less convenient to use, and you will have to balance sensitivity against utility.

Nonreactivity

A REACTIVE MEASURING INSTRUMENT is nothing more than an instrument that changes the behavior or feeling of a person that it was supposed to measure. For instance, you might have decided, in the example of Johnny, to use a device that rings a loud bell every time Johnny has a bedwetting accident.

His mother would then leap from sleep, make a check mark on the form you had provided, and fall back into a tormented doze. This would be a sensitive measure—though intrusive and thus less useful. However, it might also cause Johnny to reduce his bedwetting behavior, in accordance with behavior theory.

Clinically, this would be a good thing—unless he developed bell phobia—but it's important to make a clear distinction between an *instrument* that is designed to *measure* a behavior and an *intervention* that is designed to *change* it. If the bell wakes up Johnny so that he can go to the bathroom and thus finally eliminate his bedwetting behavior, the bell is a wonderful *intervention*. It's not a good measuring instrument, however, as it has changed the very behavior it was supposed to measure. A change in behavior resulting from the use of a measuring instrument is known as a *reactive effect*.

The ideal, then, is a *nonreactive* measuring instrument that has no effect on the variable being measured. If you want to know, for example, whether a particular intervention is effective in raising self-esteem in girls who have been sexually abused, you will need to be sure that any measured increase in self-esteem is due to the intervention and *not* to the measuring instrument you happen to be using. If you fail to make a distinction between the measuring instrument and the intervention, you will end up with no clear idea at all about what is causing what.

Sometimes, you might be tempted to use a measuring instrument as a clinical tool. If your client responded to Hudson's *Index of Self-Esteem* Item 13 (Figure 7.1) that she felt she was boring people all of the time, you might want to discuss with her the particular conversational gambits she feels are so boring in order to help her change them. This is perfectly legitimate so long as you realize that, by so doing, you have turned a measuring instrument into part of an intervention.

RELIABILITY

A GOOD MEASURING INSTRUMENT is reliable in that it gives the same score over and over again provided that the measurement is made under the same conditions and nothing about the research participant has changed. A reliable measuring instrument is obviously necessary because, if you are trying to track the increase in a client's self-esteem, for example, you need to be sure that the changes you see over time are due to changes in the client, not to inaccuracies in the measuring instrument.

Researchers are responsible for ensuring that the measuring instruments they use are reliable. Hence, it's worth looking briefly at the four main methods used to establish the reliability of a measuring instrument:

— Test-Retest Method

— Alternate Form Method

— Split-Half Method

— Observer Reliability

TEST-RETEST METHOD

The test-retest method of establishing reliability involves administering the same measuring instrument to the same group of people on two separate occasions. The two sets of results are then compared to see how similar they are; that is, how well they *correlate*. We will discuss *correlation* more fully in Chapter 15. For now, it's enough to say that correlation in this context can range from 0 to 1, where 0 means no correlation at all between the two sets of scores and 1 means a perfect correlation.

Generally, a correlation of 0.8 means that the instrument is reasonably reliable and 0.9 is very good. Note that there is a heading RELIABILITY in Figure 7.1a, which means that Hudson's *Index of Self-Esteem* has "excellent stability with a two-hour test-retest correlation of 0.92." The "two-hour" bit means, of course, that the two administrations of the instrument took place two hours apart.

The problem with completing the same instrument twice is that the answers given on the first occasion may affect the answers given on the second. This is known as a *testing effect.* For example, Ms. Smith might remember what she wrote the first time and write something different just to enliven the proceedings. She may be less anxious, or more bored or irritated the second time, just because there was a first time, and these states might affect her answers.

Obviously, the greater the testing effects, the less reliable the instrument. Moreover, the closer together the tests, the more likely testing effects become because Ms. Smith is more likely to remember the first occasion. Hence, if the instrument is reliable over an interval of two hours and you want to administer it to your study participants on occasions a day or a month apart, it should be even more reliable with respect to testing effects.

People may change their answers on a second occasion for reasons other than testing effects: they are having a good day or a bad day; or they have a cold; or there is a loud pneumatic drill just outside the window.

However, a word of caution is in order. Sometimes clients complete the same measuring instrument every few weeks for a year or more as a way of monitoring their progress over time. The more often an instrument is completed, the more likely it is to generate testing effects. Hence, social service programs that use instruments in this way need to be sure that the instruments they use are still reliable under the conditions in which they are to be used.

ALTERNATE-FORM METHOD

The second method of establishing the reliability of a measuring instrument is the alternate-form method. As the same suggests, an alternate form of an instrument is a second instrument that is as similar as possible to the original except that the wording of the items contained in the second instrument has changed. Administering the original form and then the alternate form reduces testing effects because the respondent is less likely to base the second set of answers on the first.

However, it's time-consuming to develop different but equivalent instruments, and they must still be tested for reliability using the test-retest method, both together as a pair, and separately as two distinct instruments.

SPLIT-HALF METHOD

The split-half method involves splitting one instrument in half so that it becomes two shorter instruments. Usually, all the even-numbered items, or questions, are used to make one instrument while the odd-numbered items make up the other. The point of doing this is to ensure that the original instrument is internally consistent; that is, it's homogeneous, or the same all the way through, with no longer or more difficult items appearing at the beginning or the end.

When the two halves are compared using the test-retest method, they should ideally yield the same score. If they did give the same score when one half was administered to a respondent on one occasion and the second half to the same respondent on a different occasion, they would have a perfect correlation of 1. Again, a correlation of 0.8 is thought to be good and a correlation of 0.9 very good. Figure 7.1a, under the RELIABILITY section, shows that Hudson's *Index of Self-Esteem* has an internal consistency of 0.93.

OBSERVER RELIABILITY (RELIABILITY OF THE PROCESS)

Sometimes, behaviors are measured by observing how often they occur, or how long they last, or how severe they are. The results are then recorded on a straightforward, simple form. Nevertheless, this is not as easy as it sounds because the behavior, or variable, being measured must first be very carefully defined and people observing the same behavior may have different opinions as to how severe the behavior was, or how long it lasted, or whether it occurred at all.

The level of agreement or correlation between trained observers thus provides a way of establishing the reliability of the process used to measure the behavior. Once we have established the reliability of the process, we can use the same method to as-

BOX 7.1 Major Types of Reliability	
Test-Retest Method	Does an individual respond to a measuring instrument in the same general way when the instrument is administered twice?
Alternate-Forms Method	When two forms of an instrument that are equivalent in their degree of validity are given to the same individual, is there a strong convergence in how that person responds?
Split-Half Method	Are the scores on one half of the measuring instrument similar to those obtained on the other half?
Observer Reliability	Is there an agreement between the observers who are measuring the same variable?

sess the reliability of other observers as part of their training. The level of agreement between observers is known as *inter-rater reliability*.

VALIDITY

A MEASURING INSTRUMENT is valid if it measures what it's supposed to measure—and measures it accurately. If you want to measure the variable assertiveness, for example, you don't want to mistakenly measure aggression instead.

There are several kinds of validity—in fact, we should really refer to the *validities* of an instrument—and we will look at the following four:

— Content Validity

— Criterion Validity

— Face Validity

— Construct Validity

CONTENT VALIDITY

Think for a moment about the variable self-esteem. In order to measure it accurately, you must first know what it is; that is, you must identify all the indicators (questions contained in the measuring instrument) that make up self-esteem, such as feeling that people like you, feeling that you are competent, and so on—and on and on and on ... It's probably impossible to identify *all* the indicators that contribute to self-esteem.

It's even less likely that everyone (or even most people) will agree with all the indicators identified by someone else. Arguments may arise over whether "feeling worthless," for example, is really an indicator of low self-esteem or whether it has more to do with depression, which is a separate variable altogether. Furthermore, even if agreement could be reached, a measuring instrument like Hudson's *Index of Self-Esteem* would have to include at least one item, or question, for *every* agreed-upon indicator. If just one was missed—for example, "sense of humor"—then the instrument would not be accurately measuring self-esteem.

Because it did not include all the possible content, or indicators, related to self-esteem, it would not be *content valid*. Hudson's *Index of Self-Esteem*, then, is not perfectly content valid because it's not possible to cover every indicator related to self-esteem in just 25 items. Longer instruments have a better chance of being content valid (perhaps one could do it in 25 *pages* of items), but, in general, perfect content validity cannot be achieved in any measuring instrument of a practical length. Content validity is a matter of "more or less" rather than "yes or no," and moreover it is strictly a matter of opinion.

For example, experts differ about the degree to which various instruments are content valid. It's therefore necessary to find some way of *validating* an instrument to determine how well it is, in fact, accurately measuring what it's supposed to measure. One such way is through a determination of the instrument's *criterion validity*.

CRITERION VALIDITY

An instrument has criterion validity if it gives the same result as a second instrument that is designed to measure the same variable. A client might complete Hudson's *Index of Self-Esteem*, for example, and achieve a score indicating high self-esteem. If the same client then completes a second instrument also designed to measure self-esteem and again achieves a good score, it's very likely that both instruments are, in fact, measuring self-esteem. Not only do they have good criterion validity in that they compare well with each other, but probably each instrument also has good content validity.

If the same client does not achieve similar scores on the two instruments, however, then neither of them are criterion valid, probably one is not content valid, and both will have to be compared with a third instrument to resolve the difficulty. There are two categories of criterion validity:

— Concurrent Validity

— Predictive Validity

CONCURRENT VALIDITY. Concurrent validity deals with the present. For example, suppose you have an instrument—say, a reading test—designed to distinguish between children who need remedial reading services and children who do not. To validate the measuring instrument, you ask the classroom teacher which children she thinks need remedial reading services. If the teacher and your instrument both come up with the same list of children, your instrument has criterion validity. If not, you will need to find another comparison: a different reading test or the opinion of another teacher.

In short, concurrent validity refers to the ability of a measuring instrument to predict accurately an individual's current status. An example of an instrument with concurrent validity is a psychopathology scale that is capable of distinguishing between adolescents who are *currently* in need of psychiatric treatment and those who are not.

PREDICTIVE VALIDITY. Predictive validity deals with the future. Perhaps you have an instrument (say a set of criteria) designed to predict which students will achieve high grades in their social work programs. If the students your instrument identified had indeed achieved high grades by the end of their BSW programs and the others had not, your instrument would have predictive validity.

Thus, predictive validity denotes an instrument's ability to predict future performance or status from present performance or status. An instrument has predictive validity if it can distinguish between individuals who will *differ at some point in the future.*

In sum, concurrent and predictive validity are concerned with prediction, and both make use of some external criterion that is purportedly a valid and reliable measure of the variable being studied. What differentiates the two is time. Concurrent validity predicts current performance or status, and predictive validity predicts future performance or status.

Moreover, concurrent validity involves administering an instrument and comparing its scores with an external criterion at approximately the same time, or concurrently. In contrast, predictive validity entails comparative measurement at two different (present and future) points in time.

The major concern of criterion validity, however, is not whether an instrument is valid for concurrent or future discriminations. Rather, the concern is with the use of a second measure as an independent criterion to check the validity of the first measure (Bostwick & Kyte, 1981).

FACE VALIDITY

Face validity, in fact, has nothing to do with what an instrument actually measures but only with what it *appears* to measure to the one who is completing it. Strictly speaking, it's not a form of validity. For example, suppose that you are taking a course on social work administration. You have a lazy instructor who has taken your final exam from a course he taught for business students last semester.

The exam, in fact, quite adequately tests your knowledge of administration theory, but it does not seem relevant to you because the language it uses relates to the business world not to social work situations.

You might not do very well on this exam because, although it has content validity (it adequately tests your knowledge), it does not have face validity (an appearance of relevance to the respondent). The moral here is that a measuring instrument should not only *be* content valid, to the greatest extent possible, but also should *appear* content valid to the person who completes it.

CONSTRUCT VALIDITY

What sets construct validity apart from content and criterion validity is its preoccupation with theory, explanatory constructs, and the testing of hypothesized relationships between and among variables. Construct validity is very difficult to understand because it involves determining the degree to which an instrument successfully measures a theoretical concept. The difficulty derives in part from the abstract nature of concepts.

As you know, a concept is a characteristic or trait that does not exist as an isolated, observable dimension of behavior. It cannot be seen, felt, or heard, and it cannot be measured directly—its existence must be inferred from the evidence at hand. Thus, the concept "hostility" may be inferred from observations of presumably hostile or aggressive acts; the concept "anxiety" may be inferred from test scores, galvanic skin responses, observations of anxious behaviors, and so on. Other typical concepts of concern to us are motivation, social class, delinquency, prejudice, and organizational conflict.

Construct validity is evaluated by determining the degree to which certain explanatory concepts account for variance, or individual differences, in the scores of an instrument. Put another way, it's concerned with the meaning of the instrument—that is, what it is measuring, and how and why it operates the way it does.

To assess the construct validity of the Rorschach inkblot test, for example, we would try to determine the factors, or concepts, that account for differences in responses on the test. Attempts might be made to determine whether the test measures emotional stability, sociability, or self-control and whether it also measures aggressiveness. The question would be: What proportion of the total test variance

BOX 7.2
Major Types of Validity

Content Validity	Does the measuring instrument adequately measure the major dimensions of the variable under consideration?
(Face Validity)	Does the measuring instrument appear to measure the subject matter under consideration? Not really a form of validity.
Criterion Validity	Does the individual's measuring instrument score predict the probable behavior on a second variable (criterion-related measure)?
Construct Validity	Does the measuring instrument appear to measure the general construct (element) it purports to measure

is accounted for by the concepts of emotional stability, sociability, self-control, and aggressiveness?

With construct validity, there is usually more interest in the property, or concept, being measured than in the instrument itself. Thus, it involves validation not only of the instrument but also of the theory underlying it. To establish construct validity, the meaning of the concept must be understood, and the propositions the theory makes about the relationships between this and other concepts must be identified.

We try to discover what predictions can be made on the basis of these propositions and whether the measurements obtained from the instrument will be consistent with those predictions. If the predictions are not supported, there is no clear-cut guide as to whether the shortcoming is in the instrument or in the theory.

Suppose a study is conducted to test the hypothesis that self-referred clients are more likely to have favorable attitudes toward treatment than those who come to the agency on some other basis. If the findings do not support the predicted relationship between self-referral and attitude toward treatment, should it be concluded that the measure is not valid or that the hypothesis is incorrect?

In such a situation, the concept of attitude toward treatment and the network of propositions that led to this prediction should be reexamined. Then the concept might be refined with more detailed hypotheses about its relationship to other concepts, and changes might be made in the instrument.

Construct validation makes use of data from a variety of sources. It is a painstaking building process much like theory construction—an attempt to ferret out the dimensions that an instrument is tapping and thereby to validate the theory underlying the instrument.

RELIABILITY AND VALIDITY REVISITED

Before we leave reliability and validity, we should say something about the relationship between them. If an instrument is not reliable, it cannot be valid. That is, if the same person completes it a number of times under the same conditions and it gives different results each time, it cannot be measuring anything accurately.

However, if an instrument *is* reliable, that does not necessarily mean it's valid. It could be reliably and consistently measuring something other than what it's supposed to measure, in the same way that people can be reliably late or watches can be reliably slow. The relationship between validity and reliability can be illustrated with a simple analogy. Suppose that you are firing five rounds from a rifle at three different targets, as illustrated in Figure 7.2:

* In Figure 7.2a, the bullet holes are scattered, representing a measuring instrument that is neither reliable nor valid.

* In Figure 7.2b, you have adjusted your sights, and now all the bullet holes are in the same place but not in the center as you intended. This represents a measuring instrument that is reliable but not valid.

* In Figure 7.2c, all the shots have hit the bull's eye: the instrument is both reliable and valid.

MEASUREMENT ERRORS

No matter how good the reliability and validity of a measuring instrument, no measurement is entirely without error. You can make two errors when you measure variables. Your measurements can contain:

— Constant Errors

— Random Errors

CONSTANT ERRORS

CONSTANT ERRORS, as the name suggests, are those errors that stay constant throughout the research study. They stay constant because they come from an un- varying source. That source may be the measuring instruments used, the research participants, or the researchers themselves. Because we have already spent some time discussing the limitations of measuring instruments, we will focus this discus- sion on errors caused by the researchers and their research participants.

Research participants, with all the best will in the world, may still have personal styles that lead to error in research results. If they are being interviewed, for example, they may exhibit *acquiescence* (a tendency to agree with everything the researcher

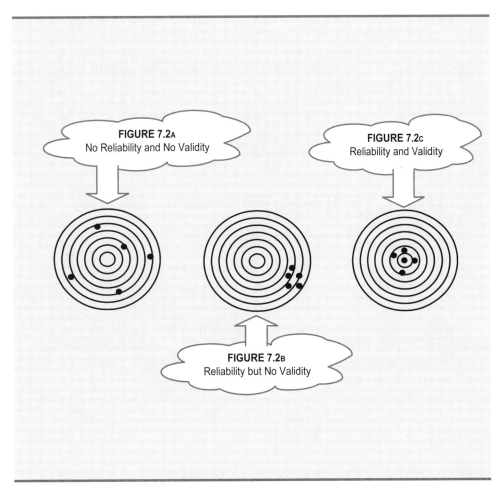

FIGURE 7.2

Targets Illustrating the Validity/Reliability Relationship

says, no matter what it is), or *social desirability* (a tendency to say anything that they think makes them look good), or *deviation* (a tendency to seek unusual responses).

If they are filling out a self-administered instrument, such as Hudson's *Index of Self-Esteem*, they may show *error of central tendency*, always choosing the number in the middle and avoiding commitment to either of the ends. Moreover, they have personal characteristics with respect to gender, age, ethnic background, and knowledge of the English language that remain constant throughout the study and may affect their answers.

Researchers also have personal styles and characteristics. Interviewers can affect the answers they receive by the way they ask the questions, by the way they dress, by their accent, mannerisms, gender, age, ethnic background, or even by their hairstyles. According to Gerald Bostwick and Nancy Kyte (1981), observers who are watching and rating research participants' behavior can commit various sins in a constant fashion, for example:

- *Contrast error*—to rate others as opposite to oneself with respect to a particular characteristic

- *Halo effect*—to think that a participant is altogether wonderful or terrible because of one good or bad trait. Or to think that the trait being observed must be good or bad because the participant is altogether wonderful or terrible

- *Error of leniency*—to always give a good report

- *Error of severity*—to always give a bad report

- *Error of central tendency*—observers, like participants, can choose always to stay comfortably in the middle of a rating scale and avoid both ends

Because these errors are constant throughout the study, they are sometimes recognized, and steps can be taken to deal with them. A different interviewer or observer might be found, for example, or allowances might be made for a particular participant's characteristics or style.

RANDOM ERRORS

RANDOM ERRORS that are not constant are difficult to find and make allowances for. Random errors spring out of the dark, wreak temporary havoc, and go back into hiding. It has been suggested that eventually they cancel each other out, and indeed they might. They might not as well, but there is little researchers can do about them except to be aware that they exist. According to Bostwick and Kyte (1981), there are three types of random error:

> *Transient qualities of the research participant*—things such as fatigue or boredom, or any temporary personal state that will affect the participant's responses

> *Situational factors*—the weather, the pneumatic drill outside the window, or anything else in the environment that will affect the participant's responses

> *Administrative factors*—anything relating to the way the instrument is administered, or the interview conducted, or the observation made. These include transient qualities of the researcher (or whoever collects the data) as well as accidents like reading out the wrong set of instructions.

 # IMPROVING VALIDITY AND RELIABILITY

When a measuring instrument does not achieve acceptable levels of validity and reliability—that is, when much error occurs—researchers often attempt to redesign the instrument so that it's more valid and reliable. Below are a few techniques for improving a measuring instrument's reliability and validity (Monette, Sullivan, & DeJong, 2011):

> *Be clearer on what you are measuring.* Often, validity and reliability are compromised because the researcher is not sufficiently clear and precise about the nature of the concepts being measured and their possible indicators. Rethinking the concepts helps in revising the instrument to make it more valid.

> *Provide better training for those who will apply the measuring instruments.* This is especially useful when a measuring instrument is used to assess research participants' feelings or attitudes. Previous research studies show that people who apply an instrument can be intentionally and unintentionally biased, and thus intentionally and/or unintentionally produce error.

> *Obtain the research participants' personal reactions about the measuring instrument.* Those under study may have some insight regarding why the verbal reports, observations, or archival reports are not producing accurate measures of their behaviors, feelings, or knowledge levels. They may, for example, comment that the wording of questions is ambiguous or that members of their subculture interpret some words differently than the researcher intended.

✳ *Obtain higher measurement levels of a variable.* This does not guarantee greater validity and reliability, but a higher level of measurement can produce a more reliable measuring instrument in some cases. So when the researcher has some options in terms of how to measure a variable, it's worth considering a higher level of measurement (e.g., nominal to ordinal, ordinal to interval).

✳ *Use more indicators of a variable.* This also does not guarantee enhanced reliability and validity, but a summated measuring instrument that has many questions, or items, can produce a more valid measure than one with fewer items. Thus, the more items, the higher the reliability and validity.

✳ *Conduct an item-by-item assessment.* If the measuring instrument consists of a number of questions, or items, perhaps only one or two of them are the problem. Deleting them may improve the instrument's validity and reliability.

BOX 7.3
Culturally Sensitive Measurement

INSTRUMENT BIAS

Researchers have debated measurement issues with racial/ethnic minorities for decades. Prominent among the debates has been the issue of testing the intelligence of ethnic minority children. Some researchers have argued that scores on standardized intelligence tests are underestimates of these children's actual abilities. The primary concern pertains to the standardization of the measuring instruments themselves.

It has been suggested that the samples used to standardize the instruments did not include enough ethnic minority children to provide the valid interpretation of the instruments' scores when they were used with ethnic minority children. Also, to do well on intelligence tests, ethnic minority children must demonstrate proficiency with the European American culture.

On the other hand, there is no such requirement for European American children to demonstrate proficiency with ethnic minority cultures. By default, the European American culture is deemed "superior" to the ethnic minority culture.

MEASUREMENT SENSITIVITY

The lack of sensitivity of measuring instruments with ethnic minority populations has been well documented. However, these instruments continue to be used with populations for which they were not designed. The question of validity is apparent. As we know from this chapter, validity addresses the extent to which a measuring instrument achieves what it claims to measure.

In many cases, we have no means to determine the validity of measuring instruments or procedures with ethnic minorities because ethnic minorities were not included in the development of instruments or procedures. Nevertheless, researchers have attempted to interpret results using culturally insensitive instruments. This undoubtedly has led to the misrepresentation and misunderstanding of ethnic minorities.

IMPORTANCE OF VARIABLES MEASURED

Of equal concern to the quality of measurement is whether or not the variables being measured are similarly important to all cultures and ethnic groups. The assumption that all groups value variables equally is another potential misuse of measurement and could assert the superiority of one group's values and beliefs over those of another. For example, when spirituality, a variable, is studied, it may be of greater importance for Native Americans than for other groups.

For a group who values spirituality, attainment of material possessions may be of lesser importance than spirituality. We know that there are often competing values in research. Thus, we need to study those variables that are important to each group—not only important to the researcher—and attempt to further our understanding of the importance placed on their valued beliefs, attitudes, and lifestyles.

LANGUAGE

Language also creates measurement issues. Some ethnic minorities lack facility with the English language, yet they are assessed with measuring instruments that assume English is their primary language. There have been some efforts to translate measuring instruments into other languages, but few studies have been conducted regarding the equivalency of the translations from the original instruments to the newly translated ones. The results of translated versions may be different from those with the English versions.

Translators and interpreters also have been used to bridge the language barriers with ethnic minority populations. Some suggest that the presence of interpreters and translators influences the participants' responses. The extent to which interpreters and translators influence the research participants' responses remains a contentious issue.

OBSERVATIONS

Qualitative studies using observational data collection methods are subject to misinterpretation as well. In observing nonverbal communication such as body language, for example, a researcher can easily misinterpret research participants' behaviors. In some Native American cultures, for example, a subordinate making direct eye contact with a person in authority would be deemed disrespectful. But in European American culture, direct eye contact indicates respect. In this case, unfamiliarity with the culture could easily lead us to incorrectly interpret the eye-contact behavior.

In short, measuring instruments and procedures remain problematic with research studies that focus on ethnic minorities. The validity of studies using instruments insensitive to ethnic minorities has created erroneous and conflicting reports. Refinement of the instruments (and their protocols) is necessary to improve the understanding of ethnic minorities with respect to their own values, beliefs, and behaviors.

SUMMARY

Measurement serves as a bridge between theory and reality. Our variables within a positivist study must be operationalized in such a way that they can be measured. The measuring instrument we select will depend on why we need to make the measurement and under what circumstances it will be administered. Provided that a number of instruments can be found that seem to meet our needs, the next step is to evaluate them.

Measurement error refers to variations in an instrument's score that cannot be attributed to the variable being measured. Basically, all measurement errors can be categorized as constant errors or random errors. The next chapter is a logical extension of this one as it presents the many different types of measuring instruments that are available for our use.

Study Questions for Chapter 7

— First, answer each question only AFTER you have read the chapter.

— Second, indicate how comfortable you were in answering each question on a 5-point scale:

1	2	3	4	5
Very uncomfortable	Somewhat uncomfortable	Neutral	Somewhat comfortable	Very comfortable

If you rated any question between 1–3, please reread the section of the chapter where the information for the question can be found. If you're still uncomfortable answering the question, talk with your instructor and/or your classmates for more clarification.

Questions	Degree of comfort? (Circle one number)
1. List the four levels of measurement that a variable can take. Now, in your own words, describe each one and provide a social work example throughout your discussion.	1 2 3 4 5
2. List the four reasons why we need to describe variables as accurately as possible. Now, in your own words, discuss each one by providing a social work example throughout your discussion.	1 2 3 4 5
3. List the five criteria we can use to select a measuring instrument. Now, in your own words, discuss each criterion and provide a social work example throughout your discussion.	1 2 3 4 5

4. Describe reliability, as a concept, as it pertains to measuring instruments. Provide a social work example throughout your discussion.	1 2 3 4 5
5. List the four different forms reliability can take. Now, in your own words, discuss each form. Provide social work examples throughout your discussion.	1 2 3 4 5
6. Describe validity, as a concept, as it pertains to measuring instruments. Provide a social work example throughout your discussion.	1 2 3 4 5
7. List the four different forms validity can take. Now, in your own words, discuss each form. Provide social work examples throughout your discussion.	1 2 3 4 5
8. Look at Figure 7.2. Describe in your own words what the figure means. Provide one common social work example throughout your discussion.	1 2 3 4 5
9. List the two kinds of measurement errors. Now, in your own words, describe each one. Provide a social work example throughout your discussion.	1 2 3 4 5
10. List the five kinds of constant errors as they pertain to the measurement process. Now, in your own words, describe each one. Provide a social work example throughout your discussion.	1 2 3 4 5
11. List the three kinds of random errors as they pertain to the measurement process. Now, in your own words, describe each one. Provide a social work example throughout your discussion.	1 2 3 4 5
12. At this point in your course, how comfortable are you with discussing measurement validity with your field instructor (or your supervisor at work)? With your fellow classmates? Discuss in detail.	1 2 3 4 5
13. At this point in your course, how comfortable are you with discussing measurement reliability with your field instructor (or your supervisor at work)? With your fellow classmates? Discuss in detail.	1 2 3 4 5
14. At this point in your course, how comfortable are you with discussing the different measurement levels with your field instructor (or your supervisor at work)? With your fellow classmates? Discuss in detail.	1 2 3 4 5

Assessing Your Self-Efficacy for Chapter 7

AFTER you have read the chapter AND have completed all the study questions, please indicate how knowledgeable you feel you are for each concept listed below.

1	2	3	4	5
Very uncomfortable	Somewhat uncomfortable	Neutral	Somewhat comfortable	Very comfortable

Major Concepts in Chapter	Knowledge Level? (Circle one number)
1. Levels of measurement	1 2 3 4 5
2. Reasons for measuring variables	1 2 3 4 5
3. Criteria for selecting measuring instruments	1 2 3 4 5
4. Reliability of measuring instruments	1 2 3 4 5
5. Validity of measuring instruments	1 2 3 4 5
6. Reliability/validity relationship	1 2 3 4 5
7. Improving a measuring instrument's validity and reliability	1 2 3 4 5
8. Constant measurement errors	1 2 3 4 5
9. Random measurement errors	1 2 3 4 5
10. Culturally sensitive measurement	1 2 3 4 5
Add up your scores (Minimum = 10, Maximum = 50)	Total score =

A   45 — 50 = Social Work Manager in the making.
B   40 — 44 = Social Work Supervisor.
C   35 — 39 = Social Work Practitioner.
D   10 — 34 = Case Aide. Reread the chapter and redo the study questions.

8

Measuring Instruments

*Our incapacity to comprehend other cultures stems
from our insistence on measuring things in our own terms.*
~ Arthur Erickson

As we know from the previous chapters in this book, on a very general level, variables refine concepts, and attributes refine variables. For example, the concept "ethnicity" can be refined more specifically in terms of the existence of ethnic groups. "Ethnic group" is a variable because research participants will *vary* with respect to which ethnic group they belong to. "Ethnic group" can be refined further, via its attributes. The ethnic groups that people can belong to—Asian, Caucasian, Latino, and so on—constitute the attributes of the variable "ethnic group."

All of this refinement stuff boils down to measurement, as pure and simple as that. As we saw in the last chapter, we need to measure the variables in our research study. One easy way to measure them is through measuring instruments that are as valid and reliable as possible. Before we select a measuring instrument to measure them, however, we need to ask ourselves a few basic questions.

QUESTIONS TO ASK BEFORE MEASURING

What we want is some method of making a selection from the huge array of measuring instruments that exist. There are six questions we can ask ourselves to help us make our choice. When we have answered them, we will be able to distinguish the kind of instrument we need from the kind we do not need; hopefully, this will eliminate a large number of all those instruments lying in wait in the library and on the Internet. The six questions are:

— Why Do We Want to Make the Measurement?

— What Do We Want to Measure?

— Who Will Make the Measurement?

— What Format Do We Require?

— Where Will the Measurement Be Made?

— When Will the Measurement Be Made?

Let's take an extremely simple and offbeat example to illustrate how the use of measuring instruments can be used. Let's say we want to know whether there is a relationship between the two variables: depression and sleep patterns.

WHY DO WE WANT TO MAKE THE MEASUREMENT?

THE FIRST QUESTION is *Why do we want to make the measurement?* At first glance, this does not seem too difficult to answer. We just want to measure depression and sleep patterns with some type of measuring instruments—one for depression and one for sleep patterns—in order to study the relationship between the two variables, if any. But things are not quite as simple as they appear. There are six general reasons for using measuring instruments, and we need to select the one that applies to our study.

The point of making this selection is to discover how accurate we need the instrument to be. If our measurement is going to affect someone's life, for example, it has to be as accurate as we can possibly make it. We might be doing an assessment that will be used in making decisions about treatment interventions, referrals, placements, and so forth. On the other hand, if our measurement will not affect anyone's life directly, we can afford to be a little less rigid in our requirements. How much less rigid depends on what we are doing.

If this is to be a beginning research study (e.g., exploratory) in a relatively unexplored field, the result will only be a tentative suggestion that some variable is possibly related to some other variable—for instance, sleep patterns are related to depression. A little inaccuracy in measurement in this case is not the end of the world.

When a little more is known in our subject area (e.g., descriptive, explanatory), we might be able to formulate and test a more specific hypothesis; for example, depressed people spend less time in delta-wave NREM sleep than nondepressed people. In this case, we obviously should be able to measure sleep patterns accurately enough to distinguish between delta-wave NREM sleep and other kinds of sleep.

All in all, how accurate our measurement needs to be depends on our purpose. Because we are only doing a beginning study, we can afford to be relatively inaccurate. In general, the higher our research question is on the knowledge level continuum (Figure 2.3), the more accurate our measurements of our variables need to be.

In short, measuring instruments that measure the variables within causality-comparative interaction questions (the highest level of research questions) need to be more accurate than instruments that are used to measure existence questions (the lowest level of research questions). We have now answered the first question: *Why do we want to make the measurement?*

WHAT DO WE WANT TO MEASURE?

THE SECOND QUESTION is *What do we want to measure?* We know the answer to that one also: we simply want to measure two variables, depression and sleep patterns. But here again, it's not as simple as it may seem. Not only are measuring instruments more accurate or less accurate, they can be *wideband* or *narrowband*. *Wideband* instruments measure a broad trait or characteristic. A trait is pretty much the same thing as a characteristic, and it means some aspect of character such as bravery, gaiety, or depression.

Logically enough, *narrowband* instruments measure just a particular aspect of a particular trait. A narrowband instrument, for example, might tell us how depressed Uncle Fred feels about his daughter moving to Moose Jaw, but it will not give us an overall picture of Uncle Fred's depression. Thus, a wideband instrument will give an overall picture of Uncle Fred's depression, but it will not tell us how he feels about his daughter moving to Moose Jaw.

In our particular study, we are not interested too much in how Uncle Fred feels about his daughter moving to Moose Jaw. If he's one of our research participants, we just want to know about his overall depression so that we can relate it to his sleep patterns. We need a wideband instrument then, which does not have to be absolutely smack-on 100% accurate.

WHO WILL MAKE THE MEASUREMENT?

THE THIRD QUESTION asks, *Who will make the measurement?* We will—that seems obvious enough. However, it's not always social workers who complete the measuring instruments. More often than not, our research participants complete them. In our study, it will be the people who participate in our study who will fill out the instrument to measure their depression levels. Sometimes family members complete the measuring instruments, or teachers, specially trained outside observers, or the staff members in an institution.

The point is that different kinds of people require different kinds of measuring instruments. An instrument that could be completed easily and accurately by a trained social worker might prove too difficult for Uncle Fred, who has arthritis and cataracts and a reading level of around the fourth grade. In our simple research study, we will have to be sure the instrument we finally select is easy for our research participants to understand. So far, then, to measure the depression levels of our research participants, we need a wideband instrument, easy to complete, and not necessarily smack-on accurate.

WHAT FORMAT DO WE REQUIRE?

THE FOURTH QUESTION is *What format do we require?* A format is the way our questions will look on the page. They may appear as a simple inventory, such as:

List below the things that make you feel depressed.

_____

_____

_____

Or a checklist such as:

Check below all the things that you sometimes feel.

____ My mother gets on my nerves.

____ My father does not understand me.

_____ I do not get along very well with my sister.

_____ I think I hate my family sometimes.

Or a scale such as:

How satisfied are you with your life? (Circle one number below.)

1. Very unsatisfied

2. Somewhat satisfied

3. Satisfied

4. More than satisfied

5. Very satisfied

More often than not, measuring instruments contain a number of items, or questions, that when totaled yield more accurate results than just asking one question. These measuring instruments are called summative scales and will be discussed more thoroughly later in this chapter.

After careful thought, we decide that a wideband, easy-to-complete, not-smack-on-accurate summative scale would do the job. However, we have not finished yet. Instruments may be unidimensional or multidimensional. A unidimensional instrument only measures one variable—for example, self esteem (e.g., Figure 7.1).

By contrast, a multidimensional instrument measures a number of variables at the same time. A multidimensional instrument is nothing more than a number of unidimensional instruments stuck together. Most often these are called subscales. For example, Figure 8.1 is a multidimensional instrument that contains three subscales, or three unidimensional instruments:

✱ Relevance of received social services (Items 1–11)

✱ The extent to which the services reduced the problem (Items 12–21)

✱ The extent to which services enhanced the client's self-esteem and contributed to a sense of power and integrity (Items 22–34)

Because our study is rather simplistic, we only need two unidimensional instruments—one for depression and one for sleep patterns.

SOCIAL SERVICE SATISFACTION SCALE

Using the scale from one to five described below, please indicate at the left of each item the number that comes closest to how you feel.

1 = None of the time
2 = Very rarely
3 = A little of the time
4 = Some of the time
5 = A good part of the time
6 = Most of the time
7 = All of the time

1. ___ The social worker took my problems very seriously.
2. ___ If I had been the worker, I would have dealt with my problems in the same way.
3. ___ The worker I had could never understand anyone like me.
4. ___ Overall the agency has been very helpful to me.
5. ___ If friends of mine had similar problems I would tell them to go to the agency.
6. ___ The social worker asks a lot of embarrassing questions.
7. ___ I can always count on the worker to help if I'm in trouble.
8. ___ The agency will help me as much as it can.
9. ___ I don't think the agency has the power to really help me.
10. ___ The social worker tries hard but usually isn't too helpful.
11. ___ The problem the agency helped me with is one of the most important in my life.
12. ___ Things have gotten better since I've been going to the agency.
13. ___ Since I've been using the agency my life is more messed up than ever.
14. ___ The agency is always available when I need it.
15. ___ I got from the agency exactly what I wanted.
16. ___ The social worker loves to talk but won't really do anything for me.
17. ___ Sometimes I just tell the social worker what I think she wants to hear.
18. ___ The social worker is usually in a hurry when I see her.
19. ___ No one should have any trouble getting some help from this agency.
20. ___ The worker sometimes says things I don't understand.
21. ___ The social worker is always explaining things carefully.
22. ___ I never looked forward to my visits to the agency.
23. ___ I hope I'll never have to go back to the agency for help.
24. ___ Every time I talk to my worker I feel relieved.
25. ___ I can tell the social worker the truth without worrying.
26. ___ I usually feel nervous when I talk to my worker.
27. ___ The social worker is always looking for lies in what I tell her.
28. ___ It takes a lot of courage to go to the agency.
29. ___ When I enter the agency I feel very small and insignificant.
30. ___ The agency is very demanding.
31. ___ The social worker will sometimes lie to me.
32. ___ Generally the social worker is an honest person.
33. ___ I have the feeling that the worker talks to other people about me.
34. ___ I always feel well treated when I leave the agency.

FIGURE 8.1

Reid-Gundlach *Social Service Satisfaction Scale*

WHERE WILL THE MEASUREMENT BE MADE?

QUESTION FIVE ASKS, *Where will the measurement be made?* Well, probably in our good friend's sleep laboratory. At first glance, it may seem that it does not matter where the measurement is made, but in fact it matters a great deal. For example, we might have a child who throws temper tantrums mostly in school. In this case, measurements dealing with temper tantrums should obviously be made at school.

We can see that an instrument that is to be completed in a railway station might differ from an instrument that is to be used in the comparative serenity of our office. It should be shorter, say, and simpler, and possibly printed on paper that glows in the dark so that if it gets torn out of our hands, we can chase after it more easily. We decide that our research participants will probably be equally depressed everywhere, more or less, and that the measurements will take place in our friend's sleep laboratory.

WHEN WILL THE MEASUREMENT BE MADE?

OUR LAST QUESTION, question six, is *When will the measurement be made?* Probably sometime in August, if it all goes well. But no, the month of the year is not what is meant by *when*. *When* refers to the time or times during the study when a measurement is made.

As will be seen in Chapters 10 and 11, there are certain research designs in which we measure a client's problem, do something to change the problem, and then measure the problem again to see if we have changed it. This involves two measurements, the first and second measurements of the problem. In research jargon, we represent these measurements as *O*s (*O* stands for *O*bservation). Whatever we do to change the problem—usually a social work intervention—is represented by *X*.

In short, in research designs we represent the dependent variables by *O*s, and the independent variables by *X*s. If our research design is such that we make an initial measurement of the dependent variable (O_1), introduce an independent variable (X), and then measure the same dependent variable again (O_2), our design would look like: O_1 X O_2.

To sum up the selection of the two measuring instruments we are going to use in our study—one for depression and one for sleep patterns—we need to find instruments that are (1) wideband, (2) unidimensional, (3) summative, (4) do not necessarily have to be smack-on accurate, and (5) easy to complete in a sleep laboratory.

TYPES OF MEASURING INSTRUMENTS

The type of measuring instrument you choose to measure your variables within your research study depends on your research situation—the question you are asking, the kind of data you need, the research participants you have selected, and the time and money you have available.

Every measuring instrument you consider must be evaluated in terms of the five criteria discussed in the previous chapter; that is, it must be useful, sensitive, nonreactive, reliable, and valid. In general, there are many different types of measuring instruments. We will only discuss five:

— Journals or Diaries

— Logs

— Inventories

— Checklists

— Summative Instruments

JOURNALS OR DIARIES

JOURNALS OR DIARIES are a useful means of data collection when you are undertaking an interpretive study. They are usually not used as data collection methods within positivistic studies. Perhaps in your interpretive study you are asking the question "What are women's experiences of home birth?" and you want your research participants to keep a record of their experiences from early pregnancy to after delivery.

With respect to the five criteria mentioned in the previous chapter, a journal is *valid* in this context to the extent that it completely and accurately describes the relevant experiences and omits the irrelevant experiences. This can only be achieved if the women keeping them have reasonable language skills, can stick pretty much to the point (will they include a three-page description their cats or their geraniums?), and are willing to complete their journals on a regular basis.

A word is in order here about *retrospective data*: that is, data based on someone's memory of what occurred in the past. There is some truth to the idea that we invent our memories. At least, we might embellish or distort them, and a description is much more liable to be accurate if it's written immediately after the event it describes rather than days or weeks later.

The journal is *reliable* insofar as the same experience evokes the same written response. Over time, women may tire of describing again an experience almost identical to the one they had last week, and they may omit it (affecting validity), or change it a little to make it more interesting (again affecting validity), or try to write it in a different way (affecting reliability).

Utility very much depends on whether the woman likes to write and is prepared to continue with what may become an onerous task. Another aspect of utility relates to your own role as researcher. Will you have the time required to go through each journal and perform the kind of qualitative analysis as outlined in Chapter 16?

Sensitivity has to do with the amount of detail included in the journal. To some degree, this reflects completeness and is a validity issue, but small changes in women's experiences as the pregnancy progresses cannot be tracked unless the experiences are each described in some detail.

Journals are usually very reactive. Indeed, they are often used as therapeutic tools simply because the act of writing encourages the writer to reflect on what has been written, thus achieving deeper insights which may lead to behavior and/or affective changes. Reactivity is not desirable in a measuring instrument.

On the other hand, an interpretive study seeks to uncover not just the experiences themselves but the meaning attached to them by the research participants, and meaning may emerge more clearly if the participants are encouraged to reflect. Researchers themselves keep journals while conducting interpretive studies. Journal keeping by the researcher is discussed in Chapter 16 on qualitative data analyses.

LOGS

YOU HAVE PROBABLY used logs in your field placement, so we will not discuss their use in depth. When used in research situations, they are nothing more than a structured kind of journal, where the research participant is asked to record in note form the events related to particular experiences or behaviors.

Each note usually includes headings: the event itself, when and where the event happened, and who was there. A log may be more valid than a journal in that the headings prompt the participant to include only relevant information with no discursive wanderings into cats or geraniums.

The log may be more reliable because it's more likely that a similar experience will be recorded in a similar way. It may be more useful because it takes less time for the participant to complete and less time for the researcher to analyze. It's usually less sensitive to small changes because it includes less detail, and it may be somewhat less reactive depending on the extent to which it leads to reflection and change.

INVENTORIES

An inventory is a list made by the research participants. For example, the following is an inventory designed to measure depression:

List below the things that make you feel depressed.

_____

_____

_____

This is valid to the degree that the list is complete, and sensitive in that the addition or omission of items over time is indicative of change. It's useful if the participant is prepared to complete it carefully and truthfully, and it's probably fairly reactive in that it provokes thought. Inventories are commonly used in interpretive studies.

CHECKLISTS

A checklist is a list prepared by the researcher. For example, a checklist designed to measure depression would include more items than shown but would follow this format.

Check below all the things that you have felt during the past week.

____ A wish to be alone

____ Sadness

____ Powerlessness

____ Anxiety

With respect to the five evaluative criteria presented in the previous chapter, the same considerations apply to a checklist as to an inventory except that content validity may be compromised if the researcher does not include all the possibilities that are relevant to the participant in the context of the study.

Summative Instruments

On a general level, inventories and checklists ask for yes or no answers. In other words, they are *dichotomous* in that research participants can only respond in one of two ways: *yes,* this occurred, or *no*, this did not occur.

Summative measuring instruments provide a greater range of responses, usually asking how frequently or to what degree a particular item, or question, applies. For example, the depression checklist as shown on the previous page may be presented in the form of a summated instrument, as follows:

Indicate how often you have experienced the following feelings by circling the appropriate number.

	Never	Rarely	Sometimes	Often
A wish to be alone	1	2	3	4
Sadness	1	2	3	4
Powerlessness	1	2	3	4
Anxiety	1	2	3	4

The words "never" and "often" are known as *anchors* and serve to describe the meanings attached to their respective values. Participants circle a number for each item and the scores are summed, or totaled. With only the four items shown (an actual depression scale would contain many more), the lowest possible score is 4, and the highest possible score is 16.

This instrument is an example of a *summative instrument.* A summative measuring instrument is any instrument that allows the researcher to derive a sum or total score from a number of items, or questions. Most, but not all, summated measuring instruments are designed so that low scores indicate a low level of the variable being measured (depression, in this case) and high scores indicate a high level. Figures 7.1 and 8.1 are excellent examples of summative instruments.

When doing a positivistic study, summative measuring instruments should be used whenever possible as they are more valid and reliable that the other four types. However, you must always take into account your research question or hypothesis and from this question or hypothesis determine what type of instrument will be the best one to measure your variables.

STANDARDIZED MEASURING INSTRUMENTS

Standardized measuring instruments are used widely in social work because they have usually been extensively tested and they come complete with information on the results of that testing. Figure 7.1, via Figure 7.1a, is an excellent example of a summative standardized measuring instrument in that it provides information about itself in six areas:

- Purpose

- Description

- Norms

- Scoring

- Reliability

- Validity

Purpose is a simple statement of what the instrument is designed to measure. *Description* provides particular features of the instrument, including its length and often its *clinical cutting score*. The clinical cutting score is different for every instrument (if it has one, that is) and is the score that differentiates the respondents with a clinically significant problem from the respondents with no such problem.

In Hudson's *Index of Self-Esteem* (Figure 7.1), for example, people who score above 30 (±5 for error) have a clinically significant problem with self-esteem, and people who score less than 30 do not.

The section on *norms* tells you who the instrument was validated on. The *Index of Self-Esteem*, for example (see NORMS in Figure 7.1a), was tested on 1,745 respondents, including single and married individuals, clinical and nonclinical populations, college students and nonstudents, Caucasians, Japanese, and Chinese Americans, and a smaller number of other ethnic groups.

It's important to know this because people with different characteristics tend to respond differently to the sort of items contained in Hudson's *Index of Self-Esteem*. For instance, a woman from a culture that values modesty might be unwilling to answer that she feels she is a beautiful person all of the time (Item 3). She might not know what a wallflower is (Item 19), and she might be very eager to assert that she feels self-conscious with strangers (Item 16) because she thinks that women ought to feel that way.

It's therefore very important to use any measuring instrument *only* with people who have the same characteristics as the people who participated in testing the instrument. As another example, instruments used with children must have been developed using children.

Scoring gives instructions about how to score the instrument. *Reliability* and *validity* we have discussed already. Summated standardized instruments are usually reliable, valid, sensitive, and nonreactive. It's therefore very tempting to believe that they must be useful, whatever the research situation. More often than not, they *are* useful—provided that what the instrument measures and what the researcher *wants* to measure are the same thing.

If you want to measure family coping, for example, and come across a wonderful standardized instrument designed to measure family cohesion, you must resist the temptation to convince yourself that family cohesion is what you really wanted to measure in the first place. Just remember that the variable being measured selects the instrument, the instrument doesn't select the variable.

EVALUATING STANDARDIZED MEASURING INSTRUMENTS

THERE ARE SEVERAL CRITERIA that must be considered when it comes time to evaluating standardized measuring instruments that you think will accurately measure the variables in your research study. Jordan, Franklin, and Corcoran (2011) present four of them as follows:

THE SAMPLE FROM WHICH DATA WERE DRAWN

- Are the samples representative of pertinent populations?

- Are the sample sizes sufficiently large?

- Are the samples homogeneous?

- Are the subsamples pertinent to respondents' demographics?

- Are the data obtained from the samples up to date?

THE VALIDITY OF THE INSTRUMENT

- Is the content domain clearly and specifically defined?

- Was there a logical procedure for including the items?

- Is the criterion measure relevant to the instrument?

✴ Was the criterion measure reliable and valid?

✴ Is the theoretical construct clearly and correctly stated?

✴ Do the scores converge with other relevant measures?

✴ Do the scores discriminate from irrelevant variables?

✴ Are there cross-validation studies that conform to these concerns?

THE RELIABILITY OF THE INSTRUMENT

✴ Is there sufficient evidence of internal consistency?

✴ Is there equivalence between various forms?

✴ Is there stability over a relevant time interval?

THE PRACTICALITY OF APPLICATION

✴ Is the instrument an appropriate length?

✴ Is the content socially acceptable to respondents?

✴ Is the instrument feasible to complete?

✴ Is the instrument relatively direct?

✴ Does the instrument have utility?

✴ Is the instrument relatively nonreactive?

✴ Is the instrument sensitive to measuring change?

✴ Is the instrument feasible to score?

ADVANTAGES AND DISADVANTAGES

LIKE EVERYTHING IN LIFE, there are advantages and disadvantages to standardized measuring instruments. Judy Krysik and Jerry Finn (2011) briefly describe them as follows:

ADVANTAGES

- Standardized instruments are readily available and easy to access.

- The development work has already been done.

- They have established reliability and validity estimates.

- Norms may be available for comparison.

- Most are easy to complete and score.

- In many instances, they are available free of charge.

- They may be available in different languages.

- They specify age range and reading level.

- Time required for administration has been determined.

DISADVANTAGES

- The norms may not apply to the target population.

- The language may be difficult.

- The tone might not fit with the philosophy of the program, for example, deficit based versus strength based.

- The target population may not understand the translation.

- The scoring procedure may be overly complex.

- The instrument may not be affordable.

- Special qualifications or training might be required for use.

- The instrument may be too long or time consuming to administer.

LOCATING STANDARDIZED MEASURING INSTRUMENTS

ONCE YOU DECIDE that you want to measure a variable through the use of a standardized instrument, the next consideration is to find it. The two general sources for locating such instruments are:

— Commercial or Professional Publishers

— Professional Books and Journals

COMMERCIAL OR PROFESSIONAL PUBLISHERS

Numerous commercial and professional publishing companies specialize in the production and sale of standardized measuring instruments for use in the social services. They can be easily found on the Internet. The cost of instruments purchased from a publisher varies considerably, depending on the instrument, the number of copies needed, and the publisher.

The instruments generally are well developed, and their psychometric properties are supported by the results of several research studies. Often they are accompanied by manuals that include the normative data for the instrument. As well, publishers are expected to comply with professional standards such as those established by the American Psychological Association. These standards apply to claims made about the instrument's rationale, development, psychometric properties, administration, and interpretation of results.

Standards for the use of some instruments have been developed to protect the interests of clients. Consequently, purchasers of instruments may be required to have certain qualifications, such as possession of an advanced degree in a relevant field. A few publishers require membership in particular professional organizations.

Most publishers will, however, accept an order from a social work student if it's cosigned by a qualified person, such as an instructor, who will supervise the use of the instrument.

PROFESSIONAL BOOKS AND JOURNALS

Standardized measuring instruments are most commonly described in human service journals. The instruments usually are supported by evidence of their validity and reliability, although they often require cross-validation and normative data from more representative samples and sub-samples. More often than not, however, the complete instrument cannot be seen in the articles that describe them. However, they usually contain a few items that can be found in the actual instrument.

Locating instruments in journals or books is not easy. Of the two most common methods, computer searches of data banks and manual searches of the literature, the former is faster, unbelievably more thorough, and easier to use. Unfortunately, financial support for the development of comprehensive data banks has been limited and intermittent.

Another disadvantage is that many articles on instruments are not referenced with the appropriate indicators for computer retrieval. These limitations are being overcome by the changing technology of computers and information retrieval systems.

Several services now allow for a complex breakdown of measurement need. Data banks that include references from over 1,300 journals, updated monthly, are now available from a division of *Psychological Abstracts Information Services* and from *Bibliographic Retrieval Services*.

Nevertheless, most social workers will probably rely on manual searches of references such as *Psychological Abstracts*. Although the reference indices will be the same as those in the data banks accessible by computer, the literature search can be supplemented with appropriate seminal (original) reference volumes.

 SUMMARY

As you know, Chapter 7 discussed measurement in general. This chapter was a logical continuation of it in that we presented a few ways variables can be measured via measuring instruments. We discussed six basic questions you need to ask yourself before selecting a measuring instrument that will measure your variables within your research question or hypothesis.

We then went on to discuss the five basic types of measuring instruments that you can choose from. The last part of the chapter discussed standardized measuring instruments, highlighted how to evaluate them, and presented their advantages and disadvantages, along with a brief discussion on how to find them.

Study Questions for Chapter 8

— First, answer each question only AFTER you have read the chapter.

— Second, indicate how comfortable you were in answering each question on a 5-point scale:

1	2	3	4	5
Very uncomfortable	Somewhat uncomfortable	Neutral	Somewhat comfortable	Very comfortable

If you rated any question between 1–3, please reread the section of the chapter where the information for the question can be found. If you're still uncomfortable answering the question, talk with your instructor and/or your classmates for more clarification.

Questions	Degree of comfort? (Circle one number)
1. List the six questions that need to be answered before selecting a measuring instrument. Now, pretend you are going to find a measuring instrument that measures your research instructor's teaching effectiveness. Answer each of the six questions in relation to finding such an instrument, keeping in mind who is going to complete the instrument—which is probably you. Could your instructor also fill it out? Why or why not?	1 2 3 4 5
2. List the five types of measuring instruments and describe each one in detail. With the same assignment in Question 1, discuss how each type of measuring instrument could be used to measure your research instructor's teaching effectiveness. Provide specific examples to illustrate your points.	1 2 3 4 5
3. Find a summative measuring instrument that measures a variable of interest to you. Evaluate the instrument on the four global criteria that are presented in the book, paying particular attention to all of their sub-criteria.	1 2 3 4 5
4. Discuss the two main sources for locating measuring instruments. Provide social work examples to illustrate your points.	1 2 3 4 5
5. Go to the Web site www.walmyr.com and click on the sample scales tab, then find the short-form scales option. From the numerous variables that come up, pick an instrument that measures a variable you're interested in. Now with the help of Google, find three other measuring instruments that say they measure the same variable. Compare and contrast their features such as scoring, format, and end results.	1 2 3 4 5

6.	At this point in your course, how comfortable are you with discussing the different types of measuring instruments with your field instructor (or your supervisor at work)? With your fellow classmates? Discuss in detail.	1 2 3 4 5
7.	Select a standardized measuring instrument that measures a variable of your choice. Discuss how valid it is via the contents of Chapter 7.	1 2 3 4 5
8.	Select a standardized measuring instrument that measures a variable of your choice. Discuss how reliable it is via the contents of Chapter 7.	1 2 3 4 5
9.	Select a standardized measuring instrument that measures a variable of your choice. Using Chapter 7 as a guide, discuss the level of measurement the instrument produces. Justify your response via the use of examples.	1 2 3 4 5

Assessing Your Self-Efficacy for Chapter 8

AFTER you have read the chapter AND have completed all the study questions, please indicate how knowledgeable you feel you are for each concept listed below.

1	2	3	4	5
Very uncomfortable	Somewhat uncomfortable	Neutral	Somewhat comfortable	Very comfortable

Major Concepts in Chapter	Knowledge Level? (Circle one number)
1. Questions that need to be answered before selecting a measuring instrument	1 2 3 4 5
2. Types of measuring instruments	1 2 3 4 5
3. Standardized measuring instruments	1 2 3 4 5
4. Criteria for selecting a standardized measuring instrument	1 2 3 4 5
5. Locating standardized measuring instruments	1 2 3 4 5
6. Advantages and disadvantages of standardized measuring instruments	1 2 3 4 5

7. Unidimensional and multidimensional measuring instruments	1 2 3 4 5
Add up your scores (Minimum = 7, Maximum = 35)	Total score =

A   31 — 35 = Social Work Manager in the making.
B   28 — 30 = Social Work Supervisor.
C   24 — 27 = Social Work Practitioner.
D   7 — 23 = Case Aide. Reread the chapter and redo the study questions.

PART IV
Sampling and Research Designs

9

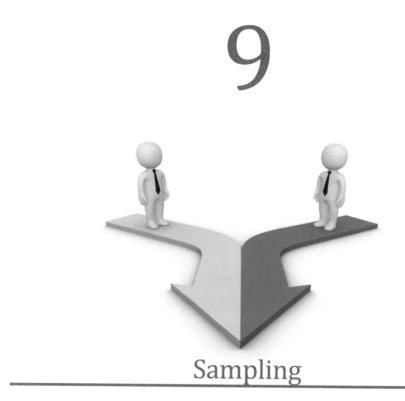

Sampling

Those market researchers . . . are playing games with you and me and with this entire country. Their so-called samples of opinion are no more accurate or reliable than my grandmother's big toe was when it came to predicting the weather.
~ Dan Rather

The last chapter discussed measuring instruments—how to select them, where to find them, and how to evaluate them. This chapter discusses who will complete them. In short, we discuss how to select the actual people, or research participants, who you will administer the measuring instruments to. Let's continue with the previous example we used in the last chapter where we are trying to discover whether there is a relationship between two variables—depression and sleep patterns. At this point, it is obviously necessary to find a few people so we can measure their depression levels (Variable 1) and sleep patterns (Variable 2).

One way of doing this is to phone our trusty social worker friend, Ken, who works with people who are depressed and ask if he will please find us some clients, or research participants, who do not mind sleeping in a laboratory once a week with wires attached to their heads. "Certainly," says Ken crisply. "How many do you want?" "Er . . ." we say, "how many have you got?"

"Oh, lots," says Ken with cheer. "Now, do you want them young or old, male or female, rich or poor, acute or chronic, severely or mildly depressed . . . ?" He adds, "Oh, and by the way, all of them are refugees from Outer Ganglinshan." We decide that we need to think about this some more. Suppose that the sleep patterns of Outer Ganglinshanians who are depressed are different from the sleep patterns of Bostonians who are depressed.

Suppose even further that men who are depressed have different sleep patterns from women who are depressed, or adolescents who are depressed from seniors who are depressed, or Anabaptists who are depressed from Theosophists who are depressed. The list of possibilities is endless.

One solution, of course, would be to assemble all the people who are depressed in the Western Hemisphere in the hope that Anabaptists and Theosophists and so forth are properly represented.

This leaves out the Eastern Hemisphere, but we have to eliminate something because our sleep laboratory has only ten beds. There is another difficulty, too. Not only are we restricted to ten sleeping people, but on our limited budget we will be hard pressed to pay them bus fare from their homes to our laboratory.

This being the case, we have to forget about the Western Hemisphere and concentrate on the area served by the city transit, within which there are probably very few Anabaptists who are depressed and no Theosophists at all to speak of.

How are we going to select ten people from this small area and still be fair to the Theosophist population? The answer is simple: we do this through the use of sampling frames.

POPULATIONS AND SAMPLING FRAMES

A *population* is the totality of persons or objects with which our research study is concerned. If, for example, we are interested in all the people who are depressed in the Western Hemisphere, then our population is all the people who are depressed in the Western Hemisphere.

If we decide to restrict our study to all the people who are depressed in the area served by city transit, then our population is all the people who are depressed in the area served by city transit. However we decide to define our population, the results of our study will apply only to that population from which our sample was drawn.

SAMPLING FRAMES

WE CANNOT DO OUR STUDY within the confines of city transit and then apply the results to the whole of the Western Hemisphere. When our population has been defined, the next step is to make a list of all the people (or other units such as case files) included in that population.

Such a list is called a *sampling frame.* For example, if our population is to be all the people who are depressed in the area served by city transit, then we must create a list, or sampling frame, of all the people who are depressed in the area served by city transit. Obtaining a sampling frame is often one of the hardest parts of a research study.

We probably will not be able to generate a list of all the people who are depressed in the area served by city transit because there is not a single person or social service program who knows about all of them. It might be better to restrict our study to all the depressed people treated by Ken—or some other source of people who are depressed that will provide us with a list.

Suppose, then, that we have decided to restrict our study to all the people who are depressed treated by Ken. We may think that "all the people who are depressed treated by Ken" is a reasonable definition of our population. But a population has to be defined exactly. "All the people who are depressed treated by Ken" is possibly not very exact, especially when we consider that Ken has been treating them for over twenty years.

The ones treated eighteen and nineteen years ago have doubtless disappeared by now over the far horizon; indeed, the fates of those treated a mere year ago might be equally veiled in mystery. Perhaps we should redefine our population as "all the people who are depressed treated by Ken over the last three months," or better yet as "all the people who are depressed treated by Ken from January 1 to March 31."

 # SAMPLING PROCEDURES

If we can make a three-month list of all the people who are depressed treated by Ken from January 1 to March 31, we have our sampling frame. The next thing is to use it to select our sample. This process is called *sampling,* and the people (or other units such as case files) picked from a sampling make up a *sample.* There are two main ways of selecting samples:

— *Probability Sampling,* which requires a sampling frame

— *Nonprobability Sampling,* which does not require a sampling frame

TABLE 9.1
Partial Page of a Random Numbers Table

02584	75844	50162	44269	76402	33228	96152	76777
66791	44653	90947	61934	79627	81621	74744	98758
44306	88222	30967	57776	90533	01276	30525	66914
01471	15131	38577	03362	54825	27705	60680	97083
65995	81864	19184	61585	19111	08641	47653	27267
45567	79547	89025	70767	25307	33151	00375	17564
27340	30215	28376	47390	11039	39458	67489	48547
02584	75844	56012	44269	76402	33228	96152	76777
66791	44653	90497	61934	79627	81621	74744	98758
44306	80722	30317	57776	90533	01276	30525	66914
65995	**81864**	19184	61585	19131	08641	47653	27267
45567	79547	89025	70767	25307	33151	00375	17564
27340	30215	23456	47390	11039	39458	67489	48547
02471	10721	30577	03362	54825	27705	60680	97083
60791	40453	90227	61934	79627	81621	74744	98758
43316	87212	36967	57576	90533	01276	30525	66914

PROBABILITY SAMPLING

THE FIRST MAIN CATEGORY of sampling procedures is probability sampling. This method of sampling is used more often in positivistic studies than in interpretive ones. A *probability sample* is one in which all the people (or units in the sampling frame) have the same known probability of being selected for the sample. By probability, we mean chance, such as the probability of winning a lottery. The selection is based on some form of random procedure of which there are four main types:

— Simple Random Sampling

— Systematic Random Sampling

— Stratified Random Sampling

— Cluster Random Sampling

Simple Random Sampling

The first type of probability sampling is simple random sampling. Suppose now that there are 100 names in our sampling frame; that is, Ken has seen 100 different clients who are depressed from January 1 to March 31. We assign each one of these clients a number; the first one on the list will be 001, the second 002, and so on until 100 is reached. Then we take a book of random numbers, open the book at random, and pick a digit on the page also at random. The first half page of such a table is shown in Table 9.1.

Suppose the digit we happen to pick on is 1, the second digit in the number in the sixth row from the bottom in the second column from the left. (That whole number is **81864** and is highlighted in **bold.**) The two digits immediately to the right of 1 are 8 and 6; thus, we have 186. We take three digits in total because 100, the highest number on our sampling frame, has three digits. The number 186 is more than 100, so we ignore it.

Going down the column, 954 is also more than 100, so we ignore it also. The next one, 021, is less than 100, so we can say that we have selected number 021 on our sampling frame to take part in our study. After 072 and 045 there are no more numbers less than 100 in the second column (middle three digits), so we go to the third column (middle three digits). Here we discover seven more people (i.e., 016, 094, 096, 049, 031, 057, 022).

We go down the columns, picking out numbers, until it occurs to us that we do not really know how many numbers should be selected. Our sleep laboratory has accommodation for ten, but then if we do a different ten each night of the week, that is seventy people. With Sundays off, to keep us sane, we have sixty. If we keep union hours, we are looking at closer to thirty-five. There has to be a better way than union hours to figure out our sample size. So, before looking at sample size, we should examine three more probability sampling procedures.

Systematic Random Sampling

The second type of probability sampling is systematic random sampling. Here, the size of our population is divided by the desired sample size to give us our sampling interval. To state it more simply, if we only want half the population to be in the sample, we select every other person. If only a third of the population is needed to be in the sample, we pick every third person; for a quarter, every fourth person; for a fifth, every fifth person; and so on.

The problem with this approach is that we need to know our sample size in order to do it. We will not really know what our sample size ought to be until later in this chapter. At this point, we can only make a guess. Let us assume that we will work at our sleep lab every weeknight. Ten sleepers every night for five nights gives us a sample size of five nights times ten sleepers which equals fifty.

The idea of a sampling interval can be expressed mathematically in the following way. Suppose that our population size is 100 and we have set our sample size—the number of people taking part in our study—at fifty. Then, dividing the former by the latter (100/50 = 2) provides the size of the sampling interval, which in this case is two.

If our sample was only going to be one-fourth of the population instead of one-half, our sampling interval would be four instead of two. We might start at the fourth person on our sampling frame and pick out, as well, the eighth, twelfth, sixteenth persons, and so on.

The problem with this method is that everyone does not have the same chance of being selected. If we are selecting every other person, starting with the second person, we select the fourth, sixth, and so on. But this means that the third and the fifth never get a chance to be chosen. This procedure introduces a potential bias that calls for caution.

Suppose, for example, we have applied for a credit card and the credit card company examines our bank account every thirtieth day. Suppose, further, that the thirtieth day falls regularly on the day after we have paid this month's rent and on the day before we receive last month's paycheck. In other words, our bank account, while miserable at all times, is particularly low every thirtieth day. This is hardly fair because we never get a chance to show the company how rich we are on days other than the thirtieth.

If we do not have to worry about this sort of bias, then a systematic sample is largely the same as a simple random sample. The selection is just a bit easier because we do not have to bother with random numbers as presented in Table 9.1.

STRATIFIED RANDOM SAMPLING

The third type of probability sampling is stratified random sampling. If, for example, our study of depression and sleeping patterns is also concerned with religious affiliation, we can look at our population and count how many of them are Christians, Jews, Muslims, Buddhists, Hindus, Theosophists, and so forth. Suppose that, in our population of 100, we found 40 Jews, 19 Christians, 10 Muslims, 10 Buddhists, 10 Hindus, 10 Sikhs, and 1 lone Theosophist.

Now, we can sample our religious categories, or strata, either proportionally or disproportionally. If we sample our population proportionally, we will choose, say, one-tenth of each category to make up our sample; that is, we will randomly select 4 Jews, 1.9 Christians, 1 Muslim, 1 Buddhist, 1 Hindu, 1 Sikh, and 0.1 of a Theosophist. This comprises a total sample of 10, as illustrated in Table 9.2.

However; the 1.9 Christians and the 0.1 of a Theosophist present a difficulty. In this case, it is necessary to sample disproportionately. For example, it may be preferable to choose one member of each religious affiliation for a total sample of seven.

In this case, the sampling fraction is not the same for each category; it is 1/40 for Jews, 1/19 for Christians, 1/10 for Muslims, Buddhists, Hindus, and Sikhs, and 1 for Theosophists. A total sample of only seven is not a good idea for reasons that will be discussed shortly.

Our population is divided into religious categories only if we believe that religious affiliation will affect either depression or sleep patterns—that is, if we really believe that Buddhists who are depressed have different sleep patterns than Muslims who are depressed, everything else being equal.

However, we must admit that we do not believe this. There is nothing in the literature or our past experience to indicate anything of the sort. And anyway, our friend's clients who are depressed, from whom the sample will be drawn, will not include anything so interesting as Buddhists and Muslims. Probably the best we can hope for is a few odd sects and the town atheist.

This method, though, could be used to look at the sleep patterns of different age groups. Our population could be divided quite sensibly into eight categories: those aged 10 to 20, 21 to 30, and 31 to 40 years, and so on until we reach 81 to 90 years. We might then sample proportionately by randomly selecting one-tenth of the people in each category.

Or we might sample disproportionately by selecting, say, six people from each category, regardless of the number of people in the category. It might be preferable to sample disproportionately, for example, because there are a small number of people in the 71 to 80 and 81 to 90 categories, but it is our belief that advanced age significantly affects sleep patterns. Therefore, we want to include in our sample more than the one or two elderly people who would be included if we took one-tenth of each category.

Categorizing people in terms of age is fairly straightforward. They have only one age, and they usually know what it is. Other types of categories, though, are more complex. Psychological labels, for instance, can be uncertain such that people fall into more than one category and the categories themselves are not homogeneous; that is, the categories are not made up of people who are all alike.

There is no point in using stratified random sampling unless the categories are both homogeneous and different from each other. In theory, the more homogeneous the categories are, the fewer people will be needed from each category to make up our sample. Suppose, for example, we had invented robots that were designed to perform various tasks. Those robots designed to be electricians were all identical, and so were all the plumbers, doctors, lawyers, and so forth. Of course, each kind of robot was different from every other kind.

If we then wanted to make some comparison between all lawyer and all doctor robots, we would only need one of each because same-kind robots are all the same; or, in other words, the robot categories are completely homogeneous. People categories are never completely homogeneous, but the more homogeneous they are, the

TABLE 9.2
Stratified Random Sample Example

Category	Number	1/10 Proportionate Sample	Number and (Disproportionate Sampling Fractions) for a Sample of 1 per Category
Jews	40	4.0	1 (1/40)
Christians	19	1.9	1 (1/19)
Muslims	10	1.0	1 (1/10)
Buddhists	10	1.0	1 (1/10)
Hindus	10	1.0	1 (1/10)
Sikhs	10	1.0	1 (1/10)
Theosophists	1	.1	1 (1)
Totals....	100	10.0	7

fewer we need from each category to make comparisons. The fewer we need, the less our study will cost.

However, we must take care not to spend the money we save in this manner on the process of categorization. If people already are in categories, as they might be in a hospital, very good. If they are easy to categorize—say, by age—that's very good, too. If they are not already categorized and are difficult to categorize, it might be more appropriate to use another sampling method.

There is one more point to be considered. The more variables we are looking at, the harder it is to create homogeneous strata. It is easy enough, for example, to categorize people as Buddhists or Hindus, or as aged between 21 and 30 or 31 and 40. It is not nearly so easy if they have to be, say, between 21 and 30 *and* Buddhist.

CLUSTER RANDOM SAMPLING

The fourth type of probability sampling is cluster random sampling. This is useful if there is difficulty creating our sampling frame. Suppose, for a moment, we want to survey all the people in the area served by city transit to see whether they are satisfied with the transit system. We do not have a list of all these people to provide a sampling frame. There is a list, however, of all the communities in the city served by the transit system, and we can use this list as an alternative sampling frame.

First, we randomly select a community, or cluster, and survey every person living there. We will be certain what this community thinks about the transit system as we talked to every member of it. But there is still the possibility that this community, in which there are a large number of families with children, has a different opinion from that of a second community, which consists largely of senior citizens.

Perhaps we ought to survey the second community as well. Then there is a third community inhabited largely by penniless writers, artists, and social work students who might have yet a different opinion. Each community is reasonably homogeneous; that is, the people within each individual community are very much like each other. But the communities themselves are totally unlike; that is, they are heterogeneous with respect to each other.

One of the problems here is that we may not be able to afford to survey everyone in the three clusters. But we could compromise. Perhaps we could survey not every street in each cluster but only some streets taken at random—and not every house on our chosen streets, but only some houses, also taken at random. This way, we survey more clusters but fewer people in each cluster.

The only difficulty here is that, because we are not surveying everyone in the community, we might happen to select people who do not give us a true picture of that community. In a community of people with small children, for example, we might randomly select a couple who does not have children and does not intend to, and whose home was demolished, moreover, to make way for the transit line. Such untypical people introduce an error into our results that is due to our sampling procedure and is therefore called a sampling error.

We will now turn our attention to the next category of sampling procedures—nonprobability sampling.

Nonprobability Sampling

In nonprobability sampling, not all the people in the population have the same probability of being included in the sample, and for each one of them the probability of inclusion is unknown. This form of sampling is often used in exploratory studies where the purpose of the study is just to collect as much data as possible. There are four types of nonprobability sampling procedures:

— Availability Sampling

— Purposive Sampling

— Quota Sampling

— Snowball Sampling

AVAILABILITY SAMPLING

The first type of nonprobability sampling is availability sampling. It is also called *accidental sampling* and *convenience sampling*. It is the simplest of the four nonprobability sampling procedures. As its name suggests, it involves selecting for our sample the first people or units who make themselves available to us. We might survey people, for example, who pass us in a shopping mall.

Or we might base our study on the caseload of a particular social worker. Or we might just seize upon the first fifty of Ken's clients who are depressed who agree to sleep in our lab with wires attached to their heads. In fact, Ken himself was selected by availability—he was a friend of ours, and he was available. There was nothing random about selecting Ken whatsoever. Not very scientific to say the least, but very practical indeed.

PURPOSIVE SAMPLING

The second type of nonprobability sampling is purposive sampling. This type is used when we want to purposely choose a particular sample. For example, if we are testing a questionnaire that must be comprehensible to less well-educated people while not offending the intelligence of better-educated people, we might present it both to doctoral candidates and to people who left school cheerfully as soon as they could.

In other words, we purposely choose the doctoral candidates and the happy school leavers to be in our two subsamples. There is nothing random about it. In the same way, if we know from previous studies that there is more family violence in the city than in the country, we might restrict our sample to those families who live in cities. Purposive sampling is used a lot in interpretive research studies.

QUOTA SAMPLING

The third type of nonprobability sampling is quota sampling. In this type of sampling, we decide, on the basis of theory, that we should include in our sample so many of a certain type of person. Suppose we wanted to relate the sleep patterns of people who are depressed to body weight and age.

We might decide to look at extremes; for example, obese and young, nonobese and young, obese and old, and nonobese and old. This gives us four categories (i.e., A, B, C, and D) as illustrated in Table 9.3. We might want, for example, fifteen people in each category, or for some reason we might need more elderly people than young.

TABLE 9.3
Quota Sampling Matrix of Body Weight by Age

	Body Weight	
Age	Obese	Nonobese
Young	Category A Obese/Young	Category B Nonobese/Young
Old	Category C Obese/Old	Category D Nonobese/Old

In this case, we may decide on ten people in each of categories A and B and twenty people in each of categories C and D.

Whatever quotas we decide on, we only have to find enough people to fill them who satisfy the two conditions of age and weight. We might discover all the obese people at a weight loss clinic, for example, or all the young, nonobese ones at a clinic for anorexics. It does not matter where or how we find them so long as we do.

SNOWBALL SAMPLING

The fourth type of nonprobability sampling is snowball sampling. If a follow-up study is to be conducted on a self-help group that broke up two years ago, for example, we might find one member of the group and ask that member to help us locate other members. The other members will then find other members and so on until the whole group has been located.

The process is a bit like telling one person a secret, with strict instructions not to tell it to anyone else. Like purposive sampling, snowball sampling is commonly used in interpretive research studies.

SAMPLE SIZE

Before our sample can be selected, we obviously have to decide on how many people are needed to take part in our study; in other words, we have to decide on our sample size. The correct sample size depends on both our population and research question.

If we are dealing with a limited population, for example, such as the victims of some rare disease, we might include the whole population in our study. Then we would not take a sample. Usually, however, the population is large enough that we do need to take a sample, the general rule being the larger the sample, the better.

As far as a minimal sample size is concerned, experts differ. Some say that a sample of 30 will allow us to perform basic statistical procedures, while others would advise a minimum sample size of 100. In fact, sample size depends on how homogeneous our population is with respect to the variables we are studying.

Recalling all those categories of robot doctors, lawyers, and so forth considered a while back, if our population of robot doctors is all the same—that is, homogeneous—we only need one robot doctor in our sample. On the other hand, if the factory messed up and our robot doctors have emerged with a wide range of medical skills, we will need a large sample to tell us anything about the medical skills of the entire robot doctor population. In this case, of course, medical skill is the variable we are studying.

Sample size must also be considered in relation to the number of categories required. If the sample size is too small, there may be only one or two people in a particular category—for example, 1.9 Christians and 0.1 of a Theosophist. This should be anticipated and the sample size adjusted. The situation can also be handled using the disproportionate stratified random sampling procedure. This procedure is the one where we selected one person from each religious category, thus neatly avoiding our 1.9 Christians and 0.1 of a Theosophist.

There are many formulas available for calculating sample size, but they are complicated and difficult to use. Usually, a sample size of one-tenth of the population is considered sufficient to provide reasonable control over sampling error. The same one-tenth convention also applies to categories of the population; we can include one-tenth of each category in our sample.

Now that you know that more confidence can be placed in the generalizability of statistics from larger samples when compared to smaller ones, you may be eager to work with random samples that are as large as possible. Unfortunately, researchers often cannot afford to sample a very large number of cases.

They therefore try to determine during the design phase of their studies how large a sample they must have to achieve their purposes. They have to consider the degree of confidence desired, the homogeneity of the population, the complexity of the analysis they plan, and the expected strength of the relationships they will measure. Russell Schutt (2008) presents a few pointers when it comes to selecting sample sizes:

- The less sampling error desired, the larger the sample size must be.

- Samples of more homogeneous populations can be smaller than samples of more diverse populations. Stratified sampling uses prior information on the population to create more homogeneous population strata from which the sample can be selected, so the sample can be smaller than if simple random sampling were used.

✸ If the only analysis planned for a survey sample is to describe the population in terms of a few variables, a smaller sample is required than if a more complex analysis involving sample subgroups is planned.

✸ When the researchers will be testing hypotheses and expect to find very strong relationships between and among the variables, they will need smaller samples to detect these relationships than if they expect weaker relationships.

BOX 9.1
Cultural Sensitivity and Sampling

Sampling—how we select people to participate in research studies—has been and remains problematic in culturally based studies. In some cases, it is very difficult to define the population to be studied, let alone draw a representative sample from the population. For example, sexual orientation remains ill defined, thereby rendering studies with this population somewhat limited. Given the limited precision with which we define groups, convenience sampling (studying those who are available) is prominent in cultural and ethnic research. Convenience samples can be problematic for a variety of reasons.

It is certain that convenience samples will be biased. For example, the literature on African Americans is focused primarily upon poor and disadvantaged individuals and families. Many poor and disadvantaged African Americans appear at public agencies to seek some type of assistance. While seeking assistance, they may participate in research studies or provide data that then are used to make inferences about all African Americans in general.

However, are we certain that data collected from poor and disadvantaged African Americans are applicable to African Americans who are not similarly disadvantaged? Probably not. Nevertheless, generalizations based upon skewed samples have been made with respect to all African Americans.

A similar predicament exists in terms of sexual orientation. The emergence of AIDS and HIV has brought much attention to gays. Sexual activity and other behaviors associated with contracting and transmitting the HIV were scrutinized. Some researchers concluded that some gays have many sexual partners and use illicit substances. This may be true for some, but not all.

Recent efforts by gays to gain legal recognition of same-sex unions and marriages suggest that some gays prefer long-term relationships over casual sexual encounters. Overgeneralizations, based upon research samples of gays with AIDS and their substance-abuse behaviors, have hindered understanding of gays and their relationships.

Research studies that have focused on women's issues are also subject to sampling errors. As mentioned previously, research samples composed of single mothers in poverty have been used to make generalizations for all women. Convenience samples drawn from women living under poverty conditions are insufficient when addressing the needs of women who may not be in poverty.

It is nearly impossible to replicate a research study that uses a convenience sample. As we know, one of the benchmarks of the scientific method is its ability to replicate research studies. Research studies that use convenience samples, however, are susceptible to local and geographic influences. The extent of the generalization of their findings is compromised because of the susceptibility to regional influences.

Although convenience samples may be better than no samples at all, recognition of the limitations of convenience samples must be observed when interpreting a study's findings. The dangers of overgeneralizations made from samples that are too small or inadequate can have far-reaching negative consequences for the populations being studied.

In a perfect world (and where would that be?), probabilistic sampling techniques are preferable to nonprobabilistic ones. Inadequate definitions of specific population parameters (or sampling frame) of minority and ethnic populations increase the difficulty associated with adequate sample selections. Sampling remains an area requiring further refinement if we are to improve research efforts with women and with ethnic and cultural groups.

Researchers can make more precise estimates of the sample size required through a method termed *statistical power analysis*. Statistical power analysis requires a good advance estimate of the strength of the hypothesized relationship in the population.

In addition, the math is complicated, so it helps to have some background in mathematics or to be able to consult a statistician. For these reasons, many researchers do not conduct formal power analyses when deciding how many cases to sample.

You can obtain some general guidance about sample sizes from the current practices of social scientists. For professional studies of the national population in which only a simple description is desired, professional social science studies typically have used a sample size of between 1,000 and 1,500, with up to 2,500 being included if detailed analyses are planned.

Studies of local or regional populations often sample only a few hundred people, in part because these studies lack sufficient funding to draw larger samples. Of course, the sampling error in these smaller studies is considerably larger than in a typical national study (Schutt, 2008).

LESSONS ABOUT SAMPLE QUALITY

RAFAEL ENGLE AND RUSSELL SCHUTT (2010) provide a few points that are implicit in the evaluation of samples:

- We can't evaluate the quality of a sample if we don't know what population it is supposed to represent. If the population is unspecified because the researchers were never clear about just what population they were trying to sample, then we can safely conclude that the sample itself is no good.

- We can't evaluate the quality of a sample if we don't know just how cases in the sample were selected from the population. If the method was specified, we then need to know whether cases were selected in a systematic fashion or on the basis of chance. In any case, we know that a haphazard method of sampling (e.g., availability sampling) undermines the generalizability of the findings.

- Sample quality is determined by the sample actually obtained, not just by the sampling method itself. If many of the people selected for our sample are nonrespondents or people (or other entities) who do not participate in the study although they have been selected for the sample, the quality of our sample is undermined—even if we chose the sample in the best possible way.

- We need to be aware that even researchers who obtain very good samples may talk about the implications of their findings for some other groups that are larger than or just different from the population they actually sampled. For example, findings from a representative sample of students in one university often are discussed as if they tell us about university students in general. And maybe they do; we just don't know.

 ## ADVANTAGES AND DISADVANTAGES

Thomas Black (1999), via Table 9.4, provides us with a brief list of the advantages and disadvantages of the various sampling techniques that can be used in social work research studies.

TABLE 9.4

Advantages and Disadvantages of Various Sampling Techniques

Type	Description	Advantages	Disadvantages
Simple random	Random sample from whole population	Highly representative if all research participants participate; the ideal	Not possible without complete list of population members; potentially uneconomical to achieve; can be disruptive to isolate members from a group; time-scale may be too long, data/sample could change
Stratified random	Random sample from identifiable groups (strata), subgroups, etc.	Can ensure that specific groups are represented, even proportionally, in the sample(s) (e.g., by gender) by selecting individuals from strata list	More complex, requires greater effort than simple random; strata must be carefully defined
Cluster	Random samples of successive clusters of research participants (e.g., by institution) until small groups are chosen as units	Possible to select randomly when no single list of population members exists, but local lists do; data collected on groups may avoid introduction of confounding by isolating members	Clusters in a level must be equivalent, and some natural ones are not for essential characteristics (e.g., geographic: numbers equal, but unemployment rates differ)
Stage	Combination of cluster (randomly selecting clusters) and random or stratified random sampling of individuals	Can make up probability sample by random at stages and within groups; possible to select random sample when population lists are very localized	Complex, combines limitations of cluster and stratified random sampling
Purposive	Handpicked research participants on the basis of specific characteristics	Ensures balance of group sizes when multiple groups are to be selected	Samples are not easily defensible as being representative of populations due to potential subjectivity of researcher

Quota	Research participants selected as they come in order to fill a quota by characteristics proportional to populations	Ensures selection of adequate numbers of research participants with appropriate characteristics	Not possible to prove that the sample is representative of designated population
Snowball	Research participants with desired traits or characteristics give names of further appropriate research participants	Possible to include members of groups where no lists or identifiable clusters even exist (e.g., drug abusers, criminals)	No way of knowing whether the sample is representative of the population from which it was drawn
Accidental	Either asking for volunteers, or the consequence of not all those selected finally participating, or a set of research participants who just happen to be available	Inexpensive way of ensuring sufficient number of research participants in a study	Can be highly unrepresentative

SUMMARY

In the course of a research study, the entire population that we are interested in is usually too big to work with, and in any case we rarely have enough money to include everyone. For these reasons, it is necessary to draw a sample. The idea is that the sample represents the population from which it was drawn; that is, the sample is identical to the population with respect to every variable that we are interested in.

When the sample is truly representative of the population, we can generalize the results received from the sample back to the population from which it was drawn. No sample is ever totally representative of the population from which it was drawn. Now that we know how to draw a sample from a population, we will turn our attention to the use of research designs that use samples—the topic of the next chapter.

Study Questions for Chapter 9

— First, answer each question only AFTER you have read the chapter.

— Second, indicate how comfortable you were in answering each question on a 5-point scale:

1	2	3	4	5
Very uncomfortable	Somewhat uncomfortable	Neutral	Somewhat comfortable	Very comfortable

If you rated any question between 1–3, please reread the section of the chapter where the information for the question can be found. If you're still uncomfortable answering the question, talk with your instructor and/or your classmates for more clarification.

Questions	Degree of comfort? (Circle one number)
1. In your own words, discuss the concepts of populations and sampling frames. Provide a single social work example throughout your discussion.	1 2 3 4 5
2. List and then discuss the various probability sampling procedures. Provide as many social work examples as you can to illustrate your main points.	1 2 3 4 5
3. List and then discuss the various nonprobability sampling procedures. Provide as many social work examples as you can to illustrate your main points.	1 2 3 4 5
4. Discuss the concept of sample size. Provide a social work example throughout your discussion.	1 2 3 4 5
5. Take a look at Table 9.4. From this table, and in your own words, discuss each advantage and disadvantage of all eight types of sampling techniques. Provide a social work example that highlights your points.	1 2 3 4 5
6. At this point in your course, how comfortable are you with discussing the various sampling methods presented in this chapter with your field instructor (or your supervisor at work)? With your fellow classmates? Discuss in detail.	1 2 3 4 5

7. Find a research article that uses one of the sampling methods discussed in this chapter. Critique the sampling method used. Could the author have used a better sampling method? If so, which one? Why?	1 2 3 4 5

Assessing Your Self-Efficacy for Chapter 9

AFTER you have read the chapter AND have completed all the study questions, please indicate how knowledgeable you feel you are for each concept listed below.

1	2	3	4	5
Very uncomfortable	Somewhat uncomfortable	Neutral	Somewhat comfortable	Very comfortable

Major Concepts in Chapter	Knowledge Level? (Circle one number)
1. Populations, sampling frames, and samples	1 2 3 4 5
2. Simple random sampling	1 2 3 4 5
3. Systematic random sampling	1 2 3 4 5
4. Stratified random sampling	1 2 3 4 5
5. Cluster random sampling	1 2 3 4 5
6. Nonprobability sampling procedures	1 2 3 4 5
7. Availability sampling	1 2 3 4 5
8. Quota sampling	1 2 3 4 5
9. Snowball sampling	1 2 3 4 5
10. Sample size	1 2 3 4 5
11. Cultural sensitivity and sampling	1 2 3 4 5
12. Advantages and disadvantages of various sampling methods	1 2 3 4 5
Add up your scores (Minimum = 12, Maximum = 60)	Total score =

A   54 — 60 = Social Work Manager in the making.
B   48 — 53 = Social Work Supervisor.
C   42 — 47 = Social Work Practitioner.
D   12 — 41 = Case Aide. Reread the chapter and redo the study questions.

10

Single-Subject Designs

"Google" is not a synonym for "research."
~ Dan Brown

The last chapter discussed how we can select research participants for our research studies. This chapter is a logical extension of the previous one in that we now discuss simple research designs that will include our selected research participants. The simplest type of research designs—the topic of this chapter—is commonly referred to as single-subject designs. They are also called *single-case designs, single-system designs, N = 1, case-level designs, single-case experimentations,* and *idiographic research.*

WHAT ARE SINGLE-SUBJECT DESIGNS?

On a very general level, single-subject designs are more "practice orientated" than group-level designs (discussed in the next chapter). That is, they are used more by social work "practitioners" than by social work "researchers."

Single-subject designs provide data about how well a treatment intervention is working so that alternative or complementary interventive strategies can be adopted if necessary. They can also indicate when a client's problem has been resolved. Single-subject designs are used to monitor client progress up to, and sometimes beyond, the point of termination.

They can also be used to evaluate the effectiveness of a social service program as a whole by aggregating or compiling the results obtained by numerous social workers serving their individual clients within the program. A family social service program might be evaluated, for example, by combining family outcomes on a number of families that have been seen by different social workers who work within the program.

According to Bloom, Fischer, and Orme (2009), the advantages of single-subject designs are as follows:

- They can be built into every social worker's practice with each and every case/situation without disruption of practice.

- They provide the tools for evaluating the effectiveness of our practice with each client, group, or system with which we work.

- They focus on individual clients or systems. If there is any variation in effect from one client or system to another, single-subject designs will be able to pick it up.

- They provide a continuous record of changes in the target problem over the entire course of intervention, not just pre- and posttest.

- They are practice-based and practitioner-oriented. Single-subject designs provide continuous assessment and outcome data to practitioners so that they can monitor progress and make changes in the nature of the intervention program if so indicated. Unlike traditional group designs—and the intervention programs they are used to evaluate—which ordinarily cannot be changed once the study has begun, single-subject designs are flexible; the worker can change the intervention and the design depending on the needs of the case.

- They can be used to test hypotheses or ideas regarding the relationship between specific intervention procedures and client changes, ruling out some alternative explanations and allowing an inference regarding causality: Was the intervention program responsible for the change in the target problem?

- They can be used to help the worker *assess* the case/situation, leading to selection of a more appropriate program of intervention by clarifying what seem to be the relevant factors involved in the problem.

They essentially are theory-free; that is, they can be applied to the practice of any practitioner regardless of the worker's theoretical orientation or approach to practice.

They are relatively easy to use and understand. They can be applied within the same time-frame the social worker is currently using in seeing clients or others. In fact, the use of single-subject designs can actually enhance the worker's efficiency by saving time and energy in trying to record and evaluate the social worker's practice.

They avoid the problem of outside researchers coming into an agency and imposing a study on the social workers. Single-subject designs are established and conducted by practitioners for their benefit and for the benefit of the client/systems.

They provide a model for demonstrating our accountability to ourselves, our clients and consumers, our funding sources, and our communities. Systematic, consistent use of single-subject designs allows practitioners and agencies to collect a body of data about the effectiveness of practice that provides more or less objective information about the success of our practice.

THE RESEARCH PROCESS

Any research design—positivistic and interpretive alike—is nothing more than a plan for conducting the entire research study from beginning to end. They all try to answer the following basic questions:

When, or over what period, should the research study be conducted?

What variables need to be measured?

How should the variables be measured?

What other variables need to be accounted for or controlled?

From whom should the data be collected?

How should the data be collected?

When should the data be collected?

How should the data be analyzed?

How should the results of the study be disseminated?

As you should know by now, these questions are highly commingled and are directly related to the research question we are trying to answer or the hypothesis we are testing. If you are exploring the concept of bereavement, for example, you will collect data from bereaved people and perhaps involved social workers, and you may also need to measure variables related to bereavement, such as grief, anger, depression, and levels of coping.

You might need to measure these variables over a period of months or years, and the way you measure them will suggest appropriate methods of how you will analyze your data. Decisions about how best to accomplish these steps depend on how much we already know about the bereavement process; that is, where your bereavement research questions fall on the knowledge level continuum as presented in Chapter 2.

 # UNIT OF ANALYSIS

Single-subject designs are used to fulfill the major purpose of social work practice: to improve the situation of a client system—*an* individual client, *a* couple, *a* family, *a* group, *an* organization, or *a* community. Any of these client configurations can be studied with a single-subject design. In short, they are used to study *one* individual or *one* group intensively, as opposed to studies that use two or more groups of research participants.

Some single-subject designs are conducted in order to study one individual or case, some to study groups of people (including families, organizations, and communities), and some to study social artifacts (such things as birth practices or divorces). The individual, group, or artifact being studied is called the *unit of analysis*.

If you are exploring the advantages and disadvantages of home birth, for example, you might be asking questions from women who have experienced homebirth, but the thing you are studying—the *unit of analysis*—is the social artifact, home birth. Conversely, if you are a social work practitioner studying the impact of home birth on a particular client, the unit of analysis is the client or individual; and if you are studying the impact on a group of women, the unit of analysis is the group of women.

 # REQUIREMENTS OF SINGLE-SUBJECT DESIGNS

The following discussion on the requirements of single-subject designs has been adapted and modified from three sources: Grinnell and Williams (1990); Williams, Tutty, and Grinnell (1995); and Williams, Unrau, and Grinnell (1998). In order to carry out a single-subject design: (1) The client's problem must be identified, (2) the desired objective to be achieved must be decided upon, (3) the intervention that is most likely to eliminate the client's problem must be selected, (4) the intervention must be implemented, and (5) the client's progress must be continually monitored to see whether the client's problem has been resolved, or at least reduced.

If practitioners are careful to organize, measure, and record what they do, via the previous five points, single-subject designs will naturally take shape in the clients' files, and the results can be used to guide future interventive efforts. Only three things are required when doing a single-subject design:

— Setting Measurable Client Objectives

— Selecting Valid and Reliable Outcome Measures

— Graphically Displaying the Resulting Data

SETTING MEASURABLE CLIENT OBJECTIVES

ONE OF THE FIRST TASKS a worker does when initially seeing a client is to establish the purpose of why they are together. Why has the client approached the worker? Or, in many nonvoluntary situations such as in probation and parole or child abuse situations, why has the worker approached the client? The two need to formulate objectives for their mutual working relationship.

TARGET PROBLEMS

A specific, measurable, client-desired outcome objective is known as a *client target problem*. Client target problems are feelings, knowledge levels, or behaviors that need to be changed. Many times clients do not have just one target problem, they have many. They sometimes have a number of interrelated problems; even when there is only one that is more important than the rest, they may not know what it is. Nevertheless, they may be quite clear about the desired outcome of their involvement with social work services.

They may want to "fix" their lives so that "Johnny listens when I ask him to do something," or "My partner pays more attention to me," or "I feel better about myself at work." Unfortunately, many clients express their desired target problems in vague, ambiguous terms, possibly because they do not know themselves exactly what they want to change; they only know that something should be different. If a worker can establish (with the guidance of the client) what should be changed, why it should be changed, how it should be changed, and to what degree it should be changed, the solution to the problem will not be far away.

CLEARLY STATING THE TARGET PROBLEM. Consider Heather, for example, who wants her partner Ben to pay more attention to her. Heather may mean sexual attention, in which case the couple's sexual relations may be the target problem. On the other hand, Heather may mean that she and Ben do not socialize enough with friends, or that Ben brings work home from the office too often or has hobbies she does not share, or any of a host of things.

Establishing clearly what the desired change would look like is the first step in developing the target problem. Without this, the worker and client could wander around forever through the problem maze, never knowing what, if anything, needs to be solved. Desired change cannot occur if no one knows what change is desired. It is, therefore, very important that the target problem to be solved be precisely stated as early as possible in the client–social worker relationship.

Continuing with the example of Heather and Ben, and after a great deal of exploration, the worker agrees that Heather and Ben have many target problems to work on, such as improving their child-discipline strategies, improving their budgeting skills, improving their communication skills, and many other issues that, when dealt with, can lead to a successful marriage.

For now, however, they agree to work on one target problem: increasing the amount of time they spend together with friends. Heather may say that she wishes she and Ben could visit friends together more often. The target problem has now become a little more specific: it has narrowed from "increasing the amount of time they spend together with friends" to "Heather and Ben visiting friends more often." "Visiting friends more often with Ben," however, is still an ambiguous phrase. It may mean once a month or every night, and the achievement of the target problem's solution cannot be known until the meaning of "more often" has been clarified.

If Heather agrees that she would be happy to visit friends with Ben once a week, the ambiguous objective may be restated as a specific, measurable objective—"to visit friends with Ben once a week." The social worker may discover later that "friends" is also an ambiguous term. Heather may have meant "her friends," but Ben may have meant "his friends," and the social worker may have imagined that "the friends" were mutual.

The disagreement about who is to be regarded as a friend may not become evident until the worker has monitored their progress for a month or so and found that no improvement was occurring. In some cases, poor progress may be due to the selection of an inappropriate interventive strategy. In other cases, it may mean that the target problem itself is not as specific, complete, and clear as it should be. Before deciding that the interventive strategy needs to be changed, it is always necessary to clarify with the client exactly what it is that specifically needs to be achieved.

SELECTING VALID AND RELIABLE OUTCOME MEASURES

A TARGET PROBLEM must be measureable with valid and reliable measuring instruments as discussed in Chapters 7 and 8. Can Heather and Ben, who wanted to visit friends more often, be trusted to report truthfully on whether the friends were visited? Suppose she says they were not visited and he says they were? Social workers must always be very conscious of what measurement methods are both available and feasible when formulating a target problem with a client.

It may be quite possible for the social worker to telephone the friends and ask if they were visited; but if the worker is not prepared to get involved with Heather's and Ben's friends, this measurement method will not be feasible. If this is the case, and if Heather and/or Ben cannot be trusted to report accurately and truthfully, there is little point in setting the target problem.

Heather's and Ben's target problem can be easily observed and measured. However, quite often a client's target problem involves feelings, attitudes, knowledge levels, or events that are known only to the client and cannot be easily observed and/or measured.

Consider Bob, a client who comes to a social worker because he is depressed. The worker's efforts may be simply to lessen his target problem, depression, but how will the worker and/or Bob know when his depression has been alleviated or reduced?

Perhaps he will say that he feels better, or his partner may say that Bob cries less, or the worker may note that he spends less time in therapy staring at his feet. All these are indicators that his depression is lessening, but they are not very valid and reliable indicators. What is needed is a more "scientific method" of measuring depression. Fortunately, a number of paper-and-pencil standardized measuring instruments have been developed that can be filled out by the client in a relatively short period of time, can be easily scored, and can provide a fairly accurate picture of the client's condition.

One such widely used instrument that measures depression is Hudson's *General Contentment Scale* (*GCS*). Because higher scores indicate higher levels of depression, and lower scores indicate lower levels of depression, the target problem in Bob's case would be to reduce his score on the *GCS* to a level at which he can adequately function. People who are not depressed will still not score zero on the *GCS*. Everyone occasionally feels blue (Item 2) or downhearted (Item 10). There is a clinical cutting score that differentiates a clinically significant problem level from a non-clinically significant problem level, and it will often be this score that the client aims to achieve.

If the target problem is "to reduce Bob's score on the *GCS* to or below the clinical cutting score of 30," the worker will know not only what the target problem is, but also precisely how Bob's success is to be measured. Usually, client success, sometimes referred to as client outcome, can be measured in a variety of ways. Bob's partner, Maria, for example, may be asked to record the frequency of his crying spells, and the target problem here may be to reduce the frequency of these spells to once a week or less.

Again, it would be important to further refine the term "crying spell" so that Maria knows exactly what it was she has to measure. Perhaps "crying spell" could be defined as ten minutes or more of continuous crying, and a gap of at least ten minutes without crying would define the difference between one "spell" and another.

There are now two independent and complementary indicators of Bob's level of depression: the *GCS* as rated by Bob, and the number of his ten-minute crying spells per day as rated by Maria. If future scores on both indicators display improvement (that is, they both go down), the worker can be reasonably certain that Bob's depression is lessening and the intervention is effective.

If the two indicators do not agree, however, the worker will need to find out why. Perhaps Bob wishes to appear more depressed than he really is, and this is an area that needs to be explored. Or perhaps Maria is not sufficiently concerned to keep an accurate recording of the number of Bob's ten-minute crying spells per day; and it may be Maria's attitude that has caused Bob's crying in the first place.

Accurate measurements made over time can do more than reveal the degree of a client's improvement. They can cast light on the problem itself and suggest new avenues to be explored, possibly resulting in the utilization of different interventive strategies.

Be that as it may, a client's target problem cannot be dealt with until it has been expressed in specific measurable indicators. These indicators cannot be said to be measurable until it has been decided how they will be measured. Specification of the target problem will, therefore, often include mention of an instrument that will be used to measure it. It will also include who is to do the measuring and under what circumstances.

It may be decided, for example, that Bob will rate himself on the *GCS* daily after dinner or once a week on Saturday morning, or that Maria will make a daily record of all crying spells that occurred in the late afternoon after he returned home from work. The physical record itself is very important, both as an aid to memory and to track Bob's progress. In a single-subject design, progress is usually monitored by displaying the measurements made in the form of graphs.

GRAPHICALLY DISPLAYING THE RESULTING DATA

AS WE KNOW from Chapter 7, the word *measurement* can be simply defined as the process of assigning a number or value to a variable. If the variable, or target problem, being considered is depression as measured by Hudson's *Generalized Contentment Scale* (*GCS*), and if Bob scores, say 62, then 62 is the number assigned to Bob's initial level of depression.

The worker will try to reduce his initial score of 62 to at least 30—the desired *minimum* score. The worker can then select and implement an intervention and ask Bob to complete the *GCS* again—say, once a week—until the score of 30 has been reached. Bob's depression levels can be plotted over time on a graph such as the ones displayed in this chapter.

EXPLORATORY DESIGNS

Suppose you have a client—Cecilia—whose underlying problem, you believe, is her high anxiety level. She will be the "subject" in your single-subject design. Before you go ahead with an intervention designed to decrease her social anxiety—an intervention Cecilia doesn't need if your belief is wrong—you will have to answer the simple question, "Does Cecilia really have a clinically significant problem with anxiety?" In other words, does the "anxiety problem" you think she has really exist in the first place?

In order to answer this question, you select a measuring instrument to measure her social anxiety level that is valid, reliable, sensitive, nonreactive, and useful in this particular situation. Say you choose the *Interaction and Audience Anxiousness Scale* (*IASS*). On this particular measuring instrument, higher scores indicate higher social anxiety levels, and the minimal clinical cutting score is 40. Clinical cutting scores are usually displayed as dashed lines, as can be seen in Figure 10.1. You administer the *IASS* to Cecilia, and she scores 62 as shown in Figure 10.1.

Scores above the clinical cutting score indicate a clinically significant problem. You might think "Ah-ha! She has a problem since her score was 22 points higher than the 'minimum clinical cutting score,'" and you rush forward with your intervention.

On the other hand, any social work intervention has the potential to harm as well as help (in the same way that any medication does), and you first want to be sure that this is a persisting problem and not just a reflection of Cecilia's high anxiety today. You might also want to be sure that her high anxiety problem will not go away by itself. Doctors usually do not treat conditions that resolve themselves, given time, and the same is true for social workers.

In order to see if Cecilia meets these three criteria for treatment—first, there really is a problem; second, the problem is persisting; and third, the problem is either stable at an unacceptable level or getting worse—you will need to administer the same measuring instrument two or three times more at intervals of, say, a week. You might then graph your results as shown in Figure 10.1. This figure constitutes a baseline measure of Cecilia's social anxiety level over a seven-week period and is a very simple example of an *A* design.

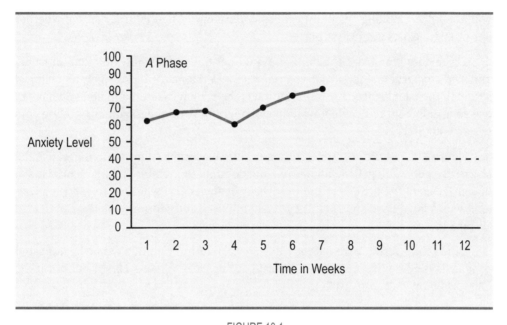

FIGURE 10.1

**A Design: Cecilia's Social Anxiety Scores for the First Seven Weeks
(Indicating that an intervention is warranted)**

There are four exploratory designs:

— *A* Design

— *B* Design

— *BB*₁ Design

— *BC* Design

A DESIGN

AT THE RISK of sounding a bit ridiculous, we'll note that the letter *A* simply designates "a research study" where the intention is to establish, via measurement, a baseline for an individual client's problem. Perhaps "research study" is a grandiose term to describe a routine assessment, but the word *re-search* does mean *to look again,* and you are indeed looking again at Cecilia's potential problem in order to see whether her problem exists in the first place.

Three data points are the minimum number needed to show any kind of trend, and some experts maintain that you need no less than seven. However, in a clinical situation the client's need for intervention is the primary factor, and you will have to use your judgment to decide how long you ought to continue to gather baseline data before you intervene.

Figure 10.1b indicates a worsening problem, needing intervention, because the scores are generally getting higher as time goes on. Remember, higher scores mean higher levels of the problem. Had the scores been generally getting lower, the problem would have been improving by itself, and no intervention would be indicated (Figure 10.1a).

If the scores fell more or less on a horizontal line, intervention would be indicated so long as the line was above the clinical cutting score (Figure 10.1b) but not if the line was below it (Figure 10.1c).

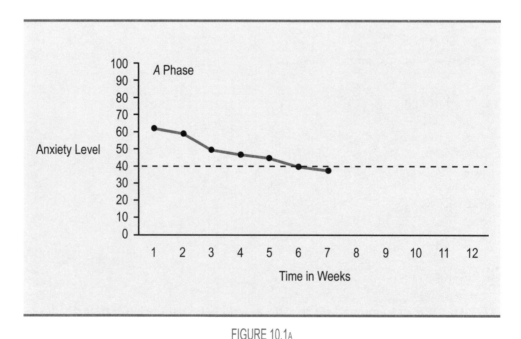

FIGURE 10.1A

A Design: Cecilia's Social Anxiety Scores for the First Seven Weeks (Indicating that an intervention is NOT warranted)

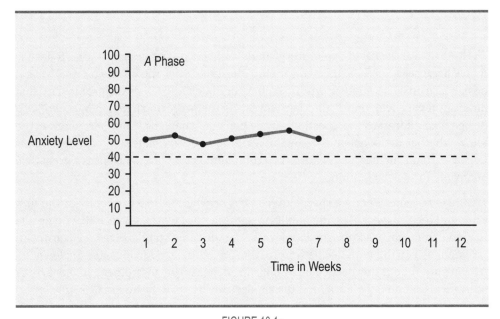

FIGURE 10.1B

A Design: Cecilia's Social Anxiety Scores for the First Seven Weeks
(Indicating that an intervention IS warranted)

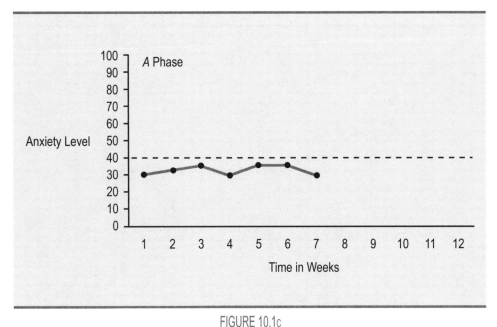

FIGURE 10.1c

A Design: Cecilia's Social Anxiety Scores for the First Seven Weeks
(Indicating that an intervention is NOT warranted)

B DESIGN

THE SECOND TYPE of exploratory single-subject research design is the *B* design. As we have seen, an *A* design answers the question "Does the problem exist?" The *A* design also answers another type of exploratory question: "Does the problem exist at different levels over time?" In other words, "Is the problem changing *by itself?*" A *B* design also addresses the question "Is the problem changing?" but here we want to know whether the problem is changing *while an intervention is being applied.* Bob is Cecilia's friend and has also come to you complaining that he experiences a great deal of anxiety in social situations.

He is nervous when he speaks to his boss or when he meets people for the first time, and the prospect of giving public presentations at work appalls him. You decide that you will measure Bob's anxiety level using the same standardized measuring instrument as you did with Cecilia (Interaction and Audience Anxiousness Scale, *IASS*). As you know about this particular standardized measuring instrument, higher scores indicate higher anxiety levels, and the clinical cutting score for the *IASS* is 40.

Bob, like Cecilia, scores 62. This one score is more of a base point rather than a baseline, but you decide that it would be inappropriate to collect baseline data over time in Bob's case as he is experiencing a great deal of discomfort at work, is highly nervous in your presence (you are a stranger, after all), and probably will not be able

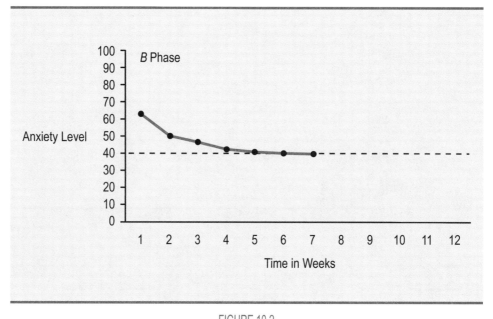

FIGURE 10.2

B Design: Bob's Anxiety Scores for the First Seven Weeks

to bring himself to seek help in the future if he does not receive some kind of intervention now.

You therefore begin your intervention, engaging Bob to the extent that he returns the following week, when you administer the *IASS* again. Now he scores 52. In the third week, he scores 49, as shown in Figure 10.2. Figure 10.2 is a simple example of a *B* design, in which you track change in the problem level at the same time as you are intervening. You do not know, from this graph, whether your intervention *caused* the change you see. Anything else could have caused it.

Perhaps Bob is having a weekly massage to reduce muscle tension, or his boss has been fired, or the public presentation that he was supposed to do has been postponed. Therefore, you cannot use the *B* design to answer explanatory research questions that come quite high on the knowledge continuum (refer to Figure 2.1).

On the other hand, you might make the clinical decision that it is worth trying a variation on your intervention: you might apply it more *frequently* by having Bob come twice a week instead of once, or you might apply it more *intensively* by increasing the amount of time Bob is expected to spend each evening on relaxation exercises. You can graph the changes that occur while you are applying the variation, as shown in Figure 10.3.

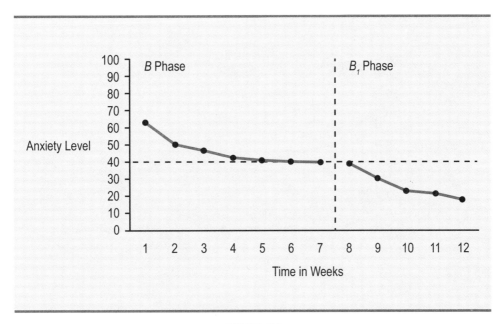

FIGURE 10.3

Bob's Anxiety Scores for the *B* Phase and *B₁* Phase

BB_1 DESIGN

FIGURE 10.2 shows that Bob's anxiety level has improved but it has not fallen below the clinical cutting score. Moreover, it does not look as though it will because it has been relatively stable for the last three weeks. It may be that Bob is a naturally anxious person and no intervention, however inspired, will reduce his problem to below clinically significant levels.

Figure 10.3 shows two *phases:* the *B* phase and the B_1 phase, separated by the vertical dotted line that runs between weeks 7 and 8. Week 7 marks the end of your original intervention, designated by the *B* intervention, and all the scores obtained by Bob while you were applying the *B* intervention constitute the *B* phase.

If it seems odd to call the first intervention *B* instead of *A*, remember that *A* has been used already to designate baseline scores. Week 8 marks the beginning of the variation on your original intervention, designated B_1, and all the scores obtained by Bob while you were applying the variation constitute the B_1 phase. The *B* and B_1 phases together constitute the BB_1 design.

When you look at the low scores Bob achieved in weeks 9–12, you might be tempted to think "Hallelujah! My specific intervention *did* work. All Bob needed was a bit more of it." However, the same considerations apply to the BB_1 design as apply to the *B* design. You simply cannot be sure that there is any relationship between your intervention and Bob's decreased anxiety, far less that one was the cause of the other.

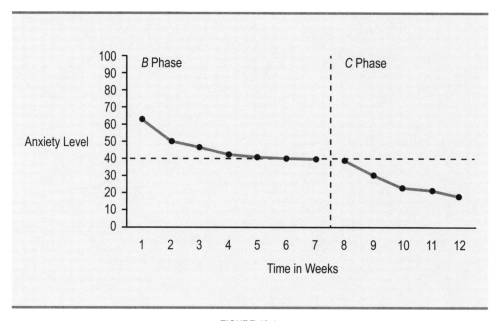

FIGURE 10.4

BC Design: Bob's Anxiety Scores for *B* Phase and *C* Phase

BC DESIGN

THE LAST exploratory single-subject research design is the *BC* design. Let us go back in time, to the point where you decided that it was worth trying a variation on your *B* intervention with Bob. Suppose you had decided instead to try an entirely different intervention, designated as *C* because it is a *different* intervention, following immediately after *B*.

Now you implement the *C* intervention, administering the *IASS* every week, graphing your results, and creating a *C* phase after the *B* phase as shown in Figure 10.4. Again, the *B* phase in Figure 10.4 is copied from Figure 10.2, and after the *C* intervention you see that Bob has succeeded in reducing his anxiety level to below the clinical cutting score of 40.

Repressing your hallelujahs, you realize that there is still no sure relationship between your intervention and Bob's success. Indeed, the waters are becoming more murky because even if your intervention was in fact related to Bob's success you would still not know whether it was the *C* intervention that did the trick, or a delayed reaction to *B,* or some combination of *B* and *C*.

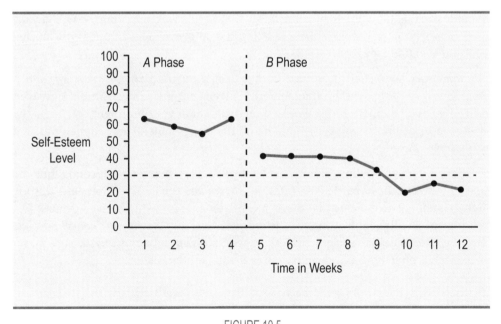

FIGURE 10.5

AB Design: Cecilia's Self-Esteem Scores for *A* Phase and *B* Phase

◈ DESCRIPTIVE DESIGNS

There are two kinds of single-subject research designs that center around answering descriptive research questions:

— *AB* Designs

— *ABC* and *ABCD* Designs

AB DESIGN

AN *AB* DESIGN is simply an *A*—or baseline phase—followed by a *B* or intervention phase. Returning to Cecilia, let's say she has a problem with low self-esteem and that you have already completed a four-week baseline phase with her, as shown in Figure 10.5, and that phase alone answered the two simple exploratory questions: "Does the problem exist?" and "Does the problem exist at different levels over time?" Now you implement a *B* intervention and find, to your pleasure, that Cecilia's self-esteem level approaches the clinical cutting score of 30 and falls below it at weeks 10–12.

What you really want to know, of course, is whether there is any relationship between your *B* intervention and Cecilia's success. You are now in a better position to hypothesize that there is because you know that Cecilia was not doing too well during the four weeks of the baseline phase and began to improve the week after you started your intervention (see Figure 10.5).

Something happened in week 5 to set Cecilia on the road to recovery, and it would be very coincidental if that something were not your intervention. However, coincidences do happen, and you cannot be certain that your intervention *caused* the change you see unless you can eliminate all the other coincidental happenings that might have caused it.

Hence, the *AB* design cannot answer explanatory research questions, but the change between the baseline data (getting worse) and the intervention data (getting better) is enough to indicate that there may be some relationship between your intervention and Cecilia's improvement. The moral to the story is to *always collect baseline data if you can* because social work ethics requires you to be reasonably sure an intervention is effective before you try it again with another client.

ABC and *ABCD* Designs

As we have discussed, you can always follow a *B* phase with a *C* phase if the *B* intervention did not achieve the desired result. An *A* phase followed by a *B* phase followed by a *C* phase constitutes an *ABC* design, and if there is a *D* intervention as well, you have an *ABCD* design. So long as there is a baseline, you can conclude fairly safely that there is a relationship between the results you see and the interventions you implemented.

However, if you have more than one intervention, you will not know which intervention—or combination of interventions—did the trick, and the more interventions you try the murkier the waters become.

Because a single intervention often comprises a package of practice techniques (e.g., active listening plus role play plus relaxation exercises), it is important to write down exactly what you did so that later on you will remember what the *B* or *C* or *D* interventions were.

 # Explanatory Designs

As we have seen, if you want to show that a particular intervention caused an observed result, you must eliminate everything else that may have caused it; in other words, you must control for intervening variables. There are two types of single-subject designs that can answer causality, or explanatory research questions:

— Reversal Designs

— Multiple-Baseline Designs.

Reversal Designs

The first type of explanatory single-subject designs are the reversal designs. There are three kinds:

— *ABA* and *ABAB* Designs

— *BAB* Designs

— *BCBC* Designs

ABA and *ABAB* Designs

Look at Figure 10.6, which illustrates Cecilia's success in getting her self-esteem score below the clinical cutting score in week 11 of the *B* intervention.

In week 12, you decide that you will withdraw your intervention related to Cecilia's self-esteem because she seems to be doing well, but you will continue to monitor her self-esteem levels to ensure that treatment gains are maintained.

Ongoing monitoring of problems that appear to be solved is something of a luxury in our profession. Too often our approach is crisis-oriented; follow-up tends to be ignored in the light of other, more pressing problems, and the result may well be a recurrence of the original problem because it had not been solved to the extent that the social worker thought.

However, with Cecilia you follow up. In weeks 12 through 16, as shown in Figure 10.6, the score hovers at the clinical cutting score. Figure 10.6 illustrates an *ABA* design where the client's scores are displayed first without an intervention (the first *A* phase), then with an intervention (the *B* phase), then without an intervention again (the second *A* phase).

The scores are not as high in the second *A* phase as they were in the first *A* phase, and this is to be expected because some of the strategies Cecilia learned in the *B* phase should remain with her even though the intervention has stopped.

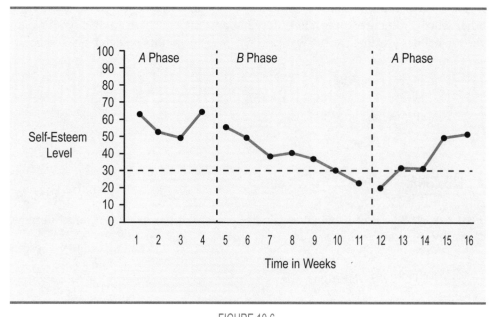

FIGURE 10.6

ABA Design: Cecilia's Self-Esteem Scores

However, from a research point of view, the very fact that her scores increased again when you stopped the intervention makes it more certain that it was your intervention that caused the improvement you saw in the *B* phase. Cecilia's improvement when the intervention started might have been a coincidence, but it is unlikely that her regression when the intervention stopped was also a coincidence.

Your certainty with respect to causality will be increased even further if you reintroduce the *B* intervention in week 17 and Cecilia's score begins to drop again as it did in the first *B* phase.

Now you have implemented two *AB* designs one after the other with the same client to produce an *ABAB* design. This design is illustrated in Figure 10.7. It is sometimes called a *reversal* design or a *withdrawal* design. Causality is established with an *ABAB* design because the same intervention has been shown to work twice with the same client and you have baseline data to show the extent of the problem when there was no intervention.

BAB DESIGN

Let's now return to Bob, with whom you implemented a *B* intervention to reduce his social anxiety as shown in Figure 10.2. When Bob's social anxiety level has fallen beneath the clinical cutting score, you might do the same thing with Bob as you did with Cecilia: withdraw the intervention and continue to monitor the problem, creating an *A* phase after the *B* phase. If the problem level worsens during the *A* phase, you intervene again in the same way as you did before, creating a second *B* phase and an overall design of *BAB*.

We have said that causality is established with an *ABAB* design because the same intervention has worked twice with the same client. We cannot say the same for a *BAB* design, however, as we do not really know that our intervention "worked" the first time. Because there was no initial baseline data (no first *A* phase), we cannot know whether the resolution of the problem on the first occasion had anything to do with the intervention.

The problem may have resolved itself or some external event (intervening variable) might have resolved it. Nor can we know the degree to which the problem changed during the first *B* phase (intervention) because there was no baseline data with which to compare the final result.

An indication of the amount of change can be obtained by comparing the first and last scores in the *B* phase, but the first score may have been an unreliable measure of Bob's problem. Bob may have felt less or more anxious that day than usual, and a baseline is necessary to compensate for such day-to-day fluctuations. Because the effectiveness of the intervention on the first occasion is unknown, there can be no way of knowing whether the intervention was just as effective the second time it was implemented, or less or more effective. All we know is that the problem improved twice, after the same intervention, and this is probably enough to warrant using the intervention again with another client.

BCBC Design

A *BCBC* design, as the name suggests, is a *B* intervention followed by a *C* intervention implemented twice in succession. The point of doing this is to compare the effectiveness of two interventions—*B* and *C*. It is unlikely that a social worker would implement this design with a client because, if the problem improved sufficiently using *B*, you would not need *C*; if you did need *C*, you would hardly return to *B* whether or not *C* appeared to do the trick.

However, if the problem has nothing to do with a client's welfare but is concerned instead with a social work program's organizational efficiency, say, as affected by organizational structure, you might try one structure *B* followed by a different structure *C* and then do the same thing again in order to show that one structure really has proved more effective in increasing efficiency when implemented twice *under the same conditions.*

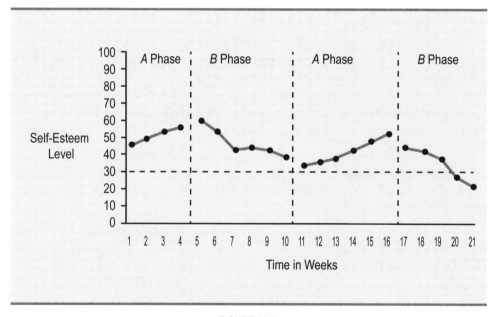

FIGURE 10.7
ABAB Design: Cecilia's Self-Esteem Scores

Multiple-Baseline Designs

The second type of explanatory single-subject designs are the multiple-baseline designs. Multiple-baseline designs are like *ABAB* designs in that the *AB* design is implemented more than once. However, whereas *ABAB* designs apply to one case with one problem in one setting, multiple-baseline designs can be used with more than:

— One Case

— One Setting

— One Problem

More Than One Case

Suppose that, instead of Bob with his social anxiety problem, you have three additional clients with anxiety problems, Breanne, Warren, and Alison. All three are residents in the same nursing home. You use the same measuring instrument to measure anxiety (the *IASS*) in all three cases, and you give all three clients the same intervention (*B* Phase).

However, you vary the number of weeks over which you collect baseline data (*A* Phase), allowing the baseline phase to last for six weeks in Breanne's case, eight weeks in Warren's case, and nine weeks for Alison. You plot your results as shown in Figure 10.8. Breanne starts to show improvement in week 7, the week you began your intervention. Had that improvement been due to some intervening variable—for example, some anxiety-reducing change in the nursing home's routine—you would expect Warren and Alison to also show improvement.

The fact that their anxiety levels continue to be high indicates that it was your intervention, not some other factor, that caused the improvement in Breanne. Causality is demonstrated again in week 9 when you begin to intervene with Warren, and Warren improves but Alison does not. Your triumph is complete when Alison, given the same intervention, begins to improve in week 10.

In a nutshell, a multiple-baseline design across clients is nothing more than stringing together a series of *AB* single-subject designs that use the same intervention and placing them on one graph. They can have differential baselines, or they can have the same. In our example, we show different baseline periods. This design simply determines whether one intervention will work with more than one client. Simple as that. We now turn our attention to see whether one intervention can work with one client in more than one setting.

More Than One Setting

Another way to conduct a multiple-baseline study is with one client in a number of settings. Suppose that your objective is to reduce the number of a child's temper tantrums at home, in school, and at the daycare center where the child goes after school. The same intervention (*B* Phase) is offered by the parents at home, the teacher in school, and the worker at the daycare center.

They are also responsible for measuring the number of tantrums that occur each day. In our example, the baseline phase continues for different lengths of time in each of the three setting as shown in Figure 10.9. Once again, baselines do not have to be of unequal lengths. If the child improves after the intervention begins in all three settings as shown in Figure 10.9, we may conclude that it was the intervention that caused the improvement in all three settings. A multiple-baseline design across settings simply determines whether one intervention will work with one client in multiple settings—in our example, at home, school, and daycare.

More Than One Problem

A third way to conduct a multiple-baseline study is to use the same intervention to tackle different target problems. Suppose that Joan is having trouble with her daughter, Anita. In addition, Joan is having trouble with her in-laws and with her boss at work.

After exploration, a worker may believe that all these troubles stem from her lack of assertiveness. Thus, the intervention would be assertiveness training. Progress with Anita might be measured by the number of times each day she is flagrantly disobedient.

Progress can be measured with Joan's in-laws by the number of times she is able to utter a contrary opinion, and so on. Because the number of occasions on which Joan has an opportunity to be assertive will vary, these figures might best be expressed in percentiles. Figure 10.10 illustrates an example of a multiple-baseline design that was used to assess the effectiveness of Joan's assertiveness training in three problem areas.

Whether it is a reversal design or a multiple-baseline design, an *ABAB* explanatory design involves establishing a baseline level for the client's target problem. This will not be possible if the need for intervention is acute, and sometimes the very thought of an *A*-type design will have to be abandoned. It is sometimes possible, however, to construct a retrospective baseline—that is, to determine what the level of the problem was before an intervention is implemented.

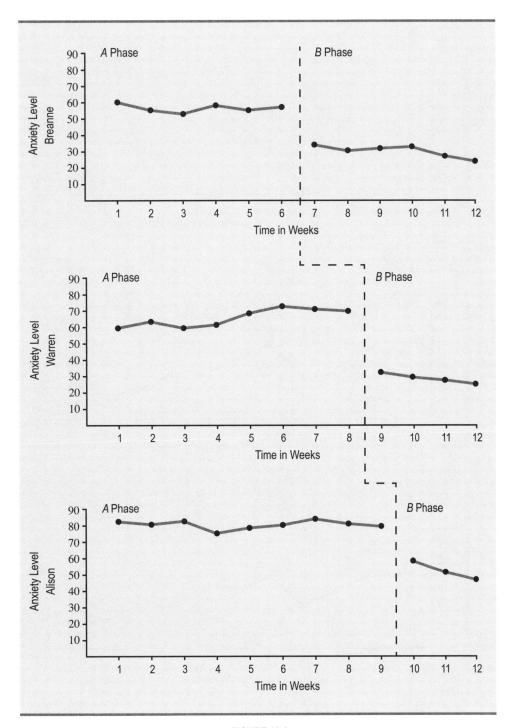

FIGURE 10.8

Multiple-Baseline Design across Clients:
Magnitude of Anxiety Levels for Three Clients

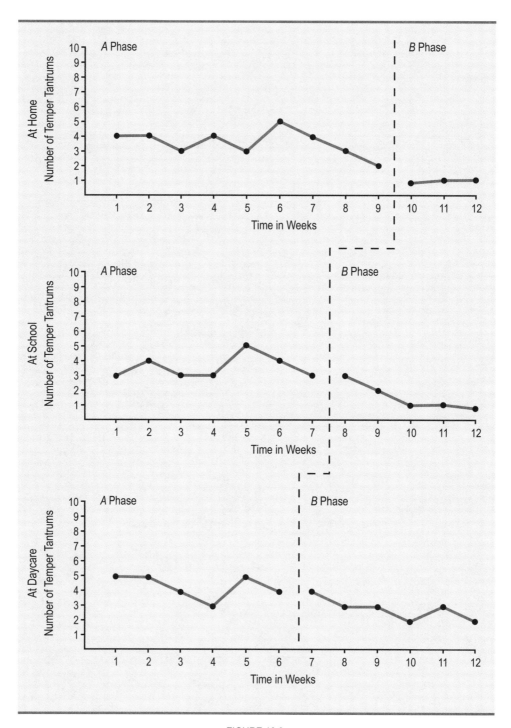

FIGURE 10.9

Multiple-Baseline Design across Settings:
Number of Temper Tantrums for One Client in Three Settings

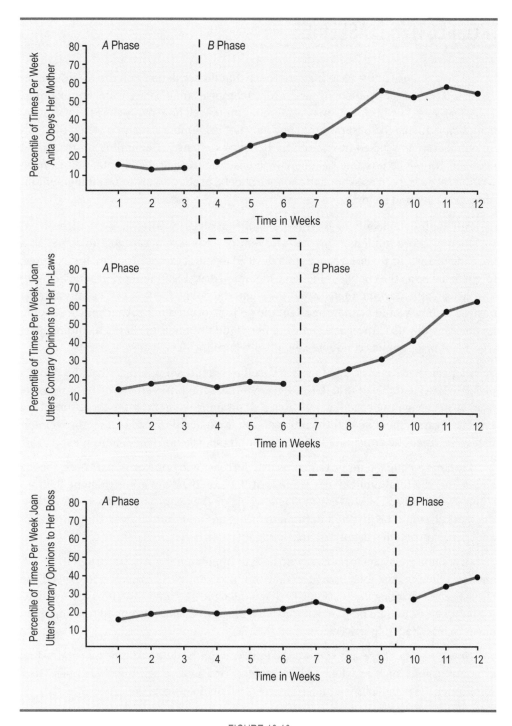

FIGURE 10.10

**Multiple-Baseline Design across Client Problems:
Magnitude of Three Client Target Problem Areas for One Client**

◆ RETROSPECTIVE BASELINES

The best retrospective baselines are those that do not depend on the client's memory. If the target problem occurs rarely, memories may be accurate. For example, Tai, a teenager, and his family may remember quite well how many times he ran away from home during the past month. They may not remember nearly so well if the family members were asked how often he behaved defiantly. Depending on the target problem, it may be possible to construct a baseline from archival data, that is, from written records, such as school attendance sheets, probation orders, employment interview forms, and so forth.

Although establishing a baseline usually involves making at least three measurements before implementing an intervention, it is also acceptable to establish a baseline of zero, or no occurrences of a desired event. A target problem, for example, might focus upon the client's reluctance to enter a drug treatment program. The baseline measurement would then be that the client did not go (zero occurrences), and the desired change would be that the client did go (one occurrence). A social worker who has successfully used the same tactics to persuade a number of clients to enter a drug treatment program has conducted a multiple-baseline design across clients.

As previously discussed, a usable baseline should show either that the client's problem level is stable or that it is growing worse. Sometimes an *A*-type design can be used even though the baseline indicates a slight improvement in the target problem. The justification must be that the intervention is expected to lead to an improvement that will exceed the anticipated improvement if the baseline trend continues.

Perhaps a child's temper tantrums are decreasing by one or two a week, for example, but the total number per week is still 18 to 20. If a worker thought the tantrums could be reduced to four or five a week, or they could be stopped altogether, the worker would be justified in implementing an intervention even though the client's target problem was improving slowly by itself.

In a similar way, a worker may be able to implement an *A*-type design if the client's baseline is unstable, provided that the intervention is expected to exceed the largest of the baseline fluctuations. Perhaps the child's temper tantrums are fluctuating between 12 and 20 per week in the baseline period, and it is hoped to bring them down to less than 10 per week.

Nevertheless, there are some occasions when a baseline cannot be established or is not usable, such as when a client's behaviors involve self-injurious ones. Also, sometimes the establishment of a baseline is totally inappropriate.

Ethical Issues

There are also a few ethical issues we need to be aware of when using single-subject designs in practice and research situations. Rafael Engel and Russell Schutt (2010) discuss some of the ethical issues as follows:

> Like any form of research, single-subject designs require the informed consent of the participant. The structure of single-subject designs for research involves particularly unique conditions that must be discussed with potential participants. As we discussed in Chapter 3, all aspects of the research study, such as the purpose, measurement, confidentiality, and data collection, are a part of the information needed for informed consent. In particular, the need for repeated baseline measurements and the possibility of premature withdrawal of treatment are particularly unique to single-subject design research.
>
> Participants must understand that the onset of the intervention is likely to be delayed until either a baseline pattern emerges or some assigned time period elapses. Until this condition is met, a needed intervention may be withheld. Furthermore, the length of the baseline also depends on the type of design. In a multiple baseline design, the delay in the intervention may be substantial. The implications of this delay must be discussed as part of obtaining informed consent.
>
> When a withdrawal or reversal design is used, there are additional considerations. The structure of such designs means that the intervention may be withdrawn just as the research subject is beginning to improve. The risks associated with prematurely ending treatment may be hard to predict. If there is a carryover effect, the subject's condition may not worsen, but it is possible that the subject's condition or status may indeed worsen. Given this possibility, the use of an *ABAB* design as opposed to the *ABA* design is preferable for the purpose of research.
>
> Obtaining informed consent may not be limited to the use of single-subject design for research purposes. As we noted in Chapter 1, the NASW *Code of Ethics* (1999) does not distinguish between the need for informed consent in research and the need for informed consent for practice evaluation. Specifically:
>
> > 5.02(e) Social workers engaged in evaluation or research should obtain voluntary and written informed consent from participants, when appropriate, without any implied or actual deprivation or penalty for refusal to participate; without undue inducement to participate; and with due regard for participants' well-being, privacy, and dignity. Informed consent should include information about the nature, extent, and duration of the participation requested and disclosure of the risks and benefits of participation in research.

Others suggest that informed consent may not be necessary. For example, Royse, Thyer, and Padgett (2009) suggest that written informed consent is not necessarily for practice evaluation because the intent is not to provide generalized knowledge or publish the results. Even if written informed consent is not required when using these tools for practice evaluation and monitoring, social workers using these tools should be guided by practice ethics.

According to the NASW *Code of Ethics,* social work practitioners should, as a part of their everyday practice with clients, provide services to clients only in the context of a professional relationship based, when appropriate, on valid informed consent. Social workers should use clear and understandable language to inform clients of the purpose of the services, risks related to the services, limits to services because of the requirements of a third party payer, relevant costs, reasonable alternatives, clients' right to refuse or withdraw consent, and the time frame covered by the consent. (NASW, 1999, 1.03[a])

Therefore, if such techniques are going to be used as part of the overall intervention, clients should be aware of the procedures.

◆ SUMMARY

This chapter presented a brief overview of single-subject designs. We categorized them as exploratory, descriptive, and explanatory. No design is inherently inferior or superior to the others. Each has advantages and disadvantages in terms of time, cost, and the data that can be obtained. The following chapter presents another kind of research design, group designs.

Study Questions for Chapter 10

— First, answer each question only AFTER you have read the chapter.

— Second, indicate how comfortable you were in answering each question on a 5-point scale:

1	2	3	4	5
Very uncomfortable	Somewhat uncomfortable	Neutral	Somewhat comfortable	Very comfortable

If you rated any question between 1–3, please reread the section of the chapter where the information for the question can be found. If you're still uncomfortable answering the question, talk with your instructor and/or your classmates for more clarification.

Questions	Degree of comfort? (Circle one number)
1. In your own words, list and discuss the advantages of single-subject designs. Provide a single social work example throughout your discussion that illustrates your main points.	1 2 3 4 5
2. In your own words, list and then discuss the questions that single-subject designs can answer. Provide a single social work example throughout your discussion that illustrates your main points.	1 2 3 4 5
3. What is a unit of analysis? Discuss the various units of analysis that single-subject designs can be used for.	1 2 3 4 5
4. In your own words, list and discuss the three requirements of using single-subject designs. Provide a single social work example throughout your discussion that illustrates your main points.	1 2 3 4 5
5. Discuss the concept of target problems. Provide a single social work example throughout your discussion that illustrates your main points.	1 2 3 4 5
6. Discuss why single-subject designs need to have valid and reliable measuring instruments. Provide a single social work example throughout your discussion that illustrates your main points.	1 2 3 4 5
7. List and then discuss the four exploratory single-subject designs. Provide a social work example throughout your discussion that illustrates your main points for each of the four designs.	1 2 3 4 5

8. List and then discuss the two descriptive single-subject designs. Provide a social work example throughout your discussion that illustrates your main points for both designs.	1 2 3 4 5
9. List and then discuss the two explanatory single-subject designs. Provide a social work example throughout your discussion that illustrates your main points for both designs.	1 2 3 4 5
10. List and then discuss the three reversal single-subject designs. Provide a social work example throughout your discussion that illustrates your main points for each of the three designs.	1 2 3 4 5
11. List and then discuss the three multiple-baseline designs. Provide a social work example throughout your discussion that illustrates your main points for each of the three designs.	1 2 3 4 5
12. In your own words discuss the concept of retrospective baselines. Provide a social work example throughout your discussion that illustrates your main points.	1 2 3 4 5

Assessing Your Self-Efficacy for Chapter 10

AFTER you have read the chapter AND have completed all the study questions, please indicate how knowledgeable you feel you are for each concept listed below.

1	2	3	4	5
Very uncomfortable	Somewhat uncomfortable	Neutral	Somewhat comfortable	Very comfortable

Major Concepts in Chapter	Knowledge Level? (Circle one number)
1. Advantages of single-subject designs	1 2 3 4 5
2. Unit of analysis	1 2 3 4 5
3. Requirements of single-subject designs	1 2 3 4 5
4. Target problems	1 2 3 4 5
5. Selecting valid and reliable outcome measures	1 2 3 4 5

6. Exploratory single-subject designs	1 2 3 4 5
7. Descriptive single-subject designs	1 2 3 4 5
8. Explanatory single-subject designs	1 2 3 4 5
9. Multiple-baseline designs	1 2 3 4 5
10. Retrospective baselines	1 2 3 4 5
Add up your scores (Minimum = 10, Maximum = 50)	Total score =

A   45 — 50 = Social Work Manager in the making.
B   40 — 44 = Social Work Supervisor.
C   35 — 39 = Social Work Practitioner.
D   10 — 34 = Case Aide. Reread the chapter and redo the study questions.

11

Group Designs

___

Design can be art. Design can be aesthetics.
Design is so simple, that's why it's so complicated.
~ Paul Rand

Now that you know how to use single-subject designs we turn our attention to the various group-level designs that research studies can take. The two most important factors in determining what group design to use in a specific study are (1) what the research question is, and (2) how much knowledge about the problem area is available.

 ## KNOWLEDGE LEVELS
___

If there is already a substantial knowledge base in your problem area, you will be in a position to address very specific research questions, the answers to which could add to the explanation of previously gathered data. If less is known about the problem area, your research questions will have to be of a more general, descriptive nature. If very little is known about the problem area, your questions will have to be even more general, at an exploratory level.

Research knowledge levels are arrayed along a continuum, from exploratory at the lowest end to explanatory at the highest (see Figures 2.1 and 2.3). Because research knowledge levels are viewed this way, the assignment of the level of knowledge accumulated in a problem area prior to a research study, as well as the level that might be attained by the research study, is totally arbitrary. There are, however, specific designs that can be used to provide us with knowledge at a certain level.

At the highest level are the explanatory designs, also called experimental designs or "ideal" experiments. These designs have the largest number of requirements (examined in the following section). They are best used in confirmatory research studies where the area under study is well developed, theories abound, and testable hypotheses can be formulated on the basis of previous work or existing theory. These designs seek to establish causal relationships between the independent and dependent variables.

In the middle range are the descriptive designs, sometimes referred to as quasi experimental. A quasi experiment resembles an "ideal" experiment in some aspects but lacks at least one of the necessary requirements. At the lowest level are the exploratory designs, also called pre-experimental or nonexperimental, which explore only the research question or problem area.

These designs do not produce statistically sound data or conclusive results, nor are they intended to. Their purpose is to build a foundation of general ideas and tentative theories, which can be explored later with more precise and hence more complex research designs and their corresponding data-gathering techniques.

The research designs that allow us to acquire knowledge at each of the three levels are described in a later section of this chapter. Before considering them, however, it's necessary to establish the characteristics that differentiate an "ideal" experiment, which leads to explanatory knowledge, from other studies that lead to the other two lower levels of knowledge (descriptive and exploratory).

CHARACTERISTICS OF "IDEAL" EXPERIMENTS

An "ideal" experiment is one in which a research study most closely approaches certainty about the relationship between the independent and dependent variables. The purpose of doing an "ideal" experiment is to ascertain whether it can be concluded from the study's findings that the independent variable is, or is not, the only cause of change in the dependent variable.

As pointed out in previous chapters, some social work research studies have no independent variable—for example, those studies that just want to find out how many people in a certain community wish to establish a community-based halfway house for people who are addicted to drugs.

The concept of an "ideal" experiment is introduced with the word "ideal" in quotation marks because such an experiment is rarely achieved in social work research situations. On a general level, in order to achieve this high degree of certainty and qualify as an "ideal" experiment, an explanatory research design must meet six conditions:

- The time order of the independent variable must be established.

- The independent variable must be manipulated.

- The relationship between the independent and dependent variables must be established.

- The research design must control for rival hypotheses.

- At least one control group should be used.

- Random assignment procedures (and if possible, random sampling from a population) must be employed in assigning research participants (or objects) to groups.

CONTROLLING THE TIME ORDER OF VARIABLES

AS YOU KNOW from Chapter 5, in an "ideal" experiment the independent variable must precede the dependent variable in time. Time order is crucial if our research study is to show that one variable causes another, because something that occurs later cannot be the cause of something that occurred earlier.

Suppose we want to study the relationship between adolescent substance abuse and gang-related behavior. The following hypothesis is formulated after some thought:

HYPOTHESIS

Adolescent substance abuse causes gang-related behavior.

In this hypothesis, the independent variable is adolescent substance abuse, and the dependent variable is gang-related behavior. The substance abuse must come *be-*

fore gang-related behavior because the hypothesis states that adolescent drug use causes gang-related behavior. We could also come up with the following hypothesis, however:

HYPOTHESIS

Adolescent gang-related behavior causes substance abuse.

In this hypothesis, adolescent gang-related behavior is the independent variable, and substance abuse is the dependent variable. According to this hypothesis, gang-related behavior must come *before* the substance abuse.

MANIPULATING THE INDEPENDENT VARIABLE

MANIPULATION of the independent variable means that we must do something with the independent variable. In the general form of the hypothesis "if X occurs, then Y will result," the independent variable (X) must be manipulated in order to effect a variation in the dependent variable (Y). There are essentially three ways in which independent variables can be manipulated:

- ✱ *X present versus X absent.* If the effectiveness of a specific treatment intervention is being evaluated, an experimental group and a control group could be used. The experimental group would be given the intervention (X), and the control group would not (no X).

- ✱ *A small amount of X versus a larger amount of X.* If the effect of treatment time on client's outcomes is being studied, two experimental groups could be used, one of which would be treated for a longer period of time.

- ✱ *X versus something else.* If the effectiveness of two different treatment interventions is being studied, Intervention X_1 could be used with Experimental Group 1 and Intervention X_2 with Experimental Group 2.

There are certain variables, such as the gender or race of our research participants, that obviously cannot be manipulated because they are fixed. They do not vary, so they are called *constants,* not variables, as was pointed out in Chapter 5. Other constants, such as socioeconomic status or IQ, may vary for research participants over their life spans, but they are fixed quantities at the beginning of the study, probably will not change during the study, and are not subject to alteration by the one doing the study. Any variable we can alter (such as treatment time) can be considered an independent variable. At least one independent variable must be manipulated in a research study if it's to be considered an "ideal" experiment.

Establishing Relationships between Variables

The relationship between the independent and the dependent variables must be established in order to infer a cause-effect relationship at the explanatory knowledge level. If the independent variable is considered to be the cause of the dependent variable, there must be some pattern in the relationship between these two variables. An example is the hypothesis "The more time clients spend in treatment (independent variable), the better their progress (dependent variable)."

Controlling Rival Hypotheses

Rival hypotheses must be identified and eliminated in an "ideal" experiment. The logic of this requirement is extremely important, because this is what makes a cause-effect statement possible.

The prime question to ask when trying to identify a rival hypothesis is "What other extraneous variables might affect the dependent variable?" (What else might affect the client's outcome besides treatment time?) At the risk of sounding redundant, "What else besides *X* might affect *Y*?"

Perhaps the client's motivation for treatment, in addition to the time spent in treatment, might affect the client's outcome. If so, motivation for treatment is an extraneous variable that could be used as the independent variable in the rival hypothesis "The higher the clients' motivation for treatment, the better their progress."

Perhaps the social worker's attitude toward the client might have an effect on the client's outcome, or the client might win the state lottery and ascend abruptly from depression to ecstasy. These extraneous variables could potentially be independent variables in other rival hypotheses. They must all be considered and eliminated before it can be said with reasonable certainty that a client's outcome resulted from the length of treatment time and not from any other extraneous variables.

Control over rival hypotheses refers to efforts on our part to identify and, if at all possible, to eliminate the extraneous variables in these alternative hypotheses. Of the many ways to deal with rival hypotheses, three of the most frequently used are:

—   Holding Extraneous Variables Constant

—   Using Correlated Variation

—   Using Analysis of Covariance

HOLDING EXTRANEOUS VARIABLES CONSTANT

The most direct way to deal with rival hypotheses is to keep constant the critical extraneous variables that might affect the dependent variable. As we know, a constant cannot affect or be affected by any other variable. If an extraneous variable can be made into a constant, then it cannot affect either the study's real independent variable or the dependent variable.

Let's take an overly simple example to illustrate this point. Suppose that a social worker who is providing a treatment intervention called cognitive behavioral therapy (CBT) to anxious clients wants to relate client outcome to length of treatment time. However, all her clients are also being seen by a consulting psychiatrist who has them on antidepressant medication.

Because medication may also affect her clients' outcomes (i.e., anxiety levels), it can be considered another independent variable that could be used in a rival hypothesis. However, because her study included her clients who all were taking medication for some time before the treatment intervention began, and who continue to take the same medicine in the same way throughout treatment, then medication can be considered a constant (in this study, anyway).

Any change in the clients' anxiety levels after the CBT intervention will, therefore, be a result of the intervention with the help of the medication. The extraneous variable of medication, which might form a rival hypothesis, has been eliminated by holding it constant. In short, this study started out with one independent variable, the CBT intervention, then added the variable of medication to it, so the final independent variable = CBT intervention + medication.

This is all very well in theory. In reality, however, a client's drug regime is usually controlled by the psychiatrist and may well be altered at any time. Even if the regimen is not altered, the effects of the drugs might not become apparent until the study is under way. In addition, the client's level of anxiety might be affected by a host of other extraneous variables over which the social worker has no control at all: for example, living arrangements, relationships with other people, the condition of the stock market, or an unexpected visit from an IRS agent. These kinds of pragmatic difficulties tend to occur frequently in social work practice and research. It's often impossible to identify all rival hypotheses, let alone eliminate them by keeping them constant.

USING CORRELATED VARIATION

Rival hypotheses can also be controlled with correlated variation of the independent variables. Suppose, for example, that we are concerned that income has an effect on a client's compulsive behavior. The client's income, which in this case is subject to variation due to seasonal employment, is identified as an independent variable. The client's living conditions—a hotel room rented by the week—are then identified as the second independent variable that might well affect the client's level of compulsive behavior.

These two variables, however, are correlated, because living conditions are highly dependent on income. Correlated variation exists if one potential independent variable can be correlated with another; then only one of them has to be dealt with in the research study.

Using Analysis of Covariance

In conducting an "ideal" experiment, we must always aim to use two or more groups that are as equivalent as possible on all important variables. Sometimes this goal is not feasible, however. Perhaps we are obliged to use existing groups that are not as equivalent as we would like.

Or perhaps during the course of the study we discover inequivalencies between the groups that were not apparent at the beginning. A statistical method called *analysis of covariance* can be used to compensate for these differences. The mathematics of the method are far beyond the scope of this text, but an explanation can be found in most statistics texts.

Using a Control Group

An "ideal" experiment should use at least one control group in addition to the experimental group. The experimental group may receive an intervention that is withheld from the control group, or equivalent groups may receive different interventions or no interventions at all.

A social worker who initiates a treatment intervention is often interested in knowing what would have happened had the intervention not been used or had some different intervention been substituted. Would members of a support group for alcoholics have recovered anyway, without the social worker's efforts? Would they have recovered faster or more completely had family counseling been used instead of the support group approach?

The answer to these questions will never be known if only the support group is studied. But what if another group of alcoholics is included in the research design? In a typical design with a control group, two equivalent groups, 1 and 2, would be formed, and both would be administered the same pretest to determine the initial level of the dependent variable (e.g., degree of alcoholism).

Then an intervention would be initiated with Group 1 but not with Group 2. The group treated—Group 1, or the experimental group—would receive the independent variable (the intervention). The group not treated—Group 2, or the control group—would not receive it. This can be easily diagramed, where:

R_a = Random assignment to a group

O_1 = First measurement of the dependent variable

X = Independent variable, or intervention

O_2 = Second measurement of the dependent variable

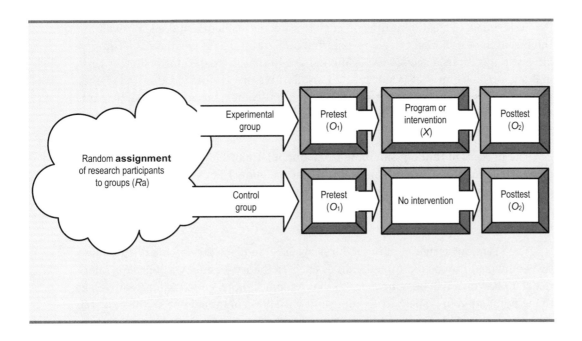

At the conclusion of the intervention, both groups would be given a posttest (the same measure as the pretest). Both the pretest and the posttest consist of the use of some sort of data-gathering procedure, such as a survey or self-report measure, to measure the dependent variable before and after the introduction of the independent variable. There are many types of group research designs, and there are many ways to graphically display them. In general, group designs can be written in symbols.

The R_a in this design indicates that the research participants were randomly assigned to each group. The symbol X, which, as usual, stands for the independent variable, indicates that an intervention is to be given to the experimental group after the pretest (O_1) and before the posttest (O_2).

The absence of X for the control group indicates that the intervention is not to be given to the control group. This design is called a classical experimental design (see Figure 11.9) because it comes closest to having all the characteristics necessary for an "ideal" experiment.

RANDOMLY ASSIGNING RESEARCH PARTICIPANTS TO GROUPS

ONCE A SAMPLE has been selected (see Chapter 9), the individuals (or objects or events) in it are randomly assigned to either an experimental or a control group in such a way that the two groups are equivalent. This procedure is known as *random assignment* or *randomization*. In random assignment, the word "equivalent" means equal in terms of the variables that are important to the study, such as the clients' motivation for treatment, or problem severity.

If the effect of treatment time on clients' outcomes is being studied, for example, the research design might use one experimental group that is treated for a comparatively longer time, a second experimental group that is treated for a shorter time, and a control group that is not treated at all. If we are concerned that the clients' motivation for treatment might also affect their outcomes, the research participants can be assigned so that all the groups are equivalent (on the average) in terms of their motivation for treatment.

The process of random sampling from a population followed by random assignment of the sample to groups can be illustrated as follows. Let's say that the research design calls for a sample size of one-tenth of the population. From a population of 10,000, therefore, a random sampling procedure is used to select a sample of 1,000 individuals.

Then random assignment procedures are used to place the sample of 1,000 into two equivalent groups of 500 individuals each. In theory, Group A will be equivalent to Group B, which will be equivalent to the random sample, which will be equivalent to the population in respect to all important variables contained within the research sample.

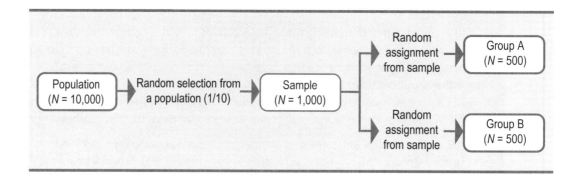

MATCHED-PAIRS METHOD

Another, more deliberate method of assigning research participants or other units to groups, a subset of randomization, involves matching. Suppose a new training program for teaching parenting skills to foster mothers is being evaluated. A standardized measuring instrument that measures parenting skill level (the dependent variable) is administered to 10 foster mothers. The scores can range from 100 (excellent parenting skills) to 0 (poor parenting skills).

The 10 women would then be matched in pairs according to their parenting skill level; the two most skilled foster mothers would be matched (Pair 1), then the next two (Pair 2), and so on. One person in the first pair would then be randomly assigned to the experimental group and the other placed in the control group. It doesn't make any difference to which group the first research participant is randomly assigned so long as there is an equal chance that she will go to either the control group or the experimental group. In this example, the first person is randomly chosen to go to the experimental group, as illustrated:

RANK ORDER OF PARENTING SKILLS SCORES (IN PARENTHESES)

First Pair
– (99) Randomly assigned to the experimental group
– (98) Assigned to the control group

Second Pair
– (97) Assigned to the control group
– (96) Assigned to the experimental group

Third Pair
– (95) Assigned to the experimental group
– (94) Assigned to the control group

Fourth Pair
– (93) Assigned to the control group
– (92) Assigned to the experimental group

Fifth Pair
– (91) Assigned to the experimental group
– (90) Assigned to the control group

As can be seen, the foster parent with the highest score (99) is randomly assigned to the experimental group, and this person's "match," with a score of 98, is assigned to the control group. This process is reversed with the next matched pair, where the first person is assigned to the control group and the match is assigned to the experimental group.

If the assignment of research participants according to scores is not reversed for every other pair, one group will be higher than the other on the variable being matched. To illustrate this point, suppose the first participant (highest score) in each match is always assigned to the experimental group. The experimental group's average score would be 95 (99 + 97 + 95 + 93 + 91 = 475/5 = 95), and the control group's average score would be 94 (98 + 96 + 94 + 92 + 90 = 470/5 = 94).

If every other matched pair is reversed, however, as in the example, the average scores of the two groups are closer together: 94.6 for the experimental group (99 + 96 + 95 + 92 + 91 = 473/5 = 94.6) and 94.4 for the control group (98 + 97 + 94 + 93 + 90 = 472/5 = 94.4). In short, 94.6 and 94.4 (difference of 0.2) are closer together than 95 and 94 (difference of 1).

CLASSIFYING GROUP RESEARCH DESIGNS

Group research designs can be classified into as many different types of classification systems as there are folks who are willing to classify them. We are going to classify them into:

— One-Group Research Designs

— Two-Group Research Designs

The main difference between the two classifications is that the one-group designs don't compare their research participants with another group; they simply don't have another group of participants to compare to. On the other hand, the two-group designs do just that: they compare one group of research participants against another group—usually to ascertain whether a particular group (experimental group) has more positive outcomes on a dependent variable then the other group (control or comparison group).

Let's begin our discussion with the simplest of all research designs—those that use only one group of research participants.

ONE-GROUP DESIGNS

One-group designs measure (1) the participants' success with an intervention (program objective) after they leave a program, and (2) any nonprogram objective at any time. One-group designs are exceptionally useful for providing a framework for gathering data—especially for needs assessments and process evaluations. In fact, two-group designs are rarely used in needs assessments and process evaluations. There are numerous types of one-group research designs, but we present only the four basic ones:

— One-Group Posttest-Only Design (Figure 11.1a)

— Cross-Sectional Survey Design (Figure 11.2a)

— Longitudinal Designs

  • Trend Studies (Figure 11.3a, Box 11.1)

  • Cohort Studies (Figure 11.4a, Box 11.2)

  • Panel Studies (Figure 11.5a, Box 11.3)

— One-Group Pretest-Posttest Design (Figure 11.6)

ONE-GROUP POSTTEST-ONLY DESIGN

THE ONE-GROUP POSTTEST-ONLY DESIGN is sometimes called the *one-shot case study* or *cross-sectional case study design*. Suppose in a particular small community there are numerous parents who are abusive toward their children. The city decides to hire a school social worker, Antonia, to implement a social service program that is supposed to reduce the number of parents who abuse their children.

She creates a 12-week child abuse prevention program (the intervention) and offers it to parents who have children in her school who wish to participate on a voluntary basis. A simple research study is then conducted to answer the rather simplistic question, "Did the parents who completed the program stop abusing their children?" The answer to this question will determine the success of her program, or intervention.

There are many different ways in which her program can be evaluated. For now, and to make matters as simple as possible, we are going to evaluate it by simply calculating the percentage of parents who said they stopped abusing their children after they attended the 12-week program—the program's objective.

At the simplest level, the program could be evaluated with a one-group posttest-only design. The basic elements of this design can be written as shown in Figure 11.1a, where:

X = Child Abuse Prevention Program, or the intervention

O = First and only measurement of the program objective

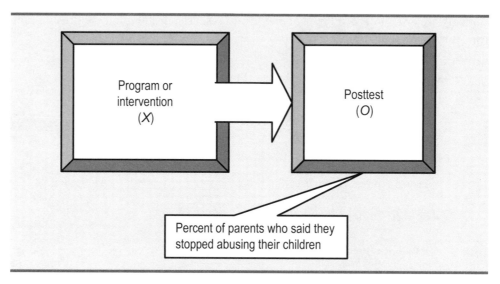

FIGURE 11.1a

One-Group Posttest-Only Study

All that this design provides is a single measure (O) of what happens when one group of people is subjected to one intervention or experience (X). It's safe to assume that all the members within the program had physically abused their children before they enrolled, because people who do not have this problem would not have enrolled in such a program. But even if the value of O indicates that some of the parents did stop being violent with their children after the program, it cannot be determined whether they quit solely because of the intervention or because something else may have caused the parents to quit.

Such somethings are called a rival hypothesis, or alternative explanation. Perhaps a law was recently passed that made it mandatory for the police to arrest folks who behave violently toward their children, or perhaps the local television station started to report such incidents on the nightly news, complete with pictures of the abusive parents.

These or other extraneous variables might have been more important in persuading the parents to cease their abusive behavior toward their children than their voluntary participation in Antonia's program. All we will know from this design is the number and percentage of the folks who self-reported that they stopped hurting their children after they successfully completed Antonia's 12-week program.

Figure 11.1b presents the results from a simple survey question that Antonia included in a mailed survey that was completed by her past participants.

SURVEY QUESTION

Do you continue to abuse your children?
1. Yes, I stopped.
2. No, I did not stop.

Notice that 85% of the parents reported they do not abuse their children after they completed Antonia's program. So Antonia could place the results of her survey question in a simple pie chart such as Figure 11.1b. And yes, we are fully aware of the problems with parents self-reporting whether or not they continue to abuse their children, but for now just go along with us. The one-group posttest-only design is also used a lot in process evaluations when it comes to the collection of client satisfaction data.

CROSS-SECTIONAL SURVEY DESIGN

Let's take another example of a design that *does not* have an intervention of some kind called a cross-sectional survey design. In doing a cross-sectional survey, we survey *only once* a cross section of some particular population.

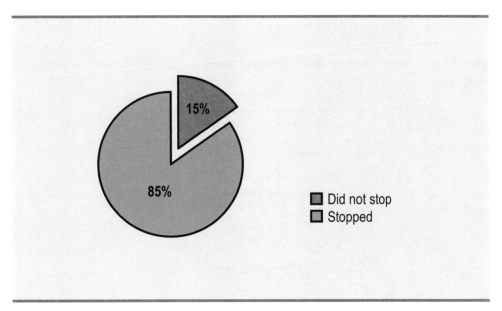

FIGURE 11.1b

Percentage of Parents Who Stopped Physically Abusing Their Children after Leaving Antonia's Program (from Figure 11.1a)

In addition to running her child abuse prevention program geared for abusive parents, Antonia may also want to start another program for children (whether they come from abusive families or not): a child abuse educational program taught to all children in her school.

Before Antonia starts her educational program geared for the children, however, she wants to know what parents think about the idea—kind of like a mini-needs assessment. She may send out questionnaires to all the parents, or she may decide to personally telephone every second parent, or every fifth or tenth, depending on how much time and money she has. She asks one simple question in her mini-needs assessment survey:

SURVEY QUESTION

Do you support our school offering a child abuse educational program that your child could enroll in on a voluntary basis and with your consent?
1. Yes
2. No

The results of her rather simplistic survey constitute a single measurement, or observation, of the parents' opinions of her proposed educational program (the one for the children) and may be written as shown in Figure 11.2a.

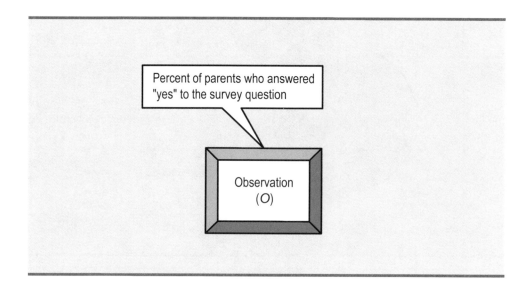

FIGURE 11.2A

Antonia's Cross-Sectional Survey Design

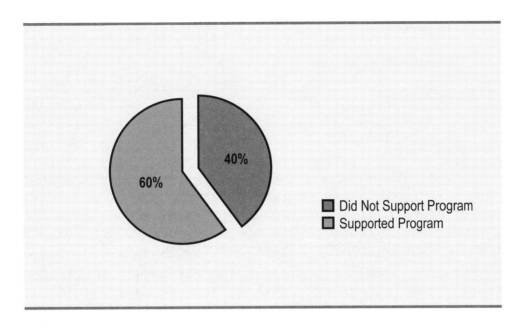

FIGURE 11.1ʙ

Percentage of Parents Who Supported a Voluntary Child Abuse Educational Program in Year 2013 (from Figure 11.2ᴀ)

The symbol O represents the entire cross-sectional survey design because such a design involves making only a single observation, or measurement, at one time period. Note that there is no X, because there is really no intervention.

Antonia wants only to ascertain the parents' attitudes toward her proposed program—nothing more, nothing less. This type of design is used a lot in needs assessment studies. Data that are derived from such a design can be displayed in a simple pie chart as in Figure 11.2b. Notice that 60% of the parents supported their children attending a voluntary child abuse educational program.

LONGITUDINAL DESIGNS

The longitudinal design provides for multiple measurements (Os) of the program objective—or some other variable of interest over time—not just at one point in time. Notice that the two previous designs—the one-group posttest-only design and the cross-sectional survey design—measured a variable only once. Not so with longitudinal designs, which measure variables more than one time, hence the name *longitudinal.* They can be broken down into three general types:

—   Trend Studies

—   Cohort Studies

—   Panel Studies

TREND STUDIES

A trend study takes different samples of people who share a similar characteristic at different points in time. Antonia may want to know whether parents of second-grade children enrolled in her school are becoming more receptive to the idea of the school offering their children a child abuse prevention education program. Her population of interest is simply the parents who have children in the second grade.

Remember, a trend study samples different groups of people at different points in time from the same population of interest. So to answer her question, she may

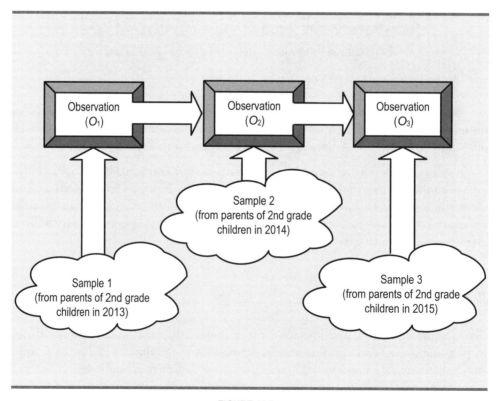

FIGURE 11.3A
Antonia's Trend Study

survey a sample of the parents of Grade 2 children this year (Sample 1), a sample of the parents of the new complement of Grade 2 children the next year (Sample 2), and so on (Sample 3) until she thinks she has sufficient data to answer her question. Each year the parents surveyed will be different, but they will all be parents of Grade 2 children—her population of interest. In this case,

O_1 = First measurement of a variable in Sample 1

O_2 = Second measurement of the same variable in Sample 2

O_3 = Third measurement of the same variable in Sample 3

Antonia will be able to determine whether parents, as a group, are becoming more receptive to the idea of introducing child abuse prevention material to their children as early as Grade 2. In other words, she will be able to measure any attitudinal trend that is, or is not, occurring.

The design can be written as shown in Figure 11.3a, and the data from Antonia's study could be displayed in a simple bar graph like Figure 11.3b. Notice that the percentage of parents desiring such a program is going up over time.

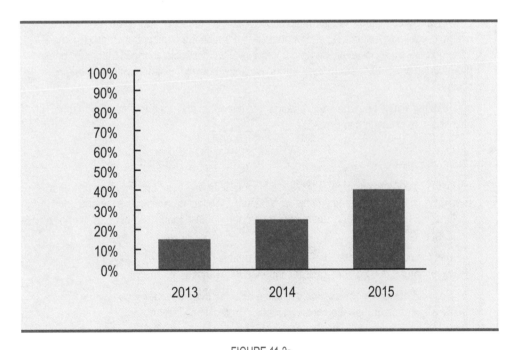

FIGURE 11.3ʙ

Displaying Data for a Trend Study (from Figure 11.3ᴀ):
Percentage of Parents Who Support a Prevention Educational Program by Year

Cohort Studies

A cohort study takes place when research participants have a certain condition and/ or receive a particular treatment are sampled over time. For example, AIDS survivors, sexual abuse survivors, or parents of children can easily be followed over time. So in

---

BOX 11.1
Trend Studies in a Nutshell

The trend study is probably the most common of the longitudinal studies. A trend study samples different groups of people at different points in time from the same population. For example, trend studies are often used with public opinion polls.

Suppose that 2 months before a year-long gun control campaign, a sample of adults is drawn: Of these adults, 64% report that they're in favor of strict gun control regulation, and 34% report that they are not. A year later, a different sample drawn from the same population shows a change: 75% report that they're in favor of gun control, and 25% report that they are not. This is a sample example of a trend study.

Trend studies provide information about net changes at an aggregate level. In the example, we know that in the period under consideration the gun control program gained 11% more support. However, we do not know how many people changed their positions (from con to pro or from pro to con), nor do we know how many stayed with their original choice.

To determine both the gross change and the net change, a panel study would be necessary, as presented in Box 11.3.

Characteristics

- Data are collected from the population at more than one point in time. (This does not always mean that the same subjects are used to collect data at more than one point in time, but that the subjects are selected from the population for data at more than one point in time.)

- There is no experimental manipulation of variables, or more specifically, the investigator has no control over the independent variable.

- This kind of study involves data collection only. No intervention is made by the investigator other than the choice of method or tool to collect data.

- In analyzing the data, the investigator draws conclusions and may attempt to find correlations between variables. Therefore, trend studies are uniquely appropriate for assessing change over time.

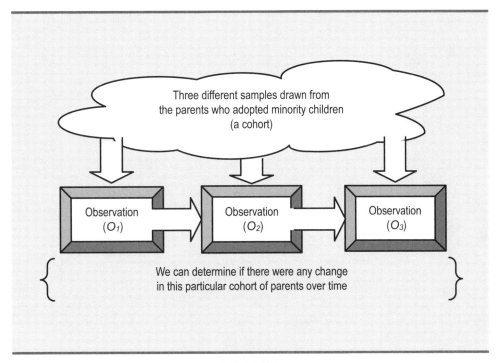

FIGURE 11.4A
Antonia's Cohort Study

a nutshell, and unlike a trend study that does not follow a particular cohort of individuals over time, a cohort study does just that: it follows a particular cohort of people who have shared a similar experience.

Antonia might select, for example, one particular group of parents who have adopted minority children, and measure their attitudes toward child abuse prevention education in successive years. Again, the design can be written as shown in Figure 11.4a, and the data could be presented in a format in a simple graph such as Figure 11.4b, where:

O_1 = First measurement of a variable for a *sample* of individuals within a given cohort

O_2 = Second measurement of the variable for a *different sample* of individuals within the same cohort *1 year later*

O_3 = Third measurement of the variable for a *different sample* of individuals within the same cohort *after 2 years*

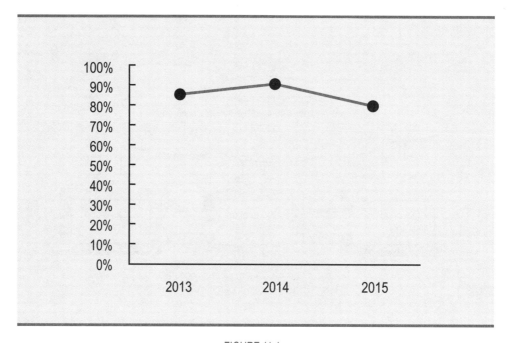

FIGURE 11.4B

Displaying Data for a Cohort Study (from Figure 11.4A):
Percentage of Parents with Minority Children Who Support a Prevention
Educational Program by Year

BOX 11.2

Cohort Studies in a Nutshell

A cohort study is a study in which subjects who presently have a certain condition and/ or receive a particular treatment are followed over time and compared with another group who are not affected by the condition under investigation. For research purposes, a cohort is any group of individuals who are linked in some way or who have experienced the same significant life event within a given period. There are many kinds of cohorts, including birth (e.g., all those who born between 1970 and 1975), disease, education, employment, family formation, and so on. Any study in which there are measures of some characteristic of one or more cohorts at two or more points in time is a cohort analysis.

In some cases, cohort studies are preferred to randomized experimental designs. For instance, because a randomized controlled study to test the effects of smoking on health would be unethical, a reasonable alternative would be a study that identifies two groups, a group of people who smoke and a group of people who do not, and follows them forward through time to see what health problems they develop.

In general, a cohort analysis attempts to identify cohort effects: Are changes in the dependent variable (health problems in this example) due to aging, or are they present because the sample members belongs to the same cohort (smoking versus nonsmoking)?

In other words, cohort studies are about the life histories of sections of populations and the individuals they comprise. They can tell us what circumstances in early life are associated with the population's characteristics in later life—what encourages the development in particular directions and what appears to impede it. We can study such developmental changes across any stage of life in any life domain: education, employment, housing, family formation, citizenship, or health.

**Group of interest
(e.g., smokers)**

**Follow
over time**

**Comparison Group
(e.g., non-smokers)**

**Follow
over time**

**Compare
outcomes**

PANEL STUDIES

In a panel study, the *same individuals* are followed over a period of time. Antonia might select one random sample of parents, for example, and measure their attitudes toward child abuse prevention education in successive years. Unlike trend and cohort studies, panel studies can reveal both net change and gross change in the program objective for the *same individuals*. Additionally panel studies can reveal shifting attitudes and patterns of behavior that might go unnoticed with other research approaches.

For example, if Bob was measured once at time 1, he would then again be measured at time 2 and so forth. We would do this for each individual in the study. Again, the design can be illustrated as in Figure 11.5a, and hypothetical data could be displayed in a simple graph as in Figure 11.5b. For example, Figure 11.5b presents the results of the percentages of the same parents who want to have a child abuse prevention education program in their children's school, as measured over a three-year period from 2013 to 2015, where:

O_1 = First measurement of attitudes toward child abuse prevention education for a sample of individuals

O_2 = Second measurement of attitudes toward child abuse prevention education for the *same individuals 1 year later*

O_3 = Third measurement of attitudes toward child abuse prevention education for the *same individuals after 2 years*

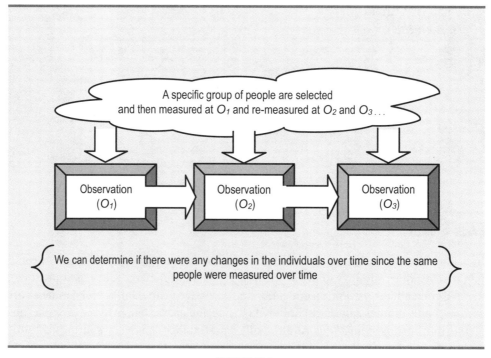

FIGURE 11.5A

Antonia's Panel Study

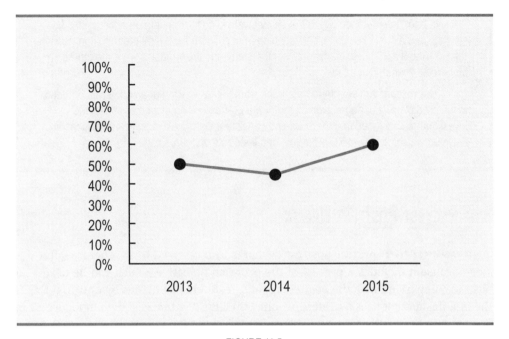

FIGURE 11.5ʙ

Displaying Data for a Panel Study (from Figure 11.5ᴀ):
Percentage of Parents Who Support a Prevention Education Program by Year

---

BOX 11.3

Panel Studies in a Nutshell

Panel studies measure the same sample of respondents at different points in time. Unlike trend studies, panel studies can reveal both net change and gross change in the variable of interest for the same people. Additionally, panel studies can reveal shifting attitudes and patterns of behavior that might go unnoticed with other research approaches.

Depending on the purpose of the study, researchers can use either a continuous panel, consisting of members who report specific attitudes or behavior patterns on a regular basis, or an interval panel, whose members agree to complete a certain number of measurement instruments only when the information is needed. In general, panel studies provide data suitable for sophisticated statistical analysis and might enable researchers to predict cause-effect relationships.

Panel data are particularly useful in predicting long-term or cumulative effects which are normally hard to analyze in a one-shot case study (or cross-sectional study). For example, in the early 80's, the National Broadcasting Company supported a panel study in order to investigate the causal influence of violent TV viewing on aggression among young people.

> In brief, the methodology in the study involved collecting data on aggression, TV viewing, and a host of sociological variables from children in several metropolitan cities in the US. About 1,200 boys participated in the study and the variables were measured six times for 3 year study period.
>
> The researchers sought to determine whether TV viewing at an earlier time added to the predictability of aggression at a later time. After looking at all the results, the investigators concluded that there was no consistent statistically significant relationship between watching violent TV programs and later acts of aggression.

ONE-GROUP PRETEST-POSTTEST DESIGN

THE ONE-GROUP pretest-posttest design is also referred to as a before–after design because it includes a pretest of the program objective, which can be used as a basis of comparison with the posttest results. It should be obvious by now that this is the first design that uses a pretest of some kind. It's written as shown in Figure 11.6, and hypothetical data could be displayed as in Table 11.1, where:

O_1 = First measurement of the program objective

X = Program, or the intervention (see Box 11.4)

O_2 = Second measurement of the program objective

BOX 11.4
Treatment: A Variable or a Constant?

For instructional purposes, group designs are displayed using symbols where X is the independent variable (treatment) and O is the measure of the dependent variable. This presentation is accurate when studies are designed with two or more groups. When one-group designs are used, however, this interpretation does not hold.

In one-group designs, the treatment or program cannot truly vary because all research participants have experienced the same event; that is, they all have experienced the program. Without a comparison or control group, treatment is considered a constant because it's a quality shared by all members in the research study. In short, time is the independent variable.

There does not necessarily have to be an independent variable in a study; we may just want to measure some variable in a particular population such as the number of people who receive a certain type of social service intervention over a ten-year period. In this situation, there is no independent or dependent variable.

The pretest-posttest design, in which a pretest precedes the introduction of the intervention and a posttest follows it, can be used to determine, on a general level, how the intervention affects a particular group. The design is used often in social work decision making. The differences between O_1 and O_2, on which these decisions are based, could be due to many other internal validity factors (to be discussed in the next section) rather than to the intervention.

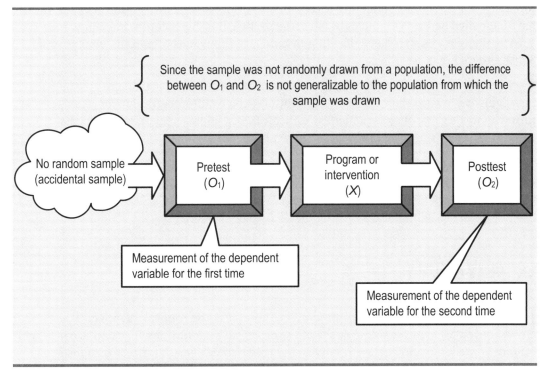

FIGURE 11.6

One-Group Pretest-Posttest Design

TABLE 11.1

Displaying Data for a One-Group Pretest-Posttest Design (from Figure 11.6)

	Pretest Average (O_1)	Posttest Average (O_2)	Difference Average $(O_2 - O_1)$
Intervention Group	50	80	30

Let's take another indicator of how Antonia's child abuse prevention program could be evaluated. Besides counting the number of parents who stopped physically abusing their children as the only indicator of her program's success, she could have a second outcome indicator such as a reduction in the parents' risk for abusive and neglectful parenting behaviors.

This program objective could be easily measured by an instrument that measures their attitudes toward physical punishment of children. Let's say that Antonia had the parents complete the instrument *before* participating in the child abuse prevention program (O_1) and *after* completing it (O_2). In this example all kinds of things could have happened between O_1 and O_2 to affect the participants' behaviors and feelings—such as the television station's deciding to publicize the names of parents who are abusive to their children.

Just the experience of taking the pretest could motivate some participants to stop being abusive toward their children. Maturation—the children becoming more mature with age so that they become less difficult to discipline—could also affect the results between the pretest and posttest measurements.

These issues are referred to as alternative explanations and rival hypotheses and can make most of us question the results of just about any outcome evaluation. The easiest way you can control for all this messy stuff is by using two groups of participants, which eliminates many of the threats to internal validity.

 INTERNAL VALIDITY

Internal validity is a term we commonly use to assess the "approximate certainty" about inferences regarding cause-effect or causal relationships. Thus, internal validity is predominantly relevant only to the research designs that try to establish causal relationships between the independent and dependent variables. In any causal study we should be able to conclude from our findings that the intervention is, or is not, the only cause of change in the dependent variable, or outcome variable, or program objective.

If our explanatory study does not have internal validity, such a conclusion is not possible, and the study's findings can be misleading. Internal validity is concerned with one of the requirements for an "ideal" research study—the control of rival hypotheses, or alternative explanations for what might bring about a change in the program objective.

In short, the higher the internal validity, the greater the extent to which rival hypotheses (or alternative explanations) can be controlled; the lower the internal validity, the less they can be controlled. We will discuss only ten threats to internal validity, which are:

— History

— Maturation

— Testing Effects

— Instrumentation Error

— Statistical Regression

— Differential Selection of Research Participants

— Mortality

— Reactive Effects of Research Participants

— Interaction Effects

— Relations between Experimental and Control Groups

History

THE FIRST THREAT to internal validity, history, refers to any outside event, either public or private, that may affect the program objective and that was not taken into account in our design. Many times, it refers to events that occur between the first and second measurement of the program objective (the pretest and the posttest). If events occur that have the potential to alter the second measurement, there is no way of knowing how much (if any) of the observed change in the program's objective is a function of the intervention and how much is attributable to these events.

Suppose, for example, we are investigating the effects of an educational program on racial tolerance. We may decide to measure the program objective (decreasing racial tolerance in the community) before introducing the intervention, the educational program. The educational program is then implemented and is represented by X. Finally, racial tolerance is measured again, after the program has run its course. This final measurement yields a posttest score, represented by O_2. As you know, the one-group pretest-posttest study design is presented in Figure 11.6.

The difference between the values O_2 and O_1 represents the difference in the degree of racial tolerance in the community before and after the educational program. If the study is internally valid, $O_2 - O_1$ will yield a crude measure of the effect of the educational program on racial tolerance, and this is what we were trying to discover. Now suppose that before the posttest could be administered, a colossal terrorist attack occurs in the United States, such as the type that occurred in New York on September 11, 2001.

It may be fair to say that terrorism can be expected to have a negative effect on racial tolerance, and the posttest scores may, therefore, show a lower level of tolerance than if the terrorist act had not occurred. The effect, $O_2 - O_1$, will now be the combined effects of the educational program *and* the terrorist act, not the effect of the program alone, as we initially intended.

Terrorism is an extraneous variable that we could not have anticipated and did not control for when we designed the study. Other examples might include an earthquake, an election, illness, divorce, or marriage—any event, public or private, that could affect the dependent variable, or program objective. Any such variable that is unanticipated and uncontrolled for is an example of history.

However, the *effects* of history are controlled for with the use of a control or comparison group; that is, the control or comparison group would theoretically have experienced the act of terrorism exactly like the experimental group. Thus, both groups would have been exposed to the extraneous terrorism variable and this would make it a constant in the research design.

So whenever a control or comparison group is used in a study, it's usually safe to say that *the effects* of history have been controlled for—not history itself as this is reserved for the person up above. The most important thing to remember as a mortal is that you cannot control history—history marches on with or without you. You can however, control for the *effects* of history by adding a control or comparison group to your research design.

MATURATION

MATURATION, the second threat to internal validity, is history's first cousin. It refers to changes, both physical and psychological, that take place in our research participants over time and can affect the dependent variable, or program objective. Suppose that we are evaluating an interventive strategy designed to improve the behavior of adolescents who engage in delinquent behavior. Because the behavior of adolescents changes naturally as they mature, the observed change may have resulted as much from their natural development as from the intervention strategy.

Maturation refers not only to physical or mental growth, however. Over time, people grow older, more or less anxious, more or less bored, and more or less motivated to take part in a study. All these factors and many more can affect the way in which people respond when the program objective is measured a second or third time.

Like history as previously discussed, the *effects* of maturation can indeed be controlled for with the use of a control or comparison group. Like history, you cannot control maturation; you can only control for the *effects* of maturation by using control or comparison groups in your designs.

Testing Effects

TESTING EFFECTS is sometimes referred to as *initial measurement effect*. Thus, the pretests that are the starting point for many research designs are another potential threat to internal validity. One of the most utilized designs involves three steps: (1) measuring some program objective, such as learning behaviors in school or attitudes toward work; (2) initiating a program to change that variable; and then (3) measuring the program objective again at the conclusion of the program. As you know, this design is known as the one-group pretest-posttest design and is illustrated in Figure 11.6.

The testing effect is the effect that taking a pretest might have on posttest scores. Suppose that Roberto, a research participant, takes a pretest to measure his initial level of racial tolerance before being exposed to a racial tolerance educational program. He might remember some of the questions on the pretest, think about them later, and change his views on racial issues before taking part in the educational program. After the program, his posttest score will reveal his changed opinions, and we may incorrectly assume that the program was *solely* responsible, whereas the true cause was his experience with the pretest *and* the intervention.

Sometimes a pretest induces anxiety in a research participant so that Roberto receives a worse score on the posttest than he should have; or boredom caused by having to respond to the same questions a second time may be a factor. To avoid the testing effect, we may wish to use a design that does not require a pretest.

If a pretest is essential, we then must consider the length of time that elapses between the pretest and posttest measurements. A pretest is far more likely to affect the posttest when the time between the two is short. The nature of the pretest is another factor. Measuring instruments that deal with factual matters, such as knowledge levels, may have large testing effects because the questions tend to be more easily recalled.

Instrumentation Error

THE FOURTH THREAT to internal validity is instrumentation error. This is simply a list of all the troubles that can afflict the measurement process. The instrument may be unreliable or invalid, as presented in Chapters 7 and 8. It may be a mechanical instrument, such as an electroencephalogram (EEG) that has malfunctioned. Occasionally, the term *instrumentation error* is used to refer to an observer whose observations are inconsistent or to measuring instruments that are valid and reliable in themselves but have not been administered properly.

Administration, with respect to a measuring instrument, means the circumstances under which the measurement is made: where, when, how, and by whom. A mother being asked about her attitudes toward her children, for example, may respond in one way in the social worker's office and in a different way at home while her children are screaming around her feet.

A mother's verbal response may differ from her written response, or she may respond differently in the morning than she would in the evening, or differently alone than she would in a group. These variations in situational responses do not indicate a true change in the feelings, attitudes, or behaviors being measured but are only examples of instrumentation error.

Statistical Regression

THE FIFTH THREAT to internal validity, statistical regression, refers to the tendency of extremely low and extremely high scores to regress, or move toward the average score for everyone in the study. Suppose an instructor makes her class take a multiple-choice exam and the average score is 50.

Now suppose that the instructor separates the low scorers from the high scorers and tries to even out the level of the class by giving the low scorers special instruction. To determine whether the special instruction has been effective, the entire class then takes another multiple-choice exam. The result of the exam is that the low scorers (as a group) do better than they did the first time, and the high scorers (as a group) do worse. The instructor believes that this has occurred because the low scorers received special instruction and the high scorers did not.

According to the logic of statistical regression, however, both the average score of the low scorers and the average score of the high scorers would move toward the total average score for both groups (i.e., 50). Even without any special instruction, and still in their state of ignorance, the low scorers (as a group) would be expected to have a higher average score than they did before. Likewise, the high scorers (as a group) would be expected to have a lower average score than they did before.

It would be easy for the instructor to assume that the low scores had increased because of the special instruction and the high scores had decreased because of the lack of it. This is not necessarily so, however; the instruction may have had nothing to do with it. It may all be due to statistical regression where the high group goes down and the low group goes up.

Differential Selection of Research Participants

The sixth threat to internal validity is differential selection of research participants. To some extent, the participants selected for a study are different from one another to begin with. "Ideal" research designs, however, require random sampling from a population (if at all possible) and random assignment to groups. This ensures that the results of a study will be generalizable to the larger population from which they were drawn (thus addressing threats to external validity, to be discussed later).

This threat, however, is present when we are working with preformed groups or groups that already exist, such as classes of students, self-help groups, or community groups. It's probable those different preformed groups will not be equivalent with respect to relevant variables and that these initial differences will invalidate the results of the posttest.

A child abuse prevention educational program for children in schools might be evaluated by comparing the prevention skills of one group of children who have experienced the educational program with the skills of a second group who have not. To make a valid comparison, the two groups must be as similar as possible with respect to age, gender, intelligence, socioeconomic status, and anything else that might affect the acquisition of child abuse prevention skills.

We would have to make every effort to form or select equivalent groups, but the groups are sometimes not as equivalent as might be hoped—especially if we are obliged to work with preformed groups, such as classes of students or community groups. If the two groups were different before the intervention was introduced, there is not much point in comparing them at the end.

Accordingly, preformed groups should be avoided whenever possible. If it's not feasible to do this, rigorous pretesting must be done to determine in what ways the groups are (or are not) equivalent, and the differences must be compensated for with the use of statistical methods.

Mortality

The seventh threat to internal validity is mortality, which simply means that research participants may drop out before the end of the study. Their absence will probably have a significant effect on the study's findings because people who drop out are likely to be different in some ways from those participants who stay to the end. People who drop out may be less motivated to participate in the intervention than are people who stay in, for example.

Because dropouts often have such characteristics in common, it cannot be assumed that the attrition occurred in a random manner. If considerably more people drop out of one group than out of the other, the result will be two groups that are no longer equivalent and cannot be usefully compared. We cannot know at the beginning of the study how many people will drop out, but we can watch to see how many do. Mortality is never problematic if dropout rates are 5% or less *and* if the dropout rates are similar for the both groups.

Reactive Effects of Research Participants

THE EIGHTH THREAT to internal validity is reactive effects. Changes in the behaviors or feelings of research participants may be caused by their reaction to the novelty of the situation or to the knowledge that they are participating in a study. The classic example of reactive effects was found in a series of studies carried out at the Hawthorne plant of the Western Electric Company, in Chicago, many years ago. Researchers were investigating the relationship between working conditions and productivity. When they increased the level of lighting in one section of the plant, productivity increased; a further increase in the lighting was followed by an additional increase in productivity.

When the lighting was then decreased, however, production levels did not fall accordingly but continued to rise. The conclusion was that the workers were increasing their productivity not because of the lighting level but because of the attention they were receiving as research participants in the study.

The term *Hawthorne effect* is still used to describe any situation in which the research participants' behaviors are influenced not by the intervention but by the knowledge that they are taking part in a research project. Another example of such a reactive effect is the placebo given to patients, which produces beneficial results because the patients believe it's medication.

Reactive effects can be controlled by ensuring that all participants in a study, in both the experimental and the control groups, appear to be treated equally. If one group is to be shown an educational film, for example, the other group should also be shown a film—some film carefully chosen to bear no relationship to the variable being investigated. If the study involves a change in the participants' routine, this in itself may be enough to change behavior, and care must be taken to continue the study until novelty has ceased to be a factor.

Interaction Effects

INTERACTION AMONG the various threats to internal validity can have an effect of its own. Any of the factors already described as threats may interact with one another, but the most common interactive effect involves differential selection and maturation.

Let's say we are studying two preformed groups of clients who are being treated for depression. The intention was for these groups to be equivalent, in terms of both their motivation for treatment and their levels of depression. It turns out that Group A is more generally depressed than Group B, however. Whereas both groups may grow less motivated over time, it's likely that Group A, whose members were more depressed to begin with, will lose motivation more completely and more quickly than Group B. Nonequivalent preformed groups thus grow less equivalent over time as a result of the interaction between differential selection and maturation.

Relations between Experimental and Control Groups

THE FINAL GROUP of threats to internal validity has to do with the effects of the use of experimental and control groups that receive different interventions. These effects include:

— Diffusion of Treatments

— Compensatory Equalization

— Compensatory Rivalry

— Demoralization

Diffusion of Treatments

Diffusion, or imitation, of treatments may occur when members of the experimental and control groups talk to each other about the study. Suppose a study is designed to present a new relaxation exercise to the experimental group and nothing at all to the control group. There is always the possibility that one of the participants in the experimental group will explain the exercise to a friend who happens to be in the control group. The friend explains it to another friend, and so on. This might be beneficial for the control group, but it undermines the study's findings.

Compensatory Equalization

Compensatory equalization of treatment occurs when the person doing the study and/or the staff member administering the intervention to the experimental group feels sorry for people in the control group who are not receiving it and attempts to compensate them. A social worker might take a control group member aside and covertly demonstrate the relaxation exercise, for example.

On the other hand, if our study has been ethically designed, there should be no need for guilt on the part of the social worker because some people are not being taught to relax. They can be taught to relax when our study is over as pointed out in Chapter 4 on ethics.

COMPENSATORY RIVALRY

Compensatory rivalry is an effect that occurs when the control group becomes motivated to compete with the experimental group. For example, a control group in a program to encourage parental involvement in school activities might get wind that something is up and make a determined effort to participate, too, on the basis that "anything they can do, we can do better." There is no direct communication between the groups, as there is in the diffusion of treatment effect, only rumors and suggestions of rumors. However, rumors are often enough to threaten the internal validity of a study.

DEMORALIZATION

In direct contrast with compensatory rivalry, demoralization refers to feelings of deprivation among the control group that may cause them to give up and drop out of the study, in which case this effect would be referred to as *mortality*. The people in the control group may also get angry.

Now that you have a sound understanding of internal validity, we turn our attention to two-group designs that have to minimize as many threats to internal validity as possible if they are to support cause-effect statements such as "my intervention caused my clients to get better."

 # TWO-GROUP DESIGNS

 Except for the one-group pretest-posttest design, one-group designs do not intend to determine cause-effect relationships. Thus, they are not concerned with internal validity issues. Two-group designs on the other hand help us produce data for coming a bit closer to proving cause-effect relationships, so now internal validity issues come readily into play. There are many two-group designs, but we will discuss only four of them.

— Comparison Group Pretest-Posttest Design

— Comparison Group Posttest-Only Design

— Classical Experimental Design

— Randomized Posttest-Only Control Group Design

COMPARISON GROUP PRETEST-POSTTEST DESIGN

THE COMPARISON GROUP pretest-posttest design simply elaborates on the one-group pretest-posttest design by adding a comparison group. This second group receives both the pretest (O_1) and the posttest (O_2) at the same time as the experimental group, but it does not receive the intervention. Also, random assignment to groups is never done in this design. This design is written as shown in Figure 11.7, and hypothetical data could look like those displayed in Table 11.2, where:

O_1 = First measurement of the program objective

X = The program, or intervention

O_2 = Second measurement of the program objective

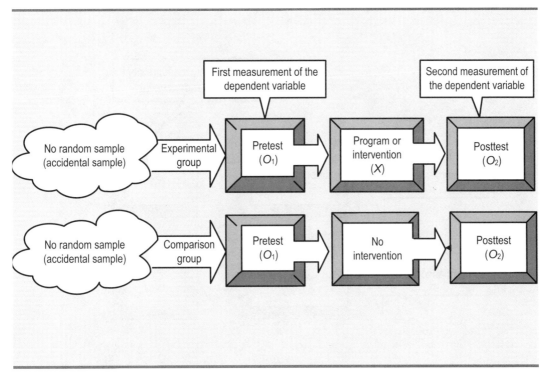

FIGURE 11.7

Comparison Group Pretest-Posttest Design

TABLE 11.2

Displaying Data for a Comparison Group Pretest-Posttest Design (from Figure 11.7)

Group	Pretest Average (O_1)	Posttest Average (O_2)	Difference Average $(O_2 - O_1)$
Intervention Group	50	80	30
Comparison Group	60	70	10
Difference....			20

The experimental and comparison groups formed under this design will probably not be equivalent because members are not randomly assigned to the two groups (notice the 10-point difference at pretest). The pretest scores, however, will indicate the extent of their differences. If the differences are not statistically significant but are still large enough to affect the posttest, the statistical technique of analysis of covariance can be used to compensate for this.

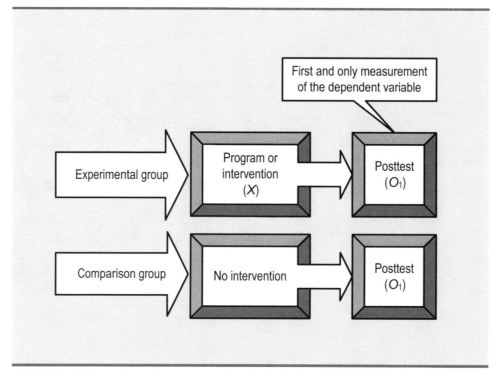

FIGURE 11.8

Comparison Group Posttest-Only Design

So long as the groups are at least somewhat equivalent at pretest, this design controls for nearly all of the threats to internal validity. But because random assignment to groups was not used, many of the external validity threats remain (to be discussed at the end of chapter).

COMPARISON GROUP POSTTEST-ONLY DESIGN

THE COMPARISON GROUP posttest-only design improves on the one-group posttest-only design by introducing a comparison group that does not receive the intervention but is subject to the same posttest as those who do (the comparison group). The basic elements of the comparison group posttest-only design are as shown in Figure 11.8, and hypothetical data could be displayed as in Table 11.3, where:

X = The program, or intervention

O_1 = First and only measurement of the program objective

TABLE 11.3
Displaying Data for a
Comparison Group Posttest-Only Design
(from Figure 11.8)

Group	Posttest Average
Intervention Group	80
Comparison Group	70
Difference....	10

In Antonia's child abuse prevention program, if the January, April, and August sections are scheduled but the August sessions are canceled for some reason, those who would have been participants in that section could be used as a comparison group. If the values of O_1 on the measuring instrument were similar for the experimental and comparison groups, it could be concluded that the program was of little use because those who had experienced it (those who had received X) were not much better or worse off than those who had not.

A problem with drawing this conclusion, however, is that there is no evidence that the groups were equivalent to begin with. Selection, mortality, and the interaction of selection and other threats to internal validity are thus the major difficulties with this design. The use of a comparison group, however, controls for the effects of history, maturation, and testing.

CLASSICAL EXPERIMENTAL DESIGN

THE CLASSICAL EXPERIMENTAL DESIGN is the basis for all the experimental designs. It involves an experimental group and a control group, both created by a random assignment method (and, if possible, by random selection from a population).

Both groups take a pretest (O_1) at the same time, after which the intervention (X) is given only to the experimental group; then both groups take the posttest (O_2) at the same time.

This design is written as shown in Figure 11.9, and the typical way to present the data is displayed in Table 11.4. Because the experimental and control groups are randomly assigned, they are equivalent with respect to all important variables. This group equivalence in the design helps control for many of the threats to internal validity because both groups will be affected by them in the same way, where:

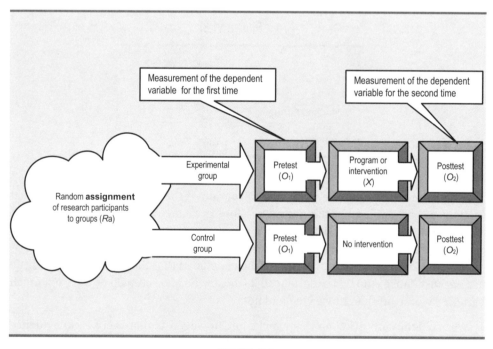

FIGURE 11.9

Classical Experimental Design

R = Random selection (R_s) from a population and random assignment (R_a) to group

O_1 = First measurement of the program objective

X = The program, or intervention

O_2 = Second measurement of the program objective

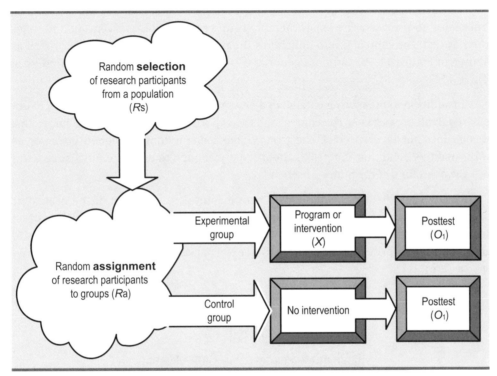

FIGURE 11.10

Randomized Posttest-Only Control Group Design

TABLE 11.4

Displaying Data for a Classical Experimental Design (from Figure 11.9)

Group	Pretest Average (O_1)	Posttest Average (O_2)	Difference Average ($O_2 - O_1$)
Intervention Group	50	80	30
Control Group	50	70	20
Difference….			10

RANDOMIZED POSTTEST-ONLY CONTROL GROUP DESIGN

THE RANDOMIZED POSTTEST-ONLY control group design is identical to the comparison group posttest-only design, except that the participants are randomly assigned to two groups. This design, therefore, has a control group rather than a comparison group.

This design usually involves only two groups, one experimental and one control. There are no pretests. The experimental group receives the intervention and takes the posttest; the control group only takes the posttest. This design can be written as shown in Figure 11.10, and data generated from this design can be presented as in Table 11.5.

In addition to measuring change in a group or groups, a pretest also helps to ensure equivalence between the control and the experimental groups. As you know, this design does not have a pretest. The groups have been randomly assigned, however, as indicated by R, and this, in itself, is theoretically enough to ensure equivalence without the need for a confirmatory pretest.

This design is useful in situations where it's not possible to conduct a pretest or where a pretest would be expected to strongly influence the results of the posttest because of the effects of testing. This design also controls for many of the threats to internal validity (previously discussed) and external validity (discussed in the following section).

TABLE 11.5
Displaying Data for a
Randomized Posttest-Only Control Group
Design (from Figure 11.10)

Group	Posttest Average
Intervention Group	80
Control Group	50
Difference....	30

EXTERNAL VALIDITY

External validity is the degree to which the results of a specific study are generalizable to another population, to another setting, and to another time. There are many threats to internal validity, but we will only discuss six of them:

— Pretest-Treatment Interaction

— Selection-Treatment Interaction

— Specificity of Variables

— Reactive Effects

— Multiple-Treatment Interference

— Researcher Bias

PRETEST-TREATMENT INTERACTION

THE FIRST THREAT to external validity, pretest-treatment interaction, is similar to the testing effects threat to internal validity. The nature of a pretest can alter the way in which research participants respond to the experimental intervention, as well as to the posttest.

It's nothing more than a situation when participants respond or react differently to a treatment because they have been pretested. Suppose, for example, that an educational program on racial tolerance is being evaluated. A pretest that measures the level of tolerance could well alert the participants to the fact that they are going to be educated into loving all their neighbors, but many people do not want to be "educated" into anything. They are satisfied with the way they feel and will resist the instruction. This will affect the level of racial tolerance registered on the posttest.

SELECTION-TREATMENT INTERACTION

THE SECOND MAJOR THREAT to external validity is selection-treatment interaction. This threat commonly occurs when a design cannot provide for random selection of participants from a population. Suppose we wanted to study the effectiveness of a family service agency staff, for example. If our research proposal was turned down by fifty agencies before it was accepted by the fifty-first, it's very likely that the accepting agency differs in certain important aspects from the other fifty. It may accept the proposal because its social workers are more highly motivated, more secure, more satisfied with their jobs, or more interested in the practical application of the study than are the average agency staff member.

As a result, we would be assessing the research participants on the very factors for which they were unwittingly (and by default) selected—motivation, job satisfaction, and so on. The study may be internally valid, but because it will not be possible to generalize the results to other family service agencies it will have little external validity.

SPECIFICITY OF VARIABLES

SPECIFICITY OF VARIABLES has to do with the fact that a research project conducted with a specific group of people at a specific time and in a specific setting may not always be generalizable to other people at different times and in different settings.

For example, a measuring instrument used to measure the IQ levels of upper-socioeconomic-level Caucasian suburban children does not provide an equally accurate measure of IQ when it's applied to lower-socioeconomic-level children of racial minorities in the inner city.

REACTIVE EFFECTS

THE FOURTH THREAT to external validity is reactive effects, which, as with internal validity, occur when the attitudes or behaviors of the research participants are affected to some degree by the very act of taking a pretest. Thus, they are no longer exactly equivalent to the population from which they were randomly selected, and it may not be possible to generalize the study's results to that population. Because pretests affect participants to some degree, the study results may be valid only for those who were pretested.

MULTIPLE-TREATMENT INTERFERENCE

THE FIFTH THREAT to external validity, multiple-treatment interference, occurs when a research participant is given two or more interventions in succession, so the results of the first intervention may affect the results of the second. A client who attends treatment sessions, for example, may not seem to benefit from one therapeutic technique, so another is tried. In fact, the client may have benefited from the first technique, but the benefit may not become apparent until the second technique has been tried.

As a result, the effects of both techniques become commingled, or the results may be erroneously ascribed to the second technique alone. Because of this threat, interventions should be given separately if possible. If the research design does not allow this, sufficient time should be allowed to elapse between the two interventions in an effort to minimize the possibility of multiple-treatment interference.

In addition, your research participants may be getting help in other places besides the program you are evaluating. They may, for example, being offered help by other caseworkers, probation officers, various self-help groups, hospitals, clinics, friends, clergy, and even their mothers and fathers in addition to the odd social work practicum student or two. All these other helping sources will affect the results of your study.

RESEARCHER BIAS

THE FINAL THREAT to external validity is researcher bias. Researchers, like people in general, tend to see what they want to see or expect to see. Unconsciously and without any thought of deceit, they may manipulate a study so that the actual results agree with the anticipated results. A practitioner may favor an intervention so strongly that the study is structured to support it, or the results may be interpreted favorably. The phrase "If I didn't believe it, I wouldn't have seen it" readily comes to mind.

If we know which individuals are in the experimental group and which are in the control group, this knowledge alone might affect the study's results. Students whom an instructor believes to be bright, for example, often are given higher grades than their performance warrants, whereas students believed to be dull are given lower grades. The way to control for researcher bias is to perform a double-blind experiment in which neither the research participants nor the evaluator knows who is in the experimental or control group.

◆ SUMMARY

Research designs cover the entire range of research questions and provide data that can be used to gain knowledge for our profession. No single design is inherently inferior or superior to the others. Each has advantages and disadvantages. Those of us who are familiar with them will be well equipped to select the one that is most appropriate to a particular evaluative effort.

Study Questions for Chapter 11

— First, answer each question only AFTER you have read the chapter.

— Second, indicate how comfortable you were in answering each question on a 5-point scale:

1	2	3	4	5
Very uncomfortable	Somewhat uncomfortable	Neutral	Somewhat comfortable	Very comfortable

If you rated any question between 1–3, please reread the section of the chapter where the information for the question can be found. If you're still uncomfortable answering the question, talk with your instructor and/or your classmates for more clarification.

Questions	Degree of comfort? (Circle one number)
1. List and then discuss all four one-group research designs. Provide as many social work examples you can think of throughout your discussion to illustrate your main points.	1 2 3 4 5
2. List the three types of longitudinal designs. Provide one common social work example throughout your discussion to illustrate your main points.	1 2 3 4 5
3. List and then discuss all four two-group research designs. Provide as many social work examples you can think of throughout your discussion to illustrate your main points.	1 2 3 4 5
4. Discuss in detail the concept of internal validity. Now list all ten threats to internal validity and provide a social work example for each threat.	1 2 3 4 5
5. Discuss in detail the concept of external validity. Now list all six threats to external validity and provide a social work example for each threat.	1 2 3 4 5
6. List the three knowledge levels. Now discuss how research designs are related to each level. Provide as many social work examples as you can to illustrate your points.	1 2 3 4 5
7. List the six criteria that an ideal experiment must contain. Provide a social work example that illustrates your main points for each of the six criterion.	1 2 3 4 5
8. Discuss how you could use the "matched pairs technique" when assigning research participants to two or more groups. Provide a social work example to illustrate your main points.	1 2 3 4 5

Assessing Your Self-Efficacy for Chapter 11

AFTER you have read the chapter AND have completed all the study questions, please indicate how knowledgeable you feel you are for each concept listed below.

1	2	3	4	5
Very uncomfortable	Somewhat uncomfortable	Neutral	Somewhat comfortable	Very comfortable

Major Concepts in Chapter	Knowledge Level? (Circle one number)
1. Knowledge levels	1 2 3 4 5
2. Characteristics of ideal experiments	1 2 3 4 5
3. Rival hypotheses	1 2 3 4 5
4. The differences between control groups, experimental groups, and comparison groups	1 2 3 4 5
5. Randomly assigning research participants to groups	1 2 3 4 5
6. Matched pairs technique	1 2 3 4 5
7. One-group research designs	1 2 3 4 5
8. Two-group research designs	1 2 3 4 5
9. Internal validity	1 2 3 4 5
10. External validity	1 2 3 4 5

Add up your scores (Minimum = 10, Maximum = 50)	Total score =

A 45 — 50 = Social Work Manager in the making.
B 40 — 44 = Social Work Supervisor.
C 35 — 39 = Social Work Practitioner.
D 10 — 34 = Case Aide. Reread the chapter and redo the study questions.

PART V
Collecting Data

12

Collecting Quantitative Data

It's a capital mistake to theorize before one has data.
~ Arthur Conan Doyle

Data collection is the heartbeat of all research studies—positivistic or interpretative. Our goal is to collect good data—qualitative data (i.e., words) for interpretive studies and quantitative data (i.e., numbers) for positivistic ones—with a steady rhythm and in a systematic manner. When data collection becomes erratic or stops prematurely, all research studies are in grave danger.

With that in mind, this chapter briefly presents a variety of data collection methods that can produce quantitative data. Likewise, the next chapter presents various data collection options that can be used with qualitative studies.

DATA COLLECTION METHODS AND DATA SOURCES

There is a critical distinction between a data collection method and a data source. This distinction must be clearly understood before we collect any data whatsoever. A *data collection method* consists of a detailed plan of procedures that aims to gather data for a specific purpose—that is, to answer a research question or to test a hypothesis.

Any data collection method can tap into a variety of *data sources*. The primary source of data in most social work research studies is people. Rarely do we use machines (e.g., biofeedback) to monitor change in people's attitudes, knowledge, or behaviors. Rather, we tend to collect data about people from the people themselves.

Data collected directly from people can be firsthand or secondhand data. Firsthand data are obtained from people who are closest to the problem we are studying. Single mothers participating in a parent support group, for example, can easily provide firsthand data to describe their own stresses as single mothers.

Secondhand data may come from people who are indirectly connected to the primary problem (i.e., stress of single mothers) we are studying. A parent support group facilitator, for example, can record secondhand observations of "stress" behaviors displayed by parents in the parent support group. The facilitator can also collect data from family members. Grandparents, for example, can provide data that reflect their perceptions of how "stressed out" their granddaughters may be (Unrau, 2011).

Regardless of the data collection method or the data source, *all* data are eventually collected, analyzed, and interpreted as part of the research process. We will discuss shortly the basic data collection methods that commonly produce quantitative data for positivistic studies. Before we do this, however, we need to understand the various types of data.

TYPES OF DATA

What exactly are data? They are recorded units of information that are used as the basis for reasoning, calculation, and discussion (a single unit of information is called a *datum*). We can collect *original data* and/or *existing data*. The distinction between the two is a simple one. We collect original data (for the first time) during the course of our study to fulfill a specific purpose: to answer our research question or test our hypothesis. Unlike original data, we can use existing data that have been previously collected and stored, either manually or in a computer, before our study was even fully conceptualized.

We can also distinguish between types of data by the research approach used. In a positivistic study, for example, we analyze *numerical data* using mathematical computations and calculations (Chapter 15). On the other hand, an interpretive study typically analyzes words or *text data* (Chapter 16).

We analyze text data by reading and rereading; our task is to look for common and differentiating characteristics and themes within the words. A single research study can easily incorporate both quantitative and qualitative types of data. In fact, interpretive and positivistic data collection methods can produce complimentary data.

As you know, quantitative data are used in research studies that utilize the positivistic research approach. The previous chapters discussed how this approach aims to reduce research topics into concepts and clearly defined variables. One of the major steps in a positivistic study is "focusing the question," which requires that we develop operational definitions for all the variables in our study. Let's revisit our two-variable research question that has been used throughout this book:

RESEARCH QUESTION

Do people who come from ethnic minority backgrounds have difficulty in accessing social services?

As we know, a positivistic research study requires that we operationally define "ethnicity" and "difficulty in accessing social services" in such a way that we can measure each variable. We could easily measure both of our study's variables using two categories each:

What is your ethnicity? *(Circle one category below.)*
1. Ethnic Minority
2. Ethnic Majority

Did you have difficulty in accessing any form of social services over the last 12-month period? *(Circle one category below.)*
1. Yes
2. No

In Chapter 5, however, we learned that our two variables (i.e., ethnicity and difficulty in accessing social services) can be operationally defined in a variety of ways. Let's consider the two-variable research question for the various data collection methods that are most often associated with producing quantitative data:

— Survey Questionnaires

— Structured Observations

— Secondary Data

— Existing Statistics

 # SURVEY QUESTIONNAIRES

Survey research or surveys in themselves are a method for researching social problems. The aim of a survey is to collect data from a population, or a sample of research participants, in order to describe them as a group. One form that a survey can take is a questionnaire, which is a carefully selected set of questions that relate to the variables in our research question (Engel & Schutt, 2011).

When data are collected using survey questionnaires, we get our research participants' perceptions about the variable being measured. Think about a survey questionnaire that you have filled out recently—a marketing survey, a consumer satisfaction questionnaire, or a teaching evaluation of your instructor. Your answers reflected your perceptions and were probably different from the perceptions of others who answered the same survey.

A survey questionnaire is one data collection method that we can use to collect data in order to answer our two-variable research question. It would have to include items that measure our two variables—ethnicity and difficulty in accessing social services. We would ask clients within our study to "self-report" what they perceive their ethnicity to be and whether they have experienced difficulty in accessing social services over the last 12-month period.

There are two basic types of survey questionnaires. Nonstandardized survey questionnaires are one type. The two questions we posed are a very basic example of a nonstandardized survey questionnaire. The two-question survey is nonstandardized because the items have not been tested for reliability or validity. We have no way of knowing whether our research participants will respond to our two questions in a uniform way. At best, we can comment on our survey questionnaire's face validity; that is, do its items "look" like they are measuring the variables we are interested in? Nonstandardized questionnaires are often developed when standardized questionnaires are not available or suited to our specific research question.

As you know from Chapter 8, most standardized survey questionnaires are scientifically constructed to measure one specific variable. Let's say we have searched the library and computer databases for a standardized survey questionnaire that measures our dependent variable, difficulty in accessing social services.

Suppose the closest standardized questionnaire we find is *Reid-Gundlach Social Service Satisfaction Scale (R-GSSSS)*, which contains 34-items and measures clients' satisfaction with social services they have received (see Figure 8.1). Clients would read each item and rate how much they agree with each item. A 5-point scale is used: 1 strongly agree, 2 agree, 3 undecided, 4 disagree, and 5 strongly disagree.

The *R-GSSSS* specifically measures satisfaction with social services, a concept that closely relates to our access variable but is not an exact measure of it. In other words, satisfaction with social services is not the same as difficulty in accessing social services, but it could be used as a proxy measure to answer our research question. Because it is a proxy measure, we would be making a humongous leap to say that the clients who are most dissatisfied with the social services are the same clients that will have the most difficulty in accessing new social services. This is a very huge leap, to say the least.

How we proceed in collecting survey questionnaire data varies depending upon whether we collect them via the mail, telephone interviews, or face-to-face interviews. When a questionnaire is sent through the mail, our research participants must also be provided with sufficient instructions to self-administer the questionnaire. This means that they must have all the necessary instructions to successfully complete the survey questionnaire alone.

When telephone or face-to-face interviews are used, the interviewer is available to assist the research participant with any difficulties in completing the questionnaire. Regardless of how our questionnaires are administered, there are some basic procedures that we can use to increase the likelihood of obtaining accurate and complete data.

ESTABLISHING PROCEDURES TO COLLECT SURVEY DATA

THERE ARE BASIC PROCEDURES that must be considered before any survey questionnaire is administered to potential research participants. First, it's essential that straightforward and simple instructions accompany the questionnaire. Our objective is to have each research participant complete the questionnaire in exactly the same way, which means they must have the same understanding of each question.

Suppose for a moment that we ask one of our two questions posed earlier: "Did you have difficulty in accessing any form of social services over the last 12-month period?" It's clear that we want our research participants to answer our question with respect to the past 12 months and not any other time frame.

A second procedure that must be established is how informed consent will be obtained from the research participants (see Chapter 3). This is a task that can be accomplished by writing a cover letter explaining the purpose of the research study and questionnaire, who the researchers are, that participation is entirely voluntary, how the data will be used, and the steps taken to guarantee confidentiality. A cover letter is usually sent out with mailed questionnaires, read aloud over the telephone, or presented in face-to-face interviews.

To decrease the likelihood of any misunderstanding, elementary language should be used in the cover letter (the same as in the questionnaire). It may even be possible to have the cover letter (and questionnaire) translated into our research participants' native language(s). In our study, we are asking about ethnicity, which suggests that English could be a second language for many of our research participants. Depending on the geographic area in which we are conducting our study, we may wish to translate our cover letter and questionnaire into the dominant language of the geographic area.

If our survey questionnaire is to be administered over the telephone or face-to-face by an interviewer, training of interviewers will be a necessary third procedure. In the same way that we want research participants to have the same understanding of the questionnaire's items, we want interviewers to handle potential queries in a consistent manner. Interviewers must be trained to ask the questions within our questionnaire in such a way that they do not influence the research participants' answers.

Basically, interviewers should refrain from discussing individual questions with research participants, from varying their tone of voice when asking the questions, and from commenting on the research participants' answers. The interviewer's task is to keep the research participant focused on answering the questions at hand, to answer questions for clarification, and to record the answers.

To save on time and resources, it may be possible to administer survey questionnaires in a group format. This usually means that we meet a group of research participants in their own environment. Suppose, for example, we were specifically interested in the accessibility of social services among Native people. We would need to travel to the reserve, then administer our questionnaire at a central location on the reserve that's convenient for our research participants.

RECORDING SURVEY DATA

THE DATA WE GATHER from questionnaires usually are in numerical form. Our question that asks whether clients had difficulty accessing any form of social services over the last 12 months will produce a number of "yes" responses and a number of "no" responses.

We can add up the total sum of responses for each category and calculate the number of clients who had difficulty accessing social services broken down by ethnicity (i.e., ethnic minority and ethnic majority).

Establishing the Reliability and Validity of Survey Data

Reliability and validity are critical to determining the credibility of any data collection instrument. Standardized questionnaires have associated with them values of both. Reliability values tell us how confident we can be in using our questionnaire over two or more time periods, across different people, and across different places. Validity values give us information about how good our questionnaire is at measuring what it purports to measure. The validity value for the *R-GSSS*, for example, is reasonably high at 0.95 (the highest possible value is 1.0).

Reports on the *R-GSSS* also note that the standardized questionnaire is useful for measuring differences in race. Specifically, African Americans and Mexican Americans are reported to predictably have lower scores. We can also assess the face validity of the *R-GSSS* by simply looking at the 34 items contained within it (see Figure 8.1). A quick glance tells us that the items reflect the "idea" of client satisfaction with social services. When using unstandardized questionnaires, we do not have the luxury of reporting reliability or validity. In this instance, we must ensure that our questionnaire, at the very least, has face validity.

Advantages and Disadvantages of Survey Data

Overall, the major advantage of survey questionnaires is that they offer a relatively inexpensive way to collect new data. In addition, they can easily reach a large number of people, provide specific data, collect data efficiently, and be input into a computer easily. An additional advantage of standardized questionnaires is that the data they generate can be compared with the data collected in other studies that used the same standardized questionnaire.

The overall disadvantages of survey questionnaires include: research participants must be literate, surveys usually get a low response rate, the research participants must have a mailing address or telephone to be reached, in-depth or open-end responses are missed, and simple questions are utilized to provide answers to complex research questions.

Structured Observations

tructured observation" is a self-explanatory data collection method. A trained observer records the interaction of others in a specific place over an agreed upon amount of time using specific procedures and measurements. Structured observation aims to observe the natural interactions between and among people that occur either in natural or in artificial settings (Polster & Collins, 2011).

If we want to observe how people of different ethnic backgrounds interact with their social worker, for example, we could set up structured observations at the social worker's offices (natural environment), or we could set up interviews to be observed from behind one-way mirrors (artificial setting).

The data collected from structured observation reflect the trained observers' perceptions of the interactions. That is, the observers do not interact with the people they are observing. They simply watch the interactions and record the presence or absence of certain behaviors. Observers could, for example, count the number of times clients (comparing ethnic minority and ethnic majority groups) mention a barrier or obstacle to accessing a social service, or monitor whether social workers engage in behaviors that specifically assist clients in accessing new services. These observations, of course, would take place during "normal" meetings between social workers and their clients.

Structured observation requires that the variables being measured are specifically defined. We must "micro-define" our variables. In our two-variable research question, for example, we have already operationally defined "ethnic" as having two categories: ethnic minority and non–ethnic minority. In measuring our difficulty in accessing social services variable, we could measure it by the number of social services referred by a social worker in a 60-minute interview.

We could then compare the results of our difficulty in accessing social services variable across our two ethnicity groups. Would we find that social workers are more or less likely to offer social service referrals to clients who are from an ethnic minority or a non–ethnic minority group?

There are three general types of recording that can be used with structured observation. Observations can be measured for frequency (e.g., count a behavior every time it occurs), for duration (e.g., how long does the behavior last each time it occurs), and for magnitude (e.g., the varying intensity of a behavior such as mild, moderate, or severe).

Whether we use frequency, duration, or magnitude (or some combination), depends on the picture we want to develop to answer our research question. Do we want to describe difficulty in accessing social services by how many times services are offered to clients (frequency), by how much time social workers spend explaining how services can be accessed (duration), or by the degree of sincerity that the workers display when offering service referrals (magnitude)?

When we record the presence or absence of behaviors during an interaction between and among people, our observations can be structured in such a way as to help the observers record the behaviors accurately. Suppose for a moment, social worker interviews with clients take an average of one hour. We could set recording intervals at every minute so that we have 60 recording intervals in one hour.

The observers would sit with a stopwatch and record whether the social workers offered any social services to their clients in the first minute, the second minute, and each minute thereafter until the interviews end. Interval recording assists the observers in making continuous observations throughout the interaction. Spot-check recording is another way to schedule observation recordings.

Unlike interval recording which is continuous, spot-check recording is a way to record intermittent observations. It may be possible to observe and record the presence or absence of a behavior for one minute every five minutes, for example.

ESTABLISHING PROCEDURES TO COLLECT OBSERVATIONAL DATA

THE PROCEDURES established for structured observation are firmly decided upon before actual observations take place. That is, the observers are specifically trained to watch for the presence or absence of specific behaviors and the recording method is set. The types of data to be recorded are selected (i.e., frequency, duration, or magnitude), and the nature of the recording is decided (i.e., continuous, interval, or spot-check).

Data generally are recorded by observers and not the persons engaging in the behaviors. As such, it's essential that observers be trained to "see" behaviors in a reliable way. Imagine that you are one of the observers and your main task is to record magnitude ratings of the degree of sincerity that social workers display when they offer social service referrals. You must decide whether the social workers' gestures are mildly, moderately, or extremely sincere. How would you know to rate a behavior that you observed as "mildly sincere" versus "moderately sincere"?

Training of observers requires that all variables be unequivocally clear. Thus, observers are usually trained using mock trials. They are selected for their ability to collect data according to the rules of the research study, not for their unique views or creative observations. In a nutshell, the observers are an instrument for data collection, and an effort is made to calibrate all instruments of the research study in the same way. To allow for several different observers to view the same situation, we may choose to videotape interactions.

A decision must also be made about who will be the best observers. Should only professionally trained outside observers be selected? This would include people who are completely unfamiliar with the context of the study but are skilled observers. How about indigenous observers—people who are familiar with the nature of the interaction to be observed?

In our example, indigenous observers could include people such as other social workers, social work supervisors, other clients, or staff from other social service offices. Who we choose to observe may depend upon availability, expense, or how important we feel it is for the observers to be familiar or unfamiliar with the situation being observed. Measurement that reflects cultural variables, for example, may require indigenous observers.

RECORDING STRUCTURED OBSERVATIONAL DATA

THE RECORDING INSTRUMENT for structured observation generally takes the form of a grid or checklist. The behaviors being observed and the method of recording are identified. The simplest recording form to construct is one that records frequency. The recording form would simply identify the period of observation and the number of times a specific behavior occurs:

Observation Period	Frequency
3:00 P.M. to 4:00 P.M.	✓✓✓✓

For duration recording, it's necessary to add the duration in minutes at each occurrence of the behavior:

Observation Period	Frequency and (Duration, in minutes)
3:00 P.M. to 4:00 P.M.	1 (5), 2 (11), 3 (15)

For magnitude recording, we record the time of occurrence and give a corresponding rating for the behavior. To simplify recording, the magnitude ratings are generally coded by assigning a number to each category. For example, 1 is mildly sincere, 2 is moderately sincere, and 3 is extremely sincere.

Observation Time	Magnitude
3:17 P.M.	1
3:25 P.M.	1
3:29 P.M.	2

ESTABLISHING THE RELIABILITY AND VALIDITY OF OBSERVATIONAL DATA

AS WE KNOW from Chapters 7 and 8, validity refers to whether we are measuring what we think we are measuring. In other words, are we really measuring or observing "difficulty in accessing social services"? Validity, in this instance, should make us think about whether our criteria for observation (i.e., how we operationalized our variable) are reasonable representations of the variable.

Reliability, on the other hand, can be assessed in more concrete ways. Once we have established an operational definition for each variable and the procedures for observation and recording, we can test their reliability. A simple method for determining reliability is to use two independent raters who observe the exact same situation. How well do their recordings match? Do the two observers produce the same frequencies? The same duration periods? The same magnitude ratings? Do they agree 100 percent or only 50 percent?

One hundred percent agreement suggests that the measure is a reliable one, compared to 50 percent, which suggests we should go back to the drawing board to come up with more precise operational definitions for both variables or more exact recording procedures.

ADVANTAGES AND DISADVANTAGES OF OBSERVATIONAL DATA

STRUCTURED OBSERVATION helps us to collect precise, valid, and reliable data within complex interactions. We are able to tease out important behaviors that are direct (or indirect) measures of the variable we are interested in. The data produced are objective observations of behaviors and thus are not tainted by our individual self-perceptions.

Think back to the survey questionnaire method of data collection that we discussed at the beginning of this chapter. The data collected using a survey questionnaire reflect the research participants' own perceptions. Structured observation, on the other hand, gives a factual account of what actually took place. It can explain one component of a social interaction with objectivity, precision, and detail.

The major disadvantage of structured observation is the time and resources needed to train skilled observers. Think about the amount of time it would take, for example, to get you and, say, two other observers to agree on what constitutes "mild," "moderate," or "extremely" sincere behavior of social workers.

Another disadvantage of structured observation is that it's a microscopic approach to dealing with complex social interactions. By focusing on one or two specific details (variables) of an interaction, we may miss out on many other important aspects of the interactions.

 # SECONDARY DATA

When existing data are used to answer a newly developed research question (or to test a hypothesis), the data are considered secondary. In other words, the data are being used for some purpose other than the original one for which they were collected. Unlike survey questionnaires or structured observation mentioned previously, collecting secondary data is unobtrusive (Rubin, 2011).

Because data already exist, it's not necessary to ask people questions (as in survey questionnaires) or to be observed (as in structured observations). Furthermore, secondary data can exist in numerical form (quantitative) or text form (qualitative). Our discussion in this section focuses on existing quantitative data.

Let's go back to our two-variable research question that asks about the relationship between clients' ethnicity and whether they have difficulty in accessing social services. So far, we have discussed data collection methods within a social service context and have focused on the interaction between social workers and their clients. Within a social service program there are many client records that could provide meaningful data to answer our simple research question. It's likely, for example, that client intake forms collect data about clients' ethnicity.

We can be assured that an ethnicity question on an existing client intake form was not thought up to answer our specific research question. Rather, the program likely had other reasons for collecting the data, such as needing to report the percentage of clients who come from an ethnic minority that they have seen in a given fiscal period. The social service program may also have records that contain data that we could use for our difficulty in accessing social services variable. Social workers, for example, may be required to record each service referral made for each client. By reading each client file, we would be able to count the number of service referrals made for each client.

Secondary data can also be accessed from existing data bases around the world. Census databases are a common example. With the advances of computer technology, databases are becoming easier to access. The Inter-University Consortium for Political and Social Research (ICPSR) is the largest data archive in the world; it holds more than 17,000 files of data from more than 130 countries.

We could use the ICPSR data, for example, to compare the accessibility of social services for clients from different ethnic groups across various countries. Of course, we could only do this if meaningful data already exist within the database to answer our research question.

ESTABLISHING PROCEDURES TO COLLECT SECONDARY DATA

GIVEN THAT SECONDARY DATA already exist, there is no need to collect them. Rather, our focus shifts to evaluating the data set's worth with respect to answering our research question. The presence of data sets has an important influence on how we formulate our research questions or test our hypotheses. When original data are collected, we design our research study and tailor our data collection procedures to gather the "best" data possible. When data exist, we can only develop a research question that is as good as the data that we have available.

Because secondary data influence how we formulate our research questions, we must firmly settle on a research question before analyzing them. Data sets can have a vertigo effect, leaving us feeling dizzy about the relationships between and among variables contained within them. It may be that we begin with a general research question, such as our two-variable question about ethnicity and difficulty in accessing social services, and move to a more specific hypothesis.

Suppose our existing data set had within it data about client ethnicity (e.g., Asians, African Americans, Caucasians, Native Americans) and data about difficulty in accessing social services (e.g., yes or no). We could return to the literature for studies that might help us formulate a directional (one-tailed) hypothesis.

A directional hypothesis would suggest that one or more of these four ethnic groups would have more (or less) difficulty accessing social services than the remaining groups. If no such literature exists, however, we would pose a nondirectional (two-tailed) hypothesis, which indicates that we have no basis to suggest that one of the four ethnic groups would have more or less difficulty accessing social services than any of the others.

Another influence of an existing data set is on how we operationally define the variables in our study. Simply put, our study's variables will have already been operationally defined for us. The definition used to collect the original data will be the definition we use in our study as well.

It's possible to create a new variable by recasting one or more of the original variables in an existing data set. For instance, suppose we are interested to know whether our clients are parents. Existing program records, however, only list the number of children in each family. We could recast these data by categorizing those clients who have one or more children versus those who have no children, thus creating a two-category variable. Clients with one or more children would be categorized as "parents" versus clients without any children who would be classified as "not parents."

One final consideration for using existing secondary data is that of informed consent. Just because data exist does not mean that we have free rein to use them in future studies. It may be that clients have provided information on intake forms because they believed it was necessary to do so in order to receive services (see Chapter 3).

Recording Secondary Data

RECORDING SECONDARY DATABASES are a simple matter because data have already been collected, organized, and checked for accuracy. Our task is to work with them and determine the best possible procedures for data analyses. One feature of existing databases is that they generally include a large number of cases and variables. Thus, some advanced knowledge of statistical software packages is required to extract the variables of interest and conduct the data analyses.

Establishing the Reliability and Validity of Secondary Data

ONCE OUR RESEARCH QUESTION is formulated and our variables have been operationally defined, it's important to establish the data set's credibility. We must remember that all data sets are not created equal, particularly with respect to their validity and reliability. Most importantly, we want to check out the data source. If ethnic status is recorded on a social service program's client intake form, for example, we would want to know how the data were obtained.

The data would be considered unreliable and even invalid if the workers simply looked at their clients and checked one of several ethnicity categories. A more reliable and valid procedure would be if they asked their clients what ethnic category they come from and at the same time showed them the categories to be selected. Data sets that are accompanied by clear data collection procedures are generally more valid and reliable than those data sets that are not.

ADVANTAGES AND DISADVANTAGES OF SECONDARY DATA

THE ADVANCEMENT of computer technology increases the likelihood that secondary data will be used more often in future social work research studies. It's a reasonably inexpensive way to gather and analyze data to answer a research question or to test a hypothesis.

Given that data sets are developing around the world, researchers can fairly easily compare data sets from different countries and across different time spans. Data sets are at our fingertips, provided that we have a research question or hypothesis to match. One major disadvantage of using an existing data set is that our research question is limited by the possibilities of the data set. We must make the best use of the data available to us, with the understanding that the "best" may not be good enough to answer our research question or test our hypothesis.

EXISTING STATISTICS

Existing statistics are a special form of secondary data. They *exist* in a variety of places. A unique feature of existing statistics is that they exist only in numerical form. We might have statistics, for example, that report 20 percent of clients served by social services were Native, 30 percent were Hispanic, and 50 percent were Caucasian.

The following provides an example of how Fran, a clinical director of a private social service agency, used existing statistics for her research question. One difference between existing statistics and secondary data is that statistics summarize data in aggregate form. The below example is from Jackie Sieppert, Steve McMurtry, & Bob McClelland (2011).

EXAMPLE OF USING EXISTING STATISTICS

FRAN IS A CLINICAL DIRECTOR of a private, nonprofit agency that provides foster care, group-home care, and residential treatment for children in a small city in Arizona. She has noticed that there is a higher number of ethnic minority children in her agency's caseload than would be expected based on the proportion of ethnic minority children in the general population. She decides to do a study of this issue using existing statistics already gathered by various sources as her data collection method.

Fran first talks with the information specialist at the local library, asking for help to conduct a computer search through the library's existing databases. The search reveals a series of reports, titled *Characteristics of Children in Substitute and Adoptive Care,* that were sponsored by the American Public Welfare Association and that provide several years of data reported by states on their populations of children in various kinds of foster and adoptive care.

She also locates an annual publication produced by the Children's Defense Fund, and this provides a variety of background data on the well-being of children in the United States. Next, Fran checks in the library's government documents section. She locates recent census data on the distribution of persons under the age of 18 across different ethnic groups in her county.

Fran now quickly turns to state-level resources, where a quick check of government listings in the telephone book reveals two agencies that appear likely to have relevant data. One is the Foster Care Review Board, which is composed of citizen volunteers who assist juvenile courts by reviewing the progress of children in foster care statewide. A call to the Board reveals that they produce an annual report that lists a variety of statistics. These include the number of foster children in the state, where they are placed, and how long they have been in care.

Fran also learns that the Board's annual reports from previous years contain similar data, thus a visit to the Board's office provides her with the historical data needed to identify trends in the statistics she is using. Finally, she discovers that two years earlier the Board produced a special issue of its annual report that was dedicated to the topic of ethnic minority children in foster care, and this issue offers additional statistics not normally recorded in most annual reports.

Another state agency is the Administration for Children, Youth, and Families, a division of the state's social services department. A call to the division connects her with a staff member who informs her that a special review of foster children was conducted by the agency only a few months before. Data from this review confirm her perception that minority children are overrepresented in foster care in the state, and it provides a range of other data that may be helpful in determining the causes of this problem.

From these sources Fran now has the data she needs to paint a detailed picture of minority foster children at the national and state levels. She also has the ability to examine the problem in terms of both point-in-time circumstances and longitudinal trends, and the latter suggest that the problem of overrepresentation has grown worse. There is also evidence to indicate that the problem is more severe in her state than nationally.

Finally, corollary data on related variables, together with the more intensive work done in the special studies by the Foster Care Review Board and the Administration for Children, Youth, and Families, gives Fran a basis for beginning to understand the causes of the problem and the type of research study that must be done to investigate solutions.

In the same way that secondary data are used for a purpose other than what was originally stated, so it is for existing statistics. With existing statistics, however, we are one step further removed from the original data. A statistic, for example, can be computed from 3,000 cases or from 30 cases—each produces only a single value.

There are two main types of statistics for us to be concerned with. The first is descriptive statistics, which simply describe the sample or population being studied. Statistics used for descriptive purposes include things like percentages, percentiles, means, standard deviations, medians, ranges, and so on.

The second type of statistics—inferential statistics—includes test statistics such as chi-square, t-test, analysis of variance (ANOVA), regression, and correlation. Do not panic; we will give an introductory discussion on statistics in Chapter 15. For now, we need only to know that descriptive statistics tell us about the characteristics of a sample or a population. Inferential statistics tell us about the likelihood of a relationship between and among variables within a population.

When using existing statistics as our "data" we proceed in much the same way as when we use secondary data. Both are unobtrusive methods of data collection in that no persons will be asked to provide data about themselves—the data already exist and have been used to calculate a statistic. Therefore, we must establish their credibility.

ESTABLISHING PROCEDURES TO COLLECT EXISTING STATISTICS

USING EXISTING STATISTICS in a research study influences our research question (and hypotheses) to a greater degree than when using secondary data. If existing statistics are to assist in developing a research question, then advanced knowledge of statistics is required. We would need to understand the purpose of each statistic, the assumptions behind it, and how it was calculated.

We would not want to gather existing statistics without also collecting information about how the original data (used to calculate our existing statistics) were collected and analyzed. This information is important to assessing the credibility of the statistics that we would use for our research study.

RECORDING EXISTING STATISTICAL DATA

RECORDING EXISTING STATISTICS is different from recording secondary data. In the case of secondary data, the data are already in a recorded form. When working with existing statistics, it's usually necessary to extract the statistics from their original sources and reconfigure them in a way that permits us to conduct an appropriate data analysis. It may be, for example, that we need to extract percentage figures from a paragraph within a published article, or mean and standard deviation scores from an already existing table in a research report.

Establishing the Reliability and Validity of Existing Statistics

Checking the reliability and validity of existing statistics requires us to look for a few basic things. First, we want to be sure that the studies or reports from which we are extracting the statistics use comparable conceptual and operational definitions. If we are to compare statistical results about the accessibility of social services to clients who are from different ethnic groups across two different studies, we want to be certain that both studies had reasonably similar operational definitions for the two variables that we are interested in.

We can also examine previously conducted studies for their own assessment of their validity and reliability. Were sound procedures used to collect the original data? Were the original data analyzed in an appropriate way? What were the limitations of each study? By asking these types of questions about previous studies, we can get clues as to the credibility of the statistics that we are about to use in our own research study.

Advantages and Disadvantages of Using Existing Statistics

The advantages of using existing statistics are many. Given that existing data are used, via the form of statistics, it's a relatively inexpensive approach and is unobtrusive. By using existing statistics, we can push the knowledge envelope of what we already know and ask more complex research questions. The use of existing statistics also provides us with the opportunity to compare the results of several research studies in an empirical way.

One disadvantage of using existing statistics is that we are not provided with data for individual cases. We can only answer research questions and test hypotheses about groups of people. Because data are already presented in a summary (i.e., statistical) form, it's difficult to assess how the data were collected and analyzed. Because the data have been handled by different individuals, there is an increased chance that human error has occurred somewhere along the way.

Summary

In this chapter we have described different methods for collecting quantitative data. We have demonstrated that one research question can be answered using any data collection method. Different data collection methods produce different types of data. Data collection methods that are more commonly associated with quantitative or numerical data are survey questionnaires, structured observation, secondary data, and existing statistics.

In the next chapter, we will look at the various data collection methods that can be used to collect qualitative data.

Study Questions for Chapter 12

— First, answer each question only AFTER you have read the chapter.

— Second, indicate how comfortable you were in answering each question on a 5-point scale:

1	2	3	4	5
Very uncomfortable	Somewhat uncomfortable	Neutral	Somewhat comfortable	Very comfortable

If you rated any question between 1–3, please reread the section of the chapter where the information for the question can be found. If you're still uncomfortable answering the question, talk with your instructor and/or your classmates for more clarification.

Questions	Degree of comfort? (Circle one number)
1. In your own words discuss the differences between a data collection method and a data source. Provide a single social work example throughout your discussion to illustrate your main points.	1 2 3 4 5
2. What are survey questionnaires? Discuss the advantages and disadvantages of using them as a data collection method. Provide social work examples throughout your discussion to illustrate your main points.	1 2 3 4 5
3. What are structured observations? Discuss the advantages and disadvantages of using them as a data collection method. Provide social work examples throughout your discussion to illustrate your main points.	1 2 3 4 5
4. What are secondary data? Discuss the advantages and disadvantages of using them as a data collection method. Provide social work examples throughout your discussion to illustrate your main points.	1 2 3 4 5
5. What are existing statistics? Discuss the advantages and disadvantages of using them as a data collection method. Provide social work examples throughout your discussion to illustrate your main points.	1 2 3 4 5

6. Find a published research article that uses one of the data collection methods covered in this chapter. Discuss the advantages and disadvantages of the data collection method when taking the study's sample into account. Could the author have used another data collection method. If so, which one?	1 2 3 4 5

Assessing Your Self-Efficacy for Chapter 12

AFTER you have read the chapter AND have completed all the study questions, please indicate how knowledgeable you feel you are for each concept listed below.

1	2	3	4	5
Very uncomfortable	Somewhat uncomfortable	Neutral	Somewhat comfortable	Very comfortable

Major Concepts in Chapter	Knowledge Level? (Circle one number)
1. Data collection methods	1 2 3 4 5
2. Data sources	1 2 3 4 5
3. Collecting data with survey questionnaires	1 2 3 4 5
4. Collecting data by structured observations	1 2 3 4 5
5. Using secondary data as a data collection method	1 2 3 4 5
6. Using existing statistics as a data collection method	1 2 3 4 5
Add up your scores (Minimum = 6, Maximum = 30)	Total score =

A   27 — 30 = Social Work Manager in the making.
B   21 — 26 = Social Work Supervisor.
C   18 — 20 = Social Work Practitioner.
D   6 — 17 = Case Aide. Reread the chapter and redo the study questions.

13

Collecting Qualitative Data

Errors using inadequate data are much less than those using no data at all.
~ Charles Babbage

As we know from the last chapter, all research studies require data—regardless of whether a positivistic or interpretive approach is used. We have already discussed that quantitative data are represented numerically, and qualitative data are expressed using words.

A second key difference between these two types of data is that qualitative data are collected to "build" a story or understanding of a concept or variable, compared to quantitative data, which narrows in on a select few variables. A third difference worth noting is that qualitative data are generally "bulkier" than quantitative data. As we will see, qualitative data can be represented by a single word, a sentence, or even an entire page of text.

The exact point in time when data are collected in the research process is another difference between quantitative and qualitative data. We have stressed that quantitative data collection can *only occur* once variables have been completely operationally defined—in fact, the reliability and validity of our measurements depend on it.

Qualitative data, on the other hand, can be collected during many different steps in the research process. We may collect data near the beginning of our study to help us focus our research question and identify key variables to be explored later on in the research process. Qualitative data collected in later steps in our study can be used to check out any assumptions we may have and any new ideas that emerge (see Chapter 6).

When collecting quantitative data, the rules for data collection are tried and tested *before* collecting any data—procedures can be outlined in a checklist format, where the data collector checks off each procedure as it's completed. For qualitative data, however, explicit procedures of data collection are not necessarily known before the data collection process starts. Rather, the procedures used are documented *as they happen*. It's only after data collection is complete that a detailed description of the procedure can be articulated.

This is not to say that in qualitative data collection we can willy-nilly change our minds or that anything goes. Research is still research, which means that a systematic approach to inquiry is used. The big difference for interpretive research is that the systematic nature of data collection applies to how we record and monitor the data collection process.

Any changes in data collection (e.g., change in questions, research participants, or literature review) are based on data already collected. More will be explained about how qualitative data collection procedures are monitored in Chapter 16. For now, let us return to our research question from the preceding chapter.

RESEARCH QUESTION

Do people who come from ethnic minority backgrounds have difficulty in accessing social services?

We have already discussed in the last chapter four different methods of collecting quantitative data to answer the above research question. Now we will turn to four data collection methods that are more commonly associated with producing qualitative data to answer the same research question.

— Narrative Interviewing

— Participant Observation

— Secondary Content Data

— Historical Data

NARRATIVE INTERVIEWING

We have seen in the previous chapter how interviewing is used to collect quantitative data via survey questionnaires, in which interviewers are trained to ask questions of research participants in a uniform way and interaction between interviewers and their research participants is minimized. Interviewing for qualitative data, on the other hand, has a completely different tone (Tutty, Rothery, & Grinnell, 1996).

The aim of narrative interviewing is to have research participants tell stories in their own words. Their stories usually begin when we ask our identified research question. For example, we could begin an interview by saying, "Could you tell me about your experiences as a Native client in terms of accessing social services?"

Qualitative interviewers are not bound by strict rules and procedures. Rather, they make every effort to engage research participants in meaningful discussions. In fact, the purpose is to have research participants tell their own stories in their own ways. The direction the interviews take may deviate from the original research problem being investigated depending on what research participants choose to tell interviewers. Data collected in one research interview can be used to develop or revise further research questions in subsequent research interviews.

The narrative interview is commonly used in case study research where numerous interviews are usually conducted to learn more about a "case," which could be defined as a person, a group of people, an event, or an organization. The narrative interview is also a basic component of other research pursuits, such as feminist research and participatory action research (Gochros, 2011).

ESTABLISHING DATA COLLECTION PROCEDURES FOR INTERVIEWING

DATA COLLECTION AND DATA ANALYSIS are intertwined in an interpretive research study. Thus, the steps we take in collecting data from a narrative interview will evolve with our study. Nevertheless, we must be clear about our starting point and the procedures that we will use to "check and balance" the decisions we make along the way. One of the aims of an interpretive research approach is to tell a story about a problem without the cobwebs of existing theories, labels, and interpretations.

As such, we may choose to limit the amount of literature we review before proceeding with data collection. The amount of literature we review is guided by the interpretive research approach we use. A grounded theory approach, for example, suggests that we review some literature at the beginning of our study in order to help frame our research question. We would then review more literature later on, taking direction from the new data that we collect.

It's necessary for us to decide when and how to approach potential research participants before data collection occurs. Think about our simple research question for a moment—Do clients who come from an ethnic minority have difficulty in accessing social services? Who would we interview first? Would we interview someone receiving multiple social services or someone not receiving any? Is there a particular ethnic group that we would want represented in our early interviews?

Remember that the data we collect in our beginning interviews will directly influence how we proceed in later interviews. It's possible for the professional literature, or our expert knowledge, to point us to a particular starting place. Regardless of where we begin, it's critical for us to document our early steps in the data collection process. The notes we take will be used later on to recall the steps we took, and more importantly, why we took them.

Let's say, for example, that our interest in our research question stems from the fact that many ethnic minority people we know in our personal lives (not our professional lives) have complained about access to social services. We may choose to begin interviewing with an individual we already know.

On the other hand, we may decide after a cursory review of the literature that most of the existing research on our research problem is based on interviews with people who, in fact, are receiving services. We may then choose to begin interviewing clients who are from an ethnic minority and who are *not* currently receiving any social services but are named on social service client lists.

We must also establish how the interview will be structured. Interviewing for qualitative data can range from informal casual conversations to more formal guided discussions. An informal interview is unplanned. The interviewer begins, for example, by asking Native clients a general question, such as the one presented earlier—could you tell me about your experiences in accessing social services?

The discussion that would follow would be based on the natural and spontaneous interaction between the interviewer and the research participant. The interviewer has no way of knowing at the outset what direction the interview will take or where it will end. A guided interview, on the other hand, has more structure. The exact amount of structure varies from one guided interview to another. In any case, the interviewer has an interview schedule, which essentially amounts to an outline of questions and/or concepts, to guide the interview with the research participant.

A loosely structured interview schedule may simply identify key concepts or ideas to include in the interview at the appropriate time. In our study, for example, we might want the interviewer to specifically ask each research participant about language barriers and social isolation, if these concepts do not naturally emerge in the interviews. A highly structured interview schedule would list each question to be asked during the interviews. The interviewer would read the question out to the research participants and record their answers.

RECORDING NARRATIVE DATA

THE MOST RELIABLE WAY to record interview data is through the use of audiotape. Videotape is also a possibility, but many people are uncomfortable with being filmed. The audiotape is an excellent record of an interview because it gives us verbatim statements made by our research participants. The tone, pace, and "atmosphere" of the interview can be recalled by simply replaying the tape.

To prepare data for analysis, however, it's necessary to transcribe every word of the interview. As we will see in Chapter 16, the transcription provides text data, which will be read (and reread) and analyzed. Because audio data are transformed into text data, verbatim statements are used. In addition, any pauses, sighs, and gestures are noted in the text. The following is an example of an excerpt of text data based on our question asked earlier.

> *Research Participant Number 6:* Being a Native in social services, huh . . . well, it's not so good, eh people don't know . . . they don't see the reserve or the kids playing . . . even when they see they don't see. The kids you know, they could have some help, especially the older ones (sighs and pauses for a few seconds). My oldest you know, he's 12 and he goes to school in the city. He comes home and doesn't know what to do. He gets into trouble. Then the social services people come with their briefcases and tell you what to do (voice gets softer). They put in stupid programs and the kids don't want to go you know, they just want to play, get into trouble stuff (laughs) . . .

> *Interviewer:* Hmmm. And how would you describe your own experiences with social services?

Because the interviewing approach to data collection is based on the interaction of the interviewer and the research participant, both parts of the discussion are included in the transcript. But data collection and recording do not stop here. The interviewer must also keep notes on the interview to record impressions, thoughts, perspectives, and any data that will shed light on the transcript during analysis. An example of the interviewer's notes from the above excerpt is:

> *September 12 (Research Participant Number 6):* I was feeling somewhat frustrated because the research participant kept talking about his children. I felt compelled to get him to talk about his own experiences but that seemed sooooo much less important to him.

As we will see in Chapter 16, the verbatim transcript and the interviewer's notes are key pieces of data that will be jointly considered when text data are analyzed.

TRUSTWORTHINESS AND TRUTH VALUE OF NARRATIVE DATA

REGARDLESS OF the type of interview or the data recording strategy that we select, we must have some way to assess the credibility of the data we collect. With quantitative data, we do this by determining the reliability and validity of the data—usually by calculating a numerical value. In contrast, with qualitative data we are less likely to generate numerical values and more likely to document our own personal observations and procedures.

An important question to assess the trustworthiness and truth value of the text data (and our interpretation of it) is whether we understand what our research participants were telling us from their points of view. Two common ways to check the credibility of interview data are triangulation and member checking. These procedures will be discussed in more detail in Chapter 16.

Briefly, triangulation involves comparing data from multiple perspectives. It may be that we interview several people (i.e., data sources) on one topic, or even that we compare quantitative and qualitative data for the same variable. Member checking simply involves getting feedback from our research participants about our interpretation of what they said.

ADVANTAGES AND DISADVANTAGES OF NARRATIVE DATA

THE MAJOR ADVANTAGE of narrative interviewing is the richness of data that are generated. Narrative interviewing allows us to remain open to learning new information or new perspectives about old ideas. Because the interviewer is usually the same person who is the researcher, there is a genuine interest expressed in the interviews.

The major disadvantage associated with narrative interviewing is that it's time consuming. Not only does it take time to conduct the interviews, but considerable time also must be allotted for transcribing the text data. Narrative interviews produce reams and reams of text, which make it difficult to conduct an analysis. Researchers can tire easily and are subject to imposing their own biases and perspectives on what the research participants say.

 # PARTICIPANT OBSERVATION

Participant observation is a way for us to be a part of something and study it at the same time. This method of data collection requires us to establish and maintain ongoing relationships with research participants in the field setting. We not only listen, observe, and record data, but also participate in events and activities as they happen. Our role in participant observation can be described on a continuum (see Figure

13.1), with one end emphasizing the *participant role* and the other end emphasizing the *observer role*.

An "observer-participant" has the dominant role of observation whereas the "participant-observer" is predominantly a participant. Suppose we were to use participant observation as a data collection method for our study. An example of an observer-participant is a researcher who joins a group of people, say Natives living on their reserve, for events related to our research study. We may travel with a community social worker, for example, and participate in community meetings on the reserve to discuss access to social services.

An example of a participant-observer could be when a social worker has the dual responsibility of conducting the meeting and observing the interactions of community members. A participant-observer could also be identified within his or her unique community.

A Native resident of the reserve, for example, could participate in the meeting as a resident and as an observer. In any case, participant observation always requires that one person assumes a dual role. For ethical reasons, the role must be made explicit to all persons participating in the research study. Whether the researcher is a social worker or a Native resident of the reserve, he or she must declare his or her dual role before the community meeting (i.e., data collection) gets under way.

PROCEDURES TO COLLECT PARTICIPANT OBSERVATIONAL DATA

GIVEN THE DUAL ROLE of researchers in participant observation, formulating steps for data collection can be tricky. It's essential for the researcher to keep a balance between "participation" and "observation." Suppose our Native resident who is a participant-observer gets so immersed in the issues of the community meeting that she forgets to look around or ask others questions related to the research study.

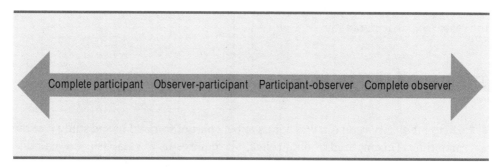

FIGURE 13.1

Continuum of Participant Observation

Someone who completely participates will not be very effective in noting important detail with respect to how other people participated in the meeting. On the other hand, if our Native researcher leans too far into her observation role, others might see her as an outsider and express their views differently than if they believed she had a vested interest within the community.

An important consideration for a participant observation study is how to gain access to the group of people being studied. Imagine who might be welcomed into a community meeting on a Native reserve and who might be rejected. Chances are that the Native people on a reserve would be more accepting of a Native person, a person known to them, or a person whom they trust as compared to a non-Native person, a stranger, or a person whom they know but do not trust. In participant observation we would need to understand the culture of the reserve in order to know who to seek permission from. In participant observation, entry and access is a process more analogous to peeling away the layers of an onion than it is to opening a door. Forming relationships with people is a critical part of data collection.

The more meaningful relationships we can establish, the more meaningful data we will collect. This is not to say, however, that we somehow trade relationship tokens for pieces of information. Rather, research participants should feel a partnership with the researcher that is characterized by mutual interest, reciprocity, trust, and cooperation.

RECORDING PARTICIPANT OBSERVATIONAL DATA

The data generated from participant observation come from observing, interviewing, using existing documents and artifacts, and reflecting on personal experiences. Below are a few examples:

Observation (September 12, 9:30 a.m. Meeting Start Time): When the social worker announced the purpose of the meeting was to discuss access to social services for people living on the reserve, there was a lot of agreement from a crowd of 42 people. Some cheered, some nodded their heads, and others made comments like, "it's about time."

Research participant's verbatim comment (September 12, 10:15 a.m.): "Native people don't use social services because they are not offered on the reserve."

Existing document: A report entitled *"The Social Service Needs of a Reserve Community"* reports that there have been three failed attempts by state social workers to keep a program up and running on the reserve. Worker turnover is identified as the main contributing factor of program failures.

Researcher's personal note (September 12, 10:44 a.m.): I feel amazed at the amount of positive energy in the room. I can sense peoples' frustrations (including my own), yet I am in awe of the hopeful and positive outlook everyone has to want to develop something that works for our community. I am proud to be a part of this initiative to improve services in the community.

Overall, participant observers produce "participant observational" data through the use of detailed and rich notes. Several strategies can be used for documenting notes. We can take notes on an ongoing basis, for example, by being careful to observe the time and context for all written entries. A more efficient method, however, would be to carry a Dictaphone, which gives us the flexibility to state a thought, to record a conversation, and to make summary comments about what we observe.

Collecting data on an ongoing basis is preferable because it increases the likelihood of producing accurate notes and remembering key events. In some instances, however, participation prevents us from recording any data, which leaves us to record our notes after the event has ended.

TRUSTWORTHINESS OF PARTICIPANT OBSERVATIONAL DATA

GIVEN THAT multiple data sources are possible in participant observation, it's possible to check the credibility of the data through triangulation. By reviewing the four data recording examples on the previous page and at the top of this one, we can be reasonably confident that there is agreement about the state of social services on the reserve. The four separate data entries seem to agree that social services on the reserve are inadequate in terms of the community's needs.

The flexibility of participant observation allows us to seek out opportunities to check out our personal assumptions and ideas. After hearing the general response of Native community members at the beginning of the meeting, for example, we may choose to ask related questions to specific individuals. We can also check our perceptions along the way by sharing our own thoughts, asking people to comment on data summaries, or asking people how well they think two data sources fit together.

ADVANTAGES AND DISADVANTAGES

A MAJOR ADVANTAGE of participant observation is that we can collect multiple sources of data and check the credibility of the data as we go. Because of the participant role, any observations made are grounded within the context in which they were generated. A "complete participant" is more likely to pick up subtle messages, for example, than would be a "complete observer."

The disadvantages of participant observation are related to time considerations. As with narrative interviewing, a considerable amount of time must be allotted to data recording and transcription. The researcher also runs the risk of becoming too immersed as a participant or too distant as an observer—both are situations that will compromise the data collected.

SECONDARY CONTENT DATA

Secondary content data are existing text data. In the same way that existing quantitative data can be used to answer newly developed research questions, so can existing qualitative (or content) data. In this case, the text data were recorded at some other time and for some other purpose than the research question that we have posed. Let's return to our research question—Do clients who come from an ethnic minority have difficulty in accessing social services?

With the use of content data, we could answer our question using context data that already exist. It may be, for example, that social workers are mandated to record any discussion they had about barriers to accessing social services for their clients on their client files. Case notes, for example, may read "client does not have reliable transportation" or "client has expressed a strong wish for a worker who has the same ethnic background." These types of comments can be counted and categorized according to meaningful themes. In this instance, we are zeroing in on text data for specific examples of recorded behaviors, much like the microscopic approach of structured observation.

We must be aware that content data can be firsthand or secondhand. In our example, firsthand data would be generated when the social workers document their own behaviors in relation to offering services to their clients. When social workers record their own impressions about how their clients respond to offers of services, secondhand data are produced (LeCroy & Solomon, 2011).

ESTABLISHING PROCEDURES TO COLLECT SECONDARY CONTENT DATA

CONTENT DATA are restricted to what is available. That is, if 68 client files exist, then we have exactly 68 client files to work from. We do not have the luxury of collecting more data. Like secondary quantitative data, we are in a position only to compile the existing data, not to collect new data. It's possible, however, that content data are available from several sources. Client journals may be on file, or perhaps the agency recently conducted an open-ended client satisfaction survey, which has handwritten responses to satisfaction-type questions from clients.

A major consideration of content data is whether a sufficient amount exists to adequately answer our research question. If there are not enough data, we do not want to spend precious time reading and analyzing them. We must also remember that we are reading and reviewing text data for a purpose that they were not originally intended for.

Suppose, for example, you kept a daily journal of your personal experience in your research course. Would you write down the same thoughts if you knew your journal would be private compared with if you were to share your writings with your research instructor? The original intent of writing is essential to remember because it provides the context in which the writing occurred (Rogers & Bouey, 2008).

Because we are examining confidential client case files, we must establish a coding procedure to ensure that our clients' confidentiality and anonymity are maintained. In fact, it's not at all necessary for us, as researchers, to know the names of the client files we are reading. Given our research question, we need only to have access to those portions of clients' files that contain information about client ethnicity and the difficulty clients have in accessing social services.

RECORDING SECONDARY CONTENT DATA

AS WE KNOW, content data exist in text form. If they exist in handwritten form, it's necessary to type them out into transcript form. It's useful to make several copies of the transcripts to facilitate data analysis. More will be said about preparing transcripts in Chapter 16.

ESTABLISHING THE TRUSTWORTHINESS OF CONTENT DATA

CLEARLY, firsthand data are more credible than secondhand data when dealing with existing text data. Because the data are secondary, questions of credibility center more around data analysis than data collection. In our example, it may be possible to triangulate data by comparing the files of different workers or by comparing different client files with the same worker. It also may be possible to member check (Chapter 16) if workers are available and consent to it.

ADVANTAGES AND DISADVANTAGES OF CONTENT DATA

A MAJOR ADVANTAGE of content data is that they already exist. Thus, time and money are saved in the data collection process. The task of the researcher is simply to compile data that are readily available and accessible. The disadvantages of content data are that they are limited in scope. The data were recorded for some other purpose and may omit important detail that would be needed to answer our research question.

HISTORICAL DATA

Historical data are collected in an effort to study the past (Stuart, 2011). Like the participant-observation method to data collection, historical data can come from different data sources. Data collection can be obtrusive, as in the case of interviewing people about past or historical events, or unobtrusive, as in the case when existing documents (primarily content data) are compiled. When our purpose is to study history, however, special cases of content data and interviewing are required.

Suppose we recast our research question to ask, "Did clients who come from an ethnic minority have difficulty accessing social services from 1947 to 1965?" Phrased this way, our question directs us to understand *what has been* rather than *what is*. In order for us to answer our new research question, we would need to dig up remains from the past that could help us to describe the relationship, if any, between ethnicity and difficulty in accessing social services for our specified time period. We would search for documents such as related reports, memos, letters, transcriptions, client records, and documentaries, all dating back to the time period. Many libraries store this information in their archives.

We could also interview people (e.g., social workers and clients) who were part of social services between 1947 and 1965. People from the past might include clients, workers, supervisors, volunteers, funders, or ministers. The purpose of our interviews would be to have people remember the past—that is, to describe factual events from their memories. We are less interested in people's opinions about the past than we are about what "really" happened.

When collecting historical data, it's important to sort out firsthand data from secondhand data. Firsthand data, of course, are more highly valued because the data are less likely to be distorted or altered. Diaries, autobiographies, letters, home videos, photographs, and organizational minutes are all examples of firsthand data. Secondhand data, on the other hand, include documents like biographies, books, and articles.

ESTABLISHING PROCEDURES TO COLLECT HISTORICAL DATA

IT'S PROBABLY MORE ACCURATE to say that we retrieve historical data than it is to say that we collect it. The data already exist, in long-forgotten written documents, dusty videotapes, or peoples' memories. Our task is to resurface a sufficient amount of data so that we can describe, and sometimes explain, what happened (Stuart, 2011).

One of the first considerations for conducting a historical research study is to be sure that the variable being investigated is one that existed in the past. Suppose, for example, we had a specific interest in the relationship among three variables: client ethnicity, difficulty in accessing social services, and computer technology.

More specifically, let us say that we were interested in knowing about the relationship among these three variables, if any, for our specified time period, 1947 to 1965. It would be impossible to determine the relationship among these three variables from a historical perspective because computers were not (or were rarely) used in the social services from 1947 to 1965. Thus, there would be no past to describe or explain—at least not where computers are concerned.

Once we have established that our research question is relevant, we can delineate a list of possible data sources and the types of data that each can produce. The total list of data sources and types must be assessed to determine whether, in fact, sufficient data exist to answer our research question. It's possible, however, that data do exist but they are not accessible. Client records, for example, may be secured. Documents may be out of circulation, thus requiring a researcher to travel to where the data are stored.

RECORDING HISTORICAL DATA

DESPITE THE FACT that historical data, in many cases, already exist, it's usually necessary to reproduce the data. When interviews are used, interview notes are recorded and the interviews are transcribed as we have discussed in other interpretive data collection methods. When past documents are used, they ought to be duplicated to create working copies. Original documents should be protected and preserved so that they can be made available to other interested researchers.

ESTABLISHING THE TRUSTWORTHINESS OF HISTORICAL DATA

ASSESSING THE TRUSTWORTHINESS and truth value of historical data, in many ways, is the process of data analysis. Do different people recall similar facts? Do independent events from the past tell the same story? Much effort goes into triangulating pieces of data. The more corroboration we have among our data, the stronger our resulting conclusions will be.

When reconstructing the past, our conclusions can only be as good as the data we base them on. Are the data authentic? How much of our data are firsthand compared to secondhand? Do we have sufficient data to describe the entire time period of interest? Perhaps we might have to cut back a few years; or if other data emerge, perhaps we can expand our time period.

ADVANTAGES AND DISADVANTAGES OF HISTORICAL DATA

HISTORICAL DATA are unique and used for a specific purpose—to describe and explain the past. It's the only way for us to research history. When secondary data are readily available and accessible, the cost is minimized. When interviews are used, they provide us with an opportunity to probe further into the past and our area of interest.

The disadvantages of historical data are that they are not always easily available or accessible. There is also a risk of researcher bias such as when a letter or document is analyzed out of context. The past cannot be reconstructed, for example, if we impose present-day views, standards, and ideas.

 # SUMMARY

In this chapter we discussed different methods to collect qualitative data. With the previous chapter in mind we now know that that one research question can be answered using any data collection method—quantitative or qualitative. Different data collection methods produce different types of data. Data collection methods that are more commonly associated with qualitative or text data are narrative interviewing, participant observation, secondary content data, and historical data.

Study Questions for Chapter 13

— First, answer each question only AFTER you have read the chapter.

— Second, indicate how comfortable you were in answering each question on a 5-point scale:

1	2	3	4	5
Very uncomfortable	Somewhat uncomfortable	Neutral	Somewhat comfortable	Very comfortable

If you rated any question between 1–3, please reread the section of the chapter where the information for the question can be found. If you're still uncomfortable answering the question, talk with your instructor and/or your classmates for more clarification.

Questions	Degree of comfort? (Circle one number)
1. In your own words describe qualitative data in detail. Provide social work examples throughout your discussion to illustrate your main points.	1 2 3 4 5
2. What is narrative interviewing? Discuss in detail how you can use narrative interviewing as a qualitative data gathering method in social work research situations. Provide social work examples throughout your discussion to illustrate your main points.	1 2 3 4 5
3. Discuss how you would record narrative data for a hypothetical social work research study. Provide social work examples throughout your discussion to illustrate your main points.	1 2 3 4 5
4. Discuss how you would assess the trustworthiness and truth value of narrative data. Provide social work examples throughout your discussion to illustrate your main points.	1 2 3 4 5
5. Discuss the advantages and disadvantages of using narrative interviewing as a qualitative data gathering method. Provide social work examples throughout your discussion to illustrate your main points.	1 2 3 4 5
6. What is participant observation? Discuss in detail how you can use participant observation as a qualitative data gathering method in social work research situations. Provide social work examples throughout your discussion to illustrate your main points.	1 2 3 4 5

7. Discuss how you would record participant observational data for a hypothetical social work research study.	1 2 3 4 5
8. Discuss how you would assess the trustworthiness and truth value of participant observational data. Provide social work examples throughout your discussion to illustrate your main points.	1 2 3 4 5
9. Discuss the advantages and disadvantages of using participant observational data as a qualitative data gathering method. Provide social work examples throughout your discussion to illustrate your main points.	1 2 3 4 5
10. What are secondary content data? Discuss in detail how you can use secondary content data as a qualitative data gathering method in social work research situations. Provide social work examples throughout your discussion to illustrate your main points.	1 2 3 4 5
11. Discuss how you would record secondary content data for a hypothetical social work research study. Provide social work examples throughout your discussion to illustrate your main points.	1 2 3 4 5
12. Discuss how you would assess the trustworthiness and truth value of secondary content data. Provide social work examples throughout your discussion to illustrate your main points.	1 2 3 4 5
13. Discuss the advantages and disadvantages of using secondary content data as a qualitative data gathering method. Provide social work examples throughout your discussion to illustrate your main points.	1 2 3 4 5
14. Discuss the similarities and differences between secondary data as discussed in Chapter 12 and secondary content data as described in this chapter. Provide social work examples throughout your discussion to illustrate your main points.	1 2 3 4 5
15. What are historical data? Discuss in detail how you can use historical data as a qualitative data gathering method in social work research situations. Provide social work examples throughout your discussion to illustrate your main points.	1 2 3 4 5
16. Discuss how you would record historical data for a hypothetical social work research study. Provide social work examples throughout your discussion to illustrate your main points.	1 2 3 4 5

17. Discuss how you would assess the trustworthiness and truth value of historical data. Provide social work examples throughout your discussion to illustrate your main points.	1 2 3 4 5
18. Discuss the advantages and disadvantages of using historical data as a qualitative data gathering method. Provide social work examples throughout your discussion to illustrate your main points.	1 2 3 4 5

Assessing Your Self-Efficacy for Chapter 13

AFTER you have read the chapter AND have completed all the study questions, please indicate how knowledgeable you feel you are for each concept listed below.

1	2	3	4	5
Very uncomfortable	Somewhat uncomfortable	Neutral	Somewhat comfortable	Very comfortable

Major Concepts in Chapter	Knowledge Level? (Circle one number)
1. Collecting qualitative data	1 2 3 4 5
2. Narrative interviewing	1 2 3 4 5
3. Participant observation	1 2 3 4 5
4. Secondary content data	1 2 3 4 5
5. Historical data	1 2 3 4 5
Add up your scores (Minimum = 5, Maximum = 25)	Total score =

A 22 — 25 = Social Work Manager in the making.
B 20 — 23 = Social Work Supervisor.
C 17 — 19 = Social Work Practitioner.
D   5 — 16 = Case Aide. Reread the chapter and redo the study questions.

14

Selecting a Data Collection Method

It's difficult to imagine the power that you're going to have
when so many different sorts of data are available.
~ Tim Berners Lee

In the last two chapters we discussed eight methods of data collection, which were divided by the type of data that each is most likely to produce—quantitative data (Chapter 12) or qualitative data (Chapter 13). This chapter examines the data collection process from the vantage point of choosing the most appropriate data collection method and data source for a given research question.

 ## DATA COLLECTION AND THE RESEARCH PROCESS

Data collection is a critical step in the research process because it's the link between theory and practice. Our research study always begins with an idea that is molded by a conceptual framework, which mostly uses preexisting knowledge about our study's problem area. Once our research problem and question have been refined to a researchable level, data are sought from a selected source(s) and gathered using a data collection method. The data collected are then used to support or supplant our original study's conceptions about our research problem under investigation (Unrau, 2011).

The role of data collection in connecting theory and practice is understood when looking at the entire research process. As we have seen in previous chapters of this book, choosing a data collection method and data source follows the steps of selecting a research topic area, focusing the topic into a research question, and designing the research study.

Data collection comes before the steps of analyzing the data and writing the research report. Although data collection is presented in this text as a distinct phase of the research process, in reality it cannot be tackled separately or in isolation. All steps of the research process must be considered if we hope to come up with the best strategy to gather the most relevant, reliable, and valid data to answer a research question or to test a hypothesis. This section discusses the role of data collection in relation to the other steps of the generic research process as outlined in Chapters 5 and 6.

SELECTING A RESEARCH TOPIC AND RESEARCH QUESTION

OUR SPECIFIC RESEARCH QUESTION identifies the general problem area and the population to be studied. It tells us what we want to collect data about and alerts us to potential data sources. It does not necessarily specify the exact manner in which our data will be gathered, however. Let's return to our research question:

RESEARCH QUESTION

Do people who come from ethnic minority backgrounds have difficulty in accessing social services?

Our research question identifies a problem area (difficulty in accessing social services for people who are ethnic minorities) and a population (social service clients). It does not state how the question will be answered. We have seen in the last two chapters that our research question, in fact, could be answered using various data collection methods. One factor that affects how our question is answered depends upon how we conceptualize and measure the variables within it. As we know, "accessing social services" could be measured in a variety of ways.

Another factor that affects how a research question is answered (or a hypothesis is tested) is the source of data—that is, who or what is providing them. If we want to get firsthand data about the accessibility of social services, for example, we could target the clients as a potential data source. If such firsthand data sources were not a viable option, secondhand data sources could be sought.

Social workers, for example, can be asked for their perceptions of how accessible social services are to clients who come from ethnic minorities. In other instances, secondhand data can be gleaned from existing reports (secondary data or content data) written about clients (or client records) that monitor client progress and social worker–client interactions.

By listing all possible data collection methods and data sources that could provide sound data to answer a research question, we develop a fuller understanding of our initial research problem. It also encourages us to think about our research problem from different perspectives, via the data sources.

Because social work problems are complex, data collection is strengthened when two or more data sources are used. For example, if social workers and clients were to each report their perceptions of service accessibility in a similar way, then we could be more confident that the data (from both these sources) accurately reflect the problem being investigated.

DESIGNING THE RESEARCH STUDY AND COLLECTING THE DATA

AS WE KNOW, the research design flows from the research question, which flows from the problem area. A research design organizes our research question into a framework that sets the parameters and conditions of the study. As mentioned, the research question directs *what* data are collected and *who* data could be collected from. In a positivistic study, the research design refines the *what* question by operationalizing variables and the *who* question by developing a sampling strategy.

In an interpretive study, however, the research design identifies the starting point for data collection and how such procedures will be monitored and recorded along the way. In both research approaches, the research design also dictates (more or less) *when*, *where,* and *how* data will be collected.

The research design outlines how many data collection points our study will have and specifies the data sources. Each discrete data gathering activity constitutes a data collection point and defines *when* data are to be collected. Thus, using an exploratory one-group, posttest-only design, we will collect data only once from a single group of research participants. On the other hand, if a classical experimental design is used, data will be collected at two separate times with two different groups of research participants—for a total of four discrete data collection points.

Where the data are collected is also important to consider. If our research question is too narrow and begs for a broader issue that encompasses individuals living in various geographic locations, then mailed survey questionnaires would be more feasible than face-to-face interviews. If our research question focuses on a specific population where all research participants live in the same geographic location, it may be possible to use direct observations or individual or group interviews.

Because most social work studies are applied, the setting of our study usually involves clients in their natural environments where there is little control over extraneous variables. If we want to measure the clients' perceptions about their difficulty in accessing social services, for example, do we observe clients in agency waiting rooms, observe how they interact with their social workers, or have them complete a survey questionnaire of some kind? In short, we must always consider which method of data collection will lead to the most valid and reliable data to answer a research question or to test a hypothesis.

The combination of potential data collection methods and potential data sources is another important consideration. A research study can have one data collection source and still use multiple data collection methods. Our program's clients (data source 1) in our study, for example, can fill out a standardized questionnaire that measures their perceptions of how accessible social services are (data collection method 1) in addition to participating in face-to-face interviews (data collection method 2).

In the same vein, another study can have multiple data sources and one data collection method. In this case, we can collect data about difficulty in accessing social services through observation recordings by social workers (data source 1), administrators (data source 2), or other citizens (data source 3).

The combination of data collection methods should not be too taxing on any research participant or any system, such as the social service program itself. That is, data collection should not interfere greatly with the day-to-day activities of the persons providing (or responsible for collecting) the data. In some studies, there is no research design per se. Instead, we can use existing data to answer our research question.

Such is the case when a secondary or content data are used. When the data already exist, we put a lot of effort into ensuring that the research question is a good fit with the data at hand. Regardless of what data collection method is used, once the data are collected, they are subject to analysis.

ANALYZING AND INTERPRETING THE DATA

COLLECTING DATA is a resource-intensive endeavor that can be expensive and time consuming—for both interpretive and positivistic research studies. The truth of this statement is realized in the data analysis step of our research study. Without a great deal of forethought about what data to collect, data can be thrown out because they cannot be organized or analyzed in any meaningful way.

In short, data analyses should always be considered when choosing a data collection method and data source because the analysis phase must summarize, synthesize, and ultimately organize the data in an effort to have as clear-cut an answer as possible to our research question. When too much (or too little) data are collected, we can easily become bogged down (or stalled) by difficult decisions that could have been avoided with a little forethought.

After thinking through our research problem and research question and selecting a viable data collection and data source, it's worthwhile to list out the details of the type of data that will be produced. Specifically, we must think about how the data will be used in our data analysis. This exercise provides a clearer idea of the type of results we can expect.

The main variable in our research question is difficulty in accessing social services. Suppose the social worker decides to collect data about this variable by giving clients (data source) a brief standardized questionnaire (data collection method) to measure their perceptions. Many standardized questionnaires contain several subscales that, when combined, give a quantitative measure of a larger concept.

The *R-GSSSS* introduced in Chapter 8, for example, is made up of three subscales: (1) relevance, (2) impact, and (3) gratification. Thus, the *R-GSSSS* has four scores associated with it: a relevance score, an impact score, a gratification score, and a total score (which is a measure of satisfaction). With three separate subscales, we can choose to use any one subscale (one variable), all three subscales (three variables), or a total score (one variable).

Alternatively, if data about difficulty in accessing social services were to be collected using two different data sources such as social worker (data source 1) and client (data source 2) observations, we must think about how the two data sources fit together. That is, will data from the two sources be treated as two separate variables? If so, will one variable be weighted differently in our analysis than the other? Thinking about how the data will be summarized helps us to expose any frivolous data—that is, data that are not suitable to answering our research question.

Besides collecting data about our study's variables, we must also develop a strategy to collect demographic data about the people who participate in our study. Typical demographic variables include age, gender, education level, and family income. These data are not necessarily used in the analysis of the research question. Rather, they provide a descriptive context for our study. Some data collection methods, such as standardized questionnaires, include these types of data. Often, however, we are responsible for obtaining them as part of the data collection process.

PRESENTATION AND DISSEMINATION OF FINDINGS

IT'S USEFUL to think about our final research report when choosing a data collection method and data source as it forces us to visualize how our study's findings will ultimately be presented. It identifies both who the audience of the study will be and who the people interested in our findings are. Knowing who will read our research report and how it will be disseminated helps us to take more of an objective stance toward our study. In short, we can take a third-person look at what our study will finally look like.

Such objectivity helps us to think about our data collection method and data source with a critical eye. Will consumers of our research study agree that the clients in fact were the best data collection source? Were the data collection method and analysis sound? These are some of the practical questions that bring scrutiny to the data collection process.

SELECTING A DATA COLLECTION METHOD

Thinking through the steps in the research process from the vantage point of collecting data permits us to refine the conceptualization of our study and the place of data collection within it. It also sets the context within which our data will be gathered. Clearly, there are many viable data collection methods and data sources that can be used to answer any research question.

Nevertheless, there are many practical criteria that ultimately refine the final data collection method (and sources) to fit the conditions of any given research study. These criteria are:

— Size

— Scope

— Program Participation

— Worker Cooperation

— Intrusion into the Lives of Research Participants

— Resources

— Time

— Previous Research Findings

They all interact with one another, but for the sake of clarity each one is presented separately.

Size

THE SIZE OF OUR RESEARCH STUDY reflects just how many people, places, or systems are represented in it. As with any planning activity, the more people involved, the more complicated the process and the more difficult it is to arrive at a mutual agreement. Decisions about which data collection method and which data source to use can be stalled when several people, levels, or systems are involved.

This is because individuals have different interests and opinions. Imagine if our research question about whether ethnicity is related to difficulty in accessing social services were examined on a larger scale such that all social service programs in the country were included. Our study's complexity is dramatically increased because of such factors as the increased number of programs, clients, funders, government representatives, and social workers involved. The biases within each of these stakeholder groups make it much more difficult to agree upon the best data collection method and data source for our study.

Our study's sample size is also a consideration. This is particularly true for positivistic studies, which aim to have a sample that is representative of the population of interest. With respect to sample size, this means that we should strive for a reasonable representation of the sampling frame. When small-scale studies are conducted, such as a program evaluation in one social work program, the total number of people in the sampling frame may be in the hundreds or fewer. Thus, randomly selecting clients poses no real problem.

On the other hand, when large-scale studies are conducted, such as when the federal government chooses to examine a social service program that involves hundreds of thousands of people, sampling can become more problematic. If our sample is in the hundreds, it's unlikely that we would be able to successfully observe or interview all participants to collect data for our study. Rather, a more efficient manner of data collection—say a survey—may be more appropriate.

Scope

THE SCOPE OF OUR RESEARCH STUDY is another matter to consider. Scope refers to how much of our *problem area* will be covered. If in our research question, for example, we are interested in gathering data on other client-related variables such as language ability, degree of social isolation, and level of assertiveness, then three different aspects of our problem area will be covered.

In short, we need to consider whether one method of data collection and one data source can be used to collect all the data. It could be that client records, for example, are used to collect data about clients' language abilities, interviews with clients are conducted to collect data about social isolation, and observation methods are used to gather data about clients' assertiveness levels.

PROGRAM PARTICIPATION

MANY SOCIAL WORK RESEARCH EFFORTS are conducted in actual real-life program settings. Thus, it's essential that we gain the support of program personnel to conduct our study. Program factors that can impact the choice of our data collection methods and data sources include variables such as the program's clarity in its mandate to serve clients, its philosophical stance toward clients, and its flexibility in client record keeping. First, if a program is not able to clearly articulate a client service delivery plan, it will be difficult to distinguish between clinical activity and research activity, and to determine when the two overlap.

Second, some programs tend to base themselves on strong beliefs about a client population, which affect who can have access to clients and in what manner. A child sexual abuse investigation program, for example, may be designed specifically to avoid the problem of using multiple interviewers and multiple interviews of children in the investigation of an allegation of sexual abuse.

As a result, the program would be hesitant for us to conduct interviews with the children to gather data for research purposes. Finally, to save time and energy there is often considerable overlap between program client records and research data collection. The degree of willingness of a program to adapt to new record-keeping techniques will affect how we might go about collecting certain types of data.

WORKER COOPERATION

ON A GENERAL LEVEL, programs have fewer resources than they need and more clients than they can handle. Such conditions naturally lead their administrators and social workers to place intervention activity as a top priority (versus research activity). When our research study has social workers collecting data as a part of their day-to-day activities, it's highly likely that they will view data collection as additional paperwork and not as a means to expedite decision-making in their work.

Getting cooperation of social workers within a program is a priority in any research study that relies directly or indirectly on their meaningful participation. Program workers will be affected by our study whether they are involved in the data collection process or not. They may be asked to schedule additional interviews with families or adjust their intervention plans to ensure that data collection occurs at the optimal time.

Given the fiscal constraints faced by programs, the workers themselves often participate as data collectors. They may end up using new client recording forms or administering questionnaires. Whatever the level of their participation, it's important for us to strive to achieve a maximum level of their cooperation.

There are three factors to consider when trying to achieve maximum cooperation from workers. First, we should make every effort to work effectively and efficiently with the program's staff. Cooperation is more likely to be achieved when workers participate in the development of our study plan from the beginning. Thus, it's worthwhile to take time to explain the purpose of our study and its intended outcomes at an early stage in the study. Furthermore, administrators and front-line workers alike can provide valuable information about which data collection method(s) may work best.

Second, we must be sensitive to the workloads of the program's staff. Data collection methods and sources should be designed to enhance the work of professionals. Client recording forms, for example, can be designed to provide focus for supervision meetings as well as summarize facts and worker impressions about a case.

Third, a mechanism ought to be set up by which workers receive feedback based on the data they have collected. When a mechanism for feedback is put in place, for example, workers are more likely to show interest in the data collection activity. When data are reported back to the program's staff before the completion of our study, however, we must ensure that the data will not bias later measurements (if any).

INTRUSION INTO THE LIVES OF RESEARCH PARTICIPANTS

WHEN CLIENTS ARE USED as a data source, client self-determination takes precedence over research activity. As we know, clients have every right to refuse participation in a research study and cannot be denied services because they are unwilling to participate. It's unethical, for example, when a member of a group-based treatment intervention has not consented to participate in the study but participant observation is used as the data collection method.

This is unethical because the group member ends up being observed as part of the group dynamic in the data collection process after refusing to give his or her consent. The data collection method(s) we finally select must be flexible enough to allow our study to continue even with the possibility that some clients will not participate.

Ethnic and cultural consideration must also be given to the type of data collection method used. One-on-one interviewing with Cambodian refugees, for example, may be extremely terrifying for them, given the interrogation they may have experienced in their own country.

Moreover, if we, as data collectors, have different ethnic backgrounds than our research participants, it's important to ensure that interpretation of the data (e.g., their behaviors, events, or expressions) is accurate from the clients' perspectives and not our own.

We must also recognize the cultural biases of standardized measuring instruments because most are based on testing with Caucasian groups. The problems here are twofold. First, we cannot be sure whether the concept that the instrument is measuring is expressed the same way in different cultures. For instance, a standardized self-report instrument that measures family functioning may include an item such as "We have flexible rules in our household that promote individual differences," which would likely be viewed positively by North American cultures but negatively by many Asian cultures.

Second, because most of the standardized measuring instruments are written in English, research participants must have a good grasp of English to ensure that the data collected from them are valid and reliable. Another consideration comes into play when particular populations have been the subject of a considerable amount of research study already. Many aboriginal people living on reserves, for example, have been subjected to government surveys, task force inquiries, independent research projects, and perhaps even to the curiosities of social work students learning in a practicum setting.

When a population has been extensively researched, it's even more important that we consider how the data collection method will affect those people participating in the study. Has the data collection method been used previously? If so, what was the nature of the data collected? Could the data be collected using less intrusive methods?

RESOURCES

THERE ARE VARIOUS COSTS associated with collecting data in any given research study. Materials and supplies, equipment rental, transportation costs, and training for data collectors are just a few things to consider when choosing a data collection method. In addition, once the data are collected, additional expenses can arise when the data are entered into a computer or transcribed.

An efficient data collection method is one that collects credible data to answer a research question or test a hypothesis while requiring the least amount of time and money. In our example, to ask clients about their perceptions about the difficulty in accessing social services via an open-ended interview may offer rich data, but we take the risk that clients will not fully answer our questions in the time allotted for the interview.

On the other hand, having them complete a self-report questionnaire about access to social services is a quicker and less costly way to collect data, but it gives little sense about how well the clients understood the questions being asked of them or whether the data obtained reflect their true perceptions.

TIME

TIME IS A CONSIDERATION when our study has a fixed completion date. Time constraints may be self- or externally imposed. Self-imposed time constraints are personal matters we need to consider. Is our research project a part of a thesis or dissertation? What are our personal time commitments? Externally imposed time restrictions are set by someone other than the person who is doing the study. For instance, our research study may be limited by the fiscal year of a social service program and/or funding source. Other external pressures may be political, such as an administrator who wants research results for a funding proposal or to present at a conference.

PREVIOUS RESEARCH FINDINGS

HAVING REVIEWED the professional literature on our problem, we need to be well aware of other data collection methods that have been used in similar studies. We can evaluate earlier studies for the strengths and weaknesses of their data collection methods and thereby make a more informed decision as to the best data collection strategy to use in our specific situation. Further, we need to look for diversity when evaluating other data collection approaches; that is, we can triangulate results from separate studies that used different data collection methods and data sources.

 ## TRYING OUT THE DATA COLLECTION METHOD

Data collection is a particularly vulnerable time for a research study because it's the point where talk turns into action. So far, all the considerations that have been weighed in the selection of a data collection method have been in theory. All people involved in our research endeavor have conveyed their suggestions and doubts on the entire process.

Once general agreement has been reached about which data collection method and data source to use, it's time to test the waters. Trying out a data collection method can occur informally by simply testing it out with available and willing research participants or, at the very least, with anyone who has not been involved with the planning of the study. The purpose of this trial run is to ensure that those who are going to provide data understand the questions and procedures in the way that they were intended.

Data collection methods might also be tested more formally, such as when a pilot study is conducted. A pilot study involves carrying out all aspects of the data collection plan on a mini-scale. That is, a small portion of our study's actual sample is selected and run through all steps of the data collection process.

In a pilot study, we are interested in the process of the data collection as well as the content. In short, we want to know whether our chosen data collection method produces the expected data. Are there any unanticipated barriers to gathering the desired data? How do research participants respond to our data collection procedures?

IMPLEMENTATION AND EVALUATION

The data collection step of a research study can go smoothly if we act proactively. That is, we should guide and monitor the entire data collection process according to the procedures and steps that were set out in the planning stage of our study and were tested in the pilot study.

IMPLEMENTATION

THE MAIN GUIDING PRINCIPLE to implementing the selected data collection method is that a systematic approach to data collection must be used. This means that the steps to gathering data should be methodically detailed so that there is no question about the tasks of the person(s) collecting the data—the data collector(s).

This is true whether using a positivistic or interpretive research approach. As we know, the difference between these two research approaches is that the structure of the data collection process within an interpretive research study is documented as the study progresses. By contrast, in a positivistic research study the data collection process is decided at the study's outset and provides much less flexibility after the study is under way.

It must be very clear from the beginning who is responsible for collecting the data. When we take on the task, there is reasonable assurance that the data collection will remain objective and be guided by our research interests. Data collection left to only one person may be a formidable task. We must determine the amount of resources available to decide what data collection method is most realistic. Regardless of the study size, we must attempt to establish clear roles and boundaries with those involved in the data collection process.

The clearer our research study is articulated, the less difficulty there will be in moving through all the steps of the study. In particular, it is critical to identify who will and will not be involved in the data collection process. To further avoid mix-ups and complications, specific tasks must be spelled out for all persons involved in our study. Where will the data be stored? Who will collect them? How will the data collection process be monitored?

In many social work research studies, frontline social workers are involved in data collection activities as part of their day-to-day activities. They typically gather intake and referral data, write assessment notes, and even use standardized questionnaires as part of their assessments. Data collection in programs can easily be designed to serve the dual purposes of research *and* intervention inquiry.

Thus, it's important to establish data collection protocols to avoid problems of biased data. As mentioned, everyone in a research study must agree *when* data will be collected, *where*, and in *what* manner. Agreement is more likely to occur when we have fully informed and involved everyone participating in our study.

EVALUATION

THE PROCESS of selecting a chosen data collection method is not complete without evaluating it. Evaluation occurs at two levels. First, the strengths and weaknesses of a data collection method and data source are evaluated, given the research context in which our study takes place. If, for example, data are gathered by a referring social worker about clients presenting problems, it must be acknowledged that the obtained data offer a limited (or restricted) point of view about the clients' problems. The strength of this approach may be that it was the only means for collecting the data.

A second level of evaluation is monitoring the implementation of the data collection process itself. When data are gathered using several methods (or several sources), it's beneficial to develop a checklist of what data have been collected for each research participant. Developing a strategy for monitoring the data collection process is especially important when the data must be collected in a timely fashion.

If pretest data are needed before a client enters a treatment program, for example, the data collection must be complete before admission occurs. Once a client has entered the program, opportunity to collect pretest data is lost.

Another strategy for monitoring the implementation of an evaluation is to keep a journal of the data collection process. The journal records any questions or queries that arise in the data collection step. We may find, for example, that several research participants completing a questionnaire have difficulty understanding one particular question.

In addition, sometimes research participants have poor reading skills and require assistance with completion of some self-report standardized questionnaires. Documenting these idiosyncratic incidents accumulates important information by which to comment on our data's credibility.

SUMMARY

There are many possible data collection methods and data sources that can be used in any given research situation. We must weigh the pros and cons of both within the context of a particular research study to arrive at the best data collection method and data source. This process involves both conceptual and practical considerations.

TABLE 14.1

Advantages and Disadvantages of Selected Data Collection Methods

Method	Description	Advantages	Disadvantages
Questionnaire (General)	A paper and pencil method for obtaining responses to statements or questions by using a form on which participants provide opinions or factual information	Is a relatively inexpensive, quick way to collect large amounts of data from large samples in short amounts of time Is convenient for respondents to complete Can result in more honest responses via anonymity Allows use of readily available questionnaires is well suited for answering questions related to "What?" "Where?" and "How many?	Limited ability to know whether you are actually measuring what you intend to measure Limited ability to discover measurement errors Limited length and breadth of questions No opportunity to probe or obtain clarification Reliance on self-report Reliance on participants' ability to recall behaviors and events Limited capability to measure different kinds of outcomes Not well suited to answering questions related to "How?" and "Why?" Difficult to administer with low-literacy groups

One-to-One Interview (General)	An interaction between two people in which information is gathered relative to respondent's knowledge, thoughts, and feelings about different topics	Allows greater depth than a questionnaire Provides data that are deeper, richer, and have more context Allows interviewer to establish rapport with respondent Allows interviewer to clarify questions Is a good method for working with low-literacy respondents Has higher response and completion rates Allows for observation of nonverbal gestures	Need for extensive time and personnel Need for highly trained, skilled interviewers Limited number of people can be included Open to interviewer bias Prone to respondents giving answers they believe are expected or socially desirable No anonymity Potentially invasive for personal questions
One-to-One Interview (Unstructured)	An interaction between two people in which the totally free response pattern allows respondents to express ideas in their own way and time	Can elicit personal information Can gather relevant unanticipated data Permits interviewer to probe for more information	Need for great interviewer skill More prone to bias in response interpretation Time-consuming data analysis
One-to-One Interview (Semi-structured)	An interaction between two people with limited free response, building around a set of basic questions from which the interviewer may branch off	Combines efficiency of structured interview with ability to probe and investigate interesting responses	No true exploratory research permitted Predetermined questions limit ability to probe further
One-to-One Interview (Structured)	An interaction between two people with predetermined questions, often with structured responses	Is easy to administer Does not require as much training of interviewer	Less ability to probe for additional information No clarification of ambiguous responses

Focus Group	Interviews with groups of people (anywhere from 4 to 12) selected because they share certain characteristics relevant to the questions of study, in which the interviewer encourages discussion and expression of differing opinions and viewpoints	Studies participants in natural, real-life atmosphere Allows for exploration of unanticipated issues as they are discussed Increases sample size in interpretive studies Saves time and money Stimulates new ideas among participants Gains additional information from observation of group process Promotes greater spontaneity and candor	Less interviewer control than in a one-to-one interview Sometimes difficult to analyze data Context of comments must be considered Need for highly trained observer-moderators No isolation of individual's train of thought throughout
Phone Interview	One-to-one conversation over the phone	May lower costs May promote greater candor via anonymity	Phones not always available Unlisted numbers present sampling bias No opportunity to observe nonverbal gestures
Participant Observation (General)	Evaluator measures behaviors, interactions, and processes by directly watching participants	Gathers spontaneous data Codes behaviors in a natural setting such as a lunch room or a hallway Provides a check against distorted perceptions of participants Works well with a homogeneous group Is a good technique to combine with other methods Is well suited for study of body language (kinesics) and study of people's use of personal space and its relationship to culture (proxemics)	Need for highly trained observer Recording of behaviors and events potentially from memory Difficult quantification and summary of data Difficult to maintain objectives. Very time-consuming and expensive

Participant Observation (Participant as Observer)	Evaluator's role as observer is known to the group being studied, but that role is secondary to his or her role as a participant	Retains benefits of participant without ethical issues at stake for evaluator	Observer difficulty in maintaining two distinct roles Potential for resentment among other participants of observer's role Observer presence can change nature of the interactions being observed
Participant Observation (Observer as Participant)	Evaluator's role as observer is known to the group being studied, and his or her primary role is to assess the program	Allows evaluator to be more focused on observation role while still maintaining connection to other participants	Evaluator clearly an outsider Observer presence can change nature of the interactions being observed
Participant Observation (Complete Observer)	Evaluator is a silent observer with no formal role as participant; evaluator may also be hidden from the group, or his or her presence may be unnoticed and unobtrusive in a completely public setting	Permits more objective observations Does not distract evaluator with a participant role Does not interfere in any way with the group's process when evaluator is hidden	Observer presence, if known, can inhibit or change interactions of participants Use of hidden observer raises ethical questions
Document Analysis	Unobtrusive measure using analysis of diaries, logs, letters, and formal policy statements to learn about values and beliefs of participants in a setting or group, or about processes involved in a program and their impact. Examples: class reviews, letters to teachers, letters from parents, or letters from former students	Reduces problems of memory relating to when, where, with whom (diaries) Provides access to thoughts and feelings that may not otherwise be accessible Can be less threatening to participants Allows collection and analysis of data on evaluator's own schedule Is relatively inexpensive	Quality of data variation among subjects Use of diaries potentially causing change in subject behaviors Not well suited for low-literacy groups Potentially very selective data No opportunities for clarification of data

Archival Data	Analysis of archival data from a society, community, or organization. Examples: birth rates, census data, contraceptive purchase data, or logs of number of visits to hospitals for STDs	Is more accurate than self-report	Not all data available or fully reported

Difficult to match geographical or individual data |
| **Historical Data** | Analysis of historical data as a method of discovering from records and personal accounts what happened in the past; especially useful for establishing a baseline or background of a program or participants before measuring outcomes | Provides baseline data that can help with interpretation of outcome findings

Helps answer questions about why a program is or is not successful in meeting its goals

Provides a picture of the broader context within which a program is operating | Potentially difficult to obtain data

Data that may be incomplete, missing, or inaccurate

Reliance on selective memory of events and behaviors by participants

Accuracy difficult to verify |
| **Secondary Analysis** | Analysis of data that already exist (not the collection of new or original data) | Is considerably cheaper and faster than doing original studies

Offers benefit of research from some of the top scholars in the field, which for the most part ensures quality data

Has advantages of putting less strain on limited funds and time, and providing samples drawn from larger populations

Provides flexibility: you might only extract a few figures from a table, or you might use the data in a subsidiary role in your research or even in a central role

Is readily available via a network of data archives in which survey data files are collected and distributed | With national population survey data, difficulty in finding relevant data for well-defined minority subgroups

Potential for irresponsible analyses: variables and data can be manipulated and transformed in ways that lessen validity of the original research

Large data files and difficult statistical packages, particularly with large samples |

Online Surveys	Questionnaires administered online through available online resources. Example: SurveyMonkey.com	Saves money by delivering questionnaires online rather than paying for postage or for interviewers	Population and sample limited to those with access to a computer and online network
		Facilitates changes to questionnaires and the copying and sorting of data	Difficulty in guaranteeing anonymity and confidentiality of data
		Can be delivered to recipients in seconds rather than in days as with traditional mail	Initial difficulties in constructing formats for computer questionnaires
		Allows sending invitations and receiving responses in a very short time, thus allowing faster participation level estimates as well	Need to provide respondents with additional instruction and orientation for the computer system
		Has higher response rates on private networks in contrast with paper surveys or interviews	Potential for computer glitches impeding collection
		Obtains more honest answers in contrast with paper surveys or interviews	Response rates not necessarily higher. (Research has shown that e-mail response rates are higher, but those rates applied only during the first few days; thereafter, the rates were not significantly higher.)
		Allows participants to answer in minutes or hours, and permits global coverage	

Study Questions for Chapter 14

— First, answer each question only AFTER you have read the chapter.

— Second, indicate how comfortable you were in answering each question on a 5-point scale:

1	2	3	4	5
Very uncomfortable	Somewhat uncomfortable	Neutral	Somewhat comfortable	Very comfortable

If you rated any question between 1–3, please reread the section of the chapter where the information for the question can be found. If you're still uncomfortable answering the question, talk with your instructor and/or your classmates for more clarification.

Questions	Degree of comfort? (Circle one number)
1. What is a data source? What is a data collection method? Discuss the differences between a data source and data collection method. Provide social work examples throughout your discussion to illustrate your main points.	1 2 3 4 5
2. Discuss how data are collected and utilized within positivistic research studies (Chapter 5) and within interpretive research studies (Chapter 6). Provide social work examples throughout your discussion to illustrate your main points.	1 2 3 4 5
3. First, list all eight criteria that need to be addressed when selecting a data collection method. Second, for each criterion, discuss how this single criterion can influence the selection of a data collection method. Third, provide social work examples throughout your discussion to illustrate your main points.	1 2 3 4 5
4. What is meant by "trying out the selected data collection method"? Provide social work examples throughout your discussion to illustrate your main points.	1 2 3 4 5
5. Discuss in depth the main principle of implementing a data collection method. Provide social work examples throughout your discussion to illustrate your main points.	1 2 3 4 5
6. Discuss in depth how you would evaluate your chosen data collection method.	1 2 3 4 5

7. Take a look at Table 14.1. It contains 16 different types of data collection methods. Provide an example of how you could use each type within a hypothetical social work research study of your choice. You can use the same study for more than one type, or you can use different studies to illustrate how you could use each type.	1 2 3 4 5

Assessing Your Self-Efficacy for Chapter 14

AFTER you have read the chapter AND have completed all the study questions, please indicate how knowledgeable you feel you are for each concept listed below.

1	2	3	4	5
Very uncomfortable	Somewhat uncomfortable	Neutral	Somewhat comfortable	Very comfortable

Major Concepts in Chapter	Knowledge Level? (Circle one number)
1. Data source	1 2 3 4 5
2. Data collection method	1 2 3 4 5
3. The sixteen types of data collection methods	1 2 3 4 5
4. Data collection within positivistic research studies	1 2 3 4 5
5. Data collection within interpretive research studies	1 2 3 4 5
6. Designing a data collection method	1 2 3 4 5
7. The eight criteria for selecting a data collection method	1 2 3 4 5
8. Trying out a data collection method	1 2 3 4 5
9. Implementing a data collection method	1 2 3 4 5
10. Evaluating a data collection method	1 2 3 4 5
Add up your scores (Minimum = 10, Maximum = 50) Total score =	

A   45 — 50 = Social Work Manager in the making.
B   40 — 44 = Social Work Supervisor.
C   35 — 39 = Social Work Practitioner.
D   10 — 34 = Case Aide. Reread the chapter and redo the study questions.

PART VI
Analyzing Data

15

Analyzing Quantitative Data

You can use all the quantitative data you can get, but you still have to distrust it and use your own intelligence and judgment.
~ Alvin Toffler

After quantitative data are collected they need to be analyzed—the purpose of this chapter. To be honest, a thorough understanding of quantitative statistical methods is far beyond the scope of this book. Such comprehension necessitates more in-depth study through taking one or more statistics courses. Instead, we briefly describe a select group of basic statistical analytical methods that are used frequently in many quantitative and qualitative social work research studies. Our emphasis is not on providing and calculating formulas but rather on helping the reader to understand the underlying rationale for their use.

We present two basic groups of statistical procedures. The first group is called *descriptive statistics*, which simply describe and summarize one or more variables for a sample or population. They provide information about only the group included in the study.

The second group of statistical procedures is called *inferential statistics*, which determine whether we can generalize findings derived from a sample to the population from which the sample was drawn. In other words, knowing what we know about a particular sample, can we infer that the rest of the population is similar to the sample that we have studied?

Before you read further, we encourage you to reread Chapter 7 on levels of measurement. It's extremely important for you to have a sound understanding of the four levels of measurement before you dive into statistics.

 # ENTERING DATA INTO COMPUTERS

The use of computers has revolutionized the analysis of quantitative and qualitative data. Where previous generations of researchers had to rely on hand-cranked adding machines to calculate every small step in a data analysis, today we can enter raw scores into a personal computer and with few complications direct the computer program to execute just about any statistical test imaginable.

Seconds later, the results are available. While the process is truly miraculous, the risk is that, even though we have conducted the correct statistical analysis, we may not understand what the results mean, a factor that will almost certainly affect how we interpret the data.

We can code data from all four levels of measurement into a computer for any given data analysis. The coding of nominal data is perhaps the most complex, because we have to create categories that correspond to certain possible responses for a variable. One type of nominal-level data that is often gathered from research participants is *place of birth*. If, for the purposes of our study, we are interested in whether our research participants were born in either Canada or the United States, we would assign only three categories to *place of birth:*

1. Canada
2. United States
3. Other

The *other* category appears routinely at the end of lists of categories and acts as a catch-all, to cover any category that may have been omitted.

When entering nominal-level data into a computer, because we do not want to enter *Canada* every time the response on the questionnaire is Canada, we may assign it the code number 1 so that all we have to enter is 1. Similarly, the United States may be assigned the number 2, and "other" may be assigned the number 3.

These numbers have no mathematical meaning. We are not saying that Canada is better than the United States because it comes first, or that the United States is twice as good as Canada because the number assigned to it is twice as high. We are merely using numbers as a shorthand device to record *qualitative* differences: differences in *kind*, not in amount.

Most coding for ordinal-, interval-, and ratio-level data is simply a matter of entering the final score, or number, from the measuring instrument that was used to measure the variable directly into the computer. If a person scored a 45 on a standardized measuring instrument, for example, the number 45 would be entered into the computer. Although almost all data entered into computers are in the form of numbers, we need to know at what level of measurement the data exist so that we can choose the appropriate statistic(s) to describe and compare the variables.

Now that we know how to measure variables at four different measurement levels, let us turn to the first group of statistics that can be helpful for the analyses of data—descriptive statistics.

Descriptive Statistics

Descriptive statistics are commonly used in most quantitative and qualitative research studies. They describe and summarize a variable(s) of interest and portray how that particular variable is distributed in the sample, or population. Before looking at descriptive statistics, however, let's examine a social work research example that will be used throughout this chapter.

Thea Black is a social worker who works in a treatment foster care program. Her program focuses on children who have behavioral problems who are placed with "treatment" foster care parents. These parents are supposed to have parenting skills that will help them provide the children's special needs.

Thus, Thea's program also teaches parenting skills to these treatment foster care parents. She assumes that newly recruited foster parents are not likely to know much about parenting children who have behavioral problems. Therefore, she believes that they would benefit from a training program that teaches these skills in order to help them to deal effectively with the special needs of these children who will soon be living with them.

Thea hopes that her parenting skills training program will increase the knowledge about parental management skills for the parents who attend. She assumes that with such training the foster parents will be in a better position to support and provide clear limits for their foster children.

After offering the training program for several months, Thea became curious about whether the foster care providers who attended the program were, indeed,

TABLE 15.1

Data Collection for Four Variables from Foster Care Providers

Number	PSS Score	Gender	Previous Training?	Years of Education
01	95	Male	No	12
02	93	Female	Yes	15
03	93	Male	No	08
04	93	Female	No	12
05	90	Male	Yes	12
06	90	Female	No	12
07	84	Male	No	14
08	84	Female	No	18
09	82	Male	No	10
10	82	Female	No	12
11	80	Male	No	12
12	80	Female	No	11
13	79	Male	No	12
14	79	Female	Yes	12
15	79	Female	No	16
16	79	Male	No	12
17	79	Female	No	11
18	72	Female	No	14
19	71	Male	No	15
20	55	Female	Yes	12

lacking in knowledge of parental management skills as she first believed (her tentative hypothesis). She was fortunate to find a valid and reliable standardized instrument that measures the knowledge of such parenting skills, the Parenting Skills Scale (*PSS*). Thea decided to find out for herself how much the newly recruited parents knew about parenting skills—clearly a descriptive research question.

At the beginning of one of her training sessions (before they were exposed to her skills training program), she handed out the *PSS*, asking the 20 individuals in attendance to complete it and also to include data about their gender, years of education, and whether they had ever participated in a parenting skills training program before. All three variables could be potentially extraneous ones that might influence the level of knowledge of parenting skills of the 20 participants.

For each foster care parent, Thea calculated the *PSS* score, called a *raw score* because it has not been sorted or analyzed in any way. The total score possible on the *PSS* is 100, with higher scores indicating greater knowledge of parenting skills. The scores for the *PSS* scale, as well as the other data collected from the 20 parents, are listed in Table 15.1.

At this point, Thea stopped to consider how she could best utilize the data that she had collected. She had data at three different levels of measurement. At the nominal level, Thea had collected data on gender (3rd column), and whether the parents had any previous parenting skills training (4th column). Each of these variables can be categorized into two responses.

The scores on the *PSS* (2nd column) are ordinal because, although the data are sequenced from highest to lowest, the differences between units cannot be placed on an equally spaced continuum. Nevertheless, many measures in the social sciences are treated as if they are at an interval level, even though equal distances between scale points cannot be proved. This assumption is important because it allows for the use of inferential statistics on such data.

Finally, the data on years of formal education (5th column) that were collected by Thea are clearly at the ratio level of measurement, because there are equally distributed points and the scale has an absolute zero.

In sum, it seemed to Thea that the data could be used in at least two ways. First, the data collected about each variable could be described to provide a picture of the characteristics of the group of foster care parents. This would call for descriptive statistics. Second, she might look for relationships between some of the variables about which she had collected data, procedures that would utilize inferential statistics. For now let us begin by looking at how the first type of descriptive statistic can be used with Thea's data set.

TABLE 15.2
Frequency Distribution (from Table 15.1)

PSS Score	Absolute Frequency
95	1
93	3
90	2
84	2
82	2
80	2
79	5
72	1
71	1
55	1

FREQUENCY DISTRIBUTIONS

One of the simplest procedures that Thea can employ is to develop a frequency distribution of her data. Constructing a frequency distribution involves counting the occurrences of each value, or category, of the variable and ordering them in some fashion. This *absolute* or *simple frequency distribution* allows us to see quickly how certain values of a variable are distributed in our sample.

The *mode*, or the most commonly occurring score, can be easily spotted in a simple frequency distribution (see Table 15.2). In this example, the mode is 79, a score obtained by five parents on the *PSS* scale. The highest and the lowest scores are also quickly identifiable. The top score was 95, while the foster care parent who performed the least well on the *PSS* scored 55.

There are several other ways to present frequency data. A commonly used method that can be easily integrated into a simple frequency distribution table is the *cumulative frequency distribution*, shown in Table 15.3.

TABLE 15.3

Cumulative Frequency and Percentage Distribution of Parental Skill Scores
(from Table 15.1)

PSS Score	Frequency		Percentage Distribution
	Absolute	Cumulative	
95	1	1	5
93	3	4	15
90	2	6	10
84	2	8	10
82	2	10	10
80	2	12	10
79	5	17	25
72	1	18	5
71	1	19	5
55	1	20	5
Total....	20		100

In Thea's data set, the highest *PSS* score, 95, was obtained by only one individual. The group of individuals who scored 93 or above on the *PSS* measure includes four foster care parents. If we want to know how many scored 80 or above, if we look at the number across from 80 in the cumulative frequency column, we can quickly see that 12 of the parents scored 80 or better.

Other tables use percentages rather than frequencies, sometimes referred to as *percentage distributions*, shown in the far-right column in Table 15.3. Each of these numbers represents the percentage of participants who obtained each *PSS* value. Five individuals, for example, scored 79 on the *PSS*. Since there was a total of 20 foster care parents, 5 out of the 20, or one-quarter of the total, obtained a score of 79. This corresponds to 25 percent of the participants.

TABLE 15.4

Grouped Frequency Distribution of Parental Skill Scores (from Table 15.1)

| | Frequency | | |
PSS Score	Absolute	Cumulative	Absolute Percentage
90 –100	6	6	30
80 – 89	6	12	30
70 – 79	7	19	35
60 – 69	0	19	0
50 – 59	1	20	5

Finally, *grouped frequency distributions* are used to simplify a table by grouping the variable into equal-sized ranges, as shown in Table 15.4. Both absolute and cumulative frequencies and percentages can also be displayed using this format. Each is calculated in the same way that was previously described for nongrouped data, and the interpretation is identical.

Looking at the absolute frequency column, for example, we can quickly identify the fact that seven of the foster care parents scored in the 70–79 range on the *PSS*. By looking at the cumulative frequency column, we can see that 12 of 20 parents scored 80 or better on the *PSS*. Further, from the absolute percentage column, it's clear that 30 percent of the foster parents scored in the 80–89 range on the knowledge of parenting skills scale.

Note that each of the other variables in Thea's data set could also be displayed in frequency distributions. Displaying years of education in a frequency distribution, for example, would provide a snapshot of how this variable is distributed in Thea's sample of foster care parents. However, with two category nominal variables, such as gender (male, female) and previous parenting skills training (yes, no), cumulative frequencies become less meaningful, and the data are better described as percentages.

Thea noted that 55 percent of the foster care parents who attended the training workshop were women (obviously the other 45 percent were men) and that 20 percent of the parents had already received some form of parenting skills training (while a further 80 percent had not been trained).

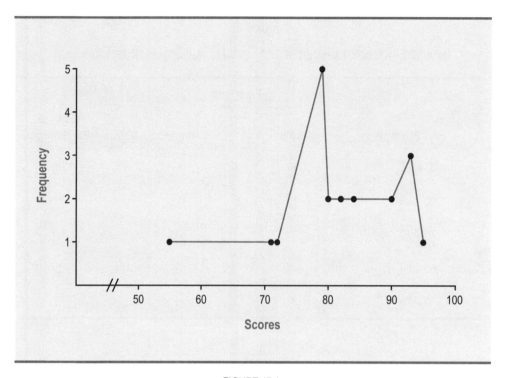

FIGURE 15.1

Frequency Polygon of Parental Scores (from Table 15.1)

MEASURES OF CENTRAL TENDENCY

We can also display the values obtained on the *PSS* in the form of a graph. A *frequency polygon* is one of the simplest ways of charting frequencies. The graph in Figure 15.1 displays the data that we had previously put in Table 15.2. The *PSS* score is plotted in terms of how many of the foster care parents obtained each score. As can be seen from Table 15.2 and Figure 15.1, most of the scores fall between 79 and 93. The one extremely low score of 55 is also quickly noticeable in such a graph because it's so far removed from the rest of the values.

A frequency polygon allows us to make a quick analysis of how closely the distribution fits the shape of a normal curve. A *normal curve*, also known as a *bell-shaped distribution* or a *normal distribution*, is a frequency polygon in which the greatest number of responses fall in the middle of the distribution and fewer scores appear at the extremes of either very high or very low scores (see Figure 15.2).

Many variables in the social sciences are assumed to be distributed in the shape of a normal curve. Low intelligence, for example, is thought to be relatively rare as

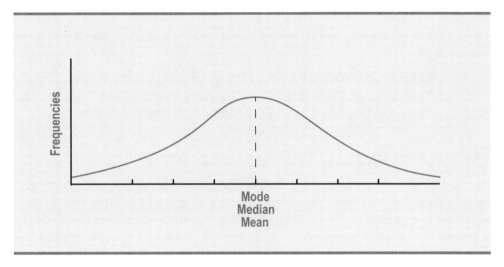

FIGURE 15.2
The Normal Distribution

compared to the number of individuals with average intelligence. On the other end of the continuum, extremely gifted individuals are also relatively uncommon.

Of course, not all variables are distributed in the shape of a normal curve. Some are such that a large number of people do very well (as Thea found in her sample of foster care parents and their parenting skill levels). Other variables, such as juggling ability, for example, would be charted showing a fairly substantial number of people performing poorly.

Frequency distributions of still other variables would show that some people do well, and some people do poorly, but not many fall in between. What is important to remember about distributions is that, although all different sorts are possible, most statistical procedures assume that there is a normal distribution of the variable in question in the population.

When looking at how variables are distributed in samples and populations it's common to use measures of *central tendency*, such as the mode, median, and mean, which help us to identify where the typical or the average score can be found. These measures are used so often because not only do they provide a useful summary of the data, they also provide a common denominator for comparing groups to each other.

MODE

As mentioned earlier, the mode is the score, or value, that occurs the most often—the value with the highest frequency. In Thea's data set of parental skills scores the mode is 79, with five foster care parents obtaining this value. The mode is particularly useful for nominal level data. Knowing what score occurred the most often, however, provides little information about the other scores and how they are distributed in the sample or population.

Because the mode is the least precise of all the measures of central tendency, the median and the mean are better descriptors of ordinal level data and above. We now turn our attention to the second measure of central tendency, the median.

MEDIAN

The median is the score that divides a distribution into two equal parts or portions. In order to do this, we must rank-order the scores, so at least an ordinal level of measurement is required. In Thea's sample of 20 *PSS* scores, the median would be the score above which the top ten scores lie and below which the bottom ten fall. As can be seen in Table 15.2, the top ten scores finish at 82, and the bottom ten scores start at 80. In this example, the median is 81, since it falls between 82 and 80.

MEAN

The mean is the most sophisticated measure of central tendency and is useful for interval or ratio levels of measurement. It's also one of the most commonly utilized statistics. A mean is calculated by summing the individual values and dividing by the total number of values. The mean of Thea's sample is $95 + 93 + 93 + 93 + 90 + 90 + ... 72 + 71 + 55/20 = 81.95$. In this example, the obtained mean of 82 (we rounded off for the sake of clarity) is larger than the mode of 79 or the median of 81.

The mean is one of the previously mentioned statistical procedures that assumes that a variable will be distributed normally throughout a population. If this is not an accurate assumption, then the median might be a better descriptor. The mean is also best used with relatively large sample sizes where extreme scores (such as the lowest score of 55 in Thea's sample) have less influence.

MEASURES OF VARIABILITY

While measures of central tendency provide valuable information about a set of scores, we are also interested in knowing how the scores scatter themselves around the center. A mean does not give a sense of how widely distributed the scores may be. This is provided by measures of variability such as the range and the standard deviation. There are many types of variability. We will only discuss two:

— Range

— Standard Deviation

RANGE

The range is simply the distance between the minimum and the maximum score. The larger the range, the greater the amount of variation of scores in the distribution. The range is calculated by subtracting the lowest score from the highest. In Thea's sample, the range is 40 (95 − 55). The range does not assume equal interval data. It is, like the mean, sensitive to deviant values because it depends on only the two extreme scores.

We could have a group of four scores ranging from 10 to 20: 10, 14, 19, and 20, for example. The range of this sample would be 10 (20 − 10). If one additional score that was substantially different from the first set of four scores was included, this would change the range dramatically. In this example, if a fifth score of 45 was added, the range of the sample would become 35 (45 − 10), a number that would suggest quite a different picture of the variability of the scores.

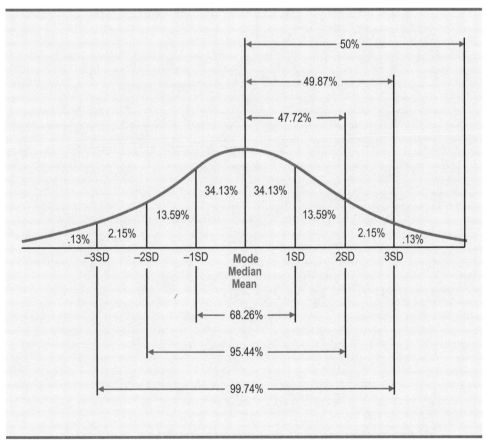

FIGURE 15.3

Proportions of the Normal Curve

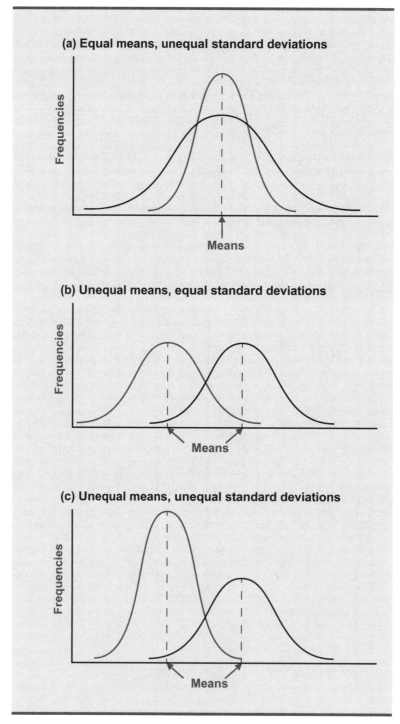

FIGURE 15.4
Variations in Normal Distributions

Standard Deviation

The standard deviation is the most utilized indicator of dispersion. It provides a picture of how the scores distribute themselves around the mean. Used in combination with the mean, the standard deviation provides a great deal of information about the sample or population without our ever needing to see the raw scores. In a normal distribution of scores (as described previously) there are six standard deviations: three below the mean and three above, as is shown in Figure 15.3

In this perfect model we always know that 34.13 percent of the scores of the sample fall within 1 standard deviation above the mean, and another 34.13 percent fall within 1 standard deviation below the mean. Thus, a total of 68.26 percent, or about two-thirds of the scores, is between +1 standard deviation and −1 standard deviation from the mean.

This leaves almost one-third of the scores to fall farther away from the mean, with 15.87 percent (50% to 34.13%) above +1 standard deviation, and 15.87 percent (50% to 34.13%) below 1 standard deviation.

In total, when we look at the proportion of scores that fall between +2 and −2 standard deviations, 95.44 percent of scores can be expected to be found within these parameters. Furthermore, 99.74 percent of the scores fall between +3 standard deviations and −3 standard deviations about the mean. Thus, finding scores that fall beyond 3 standard deviations above and below the mean should be a rare occurrence.

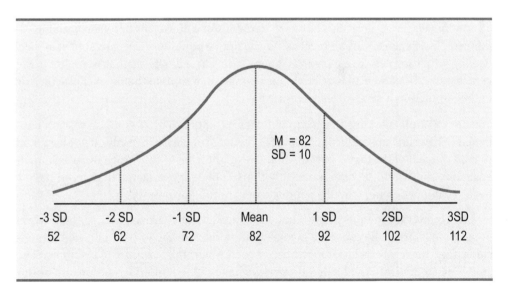

FIGURE 15.5

Distribution of Parental Skills Scores

The standard deviation has the advantage, like the mean, of taking all values into consideration in its computation. Also similar to the mean, it's utilized with interval or ratio levels of measurement and assumes a normal distribution of scores.

Several different samples of scores could have the same mean, but the variation around the mean, as provided by the standard deviation, could be quite different, as is shown in Figure 15.4a. Two different distributions could have unequal means and equal standard deviations, as in Figure 15.4b, or unequal means and unequal standard deviations, as in Figure 15.4c.

The standard deviation of the scores of Thea's foster care parents was calculated to be 10. Again, assuming that the variable of knowledge about parenting skills is normally distributed in the population of foster care parents, the results of the *PSS* scores from the sample of parents about whom we are making inferences can be shown in a distribution like Figure 15.5.

As can also be seen in Figure 15.5, the score that would include 2 standard deviations, 102, is beyond the total possible score of 100 on the test. This is because the distribution of the scores in Thea's sample of parents does not entirely fit a normal distribution. The one extremely low score of 55 (see Table 15.1) obtained by one foster care parent would have affected the mean as well as the standard deviation.

◆ INFERENTIAL STATISTICS

The goal of inferential statistical tests is to rule out chance as the explanation for finding either associations between variables or differences between variables in our samples. Because we can rarely study an entire population, we are almost always dealing with samples drawn from that population. The danger is that we might make conclusions about a particular population based on a sample that is uncharacteristic of the population it's supposed to represent.

For example, perhaps the group of foster parents in Thea's training session happened to have an unusually high level of knowledge of parenting skills. If she assumed that all the rest of the foster parents that she might train in the future were as knowledgeable, she would be overestimating their knowledge, a factor that could have a negative impact on the way she conducts her training program.

To counteract the possibility that the sample is uncharacteristic of the general population, statistical tests take a conservative position as to whether we can conclude that there are relationships between the variables within our sample. The guidelines to indicate the likelihood that we have indeed found a relationship or difference that fits the population of interest are called *probability levels*. The convention in most social science research is that variables are significantly associated or groups are significantly different if we are relatively certain that in 19 samples out of 20 (or

95 times out of 100) from a particular population, we would find the same relationship. This corresponds to a probability level of .05, written as ($p < .05$).

Probability levels are usually provided along with the results of the statistical test to demonstrate how confident we are that the results actually indicate statistically significant differences. If a probability level is greater than .05 (e.g., .06, .10), this indicates that we did not find a statistically significant difference.

Statistics That Determine Associations

THERE ARE MANY statistics that can determine whether there is an association between two variables. We will briefly discuss two:

— Chi-Square

— Correlation

Chi-Square

The *chi-square test* requires measurements of variables at only the nominal or ordinal level. Thus, it's very useful because much data in social work are gathered at these two levels of measurement. In general, the chi-square test looks at whether specific values of one variable tend to be associated with specific values of another.

In short, we use it to determine whether two variables are related. It cannot be used to determine whether one variable *caused* another, however. In thinking about the foster care parents who were in her training program, Thea was aware that women are more typically responsible for caring for their own children than men. Even if they are not mothers themselves, they are often in professions such as teaching and social work where they are caretakers.

Thus, she wondered whether there might be a relationship between gender and previous training in parenting skills, such that women were less likely to have taken such training because they already felt confident in their knowledge of parenting skills.

As a result, her one-tailed hypothesis was that fewer women than men would have previously taken parenting skills training courses. Thea could examine this possibility with her 20 foster care parents using a chi-square test. In terms of gender, Thea had data from the nine (45%) men and 11 (55%) women. Of the total group, four (20%) had previous training in foster care training, while 16 (80%) had not.

As shown in Table 15.5, the first task was for Thea to count the number of men and women who had previous training and the number of men and women who did

TABLE 15.5
Frequencies (and Percentages) of Gender by Previous Training
(from Table 15.1)

| Gender | Previous Training? | | Total |
	Yes	No	
Male	1 (11)	8 (89)	9
Female	3 (27)	8 (73)	11
Totals....	4 (20)	16 (80)	20

TABLE 15.6
Chi-Square Table for Gender by Previous Training
(from Table 15.5)

| Gender | Previous Training? | |
	Yes	No
Male		
Observed	1.0	8.0
Expected	1.8	7.2
Female		
Observed	3.0	8.0
Expected	2.2	8.8

Note: $\chi^2 = 0.8$; $df = 1$; $p > .05$

not have previous training. She put these data in one of the four categories in Table 15.5. The actual numbers are called *observed frequencies*. It's helpful to transform these raw data into percentages, making comparisons between categories much easier.

We can, however, still not tell simply by looking at the observed frequencies whether there is a statistically significant relationship between gender (male or female) and previous training (yes or no). To do this, the next step is to look at how much the observed frequencies differ from what we would expect to see if, in fact, if there was no relationship. These are called *expected frequencies*. Without going through all the calculations, the chi-square table would now look like Table 15.6 for Thea's data set.

Because the probability level of the obtained chi-square value in Table 15.6 is greater than .05, Thea did not find any statistical relationship between gender and previous training in parenting skills. Thus, statistically speaking, men were no more likely than women to have received previous training in parenting skills; her research hypothesis was not supported by the data.

CORRELATION

Tests of correlation investigate the strength of the relationship between two variables. As with the chi-square test, correlation cannot be used to imply causation, only association. Correlation is applicable to data at the interval and ratio levels of measurement. Correlational values are always decimalized numbers, never exceeding ±1.00. The size of the obtained correlation value indicates the strength of the association, or relationship, between the two variables. The closer a correlation is to zero, the less likely it is that a relationship exists between the two variables. The plus and minus signs indicate the direction of the relationship. Either high positive (close to +1.00) or high negative numbers (close to −1.00) signify strong relationships.

In positive correlations, though, the scores vary similarly, either increasing or decreasing. Thus, as parenting skills increase, so does self-esteem, for example. A negative correlation, in contrast, simply means that as one variable increases the other decreases. An example would be that as parenting skills increase the stresses experienced by foster parents decrease.

Thea may wonder whether there is a relationship between the foster parents' years of education and score on the *PSS* knowledge test. She might reason that the more years of education completed, the more likely the parents would have greater knowledge about parenting skills. To investigate the one-tailed hypothesis that years of education are positively related to knowledge of parenting skills, Thea can correlate the *PSS* scores with each person's number of years of formal education using one of the most common correlational tests, Pearson's *r*.

The obtained correlation between *PSS* score and years of education in this example is $r = -.10$ ($p > .05$). It was in the opposite direction of what she predicted. This negative correlation is close to zero, and its probability level is greater than .05. Thus, in Thea's sample, the parents' *PSS* scores are not related to their educational levels.

If the resulting correlation coefficient (*r*) had been positive and statistically significant (*p* < .05), it would have indicated that as the knowledge levels of the parents increased so would their years of formal education. If the correlation coefficient had been statistically significant but negative, this would be interpreted as showing that as years of formal education increased, knowledge scores decreased.

If a correlational analysis is misinterpreted, it's likely to be the case that the researcher implied causation rather than simply identifying an association between the two variables. If Thea were to have found a statistically significant positive correlation between knowledge and education levels and had explained this to mean that the high knowledge scores were a result of higher education levels, she would have interpreted the statistic incorrectly.

Statistics That Determine Differences

Two commonly used statistical procedures, *t*-tests and analysis of variance (ANOVA), examine the means and variances of two or more separate groups of scores to determine whether they are statistically different from one another. *T*-tests are used with only two groups of scores, whereas ANOVA is used when there are more than two groups. Both are characterized by having a dependent variable at the interval or ratio level of measurement, and an independent, or grouping, variable at either the nominal or ordinal level of measurement. Several assumptions underlie the use of both *t*-tests and ANOVA.

First, it's assumed that the dependent variable is normally distributed in the population from which the samples were drawn. Second, it's assumed that the variance of the scores of the dependent variable in the different groups is roughly the same. This assumption is called *homogeneity of variance*. Third, it's assumed that the samples are randomly drawn from the population.

Nevertheless, as mentioned in Chapter 11 on group research designs, it's a common occurrence in social work that we can neither randomly select nor randomly assign individuals to either the experimental or the control group. In many cases this is because we are dealing with already preformed groups, such as Thea's foster care parents.

Breaking the assumption of randomization, however, presents a serious drawback to the interpretation of the research findings, which must be noted in the limitations and the interpretations section of the final research report. One possible difficulty that might result from nonrandomization is that the sample may be uncharacteristic of the larger population in some manner. It's important, therefore, that the results not be used inferentially; that is, the findings must not be generalized to the general population. The design of the research study is thus reduced to an exploratory or descriptive level, being relevant to only those individuals included in the sample.

DEPENDENT *T*-TESTS

Dependent *t*-tests are used to compare two groups of scores from the same individuals. The most frequent example in social work research is looking at how a group of individuals change from before they receive a social work intervention (pre) to afterward (post). Thea may have decided that although she knew the knowledge levels of the foster care parents before receiving training was interesting, it did not give her any idea about whether her program helped the parents to improve their skill levels.

In other words her research question became "After being involved in the program, did parents know more about parenting skills than before they started?" Her hypothesis was that knowledge of parenting skills would improve after participation in her training program.

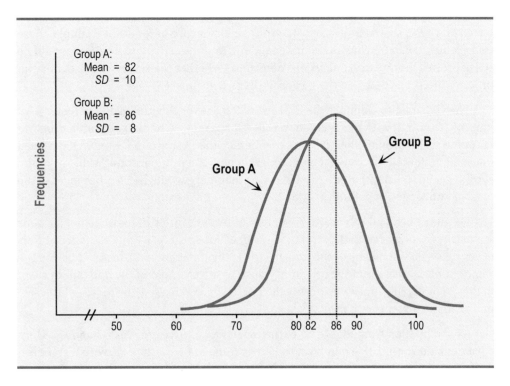

FIGURE 15.6

**Frequency Distributions of PSS Scores from
Two Groups of Foster Care Providers**

Thea managed to contact all the foster care parents in the original group (Group A) one week after they had graduated from the program and asked them to fill out the *PSS* knowledge questionnaire once again. Because it was the same group of people who were responding twice to the same questionnaire, the dependent *t*-test was appropriate.

Using the same set of scores collected by Thea previously as the pretest, the mean *PSS* was 82, with a standard deviation of 10. The mean score of the foster care parents after they completed the program was calculated as 86, with a standard deviation of 8.

A *t*-value of 3.9 was obtained, significant at the .05 level, indicating that the levels of parenting skills significantly increased after the foster care parents participated in the skills training program. The results suggest that the average parenting skills of this particular group of foster care parents significantly improved (from 82 to 86) after they had participated in Thea's program.

INDEPENDENT *T*-TESTS

Independent *t*-tests are used for two groups of scores that have no relationship to each other. If Thea had *PSS* scores from one group of foster care parents and then collected more *PSS* scores from a second group of foster care parents, for example, these two groups would be considered independent, and the independent *t*-test would be the appropriate statistical analysis to determine whether there was a statistically significant difference between the means of the two groups' *PSS* scores.

Thea decided to compare the average *PSS* score for the first group of foster care parents (Group A) with the average *PSS* score of parents in her next training program (Group B). This would allow her to see whether the first group (Group A) had been unusually talented or conversely were less well-versed in parenting skills than the second group (Group B). Her hypothesis was that there would be no differences in the level of knowledge of parenting skills between the two groups.

Because Thea had *PSS* scores from two different groups of participants (Groups A and B), the correct statistical test to identify whether there are any statistical differences between the means of the two groups is the independent *t*-test. Let us use the same set of numbers that we previously used in the example of the dependent *t*-test in this analysis, this time considering the posttest *PSS* scores as the scores of the second group of foster care parents.

As can be seen from Figure 15.6, the mean *PSS* of Group A was 82 and the standard deviation was 10. Group B scored an average of 86 on the *PSS*, with a standard deviation of 8. Although the means of the two groups are four points apart, the standard deviations in the distribution of each are fairly large, so there is considerable overlap between the two groups. This would suggest that statistically significant differences will not be found.

The obtained t-value to establish whether this four-point difference (86 – 82) between the means for two groups is statistically significant was calculated to be $t = 1.6$ with a $p > .05$. The two groups were thus not statistically different from one another, and Thea's hypothesis was supported.

Note, however, that Thea's foster care parents were not randomly assigned to each group, thus breaking one of the assumptions of the t-test. As discussed earlier, this is a serious limitation to the interpretation of the study's results. We must be especially careful not to generalize the findings beyond the groups included in the study.

Also note that in the previous example, when using the same set of numbers but a dependent t-test, we found a statistically significant difference. This is because the dependent t-test analysis is more robust than the independent t-test, because having the same participant fill out the questionnaire twice, under two different conditions, controls for many extraneous variables, such as individual differences, that could negatively influence an analysis of independent samples.

ONE-WAY ANALYSIS OF VARIANCE

A one-way ANOVA is the extension of an independent t-test that uses three or more groups. Each set of scores is from a different group of participants. For example, Thea might use the scores on the *PSS* test from the first group of foster care parents from whom she collected data before they participated in her program, but she might also collect data from a second and a third group of parents before they received the training. The test for significance of an ANOVA is called an F-test.

We could actually use an ANOVA procedure on only two groups, and the result would be identical to the t-test. Unlike the t-test, however, obtaining a significant F-value in a one-way ANOVA does not complete the analysis. Because ANOVA looks at differences between three or more groups, a significant F-value only tells us that there is a statistically significant difference among the groups. It does not tell us between which ones. To identify this, we need to do a *post-hoc* test.

A variety are available, such as Duncan's multiple range, Tukey's honestly significant difference test, and Newman-Keuls, and they are provided automatically by most computer statistics programs.

But one caution applies: a post-hoc test should be used *only after finding a significant F-value,* because some of the post-hoc tests are more sensitive than the F-test and so might find significance when the F-test does not. Generally, we should use the most conservative test first, in this case the F-test.

In the example of Thea's program, let us say that she collected data on a total of three different groups of foster care parents. The first group of foster care parents scored an average of 82 on the *PSS* (standard deviation 10). The second group scored an average of 86 (standard deviation 8), and the mean score of the third group was 88 with a standard deviation of 7.

The obtained F-value for the one-way ANOVA is 2.63, with a $p > .05$. Thus, we must conclude that there are no statistically significant differences between the means of the groups (i.e., 82, 86, and 88). Because the F-value was not significant, we would not conduct any post-hoc tests. This finding would be interesting to Thea because it suggests that all three groups of foster care parents started out with approximately the same knowledge levels, on average, before receiving training.

◆ SUMMARY

This chapter provided a beginning look at the rationale behind some of the most commonly used statistical procedures, both those that describe samples and those that analyze data from a sample in order to make inferences about the larger population. The level of measurement of the data is key to the kind of statistical procedures that can be used.

Descriptive statistics are used with data from all levels of measurement. The mode is the most appropriate measure of central tendency for measurements of this level. It's only when we have data from interval and ratio levels that we can utilize inferential statistics—those that extend the statistical conclusions made about a sample by applying them to the larger population.

Descriptive measures of central tendency, such as the mode, median, and mean of a sample or population, all provide different kinds of information, each of which is applicable only to some levels of measurement. In addition to knowing the middle or average of a distribution of scores as provided by measures of central tendency, it's useful to know the value of the standard deviation, which shows us how far away from the mean the scores are distributed.

It's assumed that most of the variables studied in social work can be found in a normal distribution in the total population. Consequently many descriptive and inferential statistics assume such a distribution for their tests to be valid.

Study Questions for Chapter 15

— First, answer each question only AFTER you have read the chapter.

— Second, indicate how comfortable you were in answering each question on a 5-point scale:

1	2	3	4	5
Very uncomfortable	Somewhat uncomfortable	Neutral	Somewhat comfortable	Very comfortable

If you rated any question between 1–3, please reread the section of the chapter where the information for the question can be found. If you're still uncomfortable answering the question, talk with your instructor and/or your classmates for more clarification.

Questions	Degree of comfort? (Circle one number)
1. In your own words describe what quantitative data are all about.	1 2 3 4 5
2. What are descriptive statistics? Discuss how they can be used in social work situations.	1 2 3 4 5
3. What are frequency distributions? Provide a social work example to illustrate your main points.	1 2 3 4 5
4. What are measures of central tendency? Provide a social work example to illustrate your main points.	1 2 3 4 5
5. List and then discuss the three measures of central tendency. Provide a social work example to illustrate your main points.	1 2 3 4 5
6. What are measures of variability? Provide a social work example to illustrate your main points.	1 2 3 4 5
7. List and then discuss the two measures of variability. Provide a social work example to illustrate your main points.	1 2 3 4 5
8. What are inferential statistics? Provide a social work example to illustrate your main points.	1 2 3 4 5
9. List and then discuss the two statistics that determine associations. Provide a social work example to illustrate your main points.	1 2 3 4 5

10. List and then discuss the two statistics that determine differences between groups. Provide a social work example to illustrate your main points.	1 2 3 4 5

Assessing Your Self-Efficacy for Chapter 15

AFTER you have read the chapter AND have completed all the study questions, please indicate how knowledgeable you feel you are for each concept listed below.

1	2	3	4	5
Very uncomfortable	Somewhat uncomfortable	Neutral	Somewhat comfortable	Very comfortable

Major Concepts in Chapter	Knowledge Level? (Circle one number)
1. Quantitative data analyses	1 2 3 4 5
2. Entering data into a computer	1 2 3 4 5
3. Descriptive statistics	1 2 3 4 5
4. Frequency distributions	1 2 3 4 5
5. Measures of central tendency	1 2 3 4 5
6. The mode	1 2 3 4 5
7. The median	1 2 3 4 5
8. The mean	1 2 3 4 5
9. Measures of variability	1 2 3 4 5
10. The range	1 2 3 4 5
11. The standard deviation	1 2 3 4 5
12. Inferential statistics	1 2 3 4 5
13. Chi-square	1 2 3 4 5
14. Correlation	1 2 3 4 5

15. Dependent *t*-tests	1 2 3 4 5
16. Independent *t*-tests	1 2 3 4 5
17. One-way analysis of variance	1 2 3 4 5

Add up your scores (Minimum = 17, Maximum = 85)	Total score =

A   76 — 85 = Social Work Manager in the making.
B   68 — 75 = Social Work Supervisor.
C   60 — 67 = Social Work Practitioner.
D   17 — 59 = Case Aide. Reread the chapter and redo the study questions.

16

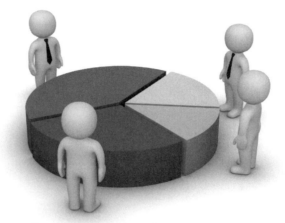

Analyzing Qualitative Data

In God we trust. All others must bring data.
~ W. Edwards Deming

The last chapter discussed the methods of analyzing quantitative data that are derived from positivistic research studies. In this chapter, we turn to the analysis of qualitative data that are derived from interpretive research studies—that is, data collected in the form of words (i.e., text data), most often from interviews, open-ended items on questionnaires, or personal logs.

Unlike *numbers*, which are used in quantitative analyses, *words* give us descriptions or opinions from the unique point of view of the person who spoke or wrote the words. Text data have both disadvantages and advantages.

The disadvantages are that words tend to be open to different interpretations and cannot be collected from large numbers of people at a time because the process of collection and analysis is much more time consuming than is the case for numerical data. The major advantage is that the material is very rich, containing multiple facets, and may provide us with a deeper understanding of the underlying meaning than would be possible if we just collected numbers (Tutty, Rothery, & Grinnell, 1996).

Purpose of Qualitative Data Analyses

Usually, we need the deeper understanding provided by qualitative data when we know very little about the problem or situation we are investigating and are not yet in a position to formulate theories about it for testing. In other words, we are at the exploratory end of the knowledge continuum, seeking to form patterns out of individual experiences so that we can develop more general theories.

The primary purpose of a qualitative data analysis is to sift and sort the masses of words we have collected from our research participants in such a way that we can derive patterns related to our research question—to identify the similarities and differences presented by individuals and the possible links between them.

Suppose for a moment that we are investigating postnatal depression among women. We may be interested in what the symptoms are, how new mothers experience them, and how they feel their depression affects their relationship with their newborns. We may also be interested in whether the women who experience postnatal depression are similar in any way with respect to various characteristics such as age, ethnic background, desire for the baby, partner or family support, socioeconomic status, medical history, and so on. Indeed, we may have structured our interviews to collect specific data related to these kinds of variables.

If we did, then we have already theorized that these characteristics or variables are related to postnatal depression, and we may, even subconsciously, look for patterns in the data that will confirm our theories. There is nothing evil about this. Researchers are human beings with a normal human tendency to make connections between events on the frailest of evidence, and it's a rare researcher who starts on a study with no preconceived notions at all.

The important thing is to be aware of our human frailties with respect to drawing unwarranted conclusions, and to organize our data collection and analysis so that these frailties are minimized as far as possible. A look at some of the assumptions underlying interpretive research might help us to accomplish this:

 We are assuming that the goal of interpretive research is to reach an in-depth understanding of each of our research participants with respect to the research question, including experiences that are unique to them. We will not achieve this goal if we do not allow participants to express their uniqueness during data collection. Neither will we achieve it if we ignore the uniqueness during data analysis because we were hoping to uncover patterns and this is an anomaly that does not quite fit.

✻ It's also easy to ignore uniqueness if it does not fit with the findings of other researchers. An exploratory topic tends to reveal little in the way of previous research, but there is usually some, and it's tempting to disregard a unique experience if it seems to contravene what others have found.

✻ Information is always provided in some context. In the case of a research study, the context is the way in which the information was elicited (e.g., the phrasing of a question). In an interview, the context is the relationship between the interviewer and the interviewee.

✻ Preconceptions on the part of the interviewer tend to elicit responses that fit with the preconceptions. Thus, it's important in analysis not to look at just the response but at the emotional atmosphere surrounding the response and the question that was responded to.

There are three major phases involved in a basic qualitative analysis:

✻ *First,* we must plan how we will do the analysis: how we will transcribe spoken or written data into a usable form and what rules we will use to fit the pieces of data together in a meaningful way.

✻ *Second,* we must do the analysis, following the general rules we set out at the beginning and perhaps revising these rules along the way if we come across some data to which our rules cannot be sensibly applied. It's important to note though that whatever rules we finally decide on must be applied to all our data.

Changing our mind about rules will mean going back over the material we have worked on already; indeed, qualitative analysis is usually a back-and-forth sort of process, involving many rereadings and reworkings as new insights appear and we begin to question our initial theories or assumptions.

✻ *Third,* we need to draw meaning from our analysis—that is, to identify relationships between the major themes that have emerged and to build theories around these for testing in the future.

PLANNING THE ANALYSIS

There are two steps involved in planning a qualitative analysis:

— Step 1: Transcribing the Data

— Step 2: Establishing General Rules for the Analysis

STEP 1: TRANSCRIBING THE DATA

TRANSCRIBING OUR DATA itself involves two tasks:

— Task 1a: Deciding What Computer Program to Use, If Any

— Task 1b: Deciding Who Will Transcribe the Data

TASK 1A: DECIDING WHAT COMPUTER PROGRAM TO USE, IF ANY

If responses are written, as in open-ended items on a questionnaire or personal logs, transcription may be a matter of typing the responses, either just for easier reading or with the aim of using a computer program to assist with the analysis. A few researchers, distrustful of computers, prefer to use a traditional cut-and-paste method, physically cutting the manuscript and grouping the cut sections together with other related sections.

A computer need not be used for transcription in this case. A typewriter would do, or even legible handwriting. Some researchers trust the computer just sufficiently to allow it to move selected passages together with other selected passages to electronically form a group of related data.

The majority of word-processing programs can accomplish this. An increasing number of researchers, however, use computer programs that have been developed specifically to assist with the analysis of qualitative data. A few familiar names are ETHNOGRAPH, HYPERQUAL, ATLAS.ti, NUD*IST, and NVivo.

New programs are always coming onto the market, so it's wise to consult colleagues or computer companies about which programs might be most helpful for a particular project. It's important to note that no computer program can do the analysis for us. The most it can do is free up time for us to spend on considering the meaning of our data.

TASK 1B: DECIDING WHO WILL TRANSCRIBE THE DATA

Some researchers are fortunate enough to have a research or administrative assistant to help them in the transcription process. If this is the case, it's necessary to lay down guidelines right at the beginning about how the material should be transcribed. If an interview has been audio- or videotaped, for example, the questions should be included in the transcript as well as the answers.

Nonverbal communications such as pauses, laughing or crying, and voice tone should be included in brackets so that the emotional context of the interview is captured as far as possible in the transcript. Those fortunate researchers with assistants are nevertheless well advised to transcribe at least the first few interviews themselves so that assistants can see what ought to be included.

Another concern is how to format the transcript so that it's easy to read and analyze. It's a good idea to leave a margin of at least two inches along the right side so that we can write notes and codes alongside the corresponding text. It's also a good idea to number each line of the transcript so that we can readily identify each segment of data.

Computer programs designed to assist in qualitative analysis will automatically do this. For example, suppose we worked in a foster care agency and we were asking foster parents who had resigned from the agency in the past year why they had resigned. A few lines from one of our interviews might be transcribed like this:

1. Sue (angrily): His behavior was just too much and nobody from the agency told

2. us that he'd set fires before and was probably going to burn our house down. I

3. suppose they thought that if they'd told us that we wouldn't have taken him but

4. I do feel that we were set up from the beginning (sounding very upset). And when

5. we called the agency, there was only an answering machine and it was a whole

6. day before the social worker called us back.

7. Interviewer: That's dreadful.

Reading these lines after the transcript is completed might immediately set us thinking about how foster parents' reasons for resigning could be separated into categories. One category might be the foster child's behavior (much worse than the foster parents had been led to expect).

Or this might be two categories: (1) the child's behavior and (2) the discrepancy between the actual behavior and the expected behavior. Another category might be negative feelings toward the agency, with two subcategories: the feeling of having been set up, and the perceived lack of support in a time of crisis. It might not take long at all for these tentative categories to harden into certainties.

Having read seven lines from one interview, we now feel we know why foster parents resign, and it only remains to confirm the reasons we have found by picking out similar sentiments from our interviews with other foster parents. Job completed!

Actually, we have barely begun. Since we cannot—and do not wish to—stop our minds from jumping ahead in this fashion, we must find some way to organize our thoughts such that our intuitive leaps do not blind us to different and perhaps contradictory insights yielded by other interviews. There are two techniques that might help us to do this: previewing the data, and keeping a journal. Both of these techniques will also help us to establish general rules for our analysis—the second and last step in the planning stage.

STEP 2: ESTABLISHING GENERAL RULES FOR THE ANALYSIS

Establishing general rules for the analysis ensures that our efforts are systematic and the same rules are applied to all our data. We use rules to decide how we could fit together pieces of data in a meaningful way and how these groups of data could be categorized and coded (to be discussed shortly).

For example, what criteria or rule do we use to decide whether a child's worsened behavior after a visit with the biological parents should be categorized under "child's behaviors" or under "relationships with biological parents"? Although we clarify and refine the rules throughout the study, by the time we have finished we should have a set of rules that have been consistently applied to every piece of data. We start to think about what rules might apply during the previewing task.

There are two basic tasks that take place when establishing rules for a qualitative data analysis:

— Task 2a: Previewing the Data

— Task 2b: Keeping a Journal

TASK 2A: PREVIEWING THE DATA

The process of transcription might be ongoing throughout the study, with each interview transcribed as soon as it's completed, or transcription might not begin until all the data have been assembled. Whichever method is used, it's important to read all the transcripts before beginning to formally identify categories.

It's also important to give all the transcripts and all parts of the transcripts the same amount of attention. We may be in peak form at the beginning of the day while reading the first few pages of the first transcript, for example, but by the end of the day and the end of the third transcript, this initial peak has waned to weary impatience.

We would be better advised to read only for as long as we remain interested in the material. This will obviously mean that the process of previewing the data extends over a longer period; qualitative data analysis takes time. It's a lengthy process of discovery, whose pace cannot be forced. If we are rereading material, it sometimes helps to read the last third of an interview at moments of high energy instead of the first third. That way, we will not lose valuable insights from later sections of the interview transcript.

Task 2b: Keeping a Journal

Some people love journals, and others hate them, but the interpretive researcher cannot afford to be without one. The journal should be started at the same time as the study is started. It should include notes on the planned method and any changes in the plan, with dates and reasons. For example, perhaps the plan was to interview all the foster parents who had resigned from the agency during the last year, but some of them would not agree to be interviewed.

We may believe that those who agreed differed in some important respects from those who refused. They were more satisfied with the agency perhaps. If this were the case, the data from our more satisfied sample might lead us to faulty conclusions, possibly causing us to place more emphasis on personal reasons for resignation such as failing health or family circumstances, and less on agency-related reasons such as poor information-sharing or support.

Whatever the difficulties we encounter and the assumptions we make, our journal should keep an accurate record of them as we move along in the data analysis. Because the work we do must be open to scrutiny by others, it's essential to keep a record of all our activities and the feelings and reasonings behind them.

When the data-collection stage begins, the journal can be used to record personal reactions to the interview situation. For example, we might feel more personal empathy with one foster parent than with another and be tempted to give more weight to the remarks of the parent with whom we sympathized. An unconscious overreliance on one research participant or one subset of research participants will hopefully reveal itself as we read through our journal entries later during the course of the analysis.

When we begin to categorize and code the data, we can use the journal to keep notes about the process, writing down the general rules, revisions to the rules, and questions or comments with respect to how particular pieces of data might be categorized. Let us now turn our attention to actually analyzing qualitative data.

 # Doing the Analysis

Once all the data have been previewed, we can start on coding. There are two levels of coding:

— Step 3: *First-level coding,* which deals with the concrete ideas evident in the transcript.

— Step 4: *Second-level coding*, which looks for and interprets the more abstract meanings underlying these concrete ideas.

Step 3: Doing First-Level Coding

There are four tasks in first-level coding:

— Task 3a: Identifying Meaning Units

— Task 3b: Creating Categories

— Task 3c: Assigning Codes to Categories

— Task 3d: Refining and Reorganizing Categories

Task 3a: Identifying Meaning Units

A meaning unit is a piece of data, which we consider to be meaningful by itself. It might be a word, a partial or complete sentence, or a paragraph or more. For example, let us look once again at the interview segment presented earlier:

1. <u>Sue (angrily): His behavior was just too much and nobody from the agency told</u>

2. *us that he'd set fires before and was probably going to burn our house down. I*

3. *suppose they thought that if they'd told us that we wouldn't have taken him but*

4. **<u>I do feel that we were set up from the beginning (sounding very upset). And when</u>**

5. ***we called the agency, there was only an answering machine and it was a whole***

6. ***day before the social worker called us back.***

7. *Interviewer:* That's dreadful<u>.</u>

In this segment, we might identify four meaning units. The first unit (underlined, line 1) relates to the child's behavior. The second unit (*italics*, lines 2 and 3) relates to lack of information provided by the agency. The third (bold, line 4) relates to feeling set up by the agency. The fourth unit (*bold italics,* lines 5 and 6) relates to poor support on the part of the agency. Of course, different researchers might identify different meaning units or label the same units differently.

For example, lines 4, 5, and 6 might be identified as relating to agency response style rather than poor support and might involve two distinct meaning units, "response method" and "response time." Similarly, the partial sentence in line 2, "he'd set fires before," might be viewed as a separate meaning unit relating to the child's past rather than present behavior.

The first run-through to identify meaning units will always be somewhat tentative and subject to change. If we are not sure whether to break a large meaning unit into smaller ones, it may be preferable to leave it as a whole. We can always break it down later in the analysis, and breaking down large units tends to be easier than combining smaller ones, especially once second-level coding begins.

TASK 3B: CREATING CATEGORIES

Once we have identified meaning units in the transcript, our next task is to consider which of them fit together into categories. Perhaps we should have a category labeled "child's behavior" into which we put all meaning units related to the child's behavior, including the second meaning unit identified above, "nobody from the agency told us that he'd set fires before and was probably going to burn our house down."

Or perhaps we should have two categories, "child's present behavior" and "child's past behavior," in which case the second meaning unit might belong in the latter category. Or perhaps we feel that the vital words are "nobody told us," and this second meaning unit really belongs in a different category labeled "provision of information by agency." All other meaning units to do with foster parents being given information by the agency would then belong in this same category even though they had nothing to do with the child's behavior.

Because these kinds of decisions are often difficult to make, it's a good idea to note in our journal how we made the decisions we did and what alternatives we considered at the time. What rules did we use to decide whether a particular meaning unit was similar to or different from another meaning unit? How did we define our categories in order to decide whether a group of similar meaning units should be placed in one category or in another?

As we continue to examine new meaning units, we will use these rules to decide whether each new unit is similar to existing units and belongs in an existing category or whether it's different from existing units and needs a new separate category. The number of categories will therefore expand every time we identify meaning units that are different in important ways from those we have already categorized.

Since too many categories will make the final analysis very difficult, we should try to keep the number within manageable limits. This may mean revising our initial rules about how categories are defined and what criteria are used to decide whether meaning units are similar enough to be grouped together. Of course, any change in rules should be noted in our journal, together with the rationale for the change.

The complexity of our categorization scheme also needs to be considered. One meaning unit may, in fact, fall into more than one category, or a group of meaning units may overlap with another group. Large, inclusive categories may consist of a number of smaller, more exclusive subcategories. For example, as we saw, the meaning unit *"nobody from the agency told us that he'd set fires before and was probably going to burn our house down"* has to do both with lack of information provided by the agency and with the child's past behavior.

Sometimes meaning units cannot be clearly placed into any category and fall into the category of "miscellaneous." When we are tired, most everything may seem to be "miscellaneous," but miscellaneous units should make up no more than 10 percent of the total data set. More than that suggests that there is a problem with the original categorization scheme.

The real purpose of a miscellaneous category is to prevent our throwing out meaning units that, at first glance, appear to be irrelevant. Such throwing out is risky because at some point we may decide that our whole categorization scheme needs massive revision and we must start the whole process again from scratch.

TASK 3C: ASSIGNING CODES TO CATEGORIES

Codes are simply a shorthand form of the category name. They typically take the form of strings of letters and/or symbols. Codes used in *The Ethnograph*, for example, may be up to ten letters long and can also include symbols. Codes are usually displayed in the margins (often the right margin) of the transcribed text.

If we had a category labeled "child's behavior," we might simply code this CB where the C stands for the foster child and the B stands for behavior. If we want to distinguish between past and present behavior, we might use the codes CPASTB and CPRESB, respectively. If there is a category relating to the behavior of the foster parents' own children (perhaps this has worsened since the foster child moved in), we might use the codes FPCPASTB and FPCPRESB, respectively, where the FPC stands for the foster parents' child.

In fact, we might make it a rule that codes starting with C, FP, FPC, and A stand for things to do with the foster child, the foster parents, the foster parents' children, and the agency, respectively. Then AINF>FP might mean information provided by the agency to the foster parents, and AINF<FP might mean information provided by the foster parents to the agency. It's a good idea to keep the codes as short as possible in the beginning because they tend to become longer as the analysis grows more complex. However, there are many different ways to assign codes and so long as the code is clearly related to the category, it does not really matter which system is used.

TASK 3D: REFINING AND REORGANIZING CATEGORIES

Before moving on from first-level coding, we need to make a final sweep through the data to ensure that our analysis reflects what our research participants have said. We should consider the logic underlying the rules we made for grouping meaning units and defining categories.

We may, for example, be confused about why we created some categories, or feel uncertain about why a particular meaning unit was put into a particular category. We might find that some categories are too complex and need to be split into smaller categories; or some categories are poorly defined; or some of the categories that we expected to emerge from the data are missing altogether.

We might, for example, have expected that some foster parents would resign because of poor health, but there is no category coded FPHEA. Investigation reveals that foster parents did indeed mention their poor health but they always ascribed it to the strain of dealing with the foster child or the foster child's biological parents or the agency.

Hence, the meaning units including poor health have been categorized under "foster child's present behavior (CPRESB)" or "relationships with agency (AREL)" or "relationships with biological parents (BPREL)" and have not been broken down finely enough to isolate poor health as a separate category. We may wish to create such a category, or we may prefer to note its absence in our journal together with other categories that are incomplete or in some way unsatisfactory.

This is a good time to ask a colleague to analyze one or two of our interviews using the rules we have devised. In this way, we can check that the categories themselves and the rules that define them make sense. If our colleague organizes meaning units in a significantly different way, our categorization scheme may need to be substantially revised.

It's probably time to stop first-level coding when all our meaning units fit easily into our current categorization scheme and there are no more units that require the creation of new categories. If interviews are continuing during first-level coding, we will probably find the data becoming repetitive, yielding no new piece of information that cannot be fitted into the present scheme.

STEP 4: DOING SECOND-LEVEL CODING

The next major step in the data analysis process is second-level coding. As noted earlier, this is more abstract and involves interpreting what the first-level categories mean. During first-level coding, we derived meaning units from interviews with individuals, and we derived categories by comparing the meaning units to see which were similar enough to be grouped together. During second-level coding we will compare the categories themselves to uncover possible relationships between them. The point of doing this is to identify themes based on patterns that repeatedly occur among our categories.

Task 4a: Comparing Categories

A comparison of categories in any interpretive study will probably yield many different types of relationships. Coleman and Unrau (2011) have suggested that the following three types of relationships are among those most commonly found:

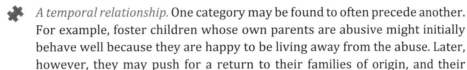 *A temporal relationship.* One category may be found to often precede another. For example, foster children whose own parents are abusive might initially behave well because they are happy to be living away from the abuse. Later, however, they may push for a return to their families of origin, and their response to the foster parents may become less positive.

A causal relationship. One category may be perceived to be the cause of another. For example, foster parents may believe that the child's bad behavior after every visit with the biological parent was the cause of their own negative attitudes toward the biological parent. However, it's always risky to assume that one category caused another when, in fact, the opposite may be true. Perhaps the foster parents started off with a negative attitude toward the child's biological parents, the child was more than usually angry about this after visits home, and the child demonstrated rage by behaving badly.

One category may be contained within another category. At this stage of the analysis, we may decide that two categories that we had thought to be separate are in fact linked. For example, foster parents may have said that they were never introduced to the child's biological parents by the agency, and we have categorized this separately from their statement that the agency was not entirely truthful with them about the child's past behavior. Now we realize that these are both examples of lack of information provided to the foster parent by the agency.

Furthermore, foster parents complained that they were not invited to agency meetings in which the child's progress was reviewed. Lack of information and nonattendance at meetings might combine to form a theme related to the agency's attitude toward the foster parents. The theme might be that the agency does not appear to accept the foster parents as equal partners in the task of helping the child.

When we have identified themes based on patterns among our categories, we code these themes in the same way as we coded our categories. If one of our themes is that the agency does not view foster parents as equal partners, for example, we might code this as A<FP-PART. Once themes have been identified and coded, the process of second-level coding is complete.

Looking for Meaning

Drawing meaning from our data is perhaps the most rewarding step of a qualitative data analysis. It involves two important steps:

— Step 5: Interpreting Data and Building Theory

— Step 6: Assessing the Trustworthiness of the Results

Step 5: Interpreting Data and Building Theory

This step involves two tasks:

— Task 5a: Developing Conceptual Classifications Systems

— Task 5b: Presenting Themes or Theory

Task 5a: Developing Conceptual Classifications Systems

The ultimate goal of an interpretive research study is to identify any relationships between the major themes that emerge from the data set. During first-level coding, we used meaning units to form categories. During second-level coding, we used categories to form themes. Now we will use themes to build theories. In order to do this, we must understand the interconnections between themes and categories. There are several strategies that might be useful in helping us to identify these connections. Miles and Huberman (1994) have suggested the following strategies for extracting meaning from a qualitative data set:

 Draw a cluster diagram. This form of diagram helps us to think about how themes and categories may or may not be related to one another. Draw and label circles for each theme and arrange them in relation to each other. Some of the circles will overlap, others will stand alone. The circles of the themes of more importance will be larger, in comparison to themes and categories that are not as relevant to our conclusions. The process of thinking about what weight to give the themes, how they interact, and how important they will be in the final scheme will be valuable in helping us to think about the meaning of our study.

�֍ *Make a matrix.* Matrix displays may be helpful for noting relations between categories or themes. Designing a two-dimensional matrix involves writing a list of categories along the left side of a piece of paper and then another list of categories across the top.

For example, along the side, we might write categories related to the theme of the degree of partnership between the agency and the foster parents. One such category might be whether the foster parents were invited to agency meetings held to discuss the child's progress. Then, along the top we might write categories related to the theme of foster parents' attitudes toward the agency.

One category here might be whether foster parents felt their opinions about the child were listened to by the agency. Where two categories intersect on the matrix, we could note with a plus sign (+) those indicators of partnership or lack of partnership that positively affect parents' attitudes. Conversely, we would mark with a minus sign (–) those that seem to have a negative effect. Such a matrix gives us a sense of to what degree and in what ways foster parents' attitudes toward the agency are molded by the agency's view of foster parents as partners.

✖ *Count the number of times a meaning unit or category appears.* Although numbers are typically associated with quantitative studies, it's acceptable to use numbers in qualitative work in order to document how many of the participants expressed a particular theme. We might be interested, for example, in finding out how many participants experienced specific problems related to lack of agency support. We would write the code names for the foster parents interviewed down the left side of a piece of paper and the list of problems across the top.

To fill in the chart, we would simply place a check mark beside each foster parent's code name if she or he experienced that particular problem. Numbers will help protect our analysis against bias that occurs when intense but rare examples of problems are presented. For example, many foster parents may have felt that they were not given sufficient information about the child's past behavior, but only one may have felt that the agency deliberately set her up. Although, we will certainly not discount this foster parent's experience, we might prefer to view it as an extreme example of the results of poor information sharing.

✖ *Create a metaphor.* Developing metaphors that convey the essence of our findings is another mechanism for extracting meaning. One example of a metaphor concerning battered women is "the cycle of violence," which effectively describes the tension building between couples until the husband beats his wife, followed by a calm, loving phase until the tension builds again.

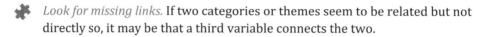 *Look for missing links.* If two categories or themes seem to be related but not directly so, it may be that a third variable connects the two.

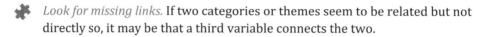 *Note contradictory evidence.* It's only natural to want to focus on evidence that supports our ideas. Because of this human tendency, it's particularly important to also identify themes and categories that raise questions about our conclusions. All contradictory evidence must be accounted for when we come to derive theories pertaining to our study area, for example, theories about why foster parents resign.

TASK 5B: PRESENTING THEMES OR THEORY

Sometimes it's sufficient to conclude an interpretive study merely by describing the major themes that emerged from the data. For example, we may have used the experiences of individual foster parents to derive reasons for resignation common to the majority of foster parents we studied.

When categorized, such reasons might relate to inadequate training; poor support from the agency; failure on the agency's part to treat the foster parents as partners; negative attitudes on the part of the foster parents' friends and extended family; unrealistic expectations on the part of the foster parents with respect to the foster child's progress and behavior; poor relations between the biological and foster parents; the perceived negative influence of the foster child on the foster parents' own children; marital discord attributed to stress; failing health attributed to stress; and so on.

We might think it sufficient in our conclusions to present and describe these categories, together with recommendations for improvement. On the other hand, we might wish to formulate questions to be answered in future studies. What would change if agencies were to view foster parents as partners rather than as clients? If we think we know what would change, we might want to formulate more specific questions. For example,

Are agencies that view foster parents as partners more likely to provide foster parents with full information regarding the child's background than agencies that do not view foster parents as partners?

Or we might want to reword this question to form a hypothesis for testing:

Agencies that view foster parents as partners are more likely to provide foster parents with full information regarding the child's background than agencies that do not view parents as partners.

In order to arrive at this hypothesis, we have essentially formulated a theory about how two of our concepts are related. We could carry this further by adding other concepts to the chain of relationships and formulating additional hypotheses:

Foster parents who have full information about the child's background are less likely to have unrealistic expectations about the child's behavior and progress than foster parents who do not have full information about the child's background.

And

Foster parents who have unrealistic expectations about the child's behavior and progress are more likely to experience marital discord (due to the fostering process) than foster parents who do not have unrealistic expectations.

Indeed, we might weave all the various woes our study has uncovered into an elaborate pattern of threads, beginning with the agency's reluctance to view foster parents as partners and ending with the foster parents' resignations. In our excitement, we might come to believe that we have solved the entire problem of resigning foster parents.

If agencies would only change their attitudes with respect to foster parents' status and behave in accordance with this change in attitude, then all foster parents would continue to be foster parents until removed by death. It's at this point that we need to focus on the second stage of our search for meaning: assessing the trustworthiness of our results.

STEP 6: ASSESSING THE TRUSTWORTHINESS OF THE RESULTS

There are three major reasons why disgruntled agencies, as well as other actors, may not agree that our results are as trustworthy as we believe. They can be broken into three tasks:

— Task 6a: Establishing Our Own Creditability

— Task 6b: Establishing the Dependability of the Data

— Task 6c: Establishing Our Control of Biases and Preconceptions

TASK 6A: ESTABLISHING OUR OWN CREDIBILITY

Because an interpretive study depends so much on human judgment, it's necessary to demonstrate that our own personal judgment is to be trusted. Part of this relates to our training and experience. Another important part is the record we made in our journal detailing the procedures we followed, the decisions we made and why we made them, and the thought processes that led to our conclusions. If we can demonstrate that we were qualified to undertake this study and we carried it out meticulously, others are far more likely to take into account our conclusions.

TASK 6B: ESTABLISHING THE DEPENDABILITY OF THE DATA

If we have been consistent in such things as interview procedures and developing rules for coding, and if we have obtained dependable data through a rigorous, recorded process, then another researcher should be able to follow the same process, make the same decisions, and arrive at essentially the same conclusions. Also, if we ourselves redo part of the analysis at a later date, the outcome should be very similar to that produced in the original analysis.

In order to ensure that we or others could duplicate our work, Coleman and Unrau (2011) have suggested we need to pay attention to the following standard issues:

 The context of the interviews. Some data-collection situations yield more credible data than others, and we may choose to weight our interviews accordingly. Some authors claim, for example, that data collected later in the study are more dependable than data collected at the beginning because our interviewing style is likely to be more relaxed and less intrusive. In addition, data obtained firsthand are considered to be more dependable than secondhand data, which are obtained through a third party.

Similarly, data offered voluntarily are thought to be stronger than data obtained through intensive questioning, and data obtained from research participants in their natural environments (e.g., home or neighborhood coffee shop) are to be more trusted than data provided by research participants in a foreign or sterile environment (e.g., researcher's office or an interviewing room).

Triangulation. Triangulation is commonly used to establish the trustworthiness of qualitative data. There are several different kinds of triangulation, but the essence of the method lies in a comparison of several perspectives. For example, we might collect data from the agency about what information was provided to foster parents in order to compare the agency's perspective with what foster parents said.

   With respect to data analysis, we might ask a colleague to use our rules to see if he or she makes the same decisions about meaning units, categories, and themes. The hope is that different perspectives will confirm each other, adding weight to the credibility of our analysis.

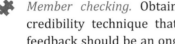 *Member checking.* Obtaining feedback from research participants is a credibility technique that is unique to interpretive studies. While such feedback should be an ongoing part of the study (e.g., interview transcripts may be presented to research participants for comment), it's particularly useful when our analysis has been completed, our interpretations made, and our conclusions drawn.

Research participants may not agree with our interpretation or conclusions, and may differ among each other. If this is the case, we need to decide whether to exclude the interpretations to which they object, or whether to leave them in, merely recording the dissenting opinions and our position in relation to them.

TASK 6C: ESTABLISHING OUR CONTROL OF BIASES AND PRECONCEPTIONS

Since all human beings inevitably have biases and preconceptions about most everything, one way to demonstrate that we are in control of ours is to list them. Such a list is useful to both ourselves and others when we want to check that our conclusions have emerged from the data rather than from our established beliefs.

   Also useful is our journal where we documented our attempts to keep ourselves open to what our research participants had to say. As Heather Coleman and Yvonne Unrau (2011) point out, we may want to consider the following points in relation to bias:

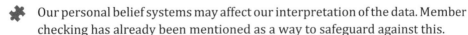 Our personal belief systems may affect our interpretation of the data. Member checking has already been mentioned as a way to safeguard against this.

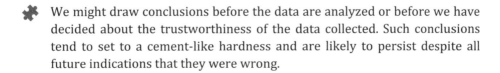 We might draw conclusions before the data are analyzed or before we have decided about the trustworthiness of the data collected. Such conclusions tend to set to a cement-like hardness and are likely to persist despite all future indications that they were wrong.

We might censor, ignore, or dismiss certain parts of the data. This may occur as a result of data overload or because the data contradict an established way of thinking.

We might make unwarranted or unsupported causal statements based on impressions rather than on solid analysis. Even when our statements are based on solid analysis, it's a good idea to actively hunt for any evidence that might contradict them. If we can demonstrate that we have genuinely searched for (but failed to find) negative evidence, looking for outliers and using extreme cases, our conclusions will be more credible.

We might be too opinionated and reduce our conclusions to a limited number of choices or alternatives.

We might unthinkingly give certain people or events more credibility than others. Perhaps we have relied too much on information that was easily accessible or we have given too much weight to research participants we personally liked. If we detect such a bias, we can interview more people, deliberately searching for atypical events and research participants who differ markedly from those we have already interviewed. Hopefully, these new data will provide a balance with the data originally collected.

Once we have assessed the trustworthiness of our results, it only remains to write the report describing our methods and findings.

EVALUATING YOUR DATA ANALYSIS PLAN

The best way to actually evaluative the quality of your qualitative data analysis plan is to evaluate your entire research study from the get-go. In short, your data analysis can only be as good as the study's research design that was used to obtain the data in the first place. Jim Raines (2011) has provided a nice list of questions that you should ask yourself before ever embarking on a qualitative research study.

Are your philosophical assumptions and values well identified?

Are the databases you searched sufficient to the research question you are trying to answer?

Is your literature review relevant to both your research problem and population?

Is the literature that you reviewed current?

* Do you use headings and subheadings to organize your ideas?

* Do you identify any differences in findings from previous research studies?

* Does your literature review support the purpose of your study?

* Is your research question crystal clear?

* Does your research question include all the major concepts that are in your study?

* Are your conceptual definitions multidimensional?

* Will your definitions evolve as participants provide their perspectives?

* Do you have a logical rationale for doing a qualitative study in the first place?

* Is there a good fit between your research question and your data-collection method?

* Does your research study demonstrate your value awareness?

* How do you plan on using informed consent procedures?

* Does your study advance the common good of your research participants?

* Do you explain the reasons for the type of sampling method you will use?

* How do you plan on reporting your subjectivity?

* How do you plan on addressing the issue of bias by you and your research participants?

* What strategies are you going to use to improve the credibility of your study's findings?

* What strategies are you going to use to improve the transferability of your study's findings?

* What strategies are you going to use to improve the dependability of your study's findings?

* What strategies are you going to use to improve the confirmability of your study's findings?

✳ What strategies are you going to use to increase the accuracy of your study's transcriptions?

✳ What is your specific plan for analyzing the data?

✳ How do you plan on developing categories for first-level coding?

✳ How do you plan on establishing relationships between categories clarified during second-level coding?

✳ How do you plan on developing themes and theories within your data analyses?

✳ How do you plan on addressing your study's limitations from an interpretivistic perspective?

✳ How do you plan on integrating your study's results with the previous literature?

✳ How do you plan on developing implications for social work theory, practice, or policy?

✳ Do you plan on making recommendations for future research studies?

✦ SUMMARY

This chapter has presented a systematic and purposeful approach to data analysis in an interpretive research study. The major steps of a data analysis include transcript preparation, planning the analysis, first-level coding, second-level coding, interpretation and theory building, and assessing the trustworthiness of the results. Although these steps have been presented in a linear fashion, any real qualitative analysis will involve moving back and forth between them in order to produce rich and meaningful findings.

Study Questions for Chapter 16

— First, answer each question only AFTER you have read the chapter.

— Second, indicate how comfortable you were in answering each question on a 5-point scale:

1	2	3	4	5
Very uncomfortable	Somewhat uncomfortable	Neutral	Somewhat comfortable	Very comfortable

If you rated any question between 1–3, please reread the section of the chapter where the information for the question can be found. If you're still uncomfortable answering the question, talk with your instructor and/or your classmates for more clarification.

Questions	Degree of comfort? (Circle one number)
1. Discuss what qualitative data are all about. Provide a social work example to illustrate your main points.	1 2 3 4 5
2. Discuss the main similarities and differences between quantitative data (Chapter 15) and qualitative data (this chapter). Provide a social work example to illustrate your main points.	1 2 3 4 5
3. What's the purpose of doing a qualitative data analysis? Provide a social work example to illustrate your main points.	1 2 3 4 5
4. Discuss the three major phases that are involved in doing a qualitative data analysis. Provide a social work example to illustrate your main points.	1 2 3 4 5
5. Discuss Step 1 in relation to doing a qualitative data analysis. Provide a social work example to illustrate your main points.	1 2 3 4 5
6. List and then discuss the two tasks contained in Step 1. Provide a social work example to illustrate your main points.	1 2 3 4 5
7. Discuss Step 2 in relation to doing a qualitative data analysis. Provide a social work example to illustrate your main points.	1 2 3 4 5
8. List and then discuss the two tasks contained in Step 2. Provide a social work example to illustrate your main points.	1 2 3 4 5
9. Discuss Step 3 in relation to doing a qualitative data analysis. Provide a social work example to illustrate your main points.	1 2 3 4 5

10. List and then discuss the four tasks contained in Step 3. Provide a social work example to illustrate your main points.	1 2 3 4 5
11. Discuss Step 4 in relation to doing a qualitative data analysis. Provide a social work example to illustrate your main points.	1 2 3 4 5
12. List and then discuss the only task contained in Step 4. Provide a social work example to illustrate your main points.	1 2 3 4 5
13. Discuss Step 5 in relation to doing a qualitative data analysis. Provide a social work example to illustrate your main points.	1 2 3 4 5
14. List and then discuss the two tasks contained in Step 5. Provide a social work example to illustrate your main points.	1 2 3 4 5
15. Discuss Step 6 in relation to doing a qualitative data analysis. Provide a social work example to illustrate your main points.	1 2 3 4 5
16. List and then discuss the three tasks contained in Step 6. Provide a social work example to illustrate your main points.	1 2 3 4 5
17. Pretend for a moment that you just completed a qualitative research study and are now ready to do a qualitative data analysis on the data you have gathered. As you know, a qualitative data analysis plan can be evaluated by answering 32 questions. List each question and then discuss how you would go about answering it based on the data you have collected in your qualitative study.	1 2 3 4 5

Assessing Your Self-Efficacy for Chapter 16

AFTER you have read the chapter AND have completed all the study questions, please indicate how knowledgeable you feel you are for each concept listed below.

1	2	3	4	5
Very uncomfortable	Somewhat uncomfortable	Neutral	Somewhat comfortable	Very comfortable

Major Concepts in Chapter	Knowledge Level? (Circle one number)
1. Qualitative data	1 2 3 4 5
2. Quantitative data	1 2 3 4 5
3. Major similarities and differences between qualitative and quantitative data	1 2 3 4 5
4. Purpose of doing a qualitative data analysis	1 2 3 4 5
5. Planning a qualitative data analysis	1 2 3 4 5
6. Transcribing qualitative data	1 2 3 4 5
7. Establishing general rules for a qualitative data analysis	1 2 3 4 5
8. First-level coding	1 2 3 4 5
9. Second-level coding	1 2 3 4 5
10. Interpreting qualitative data and building theory	1 2 3 4 5
11. Assessing the trustworthiness of the results from a qualitative data analysis	1 2 3 4 5
12. Evaluating a qualitative data analysis plan	1 2 3 4 5
Add up your scores (Minimum = 12, Maximum = 60)	Total score =

A   54 — 60 = Social Work Manager in the making.
B   48 — 53 = Social Work Supervisor.
C   42 — 47 = Social Work Practitioner.
D   12 — 41 = Case Aide. Reread the chapter and redo the study questions.

PART VII
Research Proposals and Reports

17

Positivistic Proposals and Reports

It's very difficult to decide. And I'm very open to proposals.
~ Paz Vega

This chapter discusses both how to write a positivistic research proposal, which is done *before* the study begins, and how to write its corresponding research report, which is done *after* the study is completed. They will be presented together because a research proposal describes what is *proposed* to be done, while a research report describes what *has been* done. As will be emphasized throughout the chapter, there is so much overlap between the two that a majority of the material written for a research proposal can be used in writing the final research report.

This chapter incorporates most of the contents of the preceding ones, so it is really a summary of the entire research process (and this book) up to report writing. We use an example of Lula Wilson, a social work practitioner who wants to do a research study on children who come to her women's emergency shelter with their mothers. She has been working at the shelter for the past two years. The shelter is located in a large urban city.

WRITING POSITIVISTIC RESEARCH PROPOSALS

When writing any research proposal, we must always keep in mind the purposes for its development and we must be aware of politically sensitive research topics. The purposes of the proposal are, primarily, to get permission to do the study and, second, perhaps to obtain some funds with which to do it.

There is a third purpose—to persuade the people who will review the proposal that its author, Lula, is competent to carry out the intended study. Finally, the fourth purpose of a proposal is to force Lula to write down exactly what is going to be studied, why it is going to be studied, and how it is going to be studied.

In doing this, she may think of aspects of the study that had not occurred before. For example, she may look at the first draft of her proposal and realize that some essential detail was forgotten—for instance, that the research participants (in her case, children) who are going to fill out self-report standardized measuring instruments must be able to read.

The intended readers of the proposal determine how it will be written. It is important to remember that the reviewers will probably have many proposals to evaluate at once. Some proposals will need to be turned down because there will not be sufficient funds, space, or staff time, to accept all of them. Thus, proposal reviewers are faced with some difficult decisions on which ones to accept and which ones to reject. People who review research proposals often do so on a voluntary basis.

With the above in mind, the proposal should be written so that it is easy to read, easy to follow, easy to understand, clearly organized, and brief. It must not ramble or go off into anecdotes about how Lula became interested in the subject in the first place. Rather, Lula's proposal must describe her proposed research study simply, clearly, and concisely.

Now that we know the underlying rationale for the proposal, the next step is to consider what content it should include. This depends to some extent on who will be reviewing it. If the proposal is submitted to an academic committee, for example, it will often include more of a literature review and more details of the study's research design than if it were submitted to a funding organization. Some funding bodies specify exactly what they want included and in what order; others leave it to the author's discretion.

The simplest and most logical way to write the proposal is in the same order that a research study is conducted. For example, when a research study is done, a general topic area is decided upon. This is followed by a literature review in an attempt to narrow the broad research area into more specific research questions or hypotheses. We will now go back and look at how each step of a research study leads to the writing of a parallel section in a research proposal. Let's turn to the first task of proposal writing, specifying the research topic.

PART 1: RESEARCH TOPIC (CHAPTER 2)

THE FIRST STEP in beginning any research study is to decide what the study will be about. The first procedure in writing a proposal, therefore, is to describe, in general terms, what it is that is going to be studied. Lula may describe, for example, her proposed study's general problem area as:

GENERAL PROBLEM AREA

Problems experienced by children who witness domestic violence

The first task is to convince the proposal reviewers that the general problem area is a good one to study. This task is accomplished by outlining the significance of Lula's proposed study in three specific social work areas: its practical significance, its theoretical significance, and its social policy significance. Depending on to whom the proposal is submitted, Lula may go into detail about these three areas or describe them briefly.

It may be known, for example, that the funding organization that will review the proposal is mostly interested in improving the effectiveness of individual social workers in their day-to-day practice activities. If this is the case, the reviewers will more likely be interested in the practical significance of Lula's proposed study than its theoretical and/or policy significance.

Therefore, Lula's proposal would neither go into detail about how her study might generate new social work theory, nor elaborate on the changes in social policy that might follow directly from the study's results. Because Lula is going to submit the proposal to the women's emergency shelter where she works, she would be smart to obtain informal input from the agency's executive director at this stage in writing the proposal. Informal advice at an early stage is astronomically important to proposal writers. In sum, Part 1 of the proposal describes *what* is going to be studied and *why* it should be studied.

PART 2: LITERATURE REVIEW (CHAPTER 2)

THE SECOND PART of a proposal contains the literature review. This is not simply a list of all the books and journal articles that vaguely touch on the general problem area mentioned in Part 1. When a research study is done, it is basically trying to add another piece to a jigsaw puzzle already begun by other researchers. The purpose of a literature review, then, is to show how *Lula's* study fits into the whole.

The trouble is that it might be a very big whole. There may be literally hundreds of articles and books filled with previous research studies on the study's general topic area. If Lula tries to list every one of these, the reviewers of the proposal, probably her colleagues who work with her at the shelter, will lose both interest and patience somewhere in the middle of Part 2.

The literature review has to be selective—listing enough material to show that Lula is thoroughly familiar with her topic area, but not enough to induce stupor in the reviewer. This is a delicate and sensitive balance. She should include findings from recent research studies along with any classic ones.

On the other side of the coin, another possibility is that previous research studies on Lula's general topic area may be limited. In this case, all available material is included. However, her proposal can also branch out into material that is partially related or describes a parallel topic area. Lula might find a research article, for example, that claims that children whose parents are contemplating divorce have low social interaction skills. This does not bear directly on the matter of problems children have who witnessed domestic violence (the general problem area mentioned previously). However, since marital separation can be a result of domestic violence, it might be indirectly relevant.

A literature review serves a number of purposes. First, it shows the reviewers that Lula understands the most current and central issues related to the general topic area that she proposes to study. Second, it points out in what ways her proposed study is the same as, or different from, other similar studies. Third, it describes how the results of her proposed study will contribute to solving the puzzle. Fourth, it introduces and conceptually defines all the variables that will be examined throughout the study.

At this stage, Lula does not operationally define her study's variables—that is, in such a way that allows their measurement. They are only abstractly defined. For example, if Lula is going to study the social interaction skills of children who witness domestic violence, her proposal so far introduces only the concepts of children, domestic violence, children witnessing domestic violence, and children's social interaction skills.

PART 3: CONCEPTUAL FRAMEWORK (CHAPTER 2)

A CONCEPTUAL FRAMEWORK takes the variables that have been mentioned in Part 2, illustrates their possible relationship to one another, and discusses why the relationship exists the way it is proposed and not in some other, equally possible way. The author's suppositions might be based on past professional experience.

For example, Lula has observed numerous children who accompanied their mothers to women's emergency shelters. She has made subjective observations of these children over the past two years and finally wishes to test out two hunches objectively.

First, Lula believes that children who have witnessed domestic violence *seem to* have lower social interaction skills than children who have not witnessed domestic violence. Second, Lula believes that of the children who have been a witness to domestic violence, boys *seem to* have lower social interaction skills than girls. However, these two hunches are based on only two years of subjective observations, which need to be objectively tested—the purpose of her study.

As we know, ideally, Lula's hunches should be integrated with existing theory or findings derived from previous research studies. In any case, Lula should discuss these assumptions and the reasons for believing them as the basis for the variables that are included in her proposed study.

PART 4: RESEARCH QUESTION OR HYPOTHESIS (CHAPTER 5)

GIVEN THE FIRST THREE PARTS of Lula's proposal so far, we can easily see that she wants to see whether children who have witnessed domestic violence have lower social interaction skills than those children who have not witnessed it. And of the children who have witnessed domestic violence, she wants to determine whether boys have lower social interaction skills than girls. It must be remembered that the two areas her study proposes to explore have been delineated out of her past experiences and have not been formulated on existing theory or previous research findings.

From Lula's general problem area, she formulated two related research hypotheses as follows:

RESEARCH HYPOTHESIS 1

Children who have witnessed domestic violence will have lower social interaction skills than children who have not witnessed such abuse.

RESEARCH HYPOTHESIS 2

Of those children who have witnessed domestic violence, boys will have lower social interaction skills than girls.

PART 5: METHODOLOGY

PART 5 of a research proposal contains five highly interdependent subparts:

— Part 5a: Research Design (Chapter 11)

— Part 5b: Operational Definitions (Chapters 7 and 8)

Part 5a: Research Design (Chapter 11)

In relation to Research Hypothesis 1, Lula's study would use the children who accompanied their mothers to the women's emergency shelter. These children would then be broken down into two groups: (1) those children who witnessed domestic violence, and (2) those children who did not witness it (as determined by the mother).

As presented in Chapter 11, a very simple two-group research design could be used to test Research Hypothesis 1. The average social interaction skills between the two groups can then be compared.

In relation to Research Hypothesis 2, within the group of children who have witnessed domestic violence, the children's social interaction skills between the boys and girls can be compared. This simple procedure would test Research Hypothesis 2. Once again, as presented in Chapter 11, a simple two-group research design could be used to test Research Hypothesis 2.

In Lula's study, there are two separate mini-research studies running at the same time—Research Hypotheses 1 and 2. All Lula wants to do is to see whether there is an association between the social interaction skills of children who have and have not witnessed domestic violence (Research Hypothesis 1). In addition, for those children who have witnessed domestic violence, she wants to see whether the boys have lower social interaction skills than the girls (Research Hypothesis 2).

Part 5b: Operational Definitions (Chapters 7 and 8)

As mentioned, variables are abstractly and conceptually defined in the conceptual framework part of the proposal (Part 3). Part 5b provides operational definitions of them; that is, they must be defined in ways in which they can be measurable. Let's take Lula's first simple research hypothesis previously mentioned.

RESEARCH HYPOTHESIS 1

Children who have witnessed domestic violence will have lower social interaction skills than children who have not witnessed such abuse.

In this hypothesis there are four main variables that must be operationalized before Lula's study can begin: children, domestic violence, children witnessing domestic violence, and children's social interaction skills. Each must be described in such a way that there is no ambiguity as to what they mean.

VARIABLE 1: CHILDREN.

For example, what constitutes a child? How old must the child be? Does the child have to be in a certain age range, for example, between the ages of 5 and 10? Does the child have to be a biological product of either the mother or the father? Can the child be a stepchild? Can the child be adopted? Does the child have to live full time at home?

Because Lula's study is extremely basic, she may wish to define a child operationally in such a way that permits the largest number of children to be included in the study. She would, however, go to the literature to find out how other researchers have operationally defined "children," and she would use this operational definition if it made sense to her.

However, in a simple study such as this one, a child could be operationally defined as "any person who is considered to be a child as determined by the mother." This is a very vague operational definition at best, but it is more practical than constructing one such as "a person between the ages of 5 and 17 who has resided full time with the biological mother for the last 12-month period."

If such a complex operational definition were used, Lula would have to provide answers to such questions as, why the ages of 5 and 17? Why not 4 and 18? What is the specific reason for this age range? Why must the child live at home full time? Why not part-time? Why must the mother be the biological mother? Why not a nonbiological mother? What about biological fathers? Why must the child have had to live at home for the past 12 months? Why not two years, or four years?

In short, Lula's operational definition of a child must make sense and be based on a rational or theoretical basis. For now, Lula is going to make matters simple: a child in her study will be operationally defined as any child whose mother validates their relationship. This simple operational definition makes the most practical sense to Lula.

VARIABLE 2: DOMESTIC VIOLENCE.

Let us now turn to Lula's second variable—domestic violence. What is it? Does the male partner have to shove, push, or threaten his partner? How would a child, as we have operationally defined one, know when it occurs? Does a husband yelling at his wife imply domestic violence? If so, does it have to last a long time? If it does, what is a long time? Is Lula interested in the frequency, duration, or magnitude of yelling—or all three?

A specific operational definition of domestic violence has to be established in order for the study to be of any value. Like most variables, there are as many operational definitions of domestic violence as there are people willing to define it.

For now, Lula is going to continue to make her simple study simple by operationally defining domestic violence as "women who say they have been physically abused by their partners." Lula can simply ask each woman who enters the shelter whether she believes she has been physically abused by her partner.

The data provided by the women will be "yes" or "no." Lula could have looked at the frequency, duration, or magnitude of such abuse, but for this study the variable is a dichotomous one: either domestic violence occurred, or it did not occur—as reported by the women. Questions regarding its frequency (how many times it occurred), its duration (how long each episode lasted), and its magnitude (the intensity of each episode) are not asked.

VARIABLE 3: CHILDREN WITNESSING DOMESTIC VIOLENCE.

The third variable in Lula's hypothesis is the child (or children) who witness domestic violence. Now that operational definitions of a "child" and "domestic violence" have been formulated, how will she know that a child has witnessed such an abuse? Each child could be asked directly, or a standardized checklist of possible verbal and physical abuses that a child might have witnessed can be given to the child, who is then asked how many times such abuse has been observed.

Obviously, the child would have to know what constitutes domestic violence to recognize it. In addition, the child would have to be old enough to respond to such requests, and the operational definition that is used for domestic violence must be consistent with the age of the child. For example, the child must be able to communicate to someone that domestic violence has in fact occurred—not to mention the question of whether the child could recognize it in the first place.

In Lula's continuing struggle to keep her study as simple as possible, she operationally defines "a child witnessing domestic violence" by asking the mothers who come to the women's emergency shelter whether their child(ren) witnessed the physical abuse. She is interested only in the women who come to the shelter as a result of being physically abused by their partners. Women who come to the shelter for other reasons are not included in her study. It must be kept in mind that Lula's study is focusing only upon physical abuse and not emotional or mental abuse.

So far, Lula's study is rather simple in terms of operational definitions. Up to this point she is studying mothers who bring their child(ren) with them to one women's emergency shelter. She simply asks the mother whether the person(s) with her is her child(ren), which operationally defines "child." The mother is asked whether she believes her partner physically abused her, which defines "domestic violence." The mother is also asked whether the child(ren) who accompanied her to the shelter saw the physical abuse occur, which operationally defines "children witnessing domestic violence."

VARIABLE 4: CHILDREN'S SOCIAL INTERACTION SKILLS.

VARIABLE 4: CHILDREN'S SOCIAL INTERACTION SKILLS. Let us now turn to Lula's fourth and final variable in her hypothesis—the children's social interaction skills. How will they be measured? What constitutes the social interaction skills of a child? They could be measured in a variety of ways through direct observations of parents, social work practitioners, social work researchers, social work practicum students, teachers, neighbors, and even members from the children's peer group.

They could also be measured by a standardized measuring instrument such as the ones discussed in Chapters 7 and 8. Lula decides to use one of the many standardized measuring instruments that measure social interaction skills of children, named the Social Interaction Skills of Children Assessment Instrument *(SISOCAI).*

All in all, Part 5b of a proposal provides operational definitions of all important variables that were abstractly defined in Part 3. It should be noted that the four variables that have been operationally defined should be defined from the available literature, if appropriate. (This procedure makes a study's results generalizable from one research situation to another.)

However, there may be times when this is not possible. The proposal must specify what data-gathering instruments are going to be used, including their validity and reliability, as presented in Chapters 7 and 8. In summary, let's review how Lula intends to operationally define her four key variables: child, domestic violence, child witnessing domestic violence, and children's social interaction skills:

- *Child.* Any person who the mother claims is her child.

- *Domestic Violence.* Asking the mother whether her partner physically abused her.

- *Child Witnessing Domestic Violence.* Asking the mother whether the child(ren) who accompanied her to the shelter witnessed the abuse.

- *Children's Social Interaction Skills.* The *SISOCAI* score for each child in the study.

The first three operational definitions are rather rudimentary at best. There are many more sophisticated ways of operationally defining them. However, alternative definitions will not be explored because Lula wants to keep her research proposal as uncomplicated as possible; she knows that the shelter does not want a study that would intrude too heavily into its day-to-day operations.

 On a very general level, the more complex the operational definitions of variables used in a research study, the more the study will intrude on the research participants' lives—in addition to the agency's day-to-day operations.

Part 5c: Population and Sample (Chapter 9)

The next part of the proposal presents a detailed description of who will be studied. Lula's research study will use the children who accompanied their mothers to one women's emergency shelter who wish to voluntarily participate, and whose mothers agree that they can be included in the study. The children will then each go into one of two distinct groups: those who have witnessed domestic violence, and those who have not (according to the mothers, that is).

Lula's study could have used a comparison group of children from the same local community who have never witnessed domestic violence and have never been to a women's emergency shelter. However, Lula chose to use only those children who accompanied their mothers to the shelter where she works.

There is no question of random selection from some population, and it is not possible to generalize the study's findings to any general population of children who have and have not witnessed domestic violence. The results of Lula's study will apply only to the children who participated in it.

Part 5d: Data Collection (Chapters 12 and 14)

This part presents a detailed account of how the data are going to be collected—that is, the specific data collection method(s) that will be used. As we know, data can be collected using interviews (individual or group), surveys (mail or telephone), direct observations, participant observations, secondary analyses, and content analyses.

Lula is going to collect data on the dependent variable by having her research assistant complete the *SISOCAI* for each identified child during a half-hour interview one day after the mother enters the shelter with her child(ren). Those mothers who do not bring their children with them will not be included in Lula's study.

In addition to the children, their mothers are also going to be interviewed to some small degree. Each mother will be asked by Lula whether she believes her partner physically assaulted her. These responses will then be used to operationally define "domestic violence." Each mother will also provide data on whether her child(ren) who accompanied her to the shelter saw the abuse occur. The mothers' responses will then operationally define whether the child(ren) witnessed domestic violence.

Finally, this section also should discuss ethical issues involved in data collection (Chapter 3). Chapters 12 to 14 in this book present various data collection methods that can be used in research studies. These chapters should be reread thoroughly before writing Part 5d of a research proposal.

Part 5e: Data Analysis (Chapter 15)

This part describes the way the data will be analyzed, including the statistical procedures to be used, if any. Having clearly specified the research design in Part 5a, Lula will use this part to specify exactly what statistical test(s) will be used to answer the research questions or hypotheses.

The *SISOCAI* produces interval-level data, and a child's social interaction skill score on this particular instrument can range from 0 to 100, where higher scores mean higher (better) social skills than lower scores. Because there are two groups of children who are being used to test both research hypotheses, and the dependent variable (*SISOCAI*) is at the interval-level of measurement, an independent *t*-test would be used to test both research hypotheses.

Part 6: Limitations

THERE ARE LIMITATIONS in every research study, often due to problems that cannot be eliminated entirely—even though steps can be taken to reduce them. Lula's study is certainly no exception. Limitations inherent in a study might relate to the validity and reliability of the measuring instruments, or to the generalizability of the study's findings. Sometimes the data that were needed could not be collected for some reason. In addition, this part should mention all extraneous variables that have not been controlled for.

For example, Lula may not have been able to control for all the factors that affect the children's social interaction skills. Although she believes that having witnessed domestic violence leads to lower social skills for boys as compared with girls, it may not be possible to collect reliable and valid data about whether the children saw or did not see abuse occur. In Lula's study, she is going to simply ask the mothers, so in this case she has to take the mothers' word for it. She could ask the children, however.

Asking the children would produce another set of limitations in and of itself. For example, it would be difficult for Lula to ascertain whether a child did or did not see a form of domestic violence as perceived by the child. It may be hard for a child to tell what type of abuse occurred. Also the frequency, duration, and magnitude of a particular form of domestic violence may be hard for the child to recall. All these limitations and a host of others must be delineated in this part of the proposal. In addition, asking children whether they saw the abuse occur might prove to be a traumatic experience for them.

Some limitations will not be discovered until the study is well under way. However, many problems can be anticipated, and these should be included in the proposal, together with the specific steps that are intended to minimize them.

PART 7: ADMINISTRATION

THE FINAL PART of a research proposal contains the organization and resources necessary to carry out the study. First, Lula has to find a base of operations (e.g., desk, telephone). She has to think about who is going to take on the overall administrative responsibility for the study.

How many individuals will be needed? What should their qualifications be? What will be their responsibilities? To whom are they responsible? What is the chain of command? Finally, Lula has to think about things such as a computer, stationery, telephone, travel, and parking expenses. When all the details have been put together, an organizational chart can be produced that shows what will be done, by whom, where, and in what order. The next step is to develop a time frame. By what date should each anticipated step be completed?

Optimism about completion dates should be avoided, particularly when it comes to allowing time to analyze the data and writing the final report (to be discussed shortly). Both of these activities always take far longer than anticipated, and it is important that they be properly done—which takes more time than originally planned.

When the organizational chart and time frame have been established, the final step is to prepare a budget. Lula has to figure out how much each aspect of the study—such as office space, the research assistant's time, staff time, and participants' time, if any—will cost.

We have now examined seven parts that should be included when writing a research proposal. Not all proposals are organized in precisely this way; sometimes different headings are used, or information is put in a different part of the proposal. For example, in some proposals, previous studies are discussed in the conceptual framework section rather than in the literature review. Much depends on for whom the proposal is being written and on the author's personal writing style.

Most, if not all, of the content that has been used to write the various parts of a research proposal can be used to write the final research report. Let's now turn to that discussion.

WRITING POSITIVISTIC RESEARCH REPORTS

A research report is a way of describing the completed study to other people. The findings can be reported by way of an oral presentation, a book, or a published paper. The report may be addressed solely to colleagues at work or to a worldwide audience. It may be written simply so that everyone can understand it, or it may be so highly technical that it can only be understood by a few.

The most common way of sharing a study's findings with other professionals is to publish a report in a professional journal. Most journal reports run about 25 double-spaced, typewritten pages, including figures, tables, and references. As we know, proposals are written with the proposal reviewers in mind. Similarly, a research report is written with its readers in mind.

However, some of the readers who read research reports will want to know the technical details of how the study's results were achieved, and others will only want to know how the study's results are relevant to social work practice, without the inclusion of the technical details. There are a number of ways to deal with this situation. First, a technical report can be written for those who can understand it, without worrying too much about those who cannot. In addition, a second report can be written that skims over the technical aspects of the study and concentrates mostly on the practical application of the study's findings.

Thus, two versions of the same study can be written; a technical one, and a non-technical one. The thought of writing two reports where one would suffice will not appeal to very many of us, however. Usually we try to compensate for this by including those technical aspects of the study that are necessary to an understanding of the study's findings. This is essential because readers will not be able to evaluate the study's findings without knowing how they were arrived at.

However, life can be made easier for nontechnical audiences by including some explanation of the technical aspects and, in addition, paying close attention to the practical application of the study's results. In this way, we will probably succeed in addressing the needs of both audiences—those who want all the technical details and those who want none.

A report can be organized in many different ways depending on the intended audience and the author's personal style. Often, however, the same common-sense sequence is followed as in the basic problem-solving method discussed at the beginning of this book. To solve a problem, the problem must be specified, ways of solving it must be explored, a solution to solve the problem must be tried, and an evaluation must take place to see whether the solution worked.

In general, this is the way to solve practice and research problems. It is also the order in which a research report is written. First, a research problem is defined. Then, the method used to solve it is discussed. Next, the findings are presented. Finally, the significance of the findings to the social work profession is discussed.

Part 1: Problem

PROBABLY THE BEST WAY to begin a research report is to explain simply what the research problem is. Lula might say, for example, that the study's purpose was to ascertain whether children who have witnessed domestic violence have lower social interaction skills than children who have not witnessed such abuse. In addition, the study wanted to find out whether, of those children who have witnessed domestic violence, the boys have lower social interaction skills than the girls. But why would anyone want to know about that? How would the knowledge derived from Lula's study help social workers?

Thinking back to her proposal, this question was asked and answered once before. In the first part of her proposal, when the research topic was set out, the significance of the study was discussed in the areas of practice, theory, and social policy. This material can be used, suitably paraphrased, in Part 1 of the final report.

One thing that should be remembered, though, is that a research report written for a journal is not, relatively speaking, very long. A lot of information must be included in less than 25 pages, and the author cannot afford to use too much space explaining to readers why this particular study was chosen. Sometimes the significance of the study will be apparent, and there is no room to belabor what is already obvious.

In Part 2 of the proposal, a literature review was done in which Lula's proposed study was compared with other similar studies, highlighting similarities and differences. Also, key variables were conceptually defined. In her final report, she can use both the literature review and her conceptually defined variables that she presented in her proposal. The literature review might have to be cut back if space is at a premium, but the abstract and conceptual definitions of all key variables must be included. In Part 3 of her proposal, she presented a conceptual framework. This can be used in Part 1 of the final report, where Lula must state the relationships between the variables she is studying.

In Part 4 of the research proposal, a research question to be answered or hypothesis to be tested was stated. In the final report, we started out with that, so now we have come full circle. By using the various parts of the proposal for the first part of the research report, we have managed to considerably cut down writing time.

In fact, Part 1 of a research report is nothing more than a cut-and-paste job of the first four parts of the research proposal. Actually, if the first four parts of the research proposal were done correctly, there should be very little original writing within Part 1 of a research report.

One of the most important things to remember when writing Part 1 of a report is that the study's findings have to have some form of utilization potential for social workers, or the report would not be worth writing in the first place. More specifically, the report must have some practical, theoretical, or policy significance. Part 1 of a research report tells why the study's findings would be useful to the social work profession. This is mentioned briefly but is picked up later in Part 4.

Joel Fischer (1981) has provided us with several points we need to consider when evaluating the Problem section of a published research report:

❋ Adequacy of the literature review

❋ Clarity of the problem area and research question under investigation

❋ Clarity of the statement of the hypothesis

❋ Clarity of the specification of the independent variable

❋ Clarity of the specification of the dependent variable

❋ Clarity of the definitions for major concepts

❋ Clarity of the operational definitions

❋ Reasonableness of assumption of relationship between the independent and dependent variables

❋ Number of independent variables tested

❋ Specification of independent variables in rival hypotheses

❋ Adequacy in the control of independent variables in rival hypotheses

❋ Clarity of the researcher's orientation

❋ Clarity of the study's purpose

❋ Clarity of the study's auspices

❋ Reasonableness of the author's assumptions

PART 2: METHOD

PART 2 OF A REPORT contains the method(s) used to answer the research problem. This section usually includes descriptions of the study's research design, a description of the research participants who were a part of the study (the study's sample), and a detailed description of the data-gathering procedures (who, what, when, how). It presents the operational definition of all the variables.

Once again, sections of the original research proposal can be used. For example, in Part 5b of the proposal, key variables were operationally defined; that is, they were defined in a way that would allow them to be measured. When and how the measurements would occur were also presented in Part 5d. This material can be used again in the final report.

Part 5a of the proposal described the study's research design. This section of the proposal was used—about halfway through—to link the parts of the study together into a whole. Because a research design encompasses the entire research process from conceptualizing the problem to disseminating the findings, Lula could take this opportunity to give a brief picture of the entire process. This part presents who would be studied (the research participants, or sample), what data would be gathered, how the data would be gathered, when the data would be gathered, and what would be done with the data once obtained (analysis).

In the final report, there is not a lot of space to provide this information in detail. Instead, a clear description of how the data were obtained from the measuring instruments must be presented. For example, Lula could state in this part of the report that "a research assistant rated each child on the *SISOCAI* during a half-hour interview one day after the mother entered the shelter."

Joel Fischer (1981) has provided us with several points we need to consider when evaluating the Methods section of a published research report:

- Clarity of the specification of the kinds of changes desired

- Appropriateness of the outcome measures in relation to the purpose of the study

- Degree of validity of the outcome measures

- Degree of reliability of the outcome measures

- Degree of use of a variety of outcome measures

- Clarity about how data were collected

- Clarity about who collects data

- Degree of avoidance of error in process of data collection

- Clarity of the statement of the research design

- Adequacy of the research design (in terms of its purpose)

- Clarity and adequacy of time between pretest and posttest

- Appropriateness in the use of control group(s)

- Appropriateness in the use of random assignment procedures

- Appropriateness in the use of matching procedures

- Experimental and control group equivalency at pretest

- Degree of control for effects of history

- Degree of control for effects of maturation

- Degree of control for effects of testing

- Degree of control for effects of instrumentation

- Degree of control for statistical regression

- Degree of control for differential selection of clients

- Degree of control for differential mortality

- Degree of control for temporal bias

- Degree of control for integrity of treatment

- Ability to distinguish causal variable

- Degree of control for interaction effects

- Overall degree of success in maximizing internal validity

- Adequacy of sample size

- Degree of accuracy in defining the population

- Degree of adequacy in the representativeness of the sample

- Degree of control for reactive effects of testing

- Degree of control for interaction between selection and experimental variable

- Degree of control for special effects of experimental arrangements

- Degree of control for multiple treatment interference

- Overall degree of success in maximizing external validity

PART 3: FINDINGS

PART 3 OF A REPORT presents the study's findings. Unfortunately, Lula's original proposal will not be of much help here because she did not know what she would find when it was written—only what she hoped to find.

One way to begin Part 3 of a report is to prepare whatever figures, tables, or other data displays that are going to be used. For now, let us take Lula's Research Hypothesis 1 as an example of how to write up a study's findings. Suppose that there were 80 children who accompanied their mothers to the shelter.

All of the mothers claimed they were physically abused by their partners. Lula's research assistant rated the 80 children's social skills, via the *SISOCAI*, one day after they accompanied their mothers to the shelter. Thus, there are 80 *SISOCAI* scores. What is she going to do with all that data?

The goal of tables and figures is to organize the data in such a way that the reader takes them in at a glance and says, "Ah! Well, it's obvious that the children who witnessed domestic violence had lower *SISOCAI* scores than the children who did not see such abuse."

As can be seen from Table 17.1, the average *SISOCAI* score for all of the 80 children is 60. These 80 children would then be broken down into two subgroups: those who had witnessed domestic violence and those who had not—according to their mothers, that is. For the sake of simplicity let's say there were 40 children in each subgroup. In the first subgroup, the average *SISOCAI* score for the 40 children is 45; in the second subgroup, the average *SISOCAI* score for the 40 children is 75. Table 17.1 allows the reader to quickly compare the average *SISOCAI* score for each subgroup.

The reader can see, at a glance, that there is a 30-point difference between the two average *SISOCAI* scores (75 – 45 = 30). The children who had witnessed domestic

TABLE 17.1

Means and Standard Deviations of Social Interaction Skills of Children Who Did and Did Not Witness Domestic Violence

Witness?	Mean	Standard Deviation	*n*
Yes	45	11	40
No	75	9	40
Average....	60		

violence scored 30 points lower, on the average, on the *SISOCAI* than the children who had not witnessed domestic violence. Thus, a glance at Table 17.1 shows that Lula's Research Hypothesis 1 is supported in that children who witnessed domestic violence had lower social interaction skills than children who did not witness it.

However, it is still not known from Table 17.1 whether the 30-point difference between the two average *SISOCAI* scores is large enough to be statistically significant. The appropriate statistical procedure for this design is the independent *t*-test, as described in Chapter 15. The results of the *t*-test could also be included under Table 17.1, or they could be described in the findings section:

> The result of an independent *t*-test between the *SISOCAI* scores of children who witnessed domestic violence as compared with those children who had not witnessed it was statistically significant ($t = 3.56$, $df = 78$, $p < .05$). Thus, the children who had witnessed domestic violence had statistically significantly lower social interaction skills, on the average, than the children who had not witnessed such abuse.

Table 17.2 presents the study's findings for Lula's second research hypothesis. This table uses the data from the 40 children who witnessed domestic violence (from Table 17.1). As can be seen from Tables 17.1 and 17.2, the average social skill score for the 40 children who witnessed domestic violence is 45.

Table 17.2 further breaks down these 40 children into two subgroups: boys and girls. Out of the 40 children who witnessed domestic violence, 20 were boys and 20 were girls. As can be seen from Table 17.2, boys had an average social skill score of 35 as compared with the average score for girls of 55. Thus, the boys scored, on the average, 20 points lower than the girls. So far, Lula's second research hypothesis is supported.

However, it is still not known from Table 17.2 whether the 20-point difference between the two average *SISOCAI* scores is large enough to be statistically significant. The appropriate statistical procedure for this design is the independent *t*-test, as described in Chapter 15. The results of the *t*-test could be included under Table 17.2, or they could be described in the Findings section as follows:

> The result of an independent *t*-test between the *SISOCAI* scores for boys and girls who witnessed domestic violence was statistically significant *(t* = 2.56, *df =* 38, *p* < .05). Thus, boys had statistically significant lower social interaction skills, on the average, than girls.

Once a table (or figure) is constructed, the next thing that has to be done is to describe in words what it means. Data displays should be self-explanatory if done cor-

TABLE 17.2

Means and Standard Deviations of Social Interaction Skills of Boys and Girls Who Witnessed Domestic Violence (from Table 17.1)

Gender	Mean	Standard Deviation	n
Boys	35	12	20
Girls	55	13	20
Average....	45		

rectly. It is a waste of precious space to repeat in the text something that is perfectly apparent from a table or figure.

At this point, Lula has to decide whether she is going to go into a lengthy discussion of her findings in this part of the report or whether she is going to reserve the discussion for the next part. Which option is chosen often depends on what there is to discuss. Sometimes it is more sensible to combine the findings with the discussion, pointing out the significance of what has been found as she goes along.

Joel Fischer (1981) has provided us with several points we need to consider when evaluating the Findings section of a published research report:

- Adequacy of the manipulation of the independent variable

- Appropriateness in the use of follow-up measures

- Adequacy of data to provide evidence for testing of hypotheses

- Clarity in reporting statistics

- Appropriateness in the use of statistical controls

- Appropriateness of statistics utilized

- Statistics appropriate to level of measurement

- Use of between-groups procedures

- Multivariate statistics used appropriately

Post hoc tests used appropriately

 Overall appropriateness of statistics

PART 4: DISCUSSION

THE FINAL PART OF A REPORT presents a discussion of the study's findings. Care should be taken not to merely repeat the study's findings that were already presented in Part 3. It can be tempting to repeat one finding in order to remind the reader about it preliminary to a discussion, and then another finding, and then a third . . . and, before we know it, we have written the whole of the Findings section all over again and called it a discussion. What is needed here is control and judgment—a delicate balance between not reminding the reader at all and saying everything twice.

On the other hand, Lula might be tempted to ignore her findings altogether, particularly if she did not find what she expected. If the findings did not support her hypothesis, she may have a strong urge to express her viewpoint anyway, using persuasive prose to make up for the lack of objective evidence. This temptation must be resisted at all costs.

The term "discussion" relates to what she found, not to what she thinks she ought to have found, or to what she might have found under slightly different circumstances. Perhaps she did manage to find a relationship between the variables in both of her hypotheses. However, to her dismay, the relationship was the opposite of what she predicted. For example, suppose her data indicated that children who witnessed domestic violence had higher social interaction skills than children who did not witness it (this is the opposite of what she predicted).

This unexpected result must be discussed, shedding whatever light on the surprising finding. Any relationship between two variables is worthy of discussion, particularly if they seem atypical or if they are not quite what was anticipated.

A common limitation in social work research has to do with not being able to randomly sample research participants from a population. Whenever we cannot randomly select research participants the sample cannot be considered to be truly representative of the population in question, and we cannot generalize the study's results back to the population of children who witnessed or did not witness domestic violence in the community. The simplest way to deal with this limitation is to state it directly.

Another major limitation in this study is that we will never know the social interaction skills of children who did not accompany their mothers to the shelter. The social skills of children who stay home may somehow be quite different from those children who accompanied their mothers. In fact, there are a host of other limitations in this simple study, including the simple fact that, in reference to Research Hypothesis 2, boys who did not see domestic violence may also have lower social interaction skills than girls—this was never tested in Lula's study. Nevertheless, we should also bear in mind the fact that few social work studies are based on truly representative random samples. In Lula's study, however, she still managed to collect some interesting data.

All social work researchers would like to be able to generalize their findings beyond the specific research setting and sample. From a research perspective (not a practice perspective), Lula is not really interested in the specific children in this particular study. She is more interested in children who witness domestic violence in general. Technically, the results of her study cannot be generalized to other populations of children who witness domestic violence, but she can suggest that she might find similar results with other children who accompany their mothers to similar women's shelters. She can imply and can recommend further studies into the topic area.

Sometimes we can find support for our suggestions in the results of previous studies that were not conclusive either but also managed to produce recommendations. It might even be a good idea to extract these studies from the literature review section in Part 1 of the report and resurrect them in the discussion section.

On occasion, the results of a study will not agree with the results of previous studies. In this case, we should give whatever explanations seem reasonable for the disagreement and make some suggestions whereby the discrepancy can be resolved. Perhaps another research study should be undertaken that would examine the same or different variables.

Perhaps next time a different research design should be used or the research hypothesis should be reformulated. Perhaps other operational definitions could be used. Suggestions for future studies should always be specific, not just a vague statement to the effect that more research studies need to be done in this area.

In some cases, recommendations can be made for changes in social work programs, interventions, or policies based on the results of a study. These recommendations are usually contained in reports addressed to people who have the power to make the suggested changes. When changes are suggested, the author has to display some knowledge about the policy or program and the possible consequences of implementing the suggested changes.

Finally, a report is concluded with a summary of the study's findings. This is particularly important in longer reports or when a study's findings and discussion sections are lengthy or complex. Sometimes, indeed, people reading a long report read only the summary and a few sections of the study that interests them.

Joel Fischer (1981) has provided us with several points we need to consider when evaluating the Discussion section of a published research report:

- Degree to which data support the hypothesis

- Extent to which the researcher's conclusions are consistent with data

- Degree of uniformity between tables and text

- Degree of researcher bias

- Clarity as to cause of changes in dependent variable

- Degree to which rival hypotheses were avoided in the design

- Degree to which potential rival hypotheses were dealt with in discussion

- Degree of control for threats to internal validity

- Reasonableness of opinions about implications

- Clarity as to meaning of change(s)

- Adequacy in relating findings to previous literature

- Adequacy of conclusions for generalizing beyond data

- Extent to which the research design accomplishes the purpose of the study

- Appropriateness in the handling of unexpected consequences

SUMMARY

The purpose of writing a research proposal is fourfold. A research proposal is necessary, first, to obtain permission to carry out the study and, second, to secure the funds with which to do it. Third, the researcher needs to convince the proposal reviewers that he or she is competent enough to do the study. Fourth, we need to think over precisely what we want to study, why we want to study it, what methods we should use, and what difficulties we are likely to encounter.

A proposal should be well organized and easy to read so that reviewers have a clear picture of each step of the study. The information included in most proposals can be set out under seven general headings, or parts.

Using a majority of the material from the research proposal, a research report is written that can be broken down into four general headings, or parts: problem, method, findings, and discussion. The four parts of a research report parallel the seven parts of the research proposal. This is not surprising, since both the report and the proposal are describing the same study.

Study Questions for Chapter 17

— First, answer each question only AFTER you have read the chapter.

— Second, indicate how comfortable you were in answering each question on a 5-point scale:

1	2	3	4	5
Very uncomfortable	Somewhat uncomfortable	Neutral	Somewhat comfortable	Very comfortable

If you rated any question between 1–3, please reread the section of the chapter where the information for the question can be found. If you're still uncomfortable answering the question, talk with your instructor and/or your classmates for more clarification.

Questions	Degree of comfort? (Circle one number)
1. In your own words, describe what a positivistic research proposal is all about. Provide a social work example throughout your discussion that illustrates your main points.	1 2 3 4 5
2. Discuss the role that Part 1 plays within a positivistic research proposal. Using Chapter 2 as a guide, write a hypothetical Part 1 of a positivistic research proposal with a topic area of your choice.	1 2 3 4 5
3. Discuss the role that Part 2 plays within a positivistic research proposal. Using Chapter 3 as a guide, write a hypothetical Part 2 of a positivistic research proposal with a topic area of your choice.	1 2 3 4 5
4. Discuss the role that Part 3 plays within a positivistic research proposal. Using Chapter 3 as a guide, write a hypothetical Part 3 of a positivistic research proposal with a topic area of your choice.	1 2 3 4 5
5. Discuss the role that Part 4 plays within a positivistic research proposal. Using Chapter 5 as a guide, write a hypothetical Part 5 of a positivistic research proposal with a topic area of your choice.	1 2 3 4 5
6. Discuss the role that Part 5 plays within a positivistic research proposal. Write a hypothetical Part 5 of a positivistic research proposal with a topic area of your choice.	1 2 3 4 5

7. Discuss the role that Part 6 plays within a positivistic research proposal. Write a hypothetical Part 6 of a positivistic research proposal with a topic area of your choice.	1 2 3 4 5
8. Discuss the role that Part 7 plays within a positivistic research proposal. Write a hypothetical Part 7 of a positivistic research proposal with a topic area of your choice.	1 2 3 4 5
9. In your own words, describe what a positivistic research report is all about. Provide a social work example throughout your discussion that illustrates your main points.	1 2 3 4 5
10. Discuss the role that Part 1 plays within a positivistic research report. Write a hypothetical Part 1 of a positivistic research report with a topic area of your choice.	1 2 3 4 5
11. List the15 criteria that are used to evaluate the Problem section (Part 1) of a positivistic research report. Now discuss why each criterion is important to consider when evaluating the report. Provide a social work example throughout your discussion to illustrate your main points.	1 2 3 4 5
12. List the 35 criteria that are used to evaluate the Method section (Part 2) of a positivistic research report. Now discuss why each criterion is important to consider when evaluating the report. Provide a social work example throughout your discussion to illustrate your main points.	1 2 3 4 5
13. List the 6 criteria that are used to evaluate the Findings section (Part 3) of a positivistic research report. Now discuss why each criterion is important to consider when evaluating the report. Provide a social work example throughout your discussion to illustrate your main points.	1 2 3 4 5
14. List the 14 criteria that are used to evaluate the Discussion section (Part 4) of a positivistic research report. Now discuss why each criterion is important to consider when evaluating the report. Provide a social work example throughout your discussion to illustrate your main points.	1 2 3 4 5

Assessing Your Self-Efficacy for Chapter 17

AFTER you have read the chapter AND have completed all the study questions, please indicate how knowledgeable you feel you are for each concept listed below.

1	2	3	4	5
Very uncomfortable	Somewhat uncomfortable	Neutral	Somewhat comfortable	Very comfortable

Major Concepts in Chapter	Knowledge Level? (Circle one number)
1. The seven common sections of a positivistic social work research proposal	1 2 3 4 5
2. The Research Topic section of a positivistic social work research proposal	1 2 3 4 5
3. The Literature Review section of a positivistic social work research proposal	1 2 3 4 5
4. The Conceptual Framework section of a positivistic social work research proposal	1 2 3 4 5
5. The Research Question or Hypothesis section of a positivistic social work research proposal	1 2 3 4 5
6. The Methodology section of a positivistic social work research proposal	1 2 3 4 5
7. The Limitations section of a positivistic social work research proposal	1 2 3 4 5
8. The Administration section of a positivistic social work research proposal	1 2 3 4 5
9. The four common sections of a positivistic social work research report	1 2 3 4 5
10. The Problem section of a positivistic social work research report	1 2 3 4 5
11. The Method section of a positivistic social work research report	1 2 3 4 5
12. The Findings section of a positivistic social work research report	1 2 3 4 5
13. The Discussion section of a positivistic social work research report	1 2 3 4 5

14.	The criteria used to evaluate each of the four sections of a positivistic social work research report	1 2 3 4 5
15.	How positivistic social work research reports are derived from research proposals	1 2 3 4 5

Add up your scores (Minimum = 15, Maximum = 75)	Total score =

A   67 — 75 = Social Work Manager in the making.
B   60 — 66 = Social Work Supervisor.
C   52 — 59 = Social Work Practitioner.
D   15 — 51 = Case Aide. Reread the chapter and redo the study questions.

18

Interpretive Proposals and Reports

I do not have much patience with a thing of beauty that must be explained to be understood. If it does need additional interpretation by someone other than the creator, then I question whether it has fulfilled its purpose.
~ Charlie Chaplin

Like positivistic research proposals and reports presented in the previous chapter, interpretive research proposals and their corresponding reports are also similar to one another. If we explain clearly what we intend to do when we write our proposal, for example, and we actually carry out our study as we originally planned, then writing our research report is largely a matter of changing "we will do" (as in the proposal) to "we did" (as in the report). This is true for everything but describing our study's findings in the research report.

As we will see, there is a good deal of similarity between positivistic and interpretive research proposals and reports. After all, the research process follows a logical progression whether it's positivistic (Chapters 5, 12, and 15) or interpretive (Chapters 6, 13, and 16). We need to know from the beginning of our research study what we want to study, why we want to study it, what methods we will use to study it, how long our research study will take, and how much it will cost.

In addition, we need to know what data will be collected, from whom, in what way, and how they will be analyzed. For the sake of continuity, this chapter—on interpretive proposals and reports—uses roughly the same format that was used in the last chapter which described positivistic proposals and reports. We will also use the same example: Lula Wilson, a social work practitioner who wants to do an interpretive research study on children and their mothers in the women's emergency shelter where she works.

 # WRITING INTERPRETIVE RESEARCH PROPOSALS

Before we begin to write the very first word of any research proposal we need to know why we want to write it and who will read it. As we have seen from the last chapter, knowing the purpose and our intended audience helps us to make important decisions about what we should include, in what order, and what writing style.

PURPOSE OF WRITING A PROPOSAL

THERE ARE THREE general purposes for writing a research proposal, no matter the study being proposed. (1) We need to obtain permission to do the study. (2) We need to obtain funding for the study. (3) We need to write down exactly what we intend to study, why, and how. As we know from Chapter 3, obtaining permission to do our study is often a matter of resolving ethical and informed consent issues to the satisfaction of various ethics committees.

Most universities and colleges have ethics committees, which decide whether our proposed study is designed in such a way that the interests of its research participants are ethically addressed. Many social services agencies throughout the world have their own ethics committees, which vet all proposed research endeavors that involve their clients and staff.

If Lula is associated in any way with a university, for example, and if her women's emergency shelter has its own ethics committee, she will have to obtain permission from both ethics committees before she can begin her study. Even if no ethics committees are involved, Lula will have to discuss her proposed study with her supervisor, who would probably have to obtain official permission from the shelter's Board of Directors.

All research studies require some level of funding. Even if Lula is prepared to do all the work on her own time using her own clients, there will still be direct and indirect costs such as photocopying, travel, phone, faxing, and postage. If Lula wants her shelter to cover these costs, she must include a budget in her proposal and get the budget approved before she begins her study. If it's a larger study, necessitating money from a funding body, then Lula must tailor her research proposal to meet the requirements of the particular funding body to which she is applying.

Most funding bodies have application forms that ask the applicant to supply the study's details under specific headings. Usually, funding bodies also want to know how qualified the particular applicant is to undertake the proposed study. In other words, Lula will have to convince the funding body that she personally has the experience and educational qualifications necessary to obtain meaningful and trustworthy results from her proposed study.

After permission and funding, the third purpose of writing a proposal is to force Lula to clarify her thoughts a bit more. In the process of describing her proposed study in sufficient detail in an attempt to convince others of its importance, Lula may think of aspects of her study that she has not thought of before. She may realize, for example, that she has little experience with interviewing children, and someone who has more experience with interviewing children may be in a better position to interview them.

Intended Audience

MOST RESEARCH PROPOSALS are reviewed by busy people who have a great deal of other work and probably a number of proposals to review. Thus, Lula's proposal should be as short as she can possibly make it. It should concisely describe her proposed study, its budget, and time frame in a way that is easy to read, to follow, and to understand.

Many proposals have to be rejected because there is insufficient funding or facilities to support them all, and those that are rejected are not necessarily the least worthy in terms of their importance. They are, however, often the least worthy in terms of how well they were organized and written. Lula will therefore be well advised to keep her proposal simple, clear, and brief.

Content and Writing Style

A PROPOSAL'S content and writing style will largely depend on who is going to review it. As already noted, some funding bodies stipulate on their application forms what and how much they want included, and in what format and order. If there is no such stipulation, it's simplest and most logical to write the research proposal in the order that the study will be conducted; that is, the order followed in this chapter. How much to include under what heading depends on the intended audience: A research proposal submitted to an academic committee, for example, often requires more of a literature review than a proposal submitted to a funding organization.

Style similarly depends on the recipient. In most cases, it's safest to write formally, using the third person. As we know, however, interpretive research studies are often more subjective than positivistic ones, their terminology is different, their underlying assumptions are different, and the researcher's own thoughts and feelings are an important component. It may therefore be appropriate to acknowledge the interpretive nature of the study by using a more personal writing style. As will be the case in writing the final research report, the style used depends on the proposal's intended audience and the author's personal judgment.

 # ORGANIZING THE PROPOSAL

As previously noted, if the proposal's recipients have provided no guidance as to how its contents should be organized, it's simplest to present the proposed study in the order in which it would be conducted. That is, the order that follows.

PART 1: RESEARCH TOPIC

THIS FIRST SECTION of a research proposal does nothing more than introduce the study to its readers. It examines the nature of the research question being explored and its significance, both to social work in general and to the recipient of the proposal in particular. As with positivistic studies, an interpretive study should have practical significance, theoretical significance, or significance with respect to social policy; or it may touch on all three areas.

The author's task is to explain what research question is being asked and why the answer to this question will be of benefit, paying particular attention to the interests of the proposal's reviewers. Lula may write, for example, about the general topic area in her study as follows:

GENERAL TOPIC AREA

The problems experienced by children who witness their mothers being physically abused by their fathers.

The results of such a study—knowing what these problems are—might generate new social work theory or might lead to changes in social policy. If Lula is going to submit her proposal to the women's emergency shelter where she works, however, her fellow social workers are more likely to be interested in how an understanding of the children's problems might help them to address the children's needs on a very practical level. Lula will therefore emphasize the practical significance of her study.

PART 2: LITERATURE REVIEW

As with positivistic research studies, there are four purposes in carrying out a literature review for interpretive studies:

- To assure the reviewers that Lula understands the current issues related to her research topic.

- To point out ways in which her study is similar to, or different from, other studies that have been previously conducted. Because many interpretive studies deal with topics about which little is known, Lula may not find many studies that have explored children's experiences with respect to their witnessing domestic violence. Such a paucity of information will support Lula's contention that her study needs to be conducted.

- To fit Lula's study into the jigsaw puzzle of present knowledge. Even if there is little knowledge in the area, there will still be some, and Lula's task is to explain how her study will fit with what is known already and will help to fill the knowledge gaps.

- To introduce and conceptualize the variables that will be used throughout the study. Lulu's proposal, for example, will include such concepts as children, domestic violence (or partner abuse, marital abuse, wife abuse, whichever term is preferred) and children witnessing domestic violence.

PART 3: CONCEPTUAL FRAMEWORK

AS WE KNOW, in positivistic research studies, the conceptual framework identifies the possible relationships between and among concepts to one another. Identifying the ways that concepts might be connected lays the groundwork for developing a research question or research hypothesis. In the last chapter, for example, Lula formulated the research hypothesis as follows:

RESEARCH HYPOTHESIS

Children who have witnessed domestic violence will have lower social interaction skills than children who have not witnessed such violence.

That is, her conceptual framework included the idea that a particular concept—children's social interaction skills—was directly related to another concept—whether the children witnessed the abuse or not.

In interpretive studies, the level of knowledge in the topic area will probably be too low to allow such possible connections between and among concepts to be investigated. Children's poor social interaction skills may indeed be one of the problems experienced by children who witness their mothers being physically abused by their fathers, but Lula does not know that yet. Her research question at this stage is simply, "What problems do these children experience?"

Relationships between and among concepts can still be hypothesized, however, even at an exploratory level, and even if the hypothesized relationships will not be tested during the course of the study. People reading an interpretive study, for example, are usually more interested in where the study took place and whether the influence of the clinical setting (i.e., the shelter) was appropriately acknowledged in the data analysis.

Lula must therefore take into account the possibility that the problems experienced by the children in her study may have been due to the study's setting (i.e., the shelter) and not so much from their witnessing the abuse. If she conceptualizes this possibility early, she may decide to interview the children's mothers, asking them not only to identify their children's problems but to describe each problem before and after coming into the shelter.

Similarly, she may want to explore the possibility that the children's problems may have been related to the children being abused themselves and not just to their witnessing their mothers being physically abused by their fathers.

PART 4: QUESTIONS AND HYPOTHESES

AN INTERPRETIVE RESEARCH STUDY rarely tests a research hypothesis. It is very important, however, that the questions to be answered during the course of an interpretive study be clearly formulated before it begins. Lula could formulate quite specific research questions, such as:

- What types of problems are experienced by children who have witnessed domestic violence?

- Does the type of abuse witnessed (e.g., hitting, yelling) affect the type of problems experienced by the children?

- Does the intensity of the abuse—witnessed by the children—affect the problems they experience?

- Does the frequency (e.g., daily, weekly) of the abuse—witnessed by the children—affect the problems they experience?

✱ Does the duration (e.g., over months, years) of the abuse—witnessed by the children—affect the problems they experience?

✱ Does the child's gender affect the types of problems they experience?

✱ Does the child's age affect the types of problems they experience?

✱ Do the child's problems, as perceived by the mother, affect the mother's decision to leave the abusive relationship?

✱ Do the child's problems, as perceived by the mother, affect the mother's decision about whether to return to the abusive relationship?

If Lula is going to formulate specific research questions, she will probably need to use a fairly structured interview schedule when she collects interview data from the mothers and their children. On the other hand, she may prefer to formulate just a few more general research questions, such as:

✱ What types of problems are experienced by children who have witnessed domestic violence?

✱ What effects do these problems have on the children and their mothers?

In this case, she would use an unstructured interview schedule, which would allow the mothers and children to guide the interviews themselves, relating what is important to them in their own way. Lula's decision about whether to formulate specific or general research questions depends on the level of knowledge about the study's topic area.

If enough knowledge is available to enable her to formulate specific research questions, she will probably do that. If not, one of the purposes of her study would be to gain enough knowledge to allow specific research questions to be formulated in the future.

PART 5: OPERATIONAL DEFINITIONS

AS WE KNOW, operationally defining a variable in a positivistic research study means defining the variable in such a way that it can be measured. In the last chapter, for example, Lula operationally defined the level of a child's social interaction skills in terms of the child's score derived from a standardized measuring instrument (*SISO-CIA*). The idea behind operationally defining a variable in this way is that both its definition and its measurement are consistent and objective.

Lula did not define "children's social interaction skills" herself (except insofar as she selected the measuring instrument), and she did not ask the children or their mothers what they perceived "children's social interaction skills" to be. Similarly, the measured result for each child (a numerical score) did not depend on anyone's personal perception on how well, or how badly, the child interacted socially with others.

Conversely, in interpretive studies, we are not as interested in objectively defining or measuring our concepts as we are when doing positivistic studies. Indeed, we actively encourage our research participants to provide us with their own, subjective definitions, since we are trying to understand their problems as they perceive them to be.

Similarly, we measure the extent, or effect, of a problem in terms of the research participants' subjective viewpoints. Hence, Lula will not have to worry about how to operationally define "a child" or "a child's problem," and she will not have to decide whether "a child witnessing domestic violence" means seeing it, or hearing it, or merely being aware that it's occurring. Lula might want to collect data about the ages of the children in her study, whether they are the biological children of their mothers, and whether they live full time at home, but none of these data will be used to exclude any child from the study on the grounds that the child is too old or too young, or otherwise does not fit Lula's operational definition of "a child."

Lula does not have an elaborate and complicated operational definition of a child. In her study, "a child" is operationally defined simply as "any person whom the mother considers to be her child." Similarly, "a problem" is whatever the mother and/or child considers to be problematic. "Domestic violence" is defined as whatever the research participants think it is; and children have "witnessed domestic violence" if they and/or their mothers believe that they have.

It might be as well here to put in a word about measurement. The word "measurement" is often associated with numbers, and hence with positivistic studies. To "measure" something, however, only means to describe it as accurately and completely as possible. If we cannot describe it with numbers, we may still be able to describe it with words, and this interpretive type of measurement is just as valid as a positivistic numerical measurement. Hence, Lula is measuring the problems experienced by children when she encourages the mothers and their children to describe those problems as accurately and completely as they can.

In positivistic studies, efforts are made to mitigate the effects of researcher bias through objective measurement. In interpretive studies, however, the use of measurement is to capture the subjective experiences of the research participants. Thus, it's vital for Lula to be aware of the effects of her own feelings upon the research participants she will be interviewing. Any prior assumptions she has made and any position she might hold must be clearly outlined at the beginning of her study so that the reader of her proposal can evaluate the degree to which her study's potential findings would reflect the research participants' opinions rather than Lula's opinions.

Similarly, it's important to record the interests and possible biases of the organization that is funding the study in addition to the agency where the study actually takes place. Would certain findings be more welcome to the funding body or the agency than other findings? Is the researcher under any pressure to emphasize certain aspects of the study's results to the detriment of other aspects? Again, the reader of a research proposal must be able to evaluate the degree to which the proposed study's auspices would potentially affect the study's findings.

A clear statement of the study's purpose might deflect critics who argue that the proposed study did not fulfill other purposes which the critics, themselves, may perceive as more important. Lula's research study might have a practical purpose, for example, where it would be in tune with the interests of the staff who work within the women's emergency shelter that would provide both funding for the study and access to its clients.

Lula simply wants to know what the children's problems are so that the shelter can better meet the needs of the children and their mothers. She is not overly interested in adding to social work theory or changing social policy, although her study's results may indeed have implications in both of these areas. She is less likely to be criticized for not placing sufficient emphasis on theory and policy in her discussion if she has clearly stated from the beginning that her proposed study's purpose is to inform day-to-day practice activities within her specific shelter.

Part 6: Research Design

We come now to the *how* of the study. This section includes information about what data will be collected, in what way and from whom, and how they will be analyzed. While writing about these matters, there will be many opportunities to address issues related to the study's *trustworthiness*. Evidence of a study's trustworthiness is provided by paying attention to four major concerns:

- Credibility, **or truth value**
- Transferability, **or applicability**
- Dependability, **or consistency**
- Confirmability, **or neutrality**

These four concerns are roughly equivalent to the positivistic concepts of internal validity and external validity. The first issue related to trustworthiness is credibility (akin to internal validity), which is particularly important and is built on the following aspects of an interpretive study:

- *Triangulation of data sources*—collecting data about the same thing from a number of different data sources; also engagement with research participants over a long period of time.

- *Consulting with colleagues*—consulting with them about ethical and legal matters, and about the methods chosen to select the sample of research participants and to collect and analyze the data.

- *Negative case analysis*—ensuring that information from all data sources is included in the data analysis, even when information from one data source seems to contradict themes or conclusions common to other data sources.

- *Referential adequacy*—keeping a complete and accurate record of all personal interviews and observations, such as videotapes, audiotapes, case notes, and transcriptions.

- *Member checks*—asking research participants to provide feedback on the information collected from the researcher and the conclusions drawn by the researcher.

The second issue related to trustworthiness is transferability (akin to external validity, or generalizability), which is addressed through a rich description of the study's clinical setting and the research participants. Findings from an interpretive research study are usually not generalized beyond the setting in which the study took place.

The findings may be applicable, however, to similar client populations: women and children in similar women's emergency shelters elsewhere, for example. Readers can only judge to what degree a study's findings may be applicable to their own clientele when the researcher provides a detailed description of the study's research participants in addition to their special needs and circumstances.

The third issue is dependability (akin to reliability), which relates to efforts to maintain consistency throughout the study. Were all interviews conducted in the same setting, according to the same format, and recorded in the same way? Were all research participants asked to provide feedback on the data collected, or only some? During data analysis, were rules concerning categorization and coding consistently applied? Aspects of the study related to credibility, as previously described, may be used to demonstrate dependability as well: for example, referential adequacy, providing evidence of consistent interviewing procedures, and providing evidence that all research participants were asked for their feedback.

The last issue, confirmability (akin to objectivity), has to do with Lula's awareness of her own role in influencing the data provided by the research participants and the conclusions she drew from the data. All interpretive researchers should keep journals in which they record their own thoughts and feelings about the study's research participants and about their interviews and observations.

Lula should note in her journal, for example, why she made the decisions she did about methodological matters, such as sampling procedures, and data collection and analysis techniques. While conducting the data analysis, she will record decisions and concerns about organizing and interpreting the data she collected.

These journal entries disclose the degree of impartiality she brought to the entire research process; where she was not impartial, it discloses her awareness, or lack thereof, about her own assumptions and biases. With respect to dependability (discussed previously), it provides a record of how consistent her decision making was and how consistently she conducted her interviews and analyzed her data.

PART 7: POPULATION AND SAMPLE

IN THIS PART of the proposal, Lula provides only a general description of who her research participants will be, together with a rationale for selecting these and not others. In interpretive studies, there is no attempt to select a random sample. Indeed, the sample often consists of all those persons available to be studied who fit broad criteria. Lula could draw her sample of research participants, for example, from all those women who are residents in her women's emergency shelter at a specific time.

Because Lula's study involves the effects on children who witnessed domestic violence, she will need to exclude from her sample all women who do not have children *and* all women who say that their children did not witness the abuse. Lula may personally believe that no child whose mother is being abused can remain unaware of that abuse, and the definition of "witnessing" for her may include a child's awareness as well as seeing or hearing.

In addition, it would be interesting to explore conflicting perceptions between the mothers and their children, when the children believe that they have witnessed domestic violence and their mothers believe that they have not. Lula is unlikely, however, to elicit information about the effects of witnessing domestic violence from women who do not believe that their children witnessed it; nor are these women likely to give Lula permission to interview their children on the subject.

Lula may decide to include women who do not have their children with them at the shelter. Whether she does so will depend on a number of factors. First, how many women can she interview, given her own and the women's time constraints? This will depend on how long she expects each interview to take, which, in turn, depends on such factors as the structure and depth of the interview.

In addition, she must consider the time required for transcribing and analyzing each interview in its entirety. If the number of women who have their children at the shelter is equal to, or larger than, the number of women Lula can reasonably inter-view, then she will exclude women whose children are not present.

If the number is smaller, she may consider including these women, but that deci-sion as well will depend on a number of factors. Uppermost in the mind of any inter-pretive researcher is the notion of the study's trustworthiness.

As discussed earlier, one way of establishing the trustworthiness of data is to collect data about the same thing from a number of different data sources. Data on the problems experienced by children, for example, may be collected from three data sources: (1) the children themselves, (2) their mothers, and (3) shelter staff who have observed the children. Such a triangulation of data sources allows assessment of the trustworthiness of the data obtained from any one given source. If children are not present at the shelter, then data on their problems can be obtained only from their mothers, and there will be no way to check on the "accuracy" of the data they provide.

Another way to establish trustworthiness is to ask each research participant to comment on the data gathered and the conclusions that the researcher drew from the data. Lula might want to submit the transcript of each interview to the research participant concerned to make sure that she has adequately captured what the par-ticipant was trying to say.

Then, she might want to discuss her findings with the other research participants to see if they believe that she has interpreted what they said correctly and has drawn conclusions that seem reasonable to them as well. None of this will be possible if the research participants have left the emergency shelter and disappeared before Lula has transcribed and analyzed her data.

She might, therefore, want to restrict her sample of women to those who are like-ly to remain in her shelter for a number of weeks or who will go on to a halfway house or some other traceable address. Of course, if she does this, she will lose data from women whose very transience might affect their children's problems and the way those problems are perceived.

Lula must also consider whether to interview the children and, if so, children in what age groups. She may not be skilled in interviewing young children and may feel that children under school age cannot be meaningfully interviewed at all. If there are enough women in the shelter who have older children present, she may consider restricting her sample of research participants to women whose children are, say, 10 years old or older. She will have to justify selecting age 10 instead of 8 or 12, for ex-ample, and she will lose data pertaining to the problems experienced by any excluded children.

With this in mind, she may consider enlisting the assistance of a colleague who is more skilled at eliciting information from younger children—through data collection methods such as drama, art, or play—than she is. But now she has to think about how such interview data would be analyzed and how she would integrate them with the data collected through her own personal interviews with the mothers.

The child's gender may be another consideration. Perhaps Lula has an idea that girls tend to display more internalizing problem behaviors—such as withdrawal and depression—than boys. And Lula may believe that boys tend to display more externalizing behaviors—such as hostility and aggression—than girls. She might therefore want to ensure that her study contains approximately equal numbers of girls and boys.

If she purposefully drew her sample of research participants in this way, she would have to explain that she expected to find more internalizing behaviors in girls and more externalizing behaviors in boys. This would constitute a research hypothesis, which would need to be included in the Questions and Hypotheses section and justified through the literature review. Or perhaps Lula would phrase it as a research question, simply asking whether the gender of the child was related to the type of problem behavior he or she exhibited.

Similarly, Lula might have an idea that the types of problem behaviors exhibited by children depend on their ethnic background. If she were able to conduct only a small number of interviews, for example, she might purposefully select women and children from different ethnic backgrounds to make up her sample of research participants (called *purposive sampling*, see Chapter 9). Here again, she would have to justify her choice, including a relevant research question or research hypothesis and addressing the matter in the literature review.

Lula thus has a number of factors to consider in deciding whom to include as research participants in her study. The main consideration, however, is always the willingness of the research participant to take part in the study. Like most social work populations, women in emergency shelters are an extremely vulnerable group, and it's vital to ensure that they feel freely able to refuse to participate in the study, knowing that their refusal will in no way affect the quality of the services they receive.

Similarly, the social workers within Lula's women's emergency shelter must also feel able to refuse, knowing that their refusal will not affect the terms of their employment. It is quite likely that Lula will not have the luxury of selecting her research participants in terms of the age, gender, or ethnic background of the children.

More probably, Lula will just interview those women who agree to be interviewed and who also give permission for her, or a colleague, to interview their children as well. The children will not be in a position to sign an informed consent form, as their mothers and the social workers will do, but it's still extremely important to ensure that they understand their rights with respect to refusing to take part in the study or withdrawing from it at any time.

PART 8: DATA COLLECTION

THIS PART of the interpretive research proposal provides a detailed account of how the data are going to be collected, together with a justification for using the data collection method selected rather than some other method. Lula could use focus groups, for example, rather than unstructured interviews to collect data from the women.

She could decide not to interview children, but instead to observe the children's behaviors herself, without involving a colleague or other social workers. If she does involve the shelter's social workers, she might decide just to interview them and ask how they define the children's problem behaviors and what problem behaviors they have observed in the children under study.

On the other hand, she might ask them first to define children's problem behaviors, then to purposefully observe certain children with respect to these behaviors, and finally to report their observations back to her. Whatever she decides, she must first justify her decisions and then clearly describe the methods to be used. She should state, for example, that the abused women, the shelter's workers, and the children aged 10 or over will be interviewed by herself, if that is what she has decided to do.

She should also specify where these interviews will take place, how long approximately each is expected to last, and to what degree the content will be guided by an interview schedule. She should also specify the time frame within which all the interviews will be completed and how the interviews will be recorded. Videotaping, audio taping, and taking notes during the interview all have their advantages and disadvantages, which need to be discussed.

If a colleague is to work with the younger children, for example, details of the methods used to elicit interview data from these children must be given. In addition, the colleague's credentials must be included at the beginning of the proposal, since this colleague is now a co-researcher and her experience and qualifications will affect the trustworthiness of the study's findings.

Ethical considerations that were not covered in the discussion about selecting research participants should also be addressed in this section. Should Lula obtain completed consent forms from the mothers and assent forms from their children, for example, before she asks the shelter's social workers to observe the children or to discuss their behaviors with her?

Should she share the social worker's comments with the mothers and their children and tell the social workers beforehand that this is to be done? Should she share data obtained from the children with their mothers or make it clear that such data will not be shared? Social workers might not be so honest in their comments if they know that the data will be shared: and neither might the children. In addition, children who know they are being observed might not behave as they otherwise would.

These are old dilemmas that always affect data collection methods, and Lula must specify what dilemmas she may encounter and how she plans to resolve them. It is as well to state how the mothers, children, and social workers are to be approached, and precisely what they are going to be told about her study and their own part in it. Samples of consent forms (for the mothers) and assent forms (for the children) should be included as two appendixes at the end of the proposal.

Lula's journal is also a form of data. It will include little in the way of data collected from her research participants, but it will include Lula's reactions to these data and a chronology of her study's process. Lula might therefore want to state in her proposal that she will keep a journal to record notes on the decisions she is going to make during every stage of her study, with particular reference to the study's trustworthiness.

Part 9: Data Analysis

THIS PART of the research proposal describes the way the data will be analyzed. There are usually no statistical procedures to be discussed, as there may be in a positivistic study, but there are a number of other matters. As presented in Chapter 16, a decision must be made about whether to use a software computer program to aid in the data analysis and, if so, which one. Then Lula must decide who will transcribe the interviews and how the transcripts should be formatted. She must establish a plan for her data analysis, including some plan for making journal entries.

She might want to add in her proposal that after she has analyzed the data using first- and second-level coding methods and after she has drawn conclusions, she will assess the trustworthiness of her study's findings. She will do this by documenting what she is going to do to establish credibility, transferability, dependability (consistency), and confirmability (control of biases and preconceptions).

Part 10: Limitations

ALL RESEARCH STUDIES have limitations. Some might even suggest that one of the main limitations of an interpretive study is that it is not a positivistic one, but this is simply not true. Every study is judged on how well it fulfills its own purpose, and one of the purposes of an interpretive study is usually to understand the experiences of the research participants in-depth, including experiences that are unique to them.

The purpose of Lula's study is to gain a better understanding of the problems experienced by children who have witnessed domestic violence, from the different perspectives of the mothers, their children, and the shelter's social workers, so that the needs of these children can be better identified and met.

A discussion of a study's limitations should include only factors that impede the fulfillment of this purpose. Lula's study, for example, is not limited because she did not operationally define the concepts "domestic violence" and "children witnessing domestic violence." Part of her study's purpose is to find out how the mothers and their children themselves define "domestic violence;" that is, to find out what it was that the children in her study actually witnessed, and what they and their mothers think that "witnessing" includes.

From an ideal standpoint, Lula's study is limited with respect to its transferability (generalizability, in positivistic terms). It would have been ideal if she could have constructed a sampling frame of all the children in the world who had witnessed domestic violence, taken a random sample, and interviewed all these children and their mothers in depth.

Positivistic researchers sometimes restrict their studies to manageable samples (research participants) and then generalize from the samples to the populations from which they were drawn. It is a limitation, however, if the samples did not adequately represent their populations, thus restricting the ability to generalize from the samples to their populations. It is not considered a limitation, however, that the positivist-orientated studies did not use larger populations in the first place.

Similarly, Lula does not need to apologize for having chosen to work only with those women and their children who were residents in her particular women's emergency shelter at the time she wanted to conduct her study. On the other hand, some of these women whose children had witnessed domestic violence may have refused to participate, and that would be a limitation to Lula's study: those women may have felt particularly traumatized by their children's involvement, to the point where they felt unable to discuss it. By losing them, Lula would lose a different and valuable perspective.

Another limitation to Lula's study is that many of the children who have witnessed domestic violence may have been abused themselves. It may be impossible for the mothers and/or children to distinguish between the effects of being abused themselves and the effects of witnessing the abuse. The only way Lula could deal with this is to divide her population of children who have witnessed abuse into two groups: those who have been abused, according to their mothers, and those who have not.

Of course, it might be argued that witnessing domestic violence constitutes emotional abuse. If Lula subscribes to this view, she might wish to ask the mothers specifically whether their children have been physically or sexually abused, since all the children in her sample will have been emotionally abused according to her own definition.

Nevertheless, in practical terms, Lula can form her two groups of children merely by including a question about physical or sexual abuse during her interviews with them and with their mothers. If Lula identifies this limitation early on while she is conceptualizing her study, she can include the two groups in her study's research design, mentioning the question about domestic violence in the data collection section, and noting, in the data analysis section, that she will accord each group a separate category.

Thus, her study's limitation will have ceased to be a limitation and will have become an integral part of her study. This is one of the purposes of a research design, of course: to identify and address a study's potential limitations so that they can be eliminated or at least alleviated to the greatest possible extent before the study actually starts.

Essentially, what Lula has done in thinking about children who have been abused themselves is to identify a confounding or intervening variable that might interfere with the relationship between their witnessing domestic violence and their experiencing problems, if any, due to witnessing it. Inevitably, there will be a host of other confounding variables because no one can tell for certain whether children's particular problematic behaviors are due to witnessing domestic violence or to some other factor(s). Lula will be able to conclude only that children who witnessed domestic violence experienced certain problems, not that the problems were caused by witnessing the violence in the first place.

Failure to establish causality, however, is only a limitation if the establishment of causality was one of the purposes of the study. In this case, it was not; and indeed the kind of rigorous research design needed to establish causality is usually inappropriate in an interpretive study.

Lula may find that her sample of children is not diverse enough in terms of age, gender, or ethnic background to allow her to draw conclusions about the effects of these variables on their problem behaviors. Again, this is a study limitation only if she has stated her intention to draw such a conclusion. The major limitation that Lula is likely to encounter in her study is related to the issue of credibility or truth value (internal validity, in positivistic terms).

How will she know whether the mothers and their children were truthful in relating their experiences or whether their remarks were geared more toward pleasing her or making themselves appear more socially desirable?

And if their remarks were based on memories of previous abusive behaviors, how far were those memories reliable? These are common dilemmas in both research and clinical interviews. One way to handle them is through triangulation: obtaining data on the same issue (variable) from more than one data source.

Another way is to constantly reflect on the quality of the data being obtained throughout the interview process and to record the results of these reflections in the researcher's journal. The following are examples of the kinds of questions Lula might ask herself while she is pursuing her reflections:

✲ Is the interviewee withholding something—and what should I do about it?

✲ What impact might my race, age, social status, gender, or beliefs have on my interviewee? What difference might it make that I work at the women's emergency shelter?

✲ Did what the interviewee said ring true—or did she want to please me, or look good, or protect someone else, or save herself embarrassment? Why am I feeling so stressed after this interview? Am I getting the kinds of data that are relevant for my study?

These questions might improve the quality of the data obtained by making Lula more aware of possible sources of error. Even if they do not, Lula will have shown that she has recognized her study's limitations and will take the necessary steps to deal with each limitation.

PART 11: ADMINISTRATION

THE FINAL PART of a research proposal deals with the organization and resources necessary to carry out the proposed study. Lula might want to separate her role as a researcher from her role as one of the shelter's social workers, for example, by equipping herself with a desk and computer in a room other than that which she usually uses.

If "researcher space" is not a problem, Lula will still need to think about where she should base her operations: where she will write up her notes, analyze her data, and keep the records of her interviews. Then she has to think about administrative responsibilities. Will she take on the overall responsibility for her study herself or will that fall to her supervisor? What will be the responsibilities of her colleague and the shelter's social workers? To whom will they report? What is the chain of command?

When Lula has put together the details of who does what, in what order, and who is responsible to whom, she will be in a position to consider a time frame. How long will each task take and by what date ought it to be completed? It is very easy to underestimate the amount of time needed to analyze interpretive data and to feed the information back to the research participants for their comments (member checking).

It is also easy to underestimate the time needed to write the final report. Neither of these tasks should be skimped, and it's very important to allow adequate time to complete them thoroughly—more time, that is, than the researcher believes will be necessary at the beginning of the interpretive study.

Finally, Lula must consider a budget. If she has to purchase a software computer program to help her analyze her interview data, who will pay for it? Who will cover the costs related to transcribing the data and preparing and disseminating the final report? How much money should she allocate to each of these areas? How much should she ask for overall?

When she has decided on all this, Lula will have completed her research proposal. As discussed, not all proposals are organized in this way, but all essentially contain the information that has been discussed in the preceding sections. This same information can be used to write the final research report, and it is to this that we now turn our attention.

CHECKLIST FOR EVALUATING A RESEARCH PROPOSAL

Jim Raines (2011) has provided a nice list of questions that you should ask yourself after you have completed the first draft of your interpretive research proposal:

- Are your philosophical assumptions and values well identified?

- Are the databases you searched sufficient to the research question you are trying to answer?

- Is your literature review relevant to both your research problem and population?

- Is the literature that you reviewed current at the time it was written?

- Do you use headings and subheadings to organize your ideas?

- Do you identify any differences in findings from previous research studies?

- Does your literature review support the purpose of your study?

- Is your research question crystal clear?

- Does your research question include all of the major concepts that are in your study?

- Are your conceptual definitions multidimensional?

- Will your definitions evolve as participants provide their perspectives?

- Do you have a logical rationale for doing a qualitative study in the first place?

- Is there a good fit between your research question and your data-collection method?
- Does your research study demonstrate your value awareness?
- How do you plan on using informed consent procedures?
- Does your study advance the common good of your research participants?
- Do you explain the reasons for the type of sampling method you will use?
- How do you plan on reporting your subjectivity?
- How do you plan on addressing the issue of bias by you and your research participants?
- What strategies are you going to use to improve the credibility of your study's findings?
- What strategies are you going to use to improve the transferability of your study's findings?
- What strategies are you going to use to improve the dependability of your study's findings?
- What strategies are you going to use to improve the confirmability of your study's findings
- What strategies are you going to use to increase the accuracy of your study's transcriptions?
- What is your specific plan for analyzing the data?
- How to you plan on developing categories for first-level coding?
- How to you plan on establishing relationships between categories clarified during second-level coding?
- How to you plan on developing themes and theories within your data analyses?
- How do you plan on addressing your study's limitations from an interpretivistic perspective?

❊ How do you plan on integrating your study's results with the previous literature?

❊ How do you plan on developing implications for social work theory, practice, or policy?

❊ Do you plan on making recommendations for future research studies?

WRITING INTERPRETIVE RESEARCH REPORTS

As with a positivistic research report, an interpretive one is a way of describing the research study to other people. How it's written and to some degree what it contains depend on the audience it's written for. Lula may want to present her study's findings, for example, only to the board of directors and staff of the women's emergency shelter where she works.

In this case, it will be unnecessary to describe the clinical setting (i.e., the shelter) in detail since the audience is already familiar with it. This very familiarity will also mean that Lula must take extra care to protect the identities of her research participants because personal knowledge of the women and children concerned will make it easier for her audience to identify them.

Lula will probably want to submit a written report—particularly if the shelter funded her study—but she may also want to give an oral presentation. As she imagines herself speaking the words she has written, she may find that she wants to organize the material differently or use a different style than she would if she were preparing a written report. Perhaps she will use less formal language, or include more detail about her own thoughts and feelings, or shorten the direct quotes made by the research participants.

Other possible outlets for her work include books, book chapters, journal articles, and presentations at conferences. Again, depending on the audience, she might write quite simply or she might include a wealth of technical detail, perhaps describing at length the methods she used to categorize and code her interview data.

In order to avoid writing a number of reports on the same study aimed at different audiences, she might choose to include in the main body of the report just sufficient technical detail to establish the study's trustworthiness, while putting additional technical material in appendixes for those readers who are interested. Whatever approach she chooses, it's important to remember that interpretive research studies are based on a different set of assumptions than positivistic ones.

As we know by now, the goal of an interpretive study is to understand the experiences of the study's research participants in depth, and the personal feelings of the researcher cannot be divorced from this understanding. It is therefore often appropriate to report an interpretive study using a more personal style, including both quotes from interviews with the research participants and the researcher's own reflections on the material. The aim is to produce a credible and compelling account that will be taken seriously by the reader.

The material itself can be organized in a number of ways, depending on whether it's to be presented in book form or more concisely in the form of a journal article. An article usually contains six parts: (1) an abstract, (2) an introduction, (3) a discussion of methodology, (4) a presentation of the analysis and findings, (5) a conclusion, or discussion of the significance of the study's findings, and (6) a list of references.

ABSTRACT

AN ABSTRACT is a short statement—often about 200 words—that summarizes the purpose of the study, its methodology, its findings, and its conclusions. Journal readers often decide on the basis of the abstract whether they are sufficiently interested in the topic to want to read further. Thus, the abstract must provide just enough information to enable readers to assess the relevance of the study to their own work. A statement of the study's research question, with enough context to make it meaningful, is usually followed by a brief description of the study's methodology that was used to answer the research question.

Lula might say, for example, that she interviewed eight women and eleven children who were residents in a women's emergency shelter in a small town in Alberta, Canada, plus three of the shelter's social workers. She might go on to identify the problems experienced by the children who had witnessed domestic violence, stating that these problems were derived from analyses of interview data. Finally, she would outline the practical implications from the study for social work practice, resulting from a greater understanding of the children's problems.

INTRODUCTION

THE MAIN BODY of the report begins with the introduction. It describes the *what* and *why* components of the study, which Lula has already written about in the first five parts of her research proposal. If she goes back to what she wrote before, she will see that she has already identified her research question and put it into the context of previous work through a literature review. She has discussed why she thinks this question needs to be answered, clarified her own orientation and assumptions, and commented on the interests of the women's emergency shelter or other funding organizations.

In addition, she has identified the variables relevant to her study and placed them within an appropriate framework. In short, she has already gathered the material needed for her introduction, and all that remains is to ensure that it's written in an appropriate style.

Method

After the *what* and the *why* components of the study comes the *how*. In the methods section, Lula describes how she selected her sample of research participants and how she collected her data. She would provide a justification for why she chose to use the particular sampling and data collection methods.

Again, if she looks back at her research proposal, she will see that she has already written about this in Parts 6, 7, and 8: research design, population and sample, and data collection, respectively. As before, she can use this same material, merely ensuring that it's written in a coherent and appropriate style.

Analysis and Findings

Materials on data analysis and findings are often presented together. Descriptive profiles of research participants and direct quotes from their interviews are used to answer the research question being explored. In her proposal, Lula has already written the part on data analysis in her research proposal, which stated what computer programs she was going to use (if any) and what first- and second-level coding methods.

In her research report, however, she would want to identify and provide examples of the meaning units she derived from the first-level coding process. One segment from one of her interviews might have gone as follows:

1. **Pam (sounding upset): The poor kid was never the same after that. The**

2. **first time, you know, it was just a slap on the butt that she might even**

3. **have mistaken for affection, but that second time he slammed me right**

4. **against the wall and he was still hitting my face after I landed. (pause) No**

5. mistaking that one, is there, even for a four-year old? (longer pause) No, well,

6. I guess I'm kidding myself about that first time. She knew all right. *She was*

7. *an outgoing sort of kid before, always out in the yard with friends,* but then

8. she stopped going out, and she'd follow me around, kind of, as if she was

9. afraid to let me out of her sight.

Lula may have identified three meaning units in this data segment. The first (in bold, lines 1–4) relates to what might and might not constitute domestic violence in the mind of a 4-year-old child. The second (in *italics*, lines 6 and 7) relates to the child's behavior before witnessing the abuse; and the third (underlined, lines 7–9) relates to the child's behavior after witnessing the abuse. In her report, Lula might want to identify and briefly describe the meaning units she derived from all her interviews, occasionally illustrating a unit with a direct quote to provide context and meaning.

As discussed in Chapter 16, Lula's next task in the analysis is to identify categories, assign each meaning unit to a category, and assign codes to the categories. A description of these categories will also come next in her report. She may have found, for example, that a number of mothers interpreted their child's behavior after witnessing domestic violence as indicative of fear for the mother's safety.

Instead of one large category "child's behavior after witnessing domestic violence," Lula may have chosen instead to create a number of smaller categories reflecting distinct types of behavior. One of these was "after witnessing domestic violence, child demonstrates fear for mother's safety," and Lula coded it as *CAWFMSAF,* where *C* stands for "the child," *AW* stands for "after witnessing domestic violence," and *FM-SAF* stands for "fear for mother's safety."

Depending on the number and depth of the interviews conducted, Lula may have a very large number of meaning units, and may have gone through an intricate process of refining and reorganizing in order to come up with appropriate categories. In a book, there will be room to describe all this, together with Lula's own reflections on the process; but in a journal article, running to perhaps twenty-five pages overall, Lula will have to be selective about what parts of the process she describes and how much detail she provides.

Although meaning units and categories are certainly a major part of Lula's findings, the majority of readers will be more interested in the next part of the analysis: comparing and contrasting the categories to discover the relationships between and among them in order to develop tentative themes or theories.

By doing this, Lula may have been able to finally identify the problems most commonly experienced by children who have witnessed domestic violence. She may even have been able to put the children's problems in an order of importance as perceived by the mothers and their children. In addition, she may have been able to add depth by describing the emotions related to the children's problems: perhaps guilt, on the mother's part, or anger toward the father, or a growing determination not to return to the abusive relationship. These themes will constitute the larger part of Lula's analysis and findings section, and it's to these themes that she will return in her discussion.

DISCUSSION

THIS PART of the research report presents a discussion of the study's findings. Here, Lula will point out the significance of her study's findings as they relate to the original purpose. If the purpose of her study was to inform practice by enabling the shelter's social workers to better understand the needs of children who have witnessed domestic violence, then Lula must provide a link between the children's problems and their needs resulting from those problems. She must also point out exactly how the shelter's social workers' practice might be informed.

If she has found from her study, for example, that children who witnessed domestic violence tend to experience more fear for their mothers' safety than children who had not witnessed the abuse, then a related need might be to keep the mother always within sight. Social workers within the shelter who understand this need might be more willing to tolerate children underfoot in the shelter's kitchen, for example, and might be less likely to tell Mary to "give Mom a moment's peace and go and play with Sue." These kinds of connections should be made for each theme that Lula identified in her study.

The final part of a research report often has to do with suggestions for future research studies. During the process of filling knowledge gaps by summarizing the study's findings, Lula will doubtless find other knowledge gaps that she believes ought to be filled. She might frame new research questions relating to these gaps; or she might even feel that she has sufficient knowledge to enable her to formulate research hypotheses for testing in future research studies.

REFERENCES

FINALLY, both positivistic and interpretive researchers are expected to provide a list of references that will enable the reader to locate the materials used for documentation within the report. If the manuscript is accepted for publication, the journal will certainly ask for any revisions it considers appropriate with regard to its style. It is important to note that quotes from a study's research participants do not have to be referenced, and adequate steps should always be taken to conceal their identities.

SUMMARY

The purposes of writing a research proposal are threefold: to obtain permission to do the study, to obtain funding for the study, and to encourage the author to think carefully through what he or she wants to study and what difficulties are likely to be encountered.

The proposal itself should be clear, brief, and easy to read. Although proposals may be differently organized depending on who is to receive them, the information included in most proposals may be logically set out under general headings identified in this chapter. The information contained under most of these headings can also be used to write the research report. Because the proposal outlines *what will be done* and the research report describes *what was done*, the proposal and the report should parallel each other closely, unless the implementation of the study differed widely from what was planned.

Study Questions for Chapter 18

— First, answer each question only AFTER you have read the chapter.

— Second, indicate how comfortable you were in answering each question on a 5-point scale:

1	2	3	4	5
Very uncomfortable	Somewhat uncomfortable	Neutral	Somewhat comfortable	Very comfortable

If you rated any question between 1–3, please reread the section of the chapter where the information for the question can be found. If you're still uncomfortable answering the question, talk with your instructor and/or your classmates for more clarification.

Questions	Degree of comfort? (Circle one number)
1. In your own words, describe what an interpretive research proposal is all about. Provide a social work example throughout your discussion that illustrates your main points.	1 2 3 4 5
2. Discuss the role that Part 1 plays within an interpretive research proposal. Write a hypothetical Part 1 of an interpretive research proposal with a topic area of your choice.	1 2 3 4 5
3. Discuss the role that Part 2 plays within an interpretive research proposal. Write a hypothetical Part 2 of an interpretive research proposal with a topic area of your choice.	1 2 3 4 5
4. Discuss the role that Part 3 plays within an interpretive research proposal. Write a hypothetical Part 3 of an interpretive research proposal with a topic area of your choice.	1 2 3 4 5

5. Discuss the role that Part 4 plays within an interpretive research proposal. Write a hypothetical Part 4 of an interpretive research proposal with a topic area of your choice.	1 2 3 4 5
6. Discuss the role that Part 5 plays within an interpretive research proposal. Write a hypothetical Part 5 of an interpretive research proposal with a topic area of your choice.	1 2 3 4 5
7. Discuss the role that Part 6 plays within an interpretive research proposal. Write a hypothetical Part 6 of an interpretive research proposal with a topic area of your choice.	1 2 3 4 5
8. Discuss the role that Part 7 plays within an interpretive research proposal. Write a hypothetical Part 7 of an interpretive research proposal with a topic area of your choice.	1 2 3 4 5
9. Discuss the role that Part 8 plays within an interpretive research proposal. Write a hypothetical Part 8 of an interpretive research proposal with a topic area of your choice.	1 2 3 4 5
10. Discuss the role that Part 9 plays within an interpretive research proposal. Write a hypothetical Part 9 of an interpretive research proposal with a topic area of your choice.	1 2 3 4 5
11. Discuss the role that Part 10 plays within an interpretive research proposal. Write a hypothetical Part 10 of an interpretive research proposal with a topic area of your choice.	1 2 3 4 5
12. Discuss the role that Part 11 plays within an interpretive research proposal. Write a hypothetical Part 11 of an interpretive research proposal with a topic area of your choice.	1 2 3 4 5
13. List the 32 criteria that are used to evaluate an interpretive research proposal. Now discuss why each criterion is important to consider when evaluating the proposal. Provide a social work example throughout your discussion to illustrate your main points.	1 2 3 4 5
14. In your own words, describe what an interpretive research report is all about. Provide a social work example throughout your discussion that illustrates your main points.	1 2 3 4 5

Assessing Your Self-Efficacy for Chapter 18

AFTER you have read the chapter AND have completed all the study questions, please indicate how knowledgeable you feel you are for each concept listed below.

1 Very uncomfortable	2 Somewhat uncomfortable	3 Neutral	4 Somewhat comfortable	5 Very comfortable

Major Concepts in Chapter	Knowledge Level? (Circle one number)
1. The eleven common sections of an interpretive social work research proposal	1 2 3 4 5
2. The Research Topic section of an interpretive social work research proposal	1 2 3 4 5
3. The Literature Review section of an interpretive social work research proposal	1 2 3 4 5
4. The Conceptual Framework section of an interpretive social work research proposal	1 2 3 4 5
5. The Questions and Hypotheses section of an interpretive social work research proposal	1 2 3 4 5
6. The Operational Definitions section of an interpretive social work research proposal	1 2 3 4 5
7. The Research Design section of an interpretive social work research proposal	1 2 3 4 5
8. The Population and Sample section of an interpretive social work research proposal	1 2 3 4 5
9. The Data Collection section of an interpretive social work research proposal	1 2 3 4 5
10. The Data Analysis section of an interpretive social work research proposal	1 2 3 4 5
11. The Limitations section of an interpretive social work research proposal	1 2 3 4 5

12.	The Administration section of an interpretive social work research proposal	1 2 3 4 5
13.	The 35 criteria used to evaluate an interpretive social work research proposal	1 2 3 4 5
14.	The six common sections of an interpretive social work research report	1 2 3 4 5
15.	The Abstract section of an interpretive social work research report	1 2 3 4 5
16.	The Introduction section of an interpretive social work research report	1 2 3 4 5
17.	The Methods section of an interpretive social work research report	1 2 3 4 5
18.	The Analysis and Findings section of an interpretive social work research report	1 2 3 4 5
19.	The Discussion section of an interpretive social work research report	1 2 3 4 5
20.	The References section of an interpretive social work research report	1 2 3 4 5
21.	The 35 criteria used to evaluate an interpretive social work research proposal	1 2 3 4 5

Add up your scores (Minimum = 21, Maximum = 105)	Total score =

A   90 — 105 = Social Work Manager in the making.
B   80 — 89   = Social Work Supervisor.
C   70 — 79   = Social Work Practitioner.
D   21 — 69   = Case Aide. Reread the chapter and redo the study questions.

Credits

The way to get things done is not to mind who gets the credit for doing them.
~ Benjamin Jowett

BOXES: 1.1: From *Calgary Herald*, "Another kidnap bid has parents nervous," September 6, 1991, p. 6; 2.1 & 2.3: From William M.K. Trochim, *Research Methods Knowledge Base*. Retrieved July 22, 2010 at: www.socialresearch methods.net; 2.2: From *Calgary Herald*, "Show ignores Native stereotype," September 6, 1991, Section B, p. 6; 6.1: From Silverman, D. (2010). *Qualitative research* (3rd ed.). Thousand Oaks, CA: Sage; 7.1 & 7.2: From Kyte, N.S., & Bostwick, G.J., Jr. (1981). Measurement. In R.M. Grinnell, Jr. (Ed.), *Social work research and evaluation*. Itasca, IL: F.E. Peacock Publishers; 7.3, & 9.1: From McKinney, R. (2011). Research with minority and disadvantaged groups. In R.M. Grinnell, Jr., & Y.A. Unrau (Eds.). *Social work research and evaluation: Foundations of evidence-based practice* (10th ed.). New York: Oxford University Press; and, 11.1–11.3: From *Web Center for Social Research Methods*. Retrieved on July 22, 2010 at: www.socialresearch methods.net.

FIGURES: 1.3: From Duehn, W.D. (1985). Practice and research. In R.M. Grinnell, Jr. (Ed.), *Social work research and evaluation* (2nd ed.). Itasca, IL: F.E. Peacock; 7.1 &

7.1a: From Walter W. Hudson. Copyright © 1993 by WALMYR Publishing Company; 7.2: From Kyte, N.S., & Bostwick, G.J., Jr. (1981). Measurement. In R.M. Grinnell, Jr. (Ed.), *Social work research and evaluation.* Itasca, IL: F.E. Peacock Publishers; 8.1: From Reid, P.N., & Gundlach, J.H. (1983). A scale for the measurement of consumer satisfaction with social services, *Journal of Social Service Research*, 7, 37–54; 10.8–10.10 (and related text): From Polster, R., & Lynch, M. (1981). Single-subject designs. In R.M. Grinnell, Jr. (Ed.), *Social work research and evaluation.* Itasca: IL: F.E. Peacock Publishers; and 15.3 & 15.4: From Beless, D.W. (1981). Univariate analysis. In R.M. Grinnell, Jr. (Ed.), *Social work research and evaluation.* Itasca, IL: F.E. Peacock Publishers.

TABLES: 14.1: From, Debra W. Haffner and Eva S. Goldfarb. "But does it work? Improving evaluations of sexuality education," SIECUS Report, vol. 25, no. 6 (August/September, 1997).

CHAPTERS: 2: (Pages 64–77) by Vivienne Bozalek and Nelleke Bak; 3: (Pages 93–109) by Andre Ivanoff and Betty Blythe; 4: by Carol Ing; and 15 & 17: From Williams, M., Tutty, L.M., & Grinnell, R.M., Jr. (1995). *Research in social work: An introduction* (2nd ed.). Itasca, IL: F.E. Peacock.

Glossary

In three words I can sum up everything I've learned about life: it goes on.
~ Robert Frost

Abstracting indexing services Providers of specialized reference tools that make it possible to find information quickly and easily, usually through subject headings and/or author approaches.

Abstracts Reference materials consisting of citations and brief descriptive summaries from positivist and interpretive research studies.

Accountability A system of responsibility in which program administrators account for all program activities by answering to the demands of a program's stakeholders and by justifying the program's expenditures to the satisfaction of its stakeholders.

Aggregated case-level evaluation designs The collection of a number of case-level evaluations to determine the degree to which a program objective has been met.

Aggregate-level data Derived from micro-level data, aggregate-level data are grouped so that the characteristics of individual units of analysis are no longer identifiable; for example, the variable "gross national income" is an aggregation of data about individual incomes.

Alternate-forms method A method for establishing reliability of a measuring instrument by administering, in succession, equivalent forms of the same instrument to the same group of research participants.

Alternative hypothesis See Rival hypothesis.

Analytical memos Notes made by the researcher in reference to interpretive data that raise questions or make comments about meaning units and categories identified in a transcript.

Analytic generalization The type of generalizability associated with case studies; the research findings of case studies are not assumed to fit another case no matter how apparently similar; rather, research findings are tested to see if they do in fact fit; used as working hypotheses to test practice principles.

Annual report A detailed account or statement describing a program's processes and results over a given year; usually produced at the end of a fiscal year.

Antecedent variable A variable that precedes the introduction of one or more dependent variables.

Antiquarianism An interest in past events without reference to their importance or significance for the present; the reverse of presentism.

A **Phase** In case-level evaluation designs, a phase (*A* Phase) in which the baseline measurement of the target problem is established before the intervention (*B* Phase) is implemented.

Applied research approach A search for practical and applied research results that can be utilized in actual social work practice situations; complementary to the pure research approach.

Area probability sampling A form of cluster sampling that uses a three-stage process to provide the means to carry out a research study when no comprehensive list of the population can be compiled.

Assessment-related case study A type of case study that generates knowledge

about specific clients and their situations; focuses on the perspectives of the study's participants.

Audit trail The documentation of critical steps in an interpretive research study, which allows an independent reviewer to examine and verify the steps in the research process and the conclusions of the research study.

Authority The reliance on authority figures to tell us what is true; one of the ways of knowing.

Availability sampling See Convenience sampling.

Axes Straight horizontal and vertical lines in a graph upon which values of a measurement, or the corresponding frequencies, are plotted.

Back-translation The process of translating an original document into a second language, then having an independent translator conduct a subsequent translation of the first translation back into the language of origin; the second translation is then compared with the original document for equivalency.

Baseline A period of time, usually three or four data collection periods, in which the level of the client's target problem is measured while no intervention is carried out; designated as the *A* Phase in single-system designs (case-level designs).

Between research methods approach Triangulation by using different research methods available in *both* the interpretive and the positivist research approaches in a single research study.

Bias Not neutral; an inclination to some form of prejudice or preconceived position.

Biased sample A sample unintentionally selected in such a way that some members of the population are more likely than others to be picked for sample membership.

Binomial effect size display (BESD) A technique for interpreting the *r* value in a meta-analysis by converting it into a 2 by 2 table displaying magnitude of effect.

Biography Tells the story of one individual's life, often suggesting what the person's influence was on social, political, or intellectual developments of the times.

B **Phase** In case-level evaluation designs, the intervention phase, which may or may not include simultaneous measurements.

Case The basic unit of social work practice, whether it be an individual, a couple, a family, an agency, a community, a county, a state, or a country.

Case-level evaluation designs Designs in which data are collected about a single-client system—an individual, group, or community—in order to evaluate the outcome of an intervention for the client system; a form of appraisal that monitors change for individual clients; designs in which data are collected about a single-client system—an individual, group, or community—in order to evaluate the outcome of an intervention for the client system; also called single-system research designs.

Case study Using research approaches to investigate a research question or hypothesis relating to a specific case; used to develop theory and test hypotheses; an in-depth form of research in which data are gathered and analyzed about an individual unit of analysis, person, city, event, society, etc.; it allows more intensive analysis of specific details; the disadvantage is that it is hard to use the results to generalize to other cases.

Categories Groupings of related meaning units that are given one name; used to organize, summarize, and interpret qualitative data; categories in an interpretive study can change throughout the data analysis process, and the number of categories in a given study depends upon the breadth and depth the researcher aims for in the analysis.

Category In an interpretive data analysis, an aggregate of meaning units that share a common feature.

Category saturation The point in a qualitative data analysis when all identified meaning units fit easily into the existing categorization scheme and no new categories emerge; the point at which first-level coding ends.

Causality A relationship of cause and effect; the effect will invariably occur when the cause is present.

Causal relationship A relationship between two variables for which we can state that the presence of, or absence of, one variable determines the presence of, or absence of, the other variable.

CD-ROM sources Computerized retrieval systems that allow searching for indexes and abstracts stored on compact computer discs (CDs).

Census data Data from the survey of an entire population in contrast to a survey of a sample.

Citation A brief identification of a reference that includes name of author(s), title, source, page numbers, and year of publication.

Classical experimental design An explanatory research design with randomly assigned experimental and control groups in which the dependent variable is measured before and after the treatment (the independent variable) for both groups, but only the experimental group receives the treatment (the dependent variable).

Client system *An* individual client, *a* couple, *a* family, *a* group, *an* organization, or *a* community that can be studied with case- and program-level evaluation designs and with positivist and interpretive research approaches.

Closed-ended questions Items in a measuring instrument that require respondents to select one of several response categories provided; also known as fixed-alternative questions.

Cluster diagram An illustration of a conceptual classification scheme in which the researcher draws and labels circles for each theme that emerges from the data; the circles are organized in a way to depict the relationships between themes.

Cluster sampling A multistage probability sampling procedure in which the population is divided into groups (or clusters) and the groups, rather than the individuals, are selected for inclusion in the sample.

Code The label assigned to a category or theme in a qualitative data analysis; shortened versions of the actual category or theme label; used as markers in a qualitative data analysis; usually no longer than eight characters in length and can use a combination of letters, symbols, and numbers.

Codebook A device used to organize qualitative data by applying labels and descriptions that draw distinctions between different parts of the data that have been collected.

Coding (1) In data analysis, translating data from respondents onto a form that can be read by a computer; (2) in interpretive research, marking the text with codes for content categories.

Coding frame A specific framework that delineates what data are to be coded and how they are to be coded in order to prepare them for analyses.

Coding sheets In a literature review, a sheet used to record for each research study the complete reference, research design, measuring instrument(s), population and sample, outcomes, and other significant features of the study.

Cohort study A longitudinal survey design that uses successive random samples to monitor how the characteristics of a specific group of people, who share certain characteristics or experiences (cohorts), change over time.

Collaterals Professionals or staff members who serve as indigenous observers in the data collection process.

Collective biographies Studies of the characteristics of groups of people who lived during a past period and had some major factor in common.

Collectivist culture Societies that stress interdependence and seek the welfare and survival of the group above that of the individual; collectivist cultures are characterized by a readiness to be influenced by others, preference for conformity, and cooperation in relationships.

Comparative rating scale A rating scale in which respondents are asked to compare an individual person, concept, or situation with others.

Comparative research design The study of more than one event, group, or society to isolate explanatory factors; there are two basic strategies in comparative research: (1) the study of elements that differ in many ways but that have some major factor in common, and (2) the study of elements that are highly similar but different in some important aspect, such as modern industrialized nations that have different health insurance systems.

Comparison group A nonexperimental group to which research participants have not been randomly assigned for purposes of comparison with the experimental group. Not to be confused with control group.

Comparison group posttest-only design A descriptive research design with two groups, experimental and comparison, in which the dependent variable is measured once for both groups, and only the experimental group receives the treatment (the independent variable).

Comparison group pretest-posttest design A descriptive research design with two groups, experimental and comparison, in which the dependent variable is measured before and after the treatment for both groups, but only the experimental group receives the treatment.

Compensation Attempts by researchers to compensate for the lack of treatment for control group members by administering it to them; a threat to internal validity.

Compensatory rivalry Motivation of control group members to compete with experimental group members; a threat to internal validity.

Completeness One of the four criteria for evaluating research hypotheses.

Complete observer A term describing one of four possible research roles on a continuum of participant observation research; the complete observer acts simply as an observer and does not participate in the events at hand.

Complete participant The complete participant is at the far end of the continuum from the complete observer in participant observation research; this research role is characterized by total involvement.

Comprehensive qualitative review A nonstatistical synthesis of representative research studies relevant to a research problem, question, or hypothesis.

Computerized retrieval systems Systems in which abstracts, indexes, and subject bibliographies are incorporated in computerized databases to facilitate information retrieval.

Concept An understanding, an idea, or a mental image; a way of viewing and categorizing objects, processes, relations, and events.

Conceptual classification system The strategy for conceiving how units of qualitative data relate to each other; the method used to depict patterns that emerge from the various coding levels in qualitative data.

Conceptual framework A frame of reference that serves to guide a research study and is developed from theories, findings from a variety of other research studies, and the author's personal experiences and values.

Conceptualization The process of selecting the specific concepts to include in positivist and interpretive research studies.

Conceptual validity See Construct validity.

Concurrent validity A form of criterion validity that is concerned with the ability of a measuring instrument to predict accurately an individual's status by comparing concurrent ratings (or scores) on one or more measuring instruments.

Confidentiality An ethical consideration in research whereby anonymity of research participants is safeguarded by ensuring that raw data are not seen by anyone other than the research team and that data presented have no identifying marks.

Confounding variable A variable operating in a specific situation in such a way that its effects cannot be separated; the effects of an extraneous variable thus confound the interpretation of a research study's findings.

Consistency Holding steadfast to the same principles and procedures in the qualitative data analysis process.

Constant A concept that does not vary and does not change; a characteristic that has the same value for all research participants or events in a research study.

Constant comparison A technique used to categorize qualitative data; it begins after the complete set of data has been examined and meaning units have been identified; each unit is classified as similar or different from the others; similar meaning units are lumped into the same category and classified by the same code.

Constant error Systematic error in measurement; error due to factors that consistently or systematically affect the variable being measured and that are concerned with the relatively stable qualities of respondents to a measuring instrument.

Construct See Concept.

Construct validity The degree to which a measuring instrument successfully measures a theoretical construct; the degree to which explanatory concepts account for variance in the scores of an instrument; also referred to as conceptual validity in meta-analyses.

Content analysis A data collection method in which communications are analyzed in a systematic, objective, and quantitative manner to produce new data.

Content validity The extent to which the content of a measuring instrument reflects the concept that is being measured and in fact measures that concept and not another.

Contextual detail The particulars of the environment in which the case (or unit of analysis) is embedded; provides a basis for understanding and interpreting case study data and results.

Contradictory evidence Identifying themes and categories that raise questions about the conclusions reached at the end of qualitative data analysis; outliers or extreme cases that are inconsistent or contradict the conclusions drawn from qualitative data; also called negative evidence.

Contributing partner A social work role in which the social worker joins forces with others who perform different roles in positivist and interpretive research studies.

Control group A group of randomly assigned research participants in a research study who do not receive the experimental treatment and are used for comparison purposes. Not to be confused with comparison group.

Control variable A variable, other than the independent variable(s) of primary interest, whose effects we can determine; an intervening variable that has been controlled for in the study's research design.

Convenience sampling A nonprobability sampling procedure that relies on the closest and most available research participants to constitute a sample.

Convergent validity The degree to which different measures of a construct yield similar results, or converge.

Correlated variables Variables whose values are associated; values of one variable tend to be associated in a systematic way with values in the others.

Cost-benefit analysis An analytical procedure that not only determines the costs of the program itself but also considers the monetary benefits of the program's effects.

Cost-effectiveness analysis An analytical procedure that assesses the costs of the program itself; the monetary benefits of the program's effects are not assessed.

Cover letter A letter to respondents or research participants that is written under the official letterhead of the sponsoring organization and describes the research study and its purpose.

Credibility The trustworthiness of both the steps taken in qualitative data analysis and the conclusions reached.

Criterion validity The degree to which the scores obtained on a measuring instrument are comparable to scores from an external criterion believed to measure the same concept.

Criterion variable The variable whose values are predicted from measurements of the predictor variable.

Cross-cultural comparisons Research studies that include culture as a major variable; studies that compare two or more diverse cultural groups.

Cross-sectional research design A survey research design in which data are collected to indicate characteristics of a sample or population at a particular moment in time.

Cross-tabulation table A simple table showing the joint frequency distribution of two or more nominal level variables.

Cultural encapsulation The assumption that differences between groups represent some deficit or pathology.

Culturally equivalent Similarity in the meaning of a construct between two cultures.

Cultural relativity The belief that human thought and action can be judged only from the perspective of the culture out of which they have grown.

Cut-and-paste method A method of analyzing qualitative data whereby the researcher cuts segments of the typed transcript and sorts these cuttings into relevant groupings; it can be done manually or with computer assistance.

Data The numbers, words, or scores, generated by positivist and interpretive research studies; the word *data* is plural.

Data analyses The process of turning data into information; the process of reviewing, summarizing, and organizing isolated facts (data) such that they formulate a meaningful response to a research question.

Data archive A place where many data sets are stored and from which data can be accessed.

Data coding Translating data from one language or format into another, usually to make it readable for a computer.

Data collection method Procedures specifying techniques to be employed, measuring instruments to be utilized, and activities to be conducted in implementing a positivist or interpretive research study.

Data set A collection of related data items, such as the answers given by respondents to all the questions in a survey.

Data source The provider of the data, whether it be primary—the original source—or secondary—an intermediary between the research participant and the researcher analyzing the data.

Datum Singular of data.

Decision-making rule A statement that we use (in testing a hypothesis) to choose between the null hypothesis; indicates the range(s) of values of the observed statistic that leads to the rejection of the null hypothesis.

Deduction A conclusion about a specific case(s) based on the assumption that it shares a characteristic with an entire class of similar cases.

Deductive reasoning Forming a theory, making a deduction from the theory, and testing this deduction, or hypothesis, against reality; in research, applied to theory in order to arrive at a hypothesis that can be tested; a method of reasoning whereby a conclusion about specific cases is reached based on the assumption that they share characteristics with an entire class of similar cases.

Demand needs When needs are defined by only those individuals who indicate that they feel or perceive the need themselves.

Demographic data Vital and social facts that describe a sample or a population.

Demoralization Feelings of deprivation among control group members that may cause them to drop out of a research study; a threat to internal validity.

Dependability The soundness of both the steps taken in a qualitative data analysis and the conclusions reached.

Dependent events Events that influence the probability of occurrence of each other.

Dependent variable A variable that is dependent on, or caused by, another variable; an outcome variable, which is not manipulated directly but is measured to determine whether the independent variable has had an effect.

Derived scores Raw scores of research participants, or groups, converted in such a way that meaningful comparisons with other individuals, or groups, are possible.

Descriptive research Research studies undertaken to increase precision in the definition of knowledge in a problem area where less is known than at the explanatory level; situated in the middle of the knowledge continuum.

Descriptive statistics Methods used for summarizing and describing data in a clear and precise manner.

Design bias Any effect that systematically distorts the outcome of a research study so that the study's results are not representative of the phenomenon under investigation.

Determinism A contention in positivist research studies that only an event that is true over time and place and that will occur independent of beliefs about it (a predetermined event) permits the generalization of a study's findings; one of the four main limitations of the positivist research approach.

Deterministic causation When a particular effect appears, the associated cause is always present; no other variables influence the relationship between cause and effect; the link between an independent variable that brings about the occurrence of the dependent variable every time.

Dichotomous variable A variable that can take on only one of two values.

Differential scale A questionnaire-type scale in which respondents are asked to consider questions representing different positions along a continuum and to select those with which they agree.

Differential selection A potential lack of equivalency among preformed groups of research participants; a threat to internal validity.

Diffusion of treatments Problems that may occur when experimental and control group members talk to each other about a research study; a threat to internal validity.

d **Index** A measure of effect size in a meta-analysis.

Directional hypothesis See One-tailed hypotheses.

Directional test See One-tailed hypotheses.

Direct observation An obtrusive data collection method in which the focus is entirely on the behaviors of a group, or persons, being observed.

Direct observation notes The first level of field notes, usually chronologically organized, which contain a detailed description of what was seen and heard; they may also include summary notes made after an interview.

Direct relationship A relationship between two variables such that high values of one variable are found with high values of the second variable, and vice versa.

Discriminant validity The degree to which a construct can be empirically differentiated, or discriminated from other constructs.

Divergent validity The extent to which a measuring instrument differs from other instruments that measure unrelated constructs.

Double-barreled question A question in a measuring instrument that contains two questions in one, usually joined by an *and* or an *or*.

Duration recording A method of data collection that includes direct observation of the target problem and recording of the length of time each occurrence lasts within a specified observation period.

Ecological fallacy An error of reasoning committed by coming to conclusions about individuals based only on data about groups.

Edge coding Adding a series of blank lines on the right side of the response category in a measuring instrument to aid in processing the data.

Effect size In meta-analysis, the most widely used measure of the dependent variable; the effect size statistic provides a measure of the magnitude of the relationship found between the variables of interest and allows for the computation of summary statistics that apply to the analysis of all the studies considered as a whole.

Empirical Knowledge derived from one of the ways of knowing.

Error of central tendency A measurement error due to the tendency of observers to rate respondents in the middle of a variable's value range, rather than consistently too high or too low.

Error of measurement See Measurement error.

Ethical research project The systematic inquiry into a problem area in an effort to discover new knowledge or test existing ideas; the research study is conducted in accordance with professional standards.

Ethics in research Positivist and interpretive data that are collected and analyzed with careful attention to their accuracy, fidelity to logic, and respect for the feelings and rights of research participants; one of the four criteria for evaluating research problem areas *and* formulating research questions out of the problem areas.

Ethnicity A term that implies a common ancestry and cultural heritage and encompasses customs, values, beliefs, and behaviors.

Ethnocentricity Assumptions about normal behavior that are based on one's own cultural framework without taking cultural relativity into account; the failure to acknowledge alternative worldviews.

Ethnograph A computer software program that is designed for qualitative data analyses.

Ethnographic A form of content analysis used to document and explain the communication of meaning, as well as to verify theoretical relationships; any of several methods of describing social or cultural life based on direct, systematic observation, such as becoming a participant in a social system.

Ethnography The systematic study of human cultures and the similarities and dissimilarities between them.

Ethnomethodology Pioneered by Harold Garfinkel, a method of research that focuses on the common-sense understanding of social life held by ordinary people (the ethos), usually as discovered through participant observation; often the observer's own methods of making sense of the situation become the object of investigation.

Evaluation A form of appraisal using valid and reliable research methods; there are numerous types of evaluations geared to produce data that in turn produce information that helps in the decision-making process; data from evaluations are used to develop quality programs and services.

Evaluative research designs Case- and program-level research designs that apply various research designs and data collection methods to find out whether an intervention (or treatment) worked at the case level and whether a social work program worked at the program level.

Existing documents Physical records left over from the past.

Existing statistics Previously calculated numerical summaries of data that are publicly accessible.

Experience and intuition Learning what is true through personal past experiences and intuition; two of the ways of knowing.

Experiment A research study in which we have control over the levels of the independent variable and over the assignment of research participants, or objects, to different experimental conditions.

Experimental designs (1) Explanatory research designs or "ideal experiments"; (2) case-level research designs that examine the question, "Did the client system improve because of social work intervention?"

Experimental group In an experimental research design, the group of research participants exposed to the manipulation of the independent variable; also referred to as a treatment group.

Explanatory research "Ideal" research studies undertaken to infer cause-effect and directional relationships in areas where a number of substantial research findings are already in place; situated at the top end of the knowledge continuum.

Exploratory research Research studies undertaken to gather data in areas of inquiry where very little is already known; situated at the lowest end of the knowledge continuum. See Nonexperimental design.

External evaluation An evaluation that is conducted by someone who does not have any connection with the program; usually an evaluation that is requested by the agency's funding sources; this type of evaluation complements an in-house evaluation.

External validity The extent to which the findings of a research study can be generalized outside the specific research situation.

Extraneous variables See Rival hypothesis.

Face validity The degree to which a measurement has self-evident meaning and measures what it appears to measure.

Feasibility One of the four criteria for evaluating research problem areas *and* formulating research questions out of the problem areas.

Feedback When data and information are returned to the persons who originally provided or collected them; used for informed decision making at the case and program levels; a basic principle underlying the design of evaluations.

Field notes A record, usually written, of events observed by a researcher; the notes are taken as the study proceeds, and later they are used for analyses.

Field research Research conducted in a real-life setting, not in a laboratory; the researcher neither creates nor manipulates anything within the study, but observes it.

Field-tested The pilot of an instrument or research method in conditions equivalent to those that will be encountered in the research study.

File drawer problem (1) In literature searches or reviews, the difficulty in locating studies that have not been published or are not easily retrievable; (2) in meta-analyses, errors in effect size due to reliance on published articles showing statistical significance.

Firsthand data Data obtained from people who directly experience the problem being studied.

First-level coding A process of identifying meaning units in a transcript, organizing the meaning units into categories, and assigning names to the categories.

Flexibility The degree to which the design and procedures of a research study can be changed to adapt to contextual demands of the research setting.

Focus group interview A group of people brought together to talk about their lives and experiences in free-flowing, open-ended discussions that usually focus on a single topic.

Formative evaluation A type of evaluation that focuses on obtaining data that are helpful in planning the program and in improving its implementation and performance.

Frequency recording A method of data collection by direct observations in which each occurrence of the target problem is recorded during a specified observation period.

Fugitive data Informal information found outside regular publishing channels.

Gaining access A term used in interpretive research to describe the process of engagement and relationship development between the researcher and the research participants.

Generalizable explanation evaluation model An evaluation model whose proponents believe that many solutions are possible for any one social problem and that the effects of programs will differ under different conditions.

Generalizing results Extending or applying the findings of a research study to individuals or situations not directly involved in the original research study; the ability to extend or apply the findings of a research study to subjects or situations that were not directly investigated.

Goal Attainment Scale (GAS) A modified measurement scale used to evaluate case or program outcomes.

Government documents Printed documents issued by local, state, and federal governments; such documents include reports of legislative committee hearings and investigations, studies commissioned by legislative commissions and executive agencies, statistical compilations such as the census, the regular and special reports of executive agencies, and much more.

Grand tour questions Queries in which research participants are asked to provide wide-ranging background information; mainly used in interpretive research studies.

Graphic rating scale A rating scale that describes an attribute on a continuum from one extreme to the other, with points of the continuum ordered in equal intervals and then assigned values.

Grounded theory A final outcome of the interpretive research process that is reached when the insights are grounded on observations and the conclusions seem to be firm.

Group evaluation designs Evaluation designs that are conducted with groups of cases for the purpose of assessing to what degree program objectives have been achieved.

Group research designs Research designs conducted with two or more groups of cases, or research participants, for the purpose of answering research questions or testing hypotheses.

Halo effect A measurement error due to the tendency of an observer to be influenced by a favorable trait(s) of a research participant(s).

Hawthorne effect Effects on research participants' behaviors or attitudes attributable to their knowledge that they are taking part in a research study; a reactive effect; a threat to external validity.

Heterogeneity of respondents The extent to which a research participant differs from other research participants.

Heuristic A theory used to stimulate creative thought and scientific activity.

Historical research The process by which we study the past; a method of inquiry that attempts to explain past events based on surviving artifacts.

History in research design The possibility that events not accounted for in a research design may alter the second and subsequent measurements of the dependent variable; a threat to internal validity.

Homogeneity of respondents The extent to which a research participant is similar to other research participants.

Hypothesis A theory-based prediction of the expected results of a research study; a tentative explanation that a relationship between or among variables exists.

Hypothetico-deductive method A hypothesis-testing approach that a hypothesis is derived on the deductions based from a theory.

Ideographic research Research studies that focus on unique individuals or situations.

Implementation of a program The action of carrying out a program in the way that it was designed.

Independent variable A variable that is not dependent on another variable but is believed to cause or determine changes in the dependent variable; an antecedent variable that is directly manipulated in order to assess its effect on the dependent variable.

Index A group of individual measures that, when combined, are meant to indicate some more general characteristic.

Indigenous observers People who are naturally a part of the research participants' environment and who perform the data collection function; includes relevant others (e.g., family members, peers) and collaterals (e.g., social workers, staff members).

Indirect measures A substitute variable, or a collection of representative variables, used when there is no direct measurement of the variable of interest; also called a proxy variable.

Individualism A way of living that stresses independence, personal rather than group objectives, competition, and power in relationships; achievement measured through success of the individual as opposed to the group.

Individual synthesis Analysis of published studies related to the subject under study.

Inductive reasoning Building on specific observations of events, things, or processes to make inferences or more general statements; in research studies, applied to data collection and research results to make generalizations to see if they fit a theory; a method of reasoning whereby a conclusion is reached by building on specific observations of events, things, or processes to make inferences or more general statements.

Inferential statistics Statistical methods that make it possible to draw tentative conclusions about the population based on observations of a sample selected from that population and, furthermore, to make a probability statement about those conclusions to aid in their evaluation.

Information anxiety A feeling attributable to a lack of understanding of information, being overwhelmed by the amount of information to be accessed and understood, or not knowing whether certain information exists.

Informed consent Signed statements obtained from research participants before the initiation of the research study to inform them what their participation entails and that they are free to decline participation.

In-house evaluation An evaluation that is conducted by someone who works within a program; usually an evaluation for the purpose of promoting better client services; also known as an internal evaluation; this type of evaluation complements an external evaluation.

Institutional review boards (IRBs) Boards set up by institutions in order to protect research participants and to ensure that ethical issues are recognized and responded to in a study's research design.

Instrumentation Weaknesses of a measuring instrument, such as invalidity, unreliability, improper administration, or mechanical breakdowns; a threat to internal validity.

Integration Combining evaluation and day-to-day practice activities to develop a complete approach to client service delivery; a basic principle underlying the design of evaluations.

Interaction effects Effects produced by the combination of two or more threats to internal validity.

Internal consistency The extent to which the scores on two comparable halves of the same measuring instrument are similar; inter-item consistency.

Internal validity The extent to which it can be demonstrated that the independent variable within a research study is the only cause of change in the dependent variable; overall soundness of the experimental procedures and measuring instruments.

Interobserver reliability The stability or consistency of observations made by two or more observers at one point in time.

Interpretive notes Notes on the researcher's interpretations of events that are kept separate from the record of the facts noted as direct observations.

Interpretive research approach Research studies that focus on the facts of nature as they occur under natural conditions and emphasize qualitative description and generalization; a process of discovery sensitive to holistic and ecological issues; a research approach that is complementary to the positivist research approach.

Interquartile range A number that measures the variability of a data set; the distance between the 75th and 25th percentiles.

Interrater reliability The degree to which two or more independent observers,

coders, or judges produce consistent results.

Interrupted time-series design An explanatory research design in which there is only one group of research participants and the dependent variable is measured repeatedly before and after treatment; used in case- and program-evaluation designs.

Interval level of measurement The level of measurement with an arbitrarily chosen zero point that classifies its values on an equally spaced continuum.

Interval recording A method of data collection that involves a continuous direct observation of an individual during specified observation periods divided into equal time intervals.

Intervening variable See Rival hypothesis.

Interview data Isolated facts that are gathered when research participants respond to carefully constructed research questions; data, which are in the form of words, are recorded by transcription.

Interviewing A conversation with a purpose.

Interview schedule A measuring instrument used to collect data in face-to-face and telephone interviews.

Intraobserver reliability The stability of observations made by a single observer at several points in time.

Intrusion into lives of research participants The understanding that specific data collection methods can have negative consequences for research participants; a criterion for selecting a data collection method.

Itemized rating scales A measuring instrument that presents a series of statements that respondents or observers rank in different positions on a specific attribute.

Journal A written record of the process of an interpretive research study. Journal entries are made on an ongoing basis throughout the study and include study procedures as well as the researcher's reactions to emerging issues and concerns during the data analysis process.

Key informants A subpopulation of research participants who seem to know much more about "the situation" than other research participants.

Knowledge base A body of knowledge and skills specific to a certain discipline.

Knowledge creator and disseminator A social work role in which the social worker actually carries out and disseminates the results of a positivist and/or interpretive research study to generate knowledge for our profession.

Knowledge level continuum The range of knowledge levels, from exploratory to descriptive to explanatory, at which research studies can be conducted.

Latent content In a content analysis, the true meaning, depth, or intensity of a variable, or concept, under study.

Levels of measurement The degree to which characteristics of a data set can be modeled mathematically; the higher the level of measurement, the more statistical methods that are applicable.

Limited review An existing literature synthesis that summarizes in narrative form the findings and implications of a few research studies.

Literature review See Literature search and Review of the literature.

Literature search In a meta-analysis, scanning books and journals for basic, up-to-date research articles on studies relevant to a research question or hypothesis; sufficiently thorough to maximize the chance of including all relevant sources. See Review of the literature.

Logical consistency The requirement that all the steps within a positivist research study must be logically related to one another.

Logical positivism A philosophy of science holding that the scientific method of inquiry is the only source of certain knowledge; in research, focuses on testing hypotheses deduced from theory.

Logistics In evaluation, refers to getting research participants to do what they are supposed to do, getting research instruments distributed and returned; in general, the activities that ensure that procedural tasks of a research or evaluation study are carried out.

Longitudinal case study An exploratory research design in which there is only one group of research participants and the dependent variable is measured more than once.

Longitudinal design A survey research design in which a measuring instrument(s) is administered to a sample of research participants repeatedly over time; used to detect dynamic processes such as opinion change.

Magnitude recording A direct-observation method of soliciting and recording data on amount, level, or degree of the target problem during each occurrence.

Management information system (MIS) System in which computer technology is used to process, store, retrieve, and analyze data collected routinely in such processes as social service delivery.

Manifest content Content of a communication that is obvious and clearly evident.

Manipulatable solution evaluation model An evaluation model whose proponents believe that the greatest priority is to serve the public interest, not the interests of stakeholders who have vested interests in the program being evaluated; closely resembles an outcome evaluation.

Matching A random assignment technique that assigns research participants to two or more groups so that the experimental and control groups are approximately equivalent in pretest scores or other characteristics, or so that all differences except the experimental condition are eliminated.

Maturation Unplanned change in research participants due to mental, physical, or other processes operating over time; a threat to internal validity.

Meaning units In a qualitative data analysis, a discrete segment of a transcript that can stand alone as a single idea; can consist of a single word, a partial or complete sentence, a paragraph, or more; used as the basic building blocks for developing categories.

Measurement The assignment of labels or numerals to the properties or attributes of observations, events, or objects according to specific rules.

Measurement error Any variation in measurement that cannot be attributed to the variable being measured; variability in responses produced by individual differences and other extraneous variables.

Measuring instrument Any instrument used to measure a variable(s).

Media myths The content of television shows, movies, and newspaper and magazine articles; one of the six ways of knowing.

Member checking A process of obtaining feedback and comments from research participants on interpretations and conclusions made from the qualitative data they provided; asking research participants to confirm or refute the conclusions made.

Meta-analysis A research method in which mathematical procedures are applied to the positivist findings of studies located in a literature search to produce new summary statistics and to describe the findings for a meta-analysis.

Methodology The procedures and rules that detail how a single research study is conducted.

Micro-level data Data derived from individual units of analysis, whether these data sources are individuals, families, corporations, etc.; for example, age and years of formal schooling are two variables requiring micro-level data.

Missing data Data not available for a research participant about whom other data are available, such as when a respondent fails to answer one of the questions in a survey.

Missing links When two categories or themes seem to be related, but not directly so; it may be that a third variable connects the two.

Mixed research model A model combining aspects of interpretive and positivist research approaches within all (or many) of the methodological steps contained within a single research study.

Monitoring approach to evaluation Evaluation that aims to provide ongoing feedback so that a program can be improved while it is still under way; it contributes to the continuous development and improvement of a human service program; this approach complements the project approach to evaluation.

Mortality Loss of research participants through normal attrition over time in an experimental design that requires retesting; a threat to internal validity.

Multicultural research Representation of diverse cultural factors in the subjects of study; such diversity variables may include religion, race, ethnicity, language preference, or gender.

Multigroup posttest-only design An exploratory research design in which there is more than one group of research participants and the dependent variable is measured only once for each group.

Multiple-baseline design A case-level evaluation design with more than one baseline period and intervention phase, which allows the causal inferences regarding the relationship between a treatment intervention and its effect on clients' target problems and which helps control for extraneous variables. See Interrupted time-series design.

Multiple-group design An experimental research design with one control group and several experimental groups.

Multiple-treatment interference Effects of the results of a first treatment on the results of second and subsequent treatments; a threat to external validity.

Multistage probability sampling Probability sampling procedures used when a comprehensive list of the population does not exist and it is not possible to construct one.

Multivariate (1) A relationship involving two or more variables; (2) a hypothesis stating an assertion about two or more variables and how they relate to one another.

Multivariate analysis A statistical analysis of the relationship among three or more variables.

Narrowband measuring instrument Measuring instruments that focus on a single, or a few, variables.

Nationality A term that refers to country of origin.

Naturalist A person who studies the facts of nature as they occur under natural conditions.

Needs assessment Program-level evaluation activities that aim to assess the feasibility of establishing or continuing a particular social service program; an evaluation that aims to assess the need for a human service by verifying that a social problem exists within a specific client population to an extent that warrants services.

Negative case sampling Purposefully selecting research participants based on the fact that they have different characteristics than previous cases.

Nominal level of measurement The level of measurement that classifies variables by assigning names or categories that are mutually exclusive and exhaustive.

Nondirectional test See Two-tailed hypotheses.

Nonexperimental design A research design at the exploratory, or lowest, level of the knowledge continuum; also called preexperimental.

Nonoccurrence data In the structured-observation method of data collection, a recording of only those time intervals in which the target problem did not occur.

Nonparametric tests Refers to statistical tests of hypotheses about population probability distributions, but not about specific parameters of the distributions.

Nonprobability sampling Sampling procedures in which all of the persons, events, or objects in the sampling frame have an unknown, and usually different, probability of being included in a sample.

Nonreactive Methods of research that do not allow the research participants to know that they are being studied; thus, they do not alter their responses for the benefit of the researcher.

Nonresponse The rate of nonresponse in survey research is calculated by dividing the total number of respondents by the total number in the sample, minus any units verified as ineligible.

Nonsampling errors Errors in a research study's results that are not due to the sampling procedures.

Norm In measurement, an average or set group standard of achievement that can be used to interpret individual scores; normative data describing statistical properties of a measuring instrument such as means and standard deviations.

Normalization group The population sample to which a measuring instrument under development is administered in order to establish norms; also called the norm group.

Normative needs When needs are defined by comparing the objective living conditions of a target population with what society—or, at least, that segment of society concerned with helping the target population—deems acceptable or desirable from a humanitarian standpoint.

Null hypothesis A statement concerning one or more parameters that is subjected to a statistical test; a statement that there is no relationship between the two variables of interest.

Numbers The basic data unit of analysis used in positivist research studies.

Objectivity A research stance in which a study is carried out and its data are examined and interpreted without distortion by personal feelings or biases.

Observer One of four roles on a continuum of participation in participant observation research; the level of involvement of the observer participant is lower than of the complete participant and higher than of the participant observer.

Obtrusive data collection methods Direct data collection methods that can influence the variables under study or the responses of research participants; data collection methods that produce reactive effects.

Occurrence data In the structured-observation method of data collection, a recording of the first occurrence of the target problem during each time interval.

One-group posttest-only design An exploratory research design in which the dependent variable is measured only once.

One-group pretest-posttest design A descriptive research design in which the dependent variable is measured twice—before and after treatment.

One-stage probability sampling Probability sampling procedures in which the selection of a sample that is drawn from a specific population is completed in a single process.

One-tailed hypotheses Statements that predict specific relationships between independent and dependent variables.

Online sources Computerized literary retrieval systems that provide printouts of indexes and abstracts.

Open-ended questions Unstructured questions in which the response categories are not specified or detailed.

Operational definition Explicit specification of a variable in such a way that its measurement is possible.

Operationalization The process of developing operational definitions of the variables that are contained within the concepts of a positivist and/or interpretive research study.

Ordinal level of measurement The level of measurement that classifies variables by rank-ordering them from high to low or from most to least.

Outcome The effect of the manipulation of the independent variable on the dependent variable; the end product of a treatment intervention.

Outcome measure The criterion or basis for measuring effects of the independent variable or change in the dependent variable.

Outcome-oriented case study A type of case study that investigates whether client outcomes were in fact achieved.

Outside observers Trained observers who are not a part of the research participants' environment and who are brought in to record data.

Paired observations An observation on two variables, where the intent is to examine the relationship between them.

Panel research study A longitudinal survey design in which the same group of research participants (the panel) is followed over time by surveying them on successive occasions.

Parametric tests Statistical methods for estimating parameters or testing hypotheses about population parameters.

Participant observation An obtrusive data collection method in which the researcher, or the observer, participates in the life of those being observed; both an obtrusive data collection method and a research approach, this method is characterized by the one doing the study undertaking roles that involve establishing and maintaining ongoing relationships with research participants who are often in the field settings, and observing and participating with the research participants over time.

Participant observer The participant observer is one of four roles on a continuum of participation in participant observation research; the level of involvement of the participant observer is higher than of the complete observer and lower than of the observer participant.

Permanent product recording A method of data collection in which the occurrence of the target problem is determined by observing the permanent product or record of the target problem.

Pilot study See Pretest (2).

Population An entire set, or universe, of people, objects, or events of concern to a research study, from which a sample is drawn.

Positivism See Positivist research approach.

Positivist research approach A research approach to discover relationships and facts that are generalizable; research that is "independent" of subjective beliefs, feelings, wishes, and values; a research approach that is complementary to the interpretive research approach.

Posttest Measurement of the dependent variable after the introduction of the independent variable.

Potential for testing One of the four criteria for evaluating research hypotheses.

Practitioner/researcher A social worker who guides practice through the use of research findings; collects data throughout an intervention using research methods, skills, and tools; and disseminates practice findings.

Pragmatists Researchers who believe that both interpretive and positivist research approaches can be integrated in a single research study.

Predictive validity A form of criterion validity that is concerned with the ability of a measuring instrument to predict future performance or status on the basis of present performance or status.

Predictor variable The variable that, it is believed, allows us to improve our ability to predict values of the criterion variable.

Preexposure Tasks to be carried out in advance of a research study to sensitize the researcher to the culture of interest; these tasks may include participation in cultural experiences, intercultural sharing, case studies, ethnic literature reviews, value statement exercises, etc.

Preliminary plan for data analysis A strategy for analyzing qualitative data that is outlined in the beginning stages of an interpretive research study; the plan has two general steps: (1) previewing the data, and (2) outlining what to record in the researcher's journal.

Presentism Applying current thinking and concepts to interpretations of past events or intentions.

Pretest (1) Measurement of the dependent variable prior to the introduction of the independent variable; (2) administration of a measuring instrument to a group of people who will not be included in the study to determine difficulties the research participants may have in answering questions and the general impression given by the instrument; also called a pilot study.

Pretest-treatment interaction Effects that a pretest has on the responses of research participants to the introduction of the independent variable or the experimental treatment; a threat to external validity.

Previous research Research studies that have already been completed and published; they provide information about data collection methods used to investigate research questions that are similar to our own; a criterion for selecting a data collection method.

Primary data Data in its original form, as collected from the research participants; a primary data source is one that puts as few intermediaries as possible between the production and the study of the data.

Primary language The preferred language of the research participants.

Primary reference source A report of a research study by the person who conducted the study; usually an article in a professional journal.

Probability sampling Sampling procedures in which every member of the designated population has a known probability of being selected for the sample.

Problem area In social work research, a general expressed difficulty about which something researchable is unknown; not to be confused with research question.

Problem-solving process A generic method with specified phases for solving problems; also described as the scientific method.

Process-oriented case study A type of case study that illuminates the micro-steps of intervention that lead to client outcomes; describes how programs and interventions work and gives insight into the "black box" of intervention.

Professional standards Rules for making judgments about evaluation activity that are established by a group of persons who have advanced education and usually have the same occupation.

Program An organized set of political, administrative, and clinical activities that function to fulfill some social purpose.

Program development The constant effort to improve program services to better achieve outcomes; a basic principle underlying the design of evaluations.

Program efficiency Assessment of a program's outcome in relation to the costs of obtaining the outcome.

Program evaluation A form of appraisal, using valid and reliable research methods, that examines the processes or outcomes of an organization that exists to fulfill some social purpose.

Program goal A statement defining the intent of a program that cannot be directly evaluated; it can, however, be evaluated indirectly by the program's objectives, which are derived from the program goal; not to be confused with program objectives.

Program-level evaluation A form of appraisal that monitors change for groups of clients and organizational performance.

Program objectives A statement that clearly and exactly specifies the expected change, or intended result, for individuals receiving program services; qualities of well-chosen objectives are meaningfulness, specificity, measurability, and directionality; not to be confused with program goal.

Program participation The philosophy and structure of a program that will support or supplant the successful implementation of a research study within an existing social service program; a criterion for selecting a data collection method.

Program process The coordination of administrative and clinical activities that are designed to achieve a program's goal.

Program results A report on how effective a program is at meeting its stated objectives.

Project approach to evaluation Evaluation that aims to assess a completed or finished program; this approach complements the monitoring approach.

Proxy An indirect measure of a variable that a researcher wants to study; it is often used when the variable of inquiry is difficult to measure or observe directly.

Pure research approach A search for theoretical results that can be utilized to develop theory and expand our profession's knowledge bases; complementary to the applied research approach.

Purists Researchers who believe that interpretive and positivist research approaches should never be mixed.

Purpose statement A declaration of words that clearly describes a research study's intent.

Purposive sampling A nonprobability sampling procedure in which research participants with particular characteristics are purposely selected for inclusion in a research sample; also known as judgmental or theoretical sampling.

Qualitative data Data that measure a quality or kind; when referring to variables, qualitative is another term for categorical or nominal variable values; when speaking of kinds of research, qualitative refers to studies of subjects that are hard to quantify; interpretive research produces descriptive data based on spoken or written words and observable behaviors.

Quantification In measurement, the reduction of data to numerical form

in order to analyze them by way of mathematical or statistical techniques.

Quantitative data Data that measure a quantity or amount.

Quasi-experiment A research design at the descriptive level of the knowledge continuum that resembles an "ideal" experiment but does not allow for random selection or assignment of research participants to groups and often does not control for rival hypotheses.

Questionnaire-type scale A type of measuring instrument in which multiple responses are usually combined to form a single overall score for a respondent.

Quota sampling A nonprobability sampling procedure in which the relevant characteristics of the sample are identified, the proportion of these characteristics in the population is determined, and research participants are selected from each category until the predetermined proportion (quota) has been achieved.

Race A variable based on physical attributes that can be subdivided into the Caucasoid, Negroid, and Mongoloid races.

Random assignment The process of assigning individuals to experimental or control groups so that the groups are equivalent; also referred to as randomization.

Random error Variable error in measurement; error due to unknown or uncontrolled factors that affect the variable being measured and the process of measurement in an inconsistent fashion.

Randomized cross-sectional survey design A descriptive research design in which there is only one group, the dependent variable is measured only once, the research participants are randomly selected from the population, and there is no independent variable.

Randomized longitudinal survey design A descriptive research design in which there is only one group, the dependent variable is measured more than once, and research participants are randomly selected from the population before each treatment.

Randomized one-group posttest-only design A descriptive research design in which there is only one group, the dependent variable is measured only once, and research participants are randomly selected from the population.

Randomized posttest-only control group design An explanatory research design in which there are two or more randomly assigned groups, the control group does not receive treatment, and the experimental groups receive different treatments.

Random numbers table A computer-generated or published table of numbers in which each number has an equal chance of appearing in each position in the table.

Random sampling An unbiased selection process conducted so that all members of a population have an equal chance of being selected to participate in a research study.

Rank-order scale A comparative rating scale in which the rater is asked to rank specific individuals in relation to one another on some characteristic.

Rating scale A type of measuring instrument in which responses are rated on a continuum or in an ordered set of categories, with numerical values assigned to each point or category.

Ratio level of measurement The level of measurement that has a nonarbitrary, fixed zero point and classifies the values of a variable on an equally spaced continuum.

Raw scores Scores derived from administration of a measuring instrument to research participants or groups.

Reactive effect (1) An effect on outcome measures due to the research participants' awareness that they are being observed or interviewed; a threat to external and internal validity; (2) alteration of the variables being measured or the respondents' performance on the measuring instrument due to administration of the instrument.

Reactivity The belief that things being observed or measured are affected by the fact that they are being observed or measured; one of the four main limitations of the positivist research approach.

Reassessment A step in a qualitative data analysis in which the researcher interrupts the data analysis process to reaffirm the rules used to decide which meaning units are placed within different categories.

Recoding Developing and applying new variable value labels to a variable that has previously been coded; usually, recoding is done to make variables from one or more data sets comparable.

Reductionism In the positivist research approach, the operationalization of concepts by reducing them to common measurable variables; one of the four main limitations of the positivist research approach.

Relevancy One of the four criteria for evaluating research problem areas *and* formulating research questions out of the problem areas.

Reliability (1) The degree of accuracy, precision, or consistency in results of a measuring instrument, including the ability to produce the same results when the same variable is measured more than once or repeated applications of the same test on the same individual produce the same measurement; (2) the degree to which individual differences on scores or in data are due either to true differences or to errors in measurement.

Replication Repetition of the same research procedures by a second researcher for the purpose of determining whether earlier results can be confirmed.

Researchability The extent to which a research problem is in fact researchable and the problem can be resolved through the consideration of data derived from a research study; one of the four criteria for evaluating research problem areas *and* formulating research questions out of the problem areas.

Research attitude A way that we view the world. It is an attitude that highly values craftsmanship, with pride in creativity, high-quality standards, and hard work.

Research consumer A social work role reflecting the ethical obligation to base interventions on the most up-to-date research knowledge available.

Research design The entire plan of a positivist and/or interpretive research study from problem conceptualization to the dissemination of findings.

Researcher bias The tendency of researchers to find results they expect to find; a threat to external validity.

Research hypothesis A statement about a study's research question that predicts the existence of a particular relationship between the independent and dependent variables; can be used in both the positivist and interpretive approaches to research.

Research method The use of positivist and interpretive research approaches to find out what is true; one of the ways of knowing.

Research participants People utilized in research studies; also called subjects or cases.

Research question A specific research question that is formulated directly out of the general research problem area; answered by the interpretive and/or positivist research approach; not to be confused with problem area.

Resources The costs associated with collecting data in any given research study; includes materials and supplies, equipment rental, transportation, training staff, and staff time; a criterion for selecting a data collection method.

Response categories Possible responses assigned to each question in a standardized measuring instrument, with a lower value generally indicating a low level of the variable being measured and a larger value indicating a higher level.

Response rate The total number of responses obtained from potential research participants to a measuring instrument divided by the total number of responses requested, usually expressed in the form of a percentage.

Response set Personal style; the tendency of research participants to respond to a measuring instrument in a particular way, regardless of the questions asked, or the tendency of observers or interviewers to react in certain ways; a source of constant error.

Review of the literature (1) A search of the professional literature to provide background knowledge of what has already been examined or tested in a specific problem area; (2) use of any information source, such as a computerized database, to locate existing data or information on a research problem, question, or hypothesis.

Rival hypothesis A hypothesis that is a plausible alternative to the research hypothesis and might explain the results as well or better; a hypothesis involving extraneous or intervening variables other than the independent variable in the research hypothesis; also referred to as an alternative hypothesis.

Rules of correspondence A characteristic of measurement stipulating that numerals or symbols are assigned to properties of individuals, objects, or events according to specified rules.

Sample A subset of a population of individuals, objects, or events chosen to participate in or to be considered in a research study.

Sampling error (1) The degree of difference that can be expected between the sample and the population from which it was drawn; (2) a mistake in a research study's results that is due to sampling procedures.

Sampling frame A listing of units (people, objects, or events) in a population from which a sample is drawn.

Sampling plan A method of selecting members of a population for inclusion in a research study, using procedures that make it possible to draw inferences about the population from the sample statistics.

Sampling theory The logic of using methods to ensure that a sample and a population are similar in all relevant characteristics.

Scale A measuring instrument composed of several items that are logically or empirically structured to measure a construct.

Scattergram A graphic representation of the relationship between two interval- or ratio-level variables.

Science Knowledge that has been obtained and tested through use of positivist and interpretive research studies.

Scientific community A group that shares the same general norms for both research activity and acceptance of scientific findings and explanations.

Scientific determinism See Determinism.

Scientific method A generic method with specified steps for solving problems; the principles and procedures used in the systematic pursuit of knowledge.

Scope of a study The extent to which a problem area is covered in a single research study; a criterion for selecting a data collection method.

Score A numerical value assigned to an observation; also called data.

Search statement A preliminary search statement developed by the researcher prior to a literature search and which contains terms that can be combined to elicit specific data.

Secondary analysis An unobtrusive data collection method in which available data that predate the formulation of a research study are used to answer the research question or test the hypothesis.

Secondary data Data that predate the formulation of the research study and which are used to answer the research question or test the hypothesis.

Secondary data sources A data source that provides nonoriginal, secondhand data.

Secondary reference source A source related to a primary source or sources, such as a critique of a particular source item or a literature review, bibliography, or commentary on several items.

Secondhand data Data obtained from people who are indirectly connected to the problem being studied.

Selection-treatment interaction The relationship between the manner of selecting research participants and their response to the independent variable; a threat to external validity.

Self-anchored scales A rating scale in which research participants rate themselves on a continuum of values, according to their own referents for each point.

Self-disclosure Shared communication about oneself, including one's behaviors, beliefs, and attitudes.

Semantic differential scale A modified measurement scale in which research participants rate their perceptions of the variable under study along three dimensions—evaluation, potency, and activity.

Sequential triangulation When two distinct and separate phases of a research study are conducted and the results of the first phase are considered essential for planning the second phase; research questions in Phase 1 are answered before research questions in Phase 2 are formulated.

Service recipients People who use human services—individuals, couples, families, groups, organizations, and communities; also known as clients or consumers; a stakeholder group in evaluation.

Simple random sampling A one-stage probability sampling procedure in which members of a population are selected one at a time, without a chance of being selected again, until the desired sample size is obtained.

Simultaneous triangulation When the results of a positivist and interpretive research question are answered at the same time; results to the interpretive research questions, for example, are reported separately and do not necessarily relate to, or confirm, the results from the positivist phase.

Situationalists Researchers who assert that certain research approaches (interpretive or positivist) are appropriate for specific situations.

Situation-specific variable A variable that may be observable only in certain environments and under certain circumstances, or with particular people.

Size of a study The number of people, places, or systems that are included in a single research study; a criterion for selecting a data collection method.

Snowball sampling A nonprobability sampling procedure in which individuals selected for inclusion in a sample are asked to identify other individuals from the population who might be included; useful to locate people with divergent points of view.

Social desirability (1) A response set in which research participants tend to answer questions in a way that they perceive as giving a favorable impression of themselves; (2) the inclination of data providers to report data that present a socially desirable impression of themselves or their reference groups; also referred to as impression management.

Socially acceptable response Bias in an answer that comes from research participants trying to answer questions as they think a "good" person should, rather than in a way that reveals what they actually believe or feel.

Social work research Scientific inquiry in which interpretive and positivist research approaches are used to answer research questions and create new, generally applicable knowledge in the field of social work.

Socioeconomic variables Any one of several measures of social rank, usually including income, education, and occupational prestige; abbreviated "SES."

Solomon four-group design An explanatory research design with four randomly assigned groups, two experimental and two control; the dependent variable is measured before and after treatment for one experimental and one control group, but only after treatment for the other two groups, and only experimental groups receive the treatment.

Specificity One of the four criteria for evaluating research hypotheses.

Split-half method A method for establishing the reliability of a measuring instrument by dividing it into comparable halves and comparing the scores between the two halves.

Spot-check recording A method of data collection that involves direct observation of the target problem at specified intervals rather than on a continuous basis.

Stakeholder A person or group of people having a direct or indirect interest in the results of an evaluation.

Stakeholder service evaluation model Proponents of this evaluation model believe that program evaluations will be more likely to be utilized, and thus have a greater impact on social problems, when they are tailored to the needs of stakeholders; in this model, the purpose of program evaluation is not to generalize findings to other sites, but rather to restrict the evaluation effort to a particular program.

Standardized measuring instrument A professionally developed measuring instrument that provides for uniform administration and scoring and generates normative data against which later results can be evaluated.

Statistics The branch of mathematics concerned with the collection and analysis of data using statistical techniques.

Stratified random sampling A one-stage probability sampling procedure in which a population is divided into two or more strata to be sampled separately, using simple random or systematic random sampling techniques.

Structured interview schedule A complete list of questions to be asked and spaces for recording the answers; the interview schedule is used by interviewers when questioning respondents.

Structured observation A data collection method in which people are observed in their natural environments using specified methods and measurement procedures. See Direct observation.

Subscale A component of a scale that measures some part or aspect of a major construct; also composed of several items that are logically or empirically structured.

Summated scale A questionnaire-type scale in which research participants are asked to indicate the degree of their agreement or disagreement with a series of questions.

Summative evaluation A type of evaluation that examines the ultimate success of a program and assists with decisions about whether a program should be continued or chosen in the first place among alternative program options.

Survey research A data collection method that uses survey-type data collection measuring instruments to obtain opinions or answers from a population or sample of research participants in order to describe or study them as a group.

Synthesis Undertaking the search for meaning in our sources of information at every step of the research process; combining parts such as data, concepts, and theories to arrive at a higher level of understanding.

Systematic To arrange the steps of a research study in a methodical way.

Systematic error Measurement error that is consistent, not random.

Systematic random sampling A one-stage probability sampling procedure in which every person at a designated interval in a specific population is selected to be included in a research study's sample.

Target population The group about which a researcher wants to draw conclusions; another term for a population about which one aims to make inferences.

Target problem (1) In case-level evaluation designs, the problems social workers seek to solve for their clients; (2) a measurable behavior, feeling, or cognition that is either a problem in itself or symptomatic of some other problem.

Temporal research design A research study that includes time as a major variable; the purpose of this design is to investigate change in the distribution of a variable or in relationships among variables over time; there are three types of temporal research designs: cohort, panel, and trend.

Temporal stability Consistency of responses to a measuring instrument over time; reliability of an instrument across forms and across administrations.

Testing effect The effect that taking a pretest might have on posttest scores; a threat to internal validity.

Test-retest reliability Reliability of a measuring instrument established through repeated administration to the same group of individuals.

Thematic notes In observational research, a record of emerging ideas, hypotheses, theories, and conjectures; thematic notes provide a place for the researcher to speculate and identify themes, make linkages between ideas and events, and articulate thoughts as they emerge in the field setting.

Theme In a qualitative data analysis, a concept or idea that describes a single category or a grouping of categories; an abstract interpretation of qualitative data.

Theoretical framework A frame of reference that serves to guide a research study and is developed from theories, findings from a variety of other studies, and the researcher's personal experiences.

Theoretical sampling See Purposive sampling.

Theory A reasoned set of propositions, derived from and supported by established data, which serves to explain a group of phenomena; a conjectural explanation that may, or may not, be supported by data generated from interpretive and positivist research studies.

Time orientation An important cultural factor that considers whether one is future, present, or past oriented; for instance, individuals who are present oriented would not be as preoccupied with advance planning as those who are future oriented.

Time-series design See Interrupted time-series design.

Tradition Traditional cultural beliefs that we accept without question as true; one of the ways of knowing.

Transcript A written, printed, or typed copy of interview data or any other written material that have been gathered for an interpretive research study.

Transition statements Sentences used to indicate a change in direction or focus of questions in a measuring instrument.

Treatment group See Experimental group.

Trend study A longitudinal study design in which data from surveys carried out at periodic intervals on samples drawn from a particular population are used to reveal trends over time.

Triangulation The idea of combining different research methods in all steps associated with a single research study; assumes that any bias inherent in one particular method will be neutralized when used in conjunction with other research methods; seeks convergence of a study's results; using more than one research method and source of data to study the same phenomena and to enhance validity; there are several types of triangulation, but the essence of the term is that multiple perspectives are compared; it can involve multiple data sources or multiple data analyzers; the hope is that the different perspectives will confirm each other, adding weight to the credibility and dependability of qualitative data analysis.

Triangulation of analysts Using multiple data analyzers to code a single segment of transcript and comparing the amount of agreement between analyzers; a method used to verify coding of qualitative data.

Two-phase research model A model combining interpretive and positivist research approaches in a single study where each approach is conducted as a separate and distinct phase of the study.

Two-tailed hypotheses Statements that *do not* predict specific relationships between independent and dependent variables.

Unit of analysis A specific research participant (person, object, or event) or the sample or population relevant to the research question; the persons or things being studied; units of analysis in research are often persons, but may be groups, political parties, newspaper editorials, unions, hospitals, schools, etc.; a particular unit of analysis from which data are gathered is called a case.

Univariate A hypothesis or research design involving a single variable.

Universe See Population.

Unobtrusive methods Data collection methods that do not influence the variable under study or the responses of research participants; methods that avoid reactive effects.

Unstructured interviews A series of questions that allow flexibility for both the research participant and the interviewer to make changes during the process.

Validity (1) The extent to which a measuring instrument measures the variable it is supposed to measure and measures it accurately; (2) the degree to which an instrument is able to do what it is intended to do, in terms of both experimental procedures and measuring instruments (internal validity) and generalizability of results (external validity); (3) the degree to which scores on a measuring instrument correlate with measures of performance on some other criterion.

Variable A concept with characteristics that can take on different values.

Verbatim recording Recording interview data word-for-word and including significant gestures, pauses, and expressions of persons in the interview.

Wideband measuring instrument An instrument that measures more than one variable.

Within-methods research approach Triangulation by using different research methods available in *either* the interpretive *or* the positivist research approaches in a single research study.

Words The basic data unit of analysis used in interpretive research studies.

Worker cooperation The actions and attitudes of program personnel when carrying out a research study within an existing program; a criterion for selecting a data collection method.

Working hypothesis An assertion about a relationship between two or more variables that may not be true but is plausible and worth examining.

References and Further Reading

No finite point has meaning without an infinite reference point.
~ Jean-Paul Sartre

Black, T.R. (1999). *Doing quantitative research in the social sciences: An integrated approach to research design, measurement, and statistics*. Thousand Oaks, CA: Sage.

Bloom, M., Fischer, J., & Orme, J. (2009). *Evaluating practice: Guidelines for the accountable professional* (6th ed.). Englewood Cliffs, NJ: Prentice-Hall.

Bostwick, G.J., Jr., & Kyte, N.S. (1981). Measurement. In R.M. Grinnell, Jr. (Ed.), *Social work research and evaluation* (pp. 181–195). Itasca, IL: F.E. Peacock.

Calgary Herald: "Another kidnap bid has parents nervous," September 6, 1991, p. 1.

Calgary Herald: "Show ignores Native stereotype," September 6, 1991, Section B, p. 6.

Coleman, H., & Unrau, Y. (2011). Qualitative data analysis. In R.M. Grinnell, Jr., & Y.A. Unrau (Eds.), *Social work research and evaluation: Foundations of evidence-based practice* (9th ed., pp. 447–464). New York: Oxford University Press.

Colorado State University's Writing Center (2011). http://writing.colostate.edu.

Cooper, H., & Hedges, L.V. (1994). *The handbook of research synthesis*. New York: Russell Sage Foundation.

Cooper, J., Calloway-Thomas, C., & Simonds, C.J. (2007). Non-verbal communication. In P.J. Cooper, C. Calloway-Thomas, & C.J. Simonds (Eds.), *Intercultural communication: A text with readings* (pp. 132–142). Boston: Pearson.

Corcoran, K., & Hozack, N. (2010). Locating assessment instruments. In B. Thyer (Ed.). *The handbook of social work research methods* (2nd. ed.). Thousand Oaks, CA: Sage.

Council on Social Work Education (2015). *Baccalaureate and masters curriculum policy statements*. Alexandria, VA: Author.

Creswell, J.W. (2010). *Designing and conducting mixed-methods research* (2nd ed.). Thousand Oaks, CA: Sage.

Dodd, C. (1998). *Dynamics of intercultural communication* (5th ed.). New York: McGraw-Hill.

Doyle, C. (1901/1955). *A treasury of Sherlock Holmes*. Garden City, NY: Hanover House.

Duehn, W.D. (1985). Practice and research. In R.M. Grinnell, Jr. (Ed.), *Social work research and evaluation* (2nd ed., pp. 19–48). Itasca, IL: F.E. Peacock.

Engel, R., & Schutt, K. (2010). *The practice of research in social work* (2nd ed.) Thousand Oaks, CA: Sage.

Engel, R.J., & Schutt, R.K. (2011). Survey research. In R.M. Grinnell, Jr., & Y.A. Unrau (Eds.), *Social work research and evaluation: Foundations of evidence-based practice* (9th ed., pp. 326–365). New York: Oxford University Press.

Fischer, J. (1981). A framework for evaluating empirical research reports. In R.M. Grinnell, Jr. (Ed.), *Social work research and evaluation* (pp. 347–366). Itasca, IL: F.E. Peacock.

Fischer, J., & Corcoran, K. (2007). *Measures for clinical practice* (3rd ed.). *Volume 1:*

Couples, families, and children. Volume 2: *Adults.* New York: Oxford University Press.

Gochros, H.L. (2011). Qualitative interviewing. In R.M. Grinnell, Jr., & Y.A. Unrau (Eds.), *Social work research and evaluation: Foundations of evidence-based practice* (9th ed., pp. 301–325). New York: Oxford University Press.

Grinnell, F. (1987). *The scientific attitude.* Boulder, CO: Westview Press.

Grinnell, R.M., Jr. (1981). Becoming a knowledge-based social worker. In R.M. Grinnell, Jr. (Ed.), *Social work research and evaluation* (pp. 1–8). Itasca, IL: F.E. Peacock.

Grinnell, R.M., Jr. (1985). Becoming a practitioner/researcher. In R.M. Grinnell, Jr. (Ed.), *Social work research and evaluation* (5th ed., pp. 3–24). Itasca, IL: F.E. Peacock.

Grinnell, R.M., Jr. (1993). Group research designs. In R.M. Grinnell, Jr. (Ed.), *Social work research and evaluation* (4th ed., pp. 118–153). Itasca, IL: F.E. Peacock.

Grinnell, R.M., Jr. (1995). The generation of knowledge. In R.M. Grinnell, Jr. (Ed.), *Social work research and evaluation* (2nd ed., pp. 1–15). Itasca, IL: F.E. Peacock.

Grinnell, R.M., Jr. (1997a). The generation of knowledge. In R.M. Grinnell, Jr. (Ed.), *Social work research and evaluation: Quantitative and qualitative approaches* (5th ed., pp. 3–24). Itasca, IL: F.E. Peacock.

Grinnell, R.M., Jr. (1997b). Preface. In R.M. Grinnell, Jr. (Ed.), *Social work research and evaluation: Quantitative and qualitative approaches* (5th ed., pp. xvii–xxvi). Itasca, IL: F.E. Peacock.

Grinnell, R.M., Jr. (Ed.). (1997c). *Social work research and evaluation: Quantitative and qualitative approaches* (5th ed.). Itasca, IL: F.E. Peacock.

Grinnell, R.M., Jr., Rothery, M., & Thomlison, R.J. (1993). Research in social work. In R.M. Grinnell, Jr. (Ed.), *Social work research and evaluation* (4th ed., pp. 2–16). Itasca, IL: F.E. Peacock.

Grinnell, R.M., Jr., & Siegel, D.H. (1988). The place of research in social work. In R.M. Grinnell, Jr. (Ed.), *Social work research and evaluation* (3rd ed., pp. 9–24). Itasca, IL: F.E. Peacock.

Grinnell, R.M., Jr., & Stothers, M. (1988). Research designs. In R.M. Grinnell, Jr. (Ed.), *Social work research and evaluation* (3rd ed., pp. 199–239). Itasca, IL: F.E. Peacock.

Grinnell, R.M., Jr., & Unrau, Y. (1997). Group designs. In R.M. Grinnell, Jr. (Ed.), *Social work research and evaluation: Quantitative and qualitative approaches* (5th ed., pp. 259–297). Itasca, IL: F.E. Peacock.

Grinnell, R.M., Jr., & Williams, M. (1990). *Research in social work: A primer.* Itasca, IL: F.E. Peacock.

Grinnell, R.M., Jr., Williams, M., & Tutty, L.M. (1997). Case-level evaluation. In R.M. Grinnell, Jr. (Ed.), *Social work research and evaluation: Quantitative and qualitative approaches* (5th ed., pp. 529–559). Itasca, IL: F.E. Peacock.

Hall, E.T. (1983). *The dance of life: Other dimensions of time.* New York: Doubleday.

Harris, P.R., & Moran, T. (1996). *Managing cultural differences: Leadership strategies for a new world business* (4th ed.). London: Gulf.

Hoefstede, G. (1997). *Cultures and organizations: Software of the mind.* New York: McGraw-Hill.

Hudson, W.W. (1982). *The clinical measurement package: A field manual.* Chicago: Dorsey.

Institute of Medicine. (2000). *Crossing the quality chasm: A new health system for the 21st century.* Washington, DC: National Academy Press.

Ivanoff, A., & Blythe, B. (2011). Research ethics. In R.M. Grinnell, Jr., & Y.A. Unrau (Eds.). *Social work research and evaluation: Foundations of evidence-based practice* (9th ed., pp. 71–96). New York: Oxford University Press.

Jordan, C., Franklin, C., & Corcoran, K. (2011). Standardized measuring instruments. In R.M. Grinnell, Jr., & Y. Unrau (Eds.), *Social work research and evaluation: Foundations of evidence-based practice* (9th ed., pp. 196–215). New York: Oxford University Press.

Kirst-Ashman, K.K., & Hull, G.H., Jr. (2009). *Generalist practice with organizations and communities* (4th ed.). Belmont, CA: Brooks/Cole.

Koyama, T. (1992). *Japan: A handbook in intercultural communication.* Sydney: National Center for English Language and Teaching and Research.

Krysik, J.L., & Finn, J. (2011). *Research for effective social work practice* (2nd ed.). New York: Routledge.

Krysik, J., & Grinnell, R.M., Jr. (1997). Quantitative approaches to the generation of knowledge. In R.M. Grinnell, Jr., & Y.A. Unrau (Eds.), *Social work research and evaluation: Quantitative and qualitative approaches* (5th ed., pp. 67–105). Itasca, IL: F.E. Peacock.

Kumar, R. (1994). *Research methodology: A step-by-step guide for beginners.* White Plains, NY: Longman.

LeCroy, C.W., & Solomon, G. (2011). Content analysis. In R.M. Grinnell, Jr., & Y.A. Unrau (Eds.), *Social work research and evaluation: Foundations of evidence-based practice* (9th ed., pp. 379–388). New York: Oxford University Press.

Lewis, R.D. (1997). *When cultures collide: Managing successfully across cultures.* London: Nicholas Brealey.

Maschi, T., & Youdin, R. (2012). *Social worker as researcher: Integrating research with advocacy.* Boston: Pearson.

Miles, M.B., & Huberman, A.M. (1994). *Qualitative data analysis: An expanded sourcebook.* Thousand Oaks, CA: Sage.

Monette, D.R., Sullivan, T.J., & DeJong, C.R. (2011). *Applied social research: A tool for the human services.* (8th ed.). Belmont, CA: Brooks/Cole.

Morrison, T., Conway, W.A., & Borden, G.A. (1994). *Kiss, bow, or shake hands: How to do business in six countries.* Holbrook, MA: Adams Media.

Mouton, J. (2001). *How to succeed in your master's and doctoral studies.* Pretoria, South Africa: Van Schaik.

Mullen, E.J., Bellamy, J.L., & Bledsoe, S.E. (2011). Evidence-based practice. In R.M. Grinnell, Jr., & Y.A. Unrau (Eds.). *Social work research and evaluation: Foundations of evidence-based practice* (9th ed., pp. 160–176). New York: Oxford University Press.

National Association of Social Workers. (1999). *Code of ethics.* Silver Spring, MD: Author.

Neuliep, J.W. (2000). *Communication: A contextual approach.* New York: Houghton-Mifflin.

Neuman, W.L. (2009). *Understanding research.* Boston: Pearson.

Neuman, W.L. (2012). *Basics of social research: Qualitative and quantitate approaches* (3rd ed.). Boston: Pearson.

Polster, R.A., & Collins, D. (2011). Structured observation. In R.M. Grinnell, Jr., & Y.A. Unrau (Eds.), *Social work research and evaluation: Foundations of evidence-based practice* (9th ed., pp. 287–300). New York: Oxford University Press.

Porter, R.E., & Samovar, L.A. (2006). Understanding intercultural communication: An overview. In L.A. Samovar, R.E. Porter, & E.R. McDaniel (Eds.), *Intercultural communication: A reader* (11th ed., pp. 6–16). Belmont, CA: Thomson Wadsworth.

Punch. K.F. (2009). *Introduction to research methods in education.* Thousand Oaks, CA: Sage.

Raines, J.C. (2011). Evaluating qualitative research studies. In R.M. Grinnell, Jr., &

Y.A. Unrau (Eds.), *Social work research and evaluation: Foundations of evidence-based practice* (9th ed., pp. 488–503). New York: Oxford University Press.

Reid, W.J., & Smith, A.D. (1989). *Research in social work* (2nd ed.). New York: Columbia University Press.

Royse, D., Thyer, B., & Padgett, D. (2009). *Program evaluation: An introduction.* Belmont, CA: Wadsworth.

Rubin, A. (2011). Secondary analysis. In R.M. Grinnell, Jr., & Y.A. Unrau (Eds.), *Social work research and evaluation: Foundations of evidence-based practice* (9th ed., pp. 369–378). New York: Oxford University Press.

Rubin, A., & Babbie, E. (2010). *Research methods for social work* (7th ed.). Pacific Grove, CA: Wadsworth.

Sackett, D.L., Rosenberg, W.M.C., Muir Gray, J.A., Haynes, R.B., & Richardson, W.S. (1996). Evidence-based medicine: What it is and what it isn't: It's about integrating individual clinical expertise and the best external evidence. *British Medical Journal, 31,* 71–72.

Sackett, D.L., Straus, S.E., Richardson, W.S., Rosenberg, W., & Haynes, R.B. (2000). *Evidence based medicine: How to practice and teach EBM* (2nd ed.). New York: Churchill Living.

Samovar, L.A., Porter, R.E., & Stefani, L.A. (1998). *Communication between cultures.* Belmont, CA: Wadsworth.

Schutt, R. (2008). *Investigating the social world: The process and practice of research* (6th ed.). Thousand Oaks, CA: Pine Forge Press.

Sieppert, J.D., McMurtry, S.L., & McClelland, R.W. (2011). Utilizing existing statistics. In R.M. Grinnell, Jr., & Y.A. Unrau (Eds.), *Social work research and evaluation: Foundations of evidence-based practice* (9th ed., pp. 389–401). New York: Oxford University Press.

Stuart, P. (2011). Historical research. In R.M. Grinnell, Jr., & Y.A. Unrau (Eds.), *Social work research and evaluation:*

Foundations of evidence-based practice (9th ed., pp. 402–412). New York: Oxford University Press.

Thomas, D.C., & Inkson, K. (2009). *Cultural intelligence: Living and working globally* (2nd ed.). San Francisco: Berrett-Koehler.

Tutty, L.M., Grinnell, R.M., & Williams, M. (1997). Research problems and questions. In R.M. Grinnell, Jr. (Ed.), *Social work research and evaluation: Quantitative and qualitative approaches* (5th ed., pp. 49–66). Itasca, IL: F.E. Peacock.

Tutty, L.M., Rothery, M.L., & Grinnell, R.M., Jr. (Eds.). (1996). *Qualitative research for social workers: Phases, steps, and tasks.* Boston: Allyn & Bacon.

Unrau, Y.A. (2011). Selecting a data collection method and data source. In R.M. Grinnell, Jr., & Y.A. Unrau (Eds.), *Social work research and evaluation: Foundations of evidence-based practice* (9th ed., pp. 413–426). New York: Oxford University Press.

Unrau, Y.A., Grinnell, R.M., Jr., & Williams, M. (2008). The quantitative research approach. In R.M. Grinnell, Jr., & Y.A. Unrau (Eds.), *Social work research and evaluation: Foundations of evidence-based practice* (8th ed., pp. 61–81). New York: Oxford University Press.

Weinbach, R.W., & Grinnell, R.M., Jr. (2015). *Statistics for social workers* (9th ed.). Boston: Allyn & Bacon.

Williams, M., Grinnell, R.M., Jr., & Tutty, L.M. (1997). Research contexts. In R.M. Grinnell, Jr. (Ed.), *Social work research and evaluation: Quantitative and qualitative approaches* (5th ed., pp. 25–45). Itasca, IL: F.E. Peacock.

Williams, M., Tutty, L.M., & Grinnell, R.M., Jr. (1995). *Research in social work: An introduction* (2nd ed.). Itasca, IL: F.E. Peacock.

Williams, M., Unrau, Y.A., & Grinnell, R.M., Jr. (1998). *Introduction to social work research* (3rd ed.). Itasca, IL: F.E. Peacock.

Woolman, M. (2000). *Ways of knowing: An introduction to theory of knowledge.* Victoria, Australia: IBID Press.

Index